I MUST HAVE LIBERTY

The latest photograph of the author
Isabel de Palencia

I MUST HAVE LIBERTY

BY

ISABEL DE PALENCIA

LONGMANS, GREEN AND CO.

NEW YORK · TORONTO

1941

I MUST HAVE LIBERTY

COPYRIGHT · 1940

BY ISABEL DE PALENCIA

First edition November 1940
Reprinted October 1941

To

CEFITO *and* MARISSA

and

MY UNCONQUERED SPAIN

She was not sad because she was alone,
She was sad because no one understood her song.

From a Chinese poem

LIST OF ILLUSTRATIONS

Book One: A Little Rebel

CHAPTER I

I have a very early and definite impression that we, that is, my sister Maria de la Asunción, my brother Juan and I, were disapproved of. Most children have, of course, that impression at times, but in most cases the disapproval is expressed by outsiders and not by usually doting grandmothers and close relatives. This impression of mine soon worked out into a conviction that Malaga Society with a capital S was afraid that the new generation of the Oyarzábal family, of which I was the third member, was going to work havoc with a long-established good reputation for strict and faithful observance of the Malaga proprieties.

An element of most disturbing influence had entered into the sacred Oyarzábal circle in the person of my mother, who was Scottish and a Protestant, and had married my father at the age of seventeen, he being twenty years older. They had met in Malaga when she was visiting one of her school friends, a Miss MacCulloch, whose father had resided for many years in Spain but had been careful to send his children over to Scotland to be educated in the way he thought they should be.

Both in the case of my mother and in that of my father, it had been "love at first sight." She was carried away by the eloquence of the handsome, dark-eyed Spaniard who had been at school in England and who could speak her language perfectly, and he was simply entranced with the pretty, fair-haired and rather wilful, little Scots lassie.

Mother was an orphan and accustomed to do very much as she pleased, and this must have been an additional charm for my father who was perhaps tired of the usual submission of Spanish girls of his class.

The marriage was at first slightly opposed by mother's family. They were related to the Tennants of Ayrshire. They were scared to think that her choice should have fallen on a Spaniard and a Catholic, but they became quite reconciled to the idea once they had met my father.

For, in truth, it would have been difficult to find a more devoted husband than he turned out to be. Right up to the day of his death, his principal aim in life was to make mother happy and we were all called upon to collaborate in this all-absorbing achievement.

Nothing ever turned him from it. If relatives or friends remonstrated with him for allowing mother to go out unescorted by some relative or a servant as other Malaga ladies had to do, or if he let her row her boat in or out of the port, and dance, and even smoke, thus challenging all Malaga ideas of good behavior for women, he would invariably shrug his shoulders and say, "What does it matter so long as she is happy ?"

But father's delight in his choice of a wife was not, it seems, shared by all of his family, especially by his mother. A foreigner was then, and still is, often an object of distrust to Spaniards. They have reason for it, considering that they have so frequently been invaded and betrayed. But a Protestant ! A Protestant was really something beyond the pale ! The Inquisition has not done its work for nothing, and, even now, in the upper circles of Spain, one may say there are rarely any mixed marriages. At least I know of none. Protestants are tolerated when they are foreigners, especially if they are members of the diplomatic corps. But for a Spaniard to marry a Protestant then was little short of social suicide.

However, father went his way undisturbed. He was by no means a devout Catholic himself at the time and most of his friends were British residents, so mother was not allowed to feel the difference. As for his family, he felt they could be kept in order, for his widowed mother, with her naive, child-like nature, would never oppose his wishes openly. I remember my grandmother rather vaguely and my impression is that of a stout old lady who went out very rarely and then only to church. She was always dressed in black, never, it seems, having discarded her widow's mourning although my grandfather had been dead for many years. I can see her sitting in a low brocaded armchair near the window, in one of the sitting rooms of her daughter's house. She went over her beads constantly and would smile on us when we went in to see her, but those smiles were always followed up by deep sighs and muttered words such as, *Ay, Señor! Ay, Dios mio!* all of which were evidently meant as regret for the fact that we were not being brought up within the Catholic faith and were therefore in danger of becoming "heretics."

It is true that, although we had been christened in the Roman Catholic church, it was mother who took charge of our spiritual education. She took us to the Protestant chapel and taught us psalms out of her Protestant Bible. This must have been a matter of grave concern to all my father's family, and I know my poor grandmother was deeply shocked one day when my mother went in to see her with a gold filigree rosary, that Pope Pius the Ninth had sent her for a marriage present, wound around her neck in place of her usual necklace.

It seems that the Sovereign Pontiff had sent mother the rosary through the good offices of Cardinal Bucelli, a cousin of my grandmother's, who had requested special prayers from His

Holiness for his new niece's conversion. But mother had not realized the meaning attached to what she considered just a pretty little ornament. The gold cross attached to the beads was, she thought, the most appropriate finish to a Pope's present.

But it was not only these religious differences that made my grandmother so anxious. Her other grandchildren were being brought up according to the Spanish ways of that time and did as all other children belonging to our exclusive circle had to do. We would meet my cousins out in the Alameda, a long broad walk shaded by huge chestnut trees, where the *élite* of Malaga used to take exercise in the afternoon, walking sedately up and down. Our cousins were always exquisitely dressed and held on to the hand of their mother or governess, while I tore along with my brothers and perhaps some other children of foreign parentage, not caring an atom what we looked like. I must often have seemed to them sadly disheveled and untidy, yet their mother, my father's only sister, never by sign or word showed disapproval of what my brothers or I did, and so did not estrange us from her.

Aunt Maria was far too clever to be surprised at anything if she sensed it might some day be the correct thing to do, and it looked then as if English manners, however eccentric they might be considered, were going to come into fashion, for King Alfonso XII, father of the exiled King Alfonso XIII, who had been restored to the Spanish throne some years after the downfall of the first Spanish Republic and the failure of the Italian dynasty of Don Amadeo de Saboya, was trying to introduce English customs into different spheres of Spanish life.

The new sovereign had been brought up in Great Britain during his exile and was anxious to sweep away some of the old notions which he considered incompatible with progress. In Madrid many people were following the royal lead, and I am sure Aunt Maria would have loved to do so if she had dared, but living in a provincial town, this was not easy. Besides, her husband's position was an obstacle to such levities. She had been the "belle" of Malaga for many years and had seen many rich and titled men at her feet, but one fine day she surprised her family by announcing that she had made up her mind to marry an old, whiskered general who soon after became the Military Governor of Malaga, and over whom she lorded it in the lovely Moorish Castle of Gibralfáro, which became their home, being the official residence of whoever might be occupying such a post. We used to be taken up there some days to pay our respects to my grandmother and I remember being terrified for fear this, to me, strange uncle might take it into his head to kiss me. In truth, there was nothing particularly odd about him except his great height, his extreme thinness and his reserved manners. However, to our childish minds he was not the mate Aunt Maria deserved. As she was so lovely and as he seemed to us so ugly, we called them "Beauty and the Beast."

She was not only just beautiful, she was also witty and charming and clever. I shall never forget how it pleased me when mother would say, as she sometimes did, that I was my aunt's ugly likeness. Even that seemed to me to be a compliment and it is true that I did have her dark hair and eyes, and her pale complexion, but I could never hope to be called the "rose of Bengal" as she was.

My father's brothers I saw but little, for one had been living abroad for years and the other two, who were officers in the army, were stationed in different towns of Spain. As to my mother's family, except for one older sister who married an Englishman and also came to settle in Malaga, they were all living in Scotland.

But to go back to my reminiscences. . .

A little black goat, a pair of brown woolen stockings and a

sermon on "green pastures" make up the first picture I can recall in which words and happenings and things appear to be related to one another and to stand out vividly from among hundreds of other vague and unconnected childish memories with little or no meaning of their own.

The background of the picture is my home, a two-story house in Malaga, with large, high-ceilinged rooms looking out on the lovely Andalusian patio. Glistening white marble floors and flat terraced roofs, where we children were allowed to play and keep our pets under cool awnings, made of esparto grass that had to be watered on very hot days, and where we each had our own special collection of flower-pots that we were supposed to tend. Roses and carnations and sweet-smelling herbs, but not geraniums, for these are so plentiful in southern Spain that they are not considered worth cultivating.

It was Easter Sunday and my mother had sent up several messages to the nursery with orders for us to hurry or we should be late for church, and was naturally displeased when, in view of the fact that none of us went down, she rustled into our room in her new spring finery to find that I was not yet ready in spite of the efforts and encouragements of my *ama* who had taken care of me since babyhood, and who now looked after my things and petted and spoilt me to her heart's content.

"She will be ready in a minute, señora," I remember *ama* saying as she did her best to get me into the new brown dress with pink satin piping that had just arrived from London and had bonnet, gloves and stockings to match. But I refused to be hurried.

"Why, what is the matter?" said mother, seeing that I had pulled my arms out of the sleeves of the dress again.

"It's that she doesn't want to go to church," said my eldest sister, Maria, with an accusing air, while my brother Juan stepped unhappily from one foot to another, fearing the re-action such words might provoke.

"Oh, I'm sure it isn't that," mother said hurriedly, drying the tears that were already pouring down my cheeks at the thought that I was not going to manage to be late after all, that I would have to sit in that horrid new dress and prickly woolen stock-ings all through the long Protestant service which had to be held in a stuffy little room in the British consulate because the so-called "religious tolerance" embodied in the Spanish constitu-tion of that time did not really mean anything, and Protestants had to worship in improvised little chapels only frequented by British and German residents.

Above all, I hated the idea of spending the morning away from my beloved *chivita*, a little black kid that my father had bought for me at the annual sheep fair held in Malaga, and in most Andalusian cities during Easter time. The custom is probably a reminiscence of the old Jewish sacrifice of the paschal lamb and, indeed, the poor animals were sacrificed by the hundred in my town for the family Easter dinner. Not in our case, however. Our lambs were kept as pets until the summer and then sent to our house in the country, where they were probably fattened and sold, or killed, but we were not aware of this.

That particular year my choice had not fallen on the cus-tomary "snow-white lamb" but on a little black kid. With complete disregard for Bible statements, kids and goats in the fair enjoyed the same standing as the sheep, and I, for one, thought my kid was just perfect.

"She doesn't like going to church," said my sister, who had an idea it was her duty to help keep us younger ones in order.

"It is also that she doesn't like that dress," said Juan, stoutly trying to defend me, and looking at my new apparel with such evident disapproval that I hated that dress more than ever, for this brother was my hero and my idol.   He was two and a half years older than I, and I looked up to him in everything.

I remember that the bells of the cathedral were ringing as we hurried to church, and I thought how much nicer it would have been to go with father to his church instead of being taken by mother to hers.

On rare occasions mother would insist that father should take us to "his" church.

"After all, the children are Catholics," she would say to him, and I was always delighted to comply.

Father and my sister and I would walk hand in hand to the great cathedral, followed by Juan skipping along beside my *ama*, carrying two little folding chairs for Maria and Juan to sit on during the Mass.   At that time there were few benches in the Andalusian churches so women either took a seat along with them or hired a chair at the church entrance and placed it wherever they thought fit, or sat doubled up on the floor in Moorish fashion.   Men, unless they were old, preferred to stand.   My *ama* would lend me her book so that I could follow the service.   It had funny little pictures in it of a priest saying Mass, and I loved watching the minister at the altar lest he skip any of the movements recorded in that old-fashioned work, evidently destined for people who did not know how to read.

I liked the Catholic service, too, because it was so much shorter than the Protestant one.   And there was no sermon, for I was never taken to High Mass.   During the service the organ would sometimes play while the canons chanted their Holy Office and I thought the sound was like the breaking of the waves against the rocks the few times a year that we had stormy weather in Malaga.

That Easter morning, however, I had to go to church with mother, and not even the sight of the white lilies on the altar

could cheer me up.   I sat sulkily in my seat just in front of a
stiff old English lady who used to frown at me if I ever dared
to turn my head around.

Suddenly, however, my attention was attracted by some
words coming from the clergyman.   He was a skinny old
gentleman who looked something like Don Quixote, according to Juan, and whose sermons bored us terribly, but those
words about "a shepherd . . . and sheep . . . and green
pastures" on that special morning simply thrilled me.

I had left my little goat, Morenita, with Maria's and Juan's
lambs, fastidiously nibbling at a bunch of alfalfa grass from the
load the man servant was supposed to bring in for them from
the market every day.   The alfalfa was tied on to a nail so as
not to touch the ground, for in that case it would not have been
eatable, and Morenita had to strain her neck to get at it, in a
most uncomfortable way.

Those other sheep and lambs the clergyman was speaking of
evidently had green fields to graze on and run about, and I
was soon lost in a reverie of the special kind of field I should
like Morenita to have, so lost that I forgot everything else and
had to be pulled out of my thoughts and my chair by a push
from Juan, who thought that I had gone to sleep and might
disgrace the family by falling off my seat.

Going home from church that very morning, we came upon
an old woman who sold flowers, and who called us to see the
first silkworms of the season.   Several children were buying
them and Juan and I were each given ten centimos to invest in
a mulberry leaf holding ten squirming, almost invisible, little
grubs.

Like most children in the town, we were accustomed to rear
silkworms every year during the proper season.   The worms
were kept in empty cigar boxes on a layer of mulberry leaves
which had to be changed every night, and we watched them

carefully until they grew at least three inches long and were able to wind themselves into their lovely white or yellow or oránge-colored cocoons. Juan and I always had a race to see which of us could be the first to show a soft, egg-shaped, little silk ball. Of course the original number of worms was always increased to forty or even fifty, for many of our pennies found their way to the stand of the old flower woman and were exchanged for what my sister Maria described as "disgusting animals." Mother liked us to have them, however. I think now that she must have felt it developed our sense of responsibility to look after them, as well as our knowledge of Spain's possibilities, for silk has always been a source of wealth to the southern and eastern Spanish provinces.

Juan and I always kept tambourines and trumpets near our worms' boxes lest any day a storm might suddenly break out. We had been told, and of course believed, that worms die from fright in a storm ; so as long as these pets were under our care we were always ready if necessary to drown the noise of thunder in what we called "music." Once the worms were all shut up in their cocoons, we would wait patiently until the butterflies nibbled their way through, laid their eggs, and died, much to my sorrow. I do not remember ever seeing the transformation of those eggs into worms again, so I suppose they were just thrown out ; otherwise mother might have had to go through the same experience I endured, many years later, when I found my dresses covered with tiny worms from hundreds of eggs my daughter Marissa had collected in a lidless box she had carefully deposited in my closet, where they had lain, ignored and forgotten, for nearly a year.

My last memory of that faraway Easter was the dinner at my Aunt Maria's house. We always dined with her family that day and they came to us for Christmas.

My cousins, Maria, Juan, Rosario and Isabelita, were playing with their lambs in the castle courtyard when we drove up. Following the custom, the lambs were all decorated with bows of bright-colored ribbons. I liked Juan much better than his sisters or his elder brother, Rafael. He was droll and supposed to resemble his mother, so perhaps that was one reason for my preference.

Aunt Maria had followed the usual Spanish tradition and had named her first-born Rafael after her husband, and her second boy Juan after her own father and mine, and their father, and grandfather, and probably their great-grandfather, for it seems to me that the head of the Oyarzábal family has always been called Juan.

I do not know whether the dinner I remember eating was really the one we had that night, but, if not, the menu would surely be the same, for no one would have dreamt of altering the usual order of things on such a day as long as my grandmother was there to prevent it. So I suppose we had first a rich rice soup from the *cocido*, the national *pot au feu* which has always been, and is, the basic food in every Spanish home, and which, like every other dish of its kind, can be more or less nourishing according to the family means. For the workers, a stripped bone and chick-peas and vegetables was thought enough. But among the well-to-do, the *cocido* is made with plenty of ham and chicken and rice and chick-peas boiled in water for hours at a time, after which the broth is strained and served apart, while red and black sausages and vegetables are added to the rest before it is sent up as a second course. In some of the wealthier homes the family only condescended to take the soup, the rest of the menu being made up with other more select dishes.

That Easter I imagine that, like every other year, we also had lobster and fowls in *pepitória*, a luscious sauce that Spaniards love, and a whole roast lamb I tried to forget had once been alive, and swallowed down without chewing to ease my conscience, and ham boiled in rich sherry and covered with burnt sugar, and innumerable sweet dishes : custard, with its thick layer of cinnamon and almond paste, and pastry and fruit of all kinds : oranges and cherries and almonds and bananas and custard apples and plums and special grapes preserved from the last year's harvest.   Mother did not allow us to drink wine, but my cousins all had a glass of sherry with their first course and another of anisette with their dessert.

Grandmother sat at one end of the table and my uncle at the other, with mother and Tita Maria on either side of him.   I should have loved to be near my aunt, but this would have meant coming very close to the general, so I wriggled into a seat between two of my cousins and was sorry afterward for, no sooner had we begun to eat than Rosario, who had been talking to my brother across the table, suddenly accosted me.

"Why didn't you choose a lamb instead of a black kid?" she asked in a loud voice.

"Because I like a kid better," I answered.

"You can't like it better.   Kids are cheaper than lambs."

I didn't see the point.

"Only poor persons buy kids," she went on, pursing her lips.

"I don't care if they do."

"I am sure it is very ugly," piped up her sister Isabelita. "Besides, you can't put bows on kids.   They don't stay on."

"It isn't.   It's lovely," I answered, gulping down my food in my haste to defend Morenita.   "It's much prettier than your stupid lambs, and I don't want to put ribbons on it.   I don't like ribbons myself."

The last part of my answer was irrelevant but it silenced my cousin.

When the numerous staff had cleared the table we all went into the big drawing room.   The furniture was rather like what we had at home. It was made of carved rosewood, covered with blue and white brocade, but I liked the pink and white satin on ours much better. The moment our grandmother fell asleep in her particular armchair, we got ready to leave. I remember there was a moon. There must have been a moon at Easter, and mother said that we should walk home.

Maria went on alone, a little ahead of Juan and me, and father and mother walked arm in arm behind us. The thought of what Rosario had said of Morenita still rankled in my mind. The little triangular-shaped head and the dark eyes and soft ears, and the tiny horns just breaking through, were lovely to me.

"I don't care if they think she is ugly," I said.

"Of course you don't," answered Juan.

"And I don't care if only poor persons buy kids."

This did not appear to bother Juan either, but the idea that we were not supposed to do what poor people did was probably borne upon me for the first time then. I dare say my thoughts went back to the words of the clergyman that morning, for I remember that as we walked along Juan and I agreed it would be much nicer for his lamb and my kid to have a field to play on instead of the hard brick floor of the terrace. We grew so excited over the idea that by the time we reached home we had mentally pulled down a whole row of houses in the Alameda and laid out a beautiful field in their place. The plan was Juan's, so naturally I thought it grand.

I am not quite sure whether it was that year or the next that mother took us to Granada for the first time. It does not much matter because our yearly visits to the capital of the old Moorish kingdom were all cut pretty much after the same pattern. And how we loved them! The trip was made by train so we enjoyed the always thrilling sensation of going through the seventeen tunnels which pierce the Malaga Mountains, before reaching the Granada *vega,* just allowing us to have fleeting glimpses of gorgeous red and golden rocks which towered above us and were at times cut open by the deep narrow gorges in the "Paso de los Gaitanes."

Dinner on board was also exciting. There were no diners in the Spanish trains at that time so we ate in our compartment and were allowed to hold the cold chicken we always had, in our fingers.

Granada was reached in the evening and we were driven up to the Siete Suelos Hotel in the Alhambra in a big omnibus pulled by three horses. The bells on the collars of the straining animals made a lovely sound. We were put to bed at once and in the morning would wake up to the music of running water. In the course of my life I have listened to the sound of many tiny brooks and to the roar of great rivers but to me nothing has ever equaled the beauty of the Alhambra rivulets and streams. Nowhere have I found water to be so eloquent. It seems not only to sing but to speak and in my childish imagination it spoke of many things, not least of great and noble deeds, as those described by the American writer, Washington Irving, whose book, *The Conquest of Granada,* I devoured later on.

We children would play in the Alhambra gardens and roam about the marvelous halls and courtyards of the palace, watched by mother and my *ama,* from early morning until the setting sun cast a deep pink glow on the Sierra Nevada. There were other little children we might have played with but Juan and I preferred the company of a Moor who lived near and spent his days in the Alhambra with us. He was supposed to earn a livelihood selling tourists Moroccan slippers made of soft yellow or red leather, but he invariably left his basket to the care of the hotel porter and went into the Alhambra where he sat and mused by the hour. Juan and I called him "Muley

Hassen" and became very friendly with him during our many successive visits to Granada. We would all three sit together on the ground near the fountain of a beautiful little recess where the cypress trees almost shut out the sky, and Muley Hassen would tell us marvelous tales of his own childhood and of his people, mostly, I suspect, drawn from his imagination, but which enthralled us and evidently were a means of expression his own soul needed.

Sometimes we would make him take off his turban and show us what he said were sabre cuts on his shaved head that we were given to understand he had received in a war. His manner was so convincing and our ideas about history were then so confused, that Juan and I were almost persuaded he was a survivor of the great struggle between the Spaniards and Arabs that had taken place in Granada nearly five centuries before. Children have no sense of time so it seemed to us perfectly natural that our Muley Hassen should have been alive all those ages and, fortunately, our visits to Granada were interrupted before we were ever moved to question our friend's sincerity in any way. I am glad now that this illusion was never shattered and love to think of the aged Arab sitting under the cypress trees, with his hands crossed on his lap and his head bent a little forward as though he were trying to catch the meaning of those unending murmurs of the Alhambra water which to him may have seemed like a message from his race.

Mother liked to take us to Granada because it was an invigorating change from the soft balmy air of Malaga, and, as she always said, it was easy because there we were always wonderfully well-behaved. This was true. I remember no pranks nor mischief disturbing the *ama's* peace of mind in Granada. And yet we had no lessons there, nothing to hamper our complete freedom, but the place undoubtedly cast a spell over us, especially Juan and me. There was something so mysterious about it all that we were evidently overawed. The only little scrape I remember getting into was the result of another little girl's commercial instinct. She asked me one morning whether I would care to go with her to pick violets which grew wild all over the Alhambra gardens and, when I was engaged making a bouquet for mother, she told me we ought to sell the seeds to people in the hotel and make lots of money. I thought the plan quite exciting and we both spent the day taking the seeds out of the flowers and wrapping them up in little bits of paper. The next afternoon mother found me going to the hotel guests, who were chiefly English tourists, and selling them the violet seeds for a penny a packet. Mother gave me quite a lecture and ordered me to return the money to all the people who had been my clients and thereby, I truly believe, squashed my incipient business talents forever.

Just about this time or around it my position as baby of the family was taken over by my new brother who was pompously christened Ricardo Gervásio y Protásio, but was familiarly alluded to as "Chick." I do not recall being at all impressed by the arrival of this new member of the family, nor was I made to feel that I had been displaced by it in anyone's affection. Besides, I was too much taken up with a new doll that had been given me for my birthday a few days before my brother's appearance to think of anything except "Maria Luisa" as she was duly and solemnly baptized by Juan after the manner of the priest whom he had seen christen our baby brother, Ricardo Gervásio y Protásio, in our parish church of San Juan.

CHAPTER II

"Girls! Girls!"

Juan's breathless voice preceded him up the stairs and into the nursery. "Quick! You are to go down to the patio to hear what father has to say. Wash your hands first lest you are sent up again to do it," he advised, retiring into his room to wash his own paws.

"What is it all about?" inquired Maria who was never in a hurry.

"It is a surprise and I promised father I wouldn't tell, so I can't," he answered.

A surprise! I wondered if a new baby had arrived. We tidied up as quickly as we could and were overtaken by Juan as we went into the patio where mother sat in her rocking-chair reading. Father was walking up and down, smoking his cigar.

"Who wants to come to Alhaurín to see the *pasos*?" he asked. Alhaurín was the name of the village where our family country house was situated and the *pasos* was the Passion Play, performed every two years by the villagers, which we had never yet seen. "Who wants to come to Alhaurín to see the *pasos* next week?"

"I! I! I!" we all yelled.

"But are we really going?" inquired Maria, who liked to be sure of things.

"If you are good . . ."

We were ready to swear to anything.

"How are we going, father?" asked Juan. "In the carriage, or couldn't we, just for once, go in the stagecoach?"

"Well, that is exactly what I was going to propose," answered father.

"You see we can't all go in the carriage because Abuelita and mother and the baby will need most of the room. One of you might go with them, the other two will come with me."

Maria then and there decided she preferred the carriage. I thought the week would never go by. I was not so much interested in the Passion Play, but I wanted to stay an extra week in Alhaurín and, above all, to drive there in the stage-coach.

The idea of leaving my dolls behind was my only worry. They went with me everywhere, but mother said we could only take down what was absolutely necessary, and no one thought them necessary except myself. Before leaving, I explained to this much cherished family of mine that they were not allowed to come and put them all to sleep in their cots, hoping they would not waken until I came back.

We had to take the stagecoach at a little village called Cár-tama, which we reached by train. Juan and I were thrilled when father hoisted us up beside him on to the top seat on the roof of the tumbled-down old vehicle pulled by six horses and manned by a fat and burly coachman and a little slip of a *zagal*, whose chief duty was to assist the passengers and to hop off and on the footboard in order to stir up the horses when lazy, as often they were.

"Ay . . . ay . . . ay . . . Paloma! Lucero! Bonita!" the burly coachman cried out to his horses as we rolled along the highway to Alhaurín.

"Ay . . . ay . . . ay . . . Paloma! Lucero! Bonita!" piped the *zagal*; his words were echoed by me, for it was a secret desire of my heart to be a coachman.

The air was so heavy with the perfume of the orange blossoms that I grew drowsy after a while and only woke to find myself in the village plaza, surrounded by my chattering cousins. It appeared that the place was full and that everybody who was anybody in Malaga intended seeing the Passion Play that year.

The old house looked lovely as we came near. It had been recently whitewashed and the dazzlingly white walls showed off the dark iron railings that bulged out from the windows, I thought, very like the black-striped waistcoat of the little village druggist who was almost as wide as he was tall, and whom we all loved because he would tell us such delightful stories. The ground floor of the house was all given up to reception rooms and to the huge dining room and kitchen. Upstairs there were rooms for us all and to spare.

What I loved best of all, however, was the Moorish garden behind the house. The sidewalks were paved with red tiles and the flower-beds watered by means of little canals that could be opened and closed by tiny wooden sluices. And at that time of the year it was full of flowers : irises, lilies, pansies, violets, huge carnations and roses of every possible variety.

The next day being Palm Sunday we were marched into the parish church by Aunt Maria to get our palms and join in the procession. We took home the lovely, feathery, two- and three-yard-length palms and tied them on to our balconies so as to keep away evil and sickness during the year.

Dinner that day was a tremendous affair, and we partook of it with all the others because my grandmother would have been deeply offended if, in her house, we had been exiled to the nursery, which terrible English invention she considered "the Siberia of children." There were several priests present, also the village doctor and his wife, and other members of our family who were staying at their homes on the other side of the street, and the dear old fat apothecary. The meal was very long and, before it was over, Aunt Maria calmly nursed her baby before the whole party. Maternity has always been the object of such reverence to Spaniards that a woman could unblushingly expose her breast in public, though she would not allow one inch of ankle or throat to be seen on other occasions. I thought she looked more beautiful than ever as she sat with her baby in her arms, laughing and chatting, and occasionally drawing a fine lace handkerchief over her bosom to shade the baby's face.   And I wished mother would not have been so shy about nursing her baby in public, too, but she always hid away to do it.

As we came out of the dining room my cousin Rosario beckoned to me mysteriously.

"Would you like to come and see something really interesting?" she whispered.

Of course I was willing.

"We must get out of the house without being seen," she said.   "You know Abuelita does not like us to go about alone."

I followed her without a word as she led the way down to the bottom of the garden and out by a little door to the roughly cobbled street behind the house.   Once there, she took my hand and ran toward a house higher up.   A group of people were standing beside one of the grilled windows.

"It must be there," Rosario said.

When we drew near she brushed the people aside and made me peer into what at first seemed just a darkened room where two women were most audibly weeping.   As my eyes grew accustomed to the light I saw that there was a black box in which there lay a man with a terribly white face.   He was dressed in black and his patent leather shoes rose out of the box as stiff as if they had been made of wood.

"What is it, Rosario?   What is it?" I inquired in an agonized whisper.

"Can't you see for yourself?   It's a dead man, but," she

added with intense excitement as she pulled me away from the window, "he didn't just die. He was killed by another man and he wasn't able to receive the last sacraments so they don't know if he will be buried in consecrated ground."

I would hear no more. I ran down the cobbled street and into the house, looking for mother. She did not scold me for going with Rosario but seemed annoyed with my cousin for taking me with her, and tried to reassure me by saying death was like a sleep. But there was something too stiff about that body I had seen to make me accept her explanation without further discussion, as I always did. Besides, people did not go to sleep in their shoes. At least I never saw anyone. The impression of that first sight I had of death was, of course, never obliterated. It kept coming back long after the gossip about the dead man, who had been killed by a jealous husband, had worn itself out.

The Passion Play began on Wednesday evening and lasted until late on Friday night. During the daytime the performance was suspended of course.

I knew many of the people in the cast because it was usual for the characters to be played by the same persons for several years in succession, the roles often being inherited by members of the same family. Thus Abraham was always played by some one of the Roméro clan and Peter and Paul were from the García Soláno family. The Christ was personified by a priest from Malaga, and the Virgin Mother by the image of Our Lady of Sorrows which was revered in the parish church. The great difficulty was to find anyone willing to play the role of Judas. This was partially settled by letting the parish priest choose the person for each successive year, but even this method provoked great discontent and heartburn.

The stage was set up in the plaza. It was just a large open platform leading to the church door. The lighting of the stage was done by colored torches. We had reserved seats in one of the balconies of the municipal building just opposite so we could get a very good view.

I cannot say I was much impressed by what I saw the first night of the performance. I could not understand the symbolism of Abraham's sacrifice of his son Isaac, and I was chiefly worried by the fate of the ram, for the poor animal was sacrificed in our view.

Thursday evening the plaza was more crowded and the people followed with rapt attention the free verse and the even freer play of the actors who went through their parts with solemn simplicity as though performing a religious ceremony.

Nobody ever directed them. Each one did his part as he thought it ought to be done. The prayer in the garden of Gethsemane seemed long but I was thrilled with the appearance of the angel.

The climax came on Friday night. The huge crowd in the plaza followed the different scenes as Christ was taken before Caiphas and Pilate, with breathless interest but in complete silence.

When Christ was at last laid on the cross, the loud hammer blows found their echo in the women's mumbled protests, but suddenly a furious cry arose at the sight of a stooping figure, carrying a bag, that passed from one side to the other of the stage as though looking for a hiding place.

"Judas! It is Judas! The traitor!" The crowd swayed violently as the cry was taken up and passed on. "Judas! Judas! Kill him! Don't let him get away!"

I was terrified. The people's frenzy was so sincere I thought they would really kill the man on the stage and I clung to Juan's arm crying:

"What is it? What do they want?"

"It's Judas Iscariot," he answered, looking as though he, too, wanted to kill that poor man who was still turning around looking for a hiding place. At last he got away.

The scene went on but the people kept on shouting that Judas must be killed. Suddenly the cross was raised and a great silence fell on all. The doors of the church were thrown open and the image of the Virgin appeared on the threshold. She was shrouded in black velvet and great tears seemed to be falling from her wide-open eyes. Then the figure on the cross was taken down and laid between her outstretched arms. The people began to cry out again :

"Dear Holy Mother, look at your Son. Look at the Child of your heart."

Flowers began to rain upon the stage. Francisco and José, our two serving men, took up at least eight huge bouquets that had been ordered by Aunt Maria, and they were laid at the feet of the Virgin by one of the actors. I saw Francisco mopping up his tears. My cousins were loud in their lamentations ; Juan looked very grim and I wanted to know what had become of Judas.

"Where is Judas ?" I asked. "Have they killed him ?" But Juan did not answer.

After a little the body of Christ was wrapped in a white shroud and put away in what I suppose was intended to be the tomb. The image of the Virgin was taken back into the church. A voice broke into a song. The songs of Andalusia are like long trailing laments. It was taken up by another and then many more, but the play was over and we were ordered home. On the way back to the house I tried to speak to mother but there were so many grown-ups I could not get near her. I next tried Rosario. She might tell me what I wanted to know.

"What did they do to Judas ?" I asked. "Why did they want to kill him ?"

"Because he is the wickedest man that ever lived," she said with real hatred in her voice. "I would like to kill him myself. There isn't one single person in the whole world, and there never has been, who doesn't hate him."

I felt more and more unhappy. I could not forget that poor lonely figure skulking away in the midst of those terrible cries : "Kill him, kill him !"

"Well, I don't hate him," I said, "and I don't think he is as bad as you think."

"That means you are a wicked creature, too. Nobody in the world thinks well of Judas. Will you believe," she said, turning to the others, "that Isabel thinks one should be sorry for Judas ?" Everybody seemed terribly shocked and I went to bed feeling most unhappy.

"What's my ugly duckling thinking ?" asked mother, as she bent over my bed that night on her way to her own room. I hid my face from her and she, fearing I might have been over-impressed by the Passion Play, sat beside me for a little, patting my head and saying, "It's only a story you know, darling, it may have been true once, but it is only a story now." I felt the way was clear for my great question, and, pulling her head down to the level of my own, I whispered, "Mother, do you hate Judas ?" Mother looked at me, surprised.

"Poor Judas, no . . . I am rather sorry for him."

I was so relieved, now there were at least two persons in the world who were sorry for Judas.

On the way back to Alhaurín father told us that mother was not very well. The doctors had ordered her to go away from Malaga for the summer and we children were all going to Scotland with her. Juan was so pleased I thought I should be, too.

In the days that followed he did nothing but talk about Rob Roy and other Scottish characters from Sir Walter Scott's works. One day at breakfast he surprised me by asking, "Would you like one of your dolls to become a queen ?"

My ideas about royalty were rather mixed but I knew queens were usually very grand people who wore crowns.

"They are not dolls, they are babies," I said.

"Oh, well, never mind. Would you like one of them to be a queen ?"

"Would she have to be grown up ?" I inquired anxiously.

"Well, yes, a queen is grown up but — she is different from other people." And he added, "Would you like her to be Queen of Scotland ?"

I thought that might be interesting as we were leaving for Scotland within the next few days. So we agreed that after dinner one of my babies would become a queen.

I hesitated very much which I would choose, but at last I decided on my beloved Maria Luisa, the one that Juan had christened after our baby brother's arrival and that was a great pet with me. She can go back and be a baby again, I thought, as soon as she has finished being a queen.

Juan was very silent all through the meal and as soon as it was over disappeared into his own room, saying he would come and fetch me in a little while. So I took up Maria Luisa and undressed her in order to get her ready for her ascent to the throne.

Juan soon came back and we looked around for something we might use as a royal robe. The lace antimacassar from the nursery sofa and one of my best sashes proved more than sufficient to make up an imposing garment.

"She ought to have a train," said Juan, pulling at the robe so that it trailed behind. Then I was asked to hold Maria Luisa by one hand while he held her by the other and, with very slow solemn steps, accompanied by a chanting sort of march,

Juan led us into his room. The place was quite dark except for two lighted candles on the table. Two of our big ninepins stood beside them.

Suddenly Juan began to speak in a loud voice and to accuse my poor Maria Luisa in a way that terrified me. "Mary Queen of Scots," he cried, "you are a traitor !"

"She isn't," I began indignantly, but before I could say another word, Juan had taken my beloved child in his arms and had begun to shake her.

"A traitor, and therefore you must die by order of the Queen of England." And, without a moment's hesitation, he laid beautiful Maria Luisa on the table and smashed her head with one of the ninepins.

I screamed with such force that my brother, who had been behaving like someone quite different from his own self, sobered down and began to pat my back nervously.

"Hush," he said, "don't cry." Then he added reproachfully, "You said you wanted her to be a queen."

However, I would not be comforted. Maria Luisa's head and face were battered out of all recognition. She was made of wax and could not even be mended. I cried and cried till my *ama* came to see what was the matter. She was followed by Maria.

When mother heard what had happened she took me down to her room and, laying me on her bed, tried to comfort me. But it took a long time.

It wasn't only the loss of my child, which was bad enough, but the shock to my faith in my brother. Mother was very much annoyed with him. "I should never have thought you could do such a thing," she said.

He looked at me so sadly my heart began to melt.

"I asked her first if she wanted her doll to be a queen," he said, with a troubled look in his face. "And I even asked her if she would like her to be Mary Queen of Scots."

"But I didn't know what it meant," I burst in.

"I would have told you if you had asked me. Don't I always tell you everything you want to know ?"

That was true. I began to warm toward him again and that very afternoon we were playing together with his best puzzle which he had given me as a peace offering. But I don't think I ever quite got over his having executed Maria Luisa.

Fortunately the trip to England and Scotland helped to make me forget my sorrow. We went by boat from Malaga to Liverpool and there is little I can remember of the trip except that I was seasick all the time.

England and Scotland themselves did not make a very strong impression on me. Everything seemed very quiet. Our cousins were very shy and reserved and well-behaved, and I was always being called back to close the doors. We were so accustomed to leaving them open in Spain that I never could get into the new way.

We spent most of the time at Prestwick where my aunts had taken a house for the summer and where we were able to bathe in the sea and begin to learn how to play golf. One of our first Sundays we managed to get into a horrible predicament. Mother and my aunts had gone to church and left us at home with strict injunctions not to touch anything and to behave properly.

Juan and I were very bored and I thought he had had a brilliant inspiration when he proposed that we should go into the back garden and play bullfight. I was ready for anything and even Maria was willing to try.

We got two short sticks and tied them on to a large bit of wood in imitation of a bull's head. A red cloth the dog used to sleep on we thought would do for a cape, so we began the show.

We had often played like this at home.

Each one had to be the bull in turn because it was so much more fun to be a bullfighter. Maria took the bull's head first and began to pursue Juan and me up and down the back-yard. She was a fast runner and threw me down several times but she could not get hold of Juan who would stand before her defiantly and squirm and twist out of her reach like a real bullfighter.

We were so engrossed in our game that we did not realize we were being watched by our neighbors on both sides of the hedge. There were children and grown-ups and they all seemed scared to see what we were doing.

"Hi . . . bull!" cried Juan to Maria, tapping the ground with his foot as he had been told real bullfighters did. Maria pawed the ground and bellowed and was just about to launch a vicious attack on him when one of the lads who was looking on at us suddenly cried out :

"Do you know it's the Sabbath ?"

"Well," said Juan, stopping short, "and what has that got to do with it ?"

"Spaniards ! Blackamoors !" the lad cried to us.

Juan laid down his red cape and went toward him. The boy jumped over the fence and came to meet him, followed by two or three others.

One minute later the two were rolling on the grass, punching each other's heads. Maria dropped the bull's head and ran into the house. I began to scream at the top of my voice. A lady and gentleman came in through the gate and tried to separate the combatants, and, in the midst of it all, mother and the aunts came back from church.

I could not see why we should have been attacked in that

way and it took mother quite a time to make us understand that our neighbors had been outraged because we were playing in the garden on a Sunday.

"But the bullfights always take place on Sundays," said Juan, trying to stem the blood from a cut lip.

My aunts were quite upset. They believed they would never live down this violation of the Sabbath in their house and thought we might have found some other quiet game with which to entertain ourselves. Evidently we were disapproved of in Scotland, too, so we never played bullfight again while we were there. I never got over my dislike of a Scottish Sabbath.

The trip back to Spain was more exciting than we had expected. Our steamer was overtaken by a gale in the English Channel and we had to take refuge in the Isle of Wight for over twenty-four hours. Several passengers suffered accidents and no one had a good meal for days. When father met us at Gibraltar I had been so seasick that I could not walk and had to be taken down to the cab in the steward's arms.

That journey gave us all a feeling of tremendous importance and was a great help afterward when we wanted to play shipwreck. Malaga seemed to have become much smaller, the streets narrower, and everything more noisy. Our house, on the contrary, seemed bigger than ever and it was lovely to get back to the roof-garden.

CHAPTER III

A few months after we returned from Scotland we heard that mother was going to become a Roman Catholic. I was not very much interested but glad to know we would not go back to the Protestant chapel.

We children were present when she was admitted into the Catholic Church. Juan wore a new sailor suit and Maria and I were in white with pale-yellow ribbons. The ceremony took place in the chapel of the Convent of the Assumption. All our aunts and cousins were there and when we left the chapel Juan, Maria and I were embraced and made much of as though we had done something really important.

Afterward we went home and mother gave us each a rosary and told us, when we were going out for our walk, that if we met anyone we knew and they asked for her, we were to say that day had been the happiest of her life.

During the weeks that followed nothing seemed much changed. Father and mother seemed very satisfied. In the month of August, Maria and I were prepared by the superior of the Convent of the Assumption to make our first confession. The only thing I can remember is that when I went up to the confessional I was struck dumb. The priest asked me a few things and I said "yes" to everything and then he gave me a prayer to recite for a penance.

I felt quite disappointed. Everybody had told me I was going to feel so happy afterward, and I wasn't a bit.

That same fall Juan was sent to the Jesuit college just outside Malaga and Maria and I were taken into the Convent of the Assumption. I believe mother would have preferred to send me as a day boarder but the mother superior advised her not to. She thought it was not good for us to get away from the convent discipline every evening and assured mother it would really be harder for me in the end. I didn't agree with her. As a day boarder I would have seen my mother every day.

It nearly broke my heart to leave my dolls behind me, but we were not allowed to take toys into the convent.

Before going into the school we had to be provided with all kinds of things : silver mugs and forks and spoons and a special kind of sewing box and three uniforms ; two grey ones and a hideous blue one for Sundays. All our things were marked with a number, not with our initials. Maria's number was 41 and mine 35.

The uniforms were most depressing : a skirt that came far below the knees, a tight-fitting jacket with a high military collar closing over a white starched one, a black woolen apron and a little cape of the same material as the dress. The Sunday uniform was the same shape but we did not wear an apron with it.

Our hair was pulled tightly back from the forehead with a black or a dark-blue ribbon and carefully braided. The only bright note in our costume was the *capulet*, a sort of red flannel cape, such as the women in the Pyrenees wear, which we used to wear out of doors.

I cannot recollect much about those first months in the convent except that I was unhappy. So unhappy I could not even feel sorry for myself and so get some comfort. I was only just seven and everything I loved had been taken from me and nothing given me in return.

The rules of the convent were very strict. We rose at a quarter to six and were taken down to chapel for Mass and meditation. Then we were given one quarter of an hour for breakfast and sent up to our classrooms for lessons or study until eleven-thirty when we had dinner, followed by our first half hour of recreation outside. Then two hours of sewing while someone read aloud from the lives of the saints. More study and another half hour's recreation, followed by studies until our six o'clock supper, after which we had one hour of supposedly free time, but we had to employ it in singing or joining in a sort of general conversation under the control of the nun on duty.

Perhaps the schedule itself would have been more bearable if we had been allowed a little more freedom. If we had not been forced to walk in line, saying our rosary, and above all, if we had been able to speak to each other at least during meals. But talking was strictly forbidden all day, and the slightest infraction was punished with a bad mark or with having to kiss the floor in public.

I did not mind the lessons, though I can hardly say I made any effort over them. But those long hours sitting before my book, during study periods, with my hands crossed on my desk and without any kind of support to my back, were torture.

The convent was situated in beautiful grounds at the foot of the hill of the Gibralfáro and I used to look at the sun shining through the eucalyptus trees and the bright geranium hedges till I grew sick with despair at not being able to get out.

The nights were almost worse. We slept in large dormitories with the windows closed. Probably the lack of fresh air prevented me from sleeping properly. I kept tossing in my bed, just longing for mother to come and say good night to me, and thinking of my babies. Now and again one could hear the sentry's voice up in the castle, passing on the watchword, and the dogs barking when anyone came near the convent, and this made me feel more shut away than ever from everything I cared for.

Maria would sometimes look me up, but she was nearly five

years older than I and had a different schedule. Besides, smaller girls were not allowed to play with the older ones during recreation.

Games were encouraged and I liked them, though they seemed rather tame after ours at home, but it was difficult to make the other girls play. They preferred to walk about, chattering to each other. They didn't know how to run properly and easily tired.

Parents were allowed to see their children for two hours on Sundays and I was always so full of eager questions about what Juan was doing that I never seemed able to tell mother what I felt myself. Not that I would have complained, for we always obeyed her orders unquestioningly, but perhaps she might have understood a little of what I was going through.

"Juan is very well," I always heard, and it comforted me not a little.

At last Christmas came and we were allowed to go home for one short week. But I lost interest when I heard that the Jesuit college did not allow the boys to go home.

On Christmas Day we drove out to the college to see Juan. My heart beat while we waited in the stiff parlor, and when my brother appeared I did not have the courage to go to meet him. He seemed so quiet and small. Almost like a stranger. He was dressed in the black Sunday uniform of the school and his head had been shorn very closely.

It was terrible leaving him there alone.

Our next holidays were at Easter, just three days, and Juan did not come home then either. The Jesuit fathers believed it was a great mistake for the boys to go home in the middle of the school year. "They are quite as happy here with us," they would say to mother. Juan did not look happy.

At the end of my first year at school I seemed to have forgotten the little I knew and to have learnt nothing else. I tried to put it all behind me and enjoy the summer holidays. We had two months, two whole months to do as we liked.

The first few days Juan and I really thought life was going to be as it used to be, but a change we could not account for had taken place. Mother and father were very loving. They wanted us to have a good time and yet there was something different in the way they looked upon things.

I was not allowed to run about, as I had always done. Our French governess, Mademoiselle Marie, was always with us and would make us go to church for a little while every afternoon.

When I went back to the convent in the month of September I felt worse than when I first entered it. There was not even the feeling of novelty. Everything was just the same. When the sister porter locked the door behind us I had the sensation that I had been trapped. That sensation never left me altogether.

I could not understand my sister's delight in returning. She was really pleased to see the nuns again and all the girls of her class. But I had nothing to say to any of them. No one there knew Juan who, even if he had not been in the Jesuit college, would not have been allowed to come to see us. The rules of the convent forbade it.

No one knew my *ama* nor my dolls, nor our roof-garden, nor Alhaurín. What could there be for me to talk to them about ?

Most of the nuns were English or French and they would make us speak their languages all the time. I liked them better than the few Spanish nuns who thought we should sew all day, but I did not really get in close touch with any of them. There was a sweet English mother, Madame Marie Casilda, who did her best to draw me out.

"What is going on here?" she would say, patting my head, but she did not succeed in making me answer.

I must have seemed a strange, unattractive child to them. Sullen and ungrateful, I instinctively felt that is what they thought, but I could see nothing to be grateful for. My only wish was to go home and their one idea was to keep me away from it. Yet they meant well and were anxious to make me happy.

Great things were expected after I made my first communion two years later. "Many children change entirely," my mother was told. I began to hope that something was going to happen to me.

For at least three months before the day fixed for the first communion, the "first communicants" were singled out and had their meals and recreation apart from the others. I got to know one of the little girls very well. She belonged to a devout family and assured me that something would happen inside of me which would make me see everything in a new light.

I began to feel quite anxious for the day to arrive.

Mother was kept busy getting my frock and veil and all the little accessories. Everything had to be absolutely like the model given by the nuns. The dress was very simple, just white muslin with a long skirt that touched the ground, and a white muslin veil.

We all had many presents. Gold medals and crucifixes and mother-of-pearl rosaries and white prayer-books.

During the ceremony I did feel rather uplifted. The chapel was beautifully decorated with flowers and the sound of the organ made me feel inclined to cry.

That day there were no lessons nor studies for anyone and the whole school seemed to think of nothing but the "first communicants."

Then life went back to the usual round and I found myself once more shut up within myself. No miracle had happened. Outwardly I was the same and inwardly I had only one burning desire : to get away. Fortunately the summer holidays were so near I had no time to grow skeptical, and that year I did get some benefit from "the long vacation."

We spent almost the whole time in Alhaurín and although Juan was out with his friends nearly all day I found it possible to amuse myself with my dolls and with another great attraction, my new little sister, Anita, who had arrived a few months before. I was allowed to hold her as much as I liked and actually to feed her, and little by little I lost my sullenness and became more like my own self.

Mother had been told by the nuns that I was a very poor sewer and should be made to work at my embroidery all summer. I was fortunate to be put in charge of a young schoolteacher who was spending the summer in Alhaurín, too, and who initiated me into the mysteries of lace-making. She was so amusing and good-tempered that I actually came to love this new accomplishment. I also took dancing lessons. Those I loved. I would play my castanets by the hour and bend and turn and move my arms until I felt that the rhythm was part of my very being.

Altogether it was a happy summer, but it made the going back all the harder. The weeks and months went slowly by and every night I deleted one of the little lines that marked the days until the holidays.

Just after Christmas our grandmother died. My sister and I were informed of our loss by the mother superior, who advised us to go into the chapel for a little while and say a prayer for her soul.

Maria and I sat in the silent chapel but I did not pray. I thought one's first duty when any member of the family died was to weep and I could not manage to do it. I went over all the happy hours we had spent in Abuelita's room and the numerous presents she had given us, but in vain.

"Oh, poor Abuelita, poor Abuelita," I said to myself, over and over. Then I suddenly remembered the dead man I had seen lying in the long black box in Alhaurín and wondered whether Abuelita would be lying in a box, too. At the thought of it I managed to squeeze out a few tears, which made me feel better.

"Are you not going to wear mourning for your grandmother ?" said one of the girls to me a few days later.

"No," I answered, "mother does not like to see us in black and she thinks the grey uniform is enough. We are going to wear them on Sundays also."

"How strange," she said. "When my grandmother died I wore black for a whole year." And she looked very superior.

I felt that we were not doing our duty toward Abuelita at all.

I did not worry overmuch, however. Just about that time I found a wonderful substitute for my much-longed-for dolls. It was simply to have imaginary children of my own. It was very easy and interesting.

First I imagined a little girl with fair hair and dark eyes, something like my little sister. In my pretense I would buy her the most wonderful toys and the prettiest clothes. Soon I thought I should like to have more children, so I settled on twin boys. They were sweet but gave me a great deal of trouble.

I thought about them all the time. In the chapel, during sewing lessons and above all during study hours. The silence all round helped wonderfully and I began to resent being addressed by anyone.

The lessons which I had never found difficult simply because I took no trouble over those that did not interest me, like mathematics, were the only distraction. All the rest of the day I gave up to my beloved imaginary family.

Twin girls were soon added to the family party and they were followed by a lovely little dark-skinned, dark-haired girl with blue eyes.

It was the most wonderful thing in the world to see them all come out of nothing and surround me. Each one, of course, had its name and its own little peculiarities. I told no one but mother about this new development, and she was sympathetic. I vowed her to secrecy for I had a feeling that if my babies were talked about, they would disappear.

Probably I had an underlying fear of ridicule. But for the moment, they were far more real to me than any of the nuns or the girls I lived with. There was also a little feeling of revenge. They had taken everything from me but now I didn't care for I had a whole world of my own.

Ridicule was much more feared than punishment in the convent. The oppressive silence wrecked one's nerves and the slightest thing would send the girls into fits of giggling. A slight mistake when reading prayers would attract such attention and provoke such hilarity that many of the girls were positively afraid to undertake the simplest tasks.

Criticisms of one another's personal appearance verged at times on cruelty. I was pestered for a time because my mother would not allow me to wear corsets.

"You can pull your waist in when you are grown up and it won't do you any harm," she would say. The other girls prided themselves on their tiny wasplike figures.

"You will be known as the girl without a waistline," I would be told. At first it bothered me but I grew indifferent to that, too.

The nuns' vigilance over any budding vanity was extended to

the children's homes. Strong disapproval was shown toward those unfortunate girls whose mothers thought fit to have their fringe cut during the summer holidays.

In spite of the nuns' condemnation most of the girls were interested in looking as nice as possible. Great store was laid on female beauty.

"Is she pretty ?" was the first thing asked about a new student.

I never saw any great or exaggerated friendships between the girls, or boundless admiration for any of the nuns. The older students were supposed to help in keeping order. It often made them disagreeably meddlesome.

One day during the afternoon study I was called up to the teacher's desk. I rather liked her. Her name was Madame Marie Louise and she was very sweet looking.

"What is Maria Josefa Derqui doing ?" she asked me in a low voice. Maria Josefa Derqui was a fat, stodgy, mentally backward girl who sat beside me in the classroom. She was at least three years older than any of us.

"Maria Josefa Derqui ?" I inquired, looking at the girl who was bending over her desk. "She is writing, I think."

"Yes, but what is she writing ?"

"I don't know."

"Well, I wish you would find out and come and tell me afterward. Do not let her suspect you are watching her."

"Am I to look and . . . tell you, mother ?"

"Yes. I am sure that child has been writing letters to someone outside and it must be put a stop to. Now go to your place and report later."

I felt horribly nervous. Madame Marie Louise evidently wanted me to sneak on Maria Josefa. But I couldn't.

"I won't do that, mother," I said.

Madame Marie Louise looked at me severely.

"Do you mean to say you refuse to do what you are told?"
"Yes. . ."

Madame Marie Louise rose suddenly.   I wondered what she
was going to do to me.

"Stay here," she said.   Moving stealthily, she came up to
Maria Josefa's desk and laid her hand on the girl's arm.   Maria
Josefa jumped, then she pulled the paper from under the nun's
hand and crammed it into her mouth.   Madame Marie Louise
was dumbfounded.

"You are a naughty, disobedient child," she said to her.
"And I must inform reverend mother at once.   Please do not
leave this room until I come and fetch you."   Then, turning
to me, "You will come with me to see reverend mother, also."

I went back to my place and waited.   When another nun
took charge of the class Madame Marie Louise asked me to go
with her.   Reverend mother was in her little sitting room.   I
was told to wait.   Madame Marie Louise soon came out and
said I might go in.

"Come in, child," said the mother superior.   "What terrible
thing have you been up to?"

I felt there was laughter in her voice and was encouraged.
Mother Caroline, the superior of the convent, was a North
American.   She had become a Roman Catholic during a visit
to Europe and had entered the order almost at once.   She was
said to be charming but I had never seen her alone before.

"I have not been up to anything," I answered, "but I have
refused to sneak and . . ." I looked up to see how reverend
mother was taking it . . . "I am not going to."

"Don't you think that is too strong a word?   Madame
Marie Louise was only hoping you would help to keep Maria
Josefa in order.   The poor child has no sense of responsibility."

"I am quite ready to help," I said rather uncertainly, "but I
am not going to tell on her."

"Very well, we shall leave it at that. I know I can trust you to look after her a little. If you see her doing things she should not do, just tell her she must not. Will you?"

I did not feel inclined to look after Maria Josefa but I was ready to do anything to keep her out of trouble. For the first time I felt there was someone in the convent who understood.

"Now, run away, and tell Maria Josefa to come to me," the reverend mother said.

My classmate escaped with nothing more than a private reprimand. It turned out that those letters were written to an imaginary person, but I persuaded her not to write them in the convent.

That was my sister's last year at school. After the summer holidays she was to be sent to London to be "finished."

I would have to go back to the convent alone. I did not mind that very much. That year I had taken six first prizes. All the nuns except the teacher of mathematics said they were well satisfied with my work. The truth is I worked very little but I was able to grasp things and remember them.

I did not feel so desperate now. Life was very uninteresting but the time seemed to pass more quickly than before. Perhaps I was less impatient because I did not see anything worth while ahead.

"The Christmas holidays are near," I would say to myself, "and after them? The Easter holidays. And after? The summer vacation. And after that? Back to the convent again. And after? And after? And after? I shall be going home."

There I stopped. Even going home did not mean so much now. I had no ambition, no desire. I had lived for seven years with the same sixty or sixty-five girls and the same teachers and I did not know any of them. They had told me nothing and had heard nothing from me.

I was slightly interested in some of my school subjects : history, literature and geography.

The religious teaching orders were the first to do something for women's education in Spain. They introduced languages and adopted the curriculum of the state schools, but with books of their own choosing. Then they stopped and in time the state schools were far ahead.

This inertia invaded the spiritual side of me also. I enjoyed the chapel services when there was music but I preferred to think to myself rather than to sing or pray with the others. Outwardly I had become "disciplined" enough to satisfy everybody.

During my last year I was asked to help the "poor school." Down near the gates of the convent the nuns were running a little day school for some of the ragged children who lived in huts on the hillside.

The school was free. Absolute subservience to the practices and beliefs of the Roman Catholic Church on the part of the family was the only price. Most of the children's parents were indifferent to those questions so they were ready to comply, as long as their offspring received a new dress and an occasional meal and was taught to read and write. There were no primary schools in that part of the town. In fact, eighty-five per cent of the whole Malaga population was then illiterate.

I found the "poor children" much more interesting than the others, little restless monkeys up to all sorts of mischief. They, too, were "disciplined" after a while, but never quite so much as we.

At fourteen I was in the top class of the school with just one other girl, two years older than I was. When the year ended, mother was advised to take me home. The nuns had nothing more to teach me.

The day we left I peeled off my uniform and kicked it under

the bed. It was sent to me later with a little note regretting my last hour's untidiness.

We all marched into the chapel for benediction. The spiritual director of the convent, who was a famous Jesuit preacher, talked to us about the dangers and snares of the world we were going to enter.

The good-byes began. All the girls who were leaving for good wept copiously. Last-hour instructions and promises were exchanged. I felt as I did when Abuelita died, I could not weep. But I had a little heart wrench when I said good-bye to reverend mother.

She laid her hand on my head and said, "God bless you, my child." I looked up. The eyes behind the glasses were full of tears. Then she laughed and I laughed, too. We didn't need to speak to each other to understand.

CHAPTER IV

Mother thought I was too young to "come out" when I left school. So for nearly a year I did little but try to adapt myself to my new surroundings.

Two more children had arrived to enrich the family circle. Now there were seven Oyarzábals. The latest additions were José Luis and Inez. Mother was almost always ailing and Maria was away so I took it upon myself to superintend the nursery. Inez was like my own child. I bathed her and fed her every day in spite of the remonstrances of the nurse and my *ama* who thought it was their duty and not mine. My dream children disappeared.

Our house was very much changed. Juan was in training to join father in business and "Chick" became my boon companion in his stead. I had a great deal of time on my hands, in spite of the children, and read most of the day, but I found great gaps in the library. Many of our standard works had disappeared.

"What has happened to all Benito Pérez Galdós' books ?" I asked Juan one day.

"Father has burnt them," he answered.

Then I hunted high and low for Dumas' *Three Musketeers*. All this author's books, as well as Maupassant's and Balzac's, had been taken away.

On my expostulating mildly with father, he said, "Those works are disapproved of by the church and should not be read by Catholics."

"Read Dickens," mother said.

But I knew Dickens by heart and I was not in the mood for his works just then.

At last I fell upon a funny little collection of books on

chivalry that had escaped the "purge." I forget the author's name. My brain fed on narratives of brave knights and beautiful ladies and pageants and tournaments. I made up my mind that one day I would have a knight in my service and that white and crimson would be my colors.

These dreams were shattered by my father's coming unexpectedly into the house early one afternoon. "We are at war," he said, sitting down with a depressed gesture. "Spain is at war with the United States."

It was true. Next day and many after that there were street riots. The people tore down the American consulate flag. We were all very much excited and sure that we were going to win, but father looked worried. Mysterious rumors began to circulate concerning Admiral Cámara's "ghost fleet." He was a friend of father's and so was his brother who lived in Malaga. No one knew where the fleet was. People said it was going to attack some port of the United States. We were never given an explanation of the reasons that had provoked the war. Parliament to us meant nothing. After some time, bad news from Cuba began to come in. No one would believe the reports until some months later when ships full of sick soldiers arrived in Malaga. It was the first intimation I had that we had lost.

For weeks one could hardly walk through the Alameda or the principal streets of the town. Hundreds of men lay dying on the ground and could not be removed because the hospitals were crammed and there was no other place for them. We were timidly called upon to help. When a ship carrying part of the remains of the Spanish army came into port the bells of the cathedral would ring for everybody to rush food down to the landing place. I did not see a single healthy-looking man among all those thousands that were disembarked in our town after being hastily shipped off from Cuba without food or clothes. They were huddled on the decks like sheep, most of them sick with Cuba's one-time scourge, the yellow fever.

"The Atlantic is one huge grave," we would be told. "Every night fifty or sixty dead men are thrown overboard from every transport bringing the troops home."

People seemed depressed but no one protested. England was often blamed. "No one has helped Spain," was the cry.

Our house was always full of men asking for food and a little money to get home. Someone started a movement to get up entertainments to raise funds. I was asked to join a theatrical group and we made quite a little money for the evacuated soldiers. I was thrilled to hear my acting praised by the professional who came down from Madrid to train us.

After some months the miserable-looking crowd of refugees left Malaga. Many just went home to die. Soon people forgot the war. That spring one of my father's friends said to him in my presence :

"Juan, you really ought to make your daughter cover up those pretty legs of hers. They are quite a temptation."

I wished that I had no legs. Father decided I had better "come out" and wear long skirts.

The day my braids were taken up and knotted on the top of my head I felt as if I were all hairpins. My long skirts were uncomfortable and kept tripping me up, much to father's amusement.

Mother took me round to see and be seen by all our relatives and friends. I did not get many compliments. Everybody remarked on my pale complexion. For years afterward I envied every woman who could boast of having a "fine color."

It was thought better for me to "come out" although I was only fifteen because there seemed no place for me in Malaga life otherwise. Once the calls were over I was considered a "young lady." Mother told everyone a ball would be given in our house that winter after my sister Maria came home.

I rather enjoyed going round to see the family. A war was raging at that moment between my Aunt Maria and my Aunt Amalia, who was the wife of one of father's cousins, the Marqués of Casa Loring. I heard a great deal about it. Both ladies were the leading lights of the two most important political parties then struggling for supremacy in Spain.

Aunt Maria, who was the sister-in-law of General Lopez Dominguez, led the Malaga members of the so-called liberal party. Aunt Amalia, whose husband had helped the struggling young schoolmaster, Antonio Cánovas del Castillo, who afterward became Spanish premier and one of the chief supporters of the Spanish crown, led the conservatives.

Aunt Amalia had rather hard features, a beaked nose and a forbidding manner, but she could count on the allegiance of the Malaga church hierarchy and of the "well-known," that is, the "well-off," people of the town.

Aunt Maria was adored by middle-class and professional people, by the poor village priests and by peasants to whom she was ready to promise everything. The Malaga workers were not yet organized so they did not count for much.

Most of our relatives sided with Aunt Amalia. My poor father was torn between them. As far as I could make out, he was not interested in the issue of either party, but his confessor advised him to back Aunt Amalia, whereas his heart was entirely with his only and much-beloved sister.

Both Aunt Amalia and Aunt Maria spent their days writing letters to Madrid to try and get favors for their respective supporters, a job here and there, a concession for road building, a new school opened would be scored first by one side, then by the other, so the balance of popularity was pretty well kept between them.

The death of one of Aunt Amalia's nephews, who was shot in a café and, it was alleged, murdered by one of his aunt's political opponents, brought matters to a crisis. People began to fear that the family feud might create serious trouble in the town. Just about that time, too, Aunt Maria's husband began to suffer from epileptic attacks. It was said he had been sick for some time but his wife had succeeded in hiding it from everyone. The poor general had to be pensioned off by the government. Aunt Maria never got over it.

When she left the Gibralfáro Castle she retired to Alhaurín and lived there for eight years without ever leaving the house. But she continued to pull the political wires in Madrid through her brother-in-law who had become prime minister and head of the liberal Spanish party.

Aunt Amalia also went to live in Madrid and some time afterward one of her daughters married the promising young lawyer, Francisco Silvela, who in time became the leader of the conservative party of Spain and several times Premier of the Spanish Cabinet. He was succeeded by the Majorcan leader, Don Antonio Maura. Aunt Amalia also kept her influence in political circles right up to the day of her death.

I did not understand what was going on. It seemed to me that everyone was trying to get at the same thing so I did not see why they did not just join forces.

A remark by a peasant from Alhaurín suddenly made me realize the existence of many people who were left out of everything. He was waiting to see Aunt Maria and I stopped to ask after his family whom I knew.

"How do you wish them to be, señorita ?" he said. "They are hungry. Just hungry, day in and day out they are always the same. Hungry . . ."

I looked at him with astonishment. I had never before

realized that hunger could be something more than a passing discomfort.

"Well, but have you nothing to give them? Are you not working?" I asked.

"I am working, yes," he said, and his eyes had the patient look of a dog's. "I am working on the marqués' land," — his was a huge property owned by one of the innumerable absentee landlords of Spain — "but, how can I feed a family of six with fifty centimos a day? I work from sunrise to sunset for fifty centimos. We just manage to get a plate of *gazpacho* once a day."

I loved *gazpacho*, the Andalusian salad made with onion and cucumber and green peppers, oil and vinegar and grapes and broken bits of bread, all swimming in fresh spring water. But to have only *gazpacho* to eat every day!

"Such is life," he said, straightening himself up, "a bad bargain for those who are poor."

I did not know what to say. He made me feel very uncomfortable. I hoped Aunt Maria would find him a better job.

When my sister Maria came back from London there was talk of sending me away. But father thought me too young to travel alone. I was glad.

That winter we had many parties. Our house became one of the centers of social life in Malaga. I met a great many young men but I found them very uninteresting. The "gilded youth" of Malaga were not attractive. They were mostly of the classical señorito type. Sons of wealthy parents, they thought of nothing but horses, bullfights, and of marrying a rich wife.

There was a sprinkling of other youths who were not wealthy and had to work hard. Good boys — but not "knights." Sometimes British officers would come up from

Gibraltar or the visit of some foreign cruiser would enliven the town for a few days. The Duke of the Abruzzi came once on an Italian warship. He was extremely handsome — tall and slim and blue-eyed. I felt flattered when he asked me to dance with him and told me about his polar expedition from which he had just returned. One of his fingers was frostbitten. I thought he must be a hero.

I began to have some admirers. They courted me in the usual Spanish way — long and tender glances, walking up and down under my windows, trying to get as many dances with me as possible. It was rather fun.

During the summer we had a good deal of gaiety but of a different sort. There was an annual fair and battles of flowers. After the sixteenth of July, the Feast of Our Lady of Mount Carmel, who is also our patroness of the sea, people also went in sea bathing. It would not have been exciting if we had conformed to custom, for women were not supposed to leave the dreary-looking enclosures near the shore, and wore long trailing robes of heavy material in which it was impossible to swim. Fortunately, father hired a little private dressing room and took Maria and me with him to the open sea where we were joined by Juan and Ricardo. This new departure of the Oyarzábals was severely criticized and everyone looked with disapproval on our two-piece bathing-suits although they were almost high-necked and had elbow sleeves. I grew quite ashamed of my own body.

That summer I went to a bullfight for the first time. It was a benefit performance and, with five other young girls, I was asked to preside over the *fiesta*. Under the care of a chaperone, of course. It was fun dressing up in the red satin Spanish costume and mantilla. We were driven to the bullring in a large open carriage, drawn by gaily harnessed horses, escorted by a group of young men on horseback.

When we went into the bullring everybody stood up and clapped their hands and shouted compliments.

We all sat stiffly in the large presidential box, usually occupied by the Mayor of Malaga, and followed the instructions of an expert who stood behind and told us when to wave our handkerchiefs for the changes in the fight. A famous bullfighter called "el Guerra" killed the six bulls that day. His fees were very high and he was supposed to be amassing a fortune. When the bullfighters went the round of the ring before the fight began I was quite excited. Their glittering gold-and-silver embroidered costumes were magnificent but I thought their pink stockings too bright. After the *paseo*, el Guerra and two other bullfighters sent up their beautiful embroidered capes for us to lay them over the railing of our box. The performance itself was an awful shock to me. I could not bear the sight of the gored horses and the bull streaming with blood. Everybody laughed at me.

"One can see you are half English," they said disdainfully.

I told mother I hated the fight. Juan laughed at me also and that disappointed me.

"It will at any rate benefit the poor," said Maria. "They will raise several thousand pesetas."

I wondered if this would allow some families to have more than *gazpacho*. The thought made me feel quite deserving.

One evening shortly afterward there was a party at the house of one of our friends. She lived in the new section of the town quite close to the sea. It was a beautiful moonlit night. So we sat in the garden.

"Let us go down to the gate and see the moonbeams on the water," said one of the girls.

We all went, chattering gaily. Little by little silence fell upon us. The sea was very calm. Baby waves rippled up caressingly to the dark sand.

The group broke up into couples. Our chaperones had remained sitting in their rocking-chairs near the house. I was about to turn away and join them when two arms were suddenly outstretched, and two hands, grasping the railing of the gate, made me a prisoner between them. I turned around.

"Don't move," said a man's low voice. I looked up. It was one of Malaga's chief male attractions, the cousin of a girl friend of ours. He often stayed in Madrid and was supposed to be very much a man of the world. Some of the girls raved about him but I had never spoken to him.

"I have got you at last," he said. "Why don't you ever pay any attention to me ?" I was dumbfounded. He was at least ten years older than I was. "I have looked at you so often and you never paid any attention to me. Look at me now," he insisted.

"I must go," I said, trying to get away.

"No, you are going to look at me first," he said and his hands encircled my face.

I looked at him, his eyes seemed to be on fire. The heavy perfume from the magnolia trees made me feel strangely sick. The two hands left my face, they caressed my bare throat.

"Little one !" he murmured. I was petrified. "Are you happy ? Do you love me ?"

Suddenly my sister called me. I pushed him away and ran toward the house. He followed slowly. When we left he pressed my hand two or three times. I would not look at him. I felt miserable. Something strange had happened. Why had he acted so ? I hardly knew him. When mother asked us who had been at the party the night before I did not mention his name. My sister did.

"He is just a waster," said father, "and vain. He thinks every woman is in love with him."

I felt furious. Well, I wasn't in love with him. I wished

I had pushed him away at once. I could not make out what had forced me to remain there looking at him. I began to think I might have done something wrong. But there was a mixture of other feelings, too. I felt I had some power in me that I had never suspected. I avoided going to confession. I thought I would have to tell the priest and I did not want to do that.

One day I received a letter from my friend's cousin. "I wish to see you," he wrote. I hid the letter in an old clothesbasket. Another letter followed. "I am going away and must see you." I threw that letter in with the first. He was going away? That was a comfort. He did go and I never saw him again.

I went to confession at last, and gave the priest an account of what had happened. He scolded me and made me promise I would never again allow myself to be caught alone by any man. I tried to think of the convent and of the dangers that we had been told of. This must be one of them. But I was conscious of other things. This power? I looked at my admirers with different eyes. My visions of knighthood disappeared but I found that I could make men do as I wanted. It seemed very easy. I would laugh and talk and contradict them and it made them wild but they paid me a great deal of attention.

I would not listen to any proposals of marriage, however. The very idea of being "tied down" forever upset me. Sometimes I would be very depressed just thinking that one day perhaps I would have to give in. One of my new beaux was very well off. He had a black beard. I thought it looked awful.

"Everyone is telling me you ought to marry that young man," said my father one day. "He is steady and wealthy." I looked at him in dismay. "But I don't want you to marry anybody," he added laughing.

Oh, the relief ! This young man used to send me presents
of camelias and *marrons glacés*. I hated both the candy and
flowers as much as his beard but my friends asked me not to discourage him too much because they liked the gifts.

That year we celebrated my sister's birthday with a large
fancy-dress ball. I have rarely enjoyed anything so much.
No doubt I flirted outrageously, within Malaga limits, of
course. In any case, I was totally unprepared to hear my
sister Maria suddenly announce, as we were undressing for the
night, that the ball was her good-bye to the world.

"I have made up my mind to adopt a religious life," she said
with a solemn air.

I could not believe my ears. "When ? How ? What
convent ?" I managed to blurt out.

"Our convent, the Convent of the Assumption." She was
very calm about it.

"But what will father and mother say ?" I asked, not knowing whether to laugh or cry.

"They are quite willing," she answered. "I talked it all
over with them some weeks ago and reverend mother is ready
to receive me whenever I am ready to enter."

My sister's decision created quite a sensation in Malaga. It
was known that she had had no love disappointment so people
came to the conclusion it was a case of a "real vocation" and the
Oyarzábals began to be looked upon with less suspicion. I
wondered that she could bear the thought of going into the
convent forever and ever. But Maria laughed at my dismay.

"You know I have always loved to be there," she said. That
was true. During our school days Maria had never seemed
homesick or unhappy.

A few days later she left us. Father and mother took her
up to the convent and the next time I saw her she was wearing
the black habit and white cap of a postulant. Three months

Isabel Oyarzábal
at six months of age

Isabel in 1906

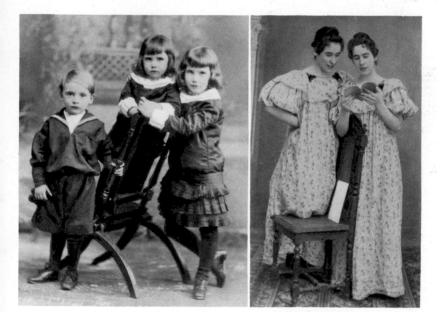

Juan, Isabel and Maria Oyarzábal   Isabel and her sister Maria

later she made her first vows. We were all present at the ceremony. I was quite upset when I saw her come into the chapel in her white bridal gown, wearing her prettiest jewels. When the priest, who was officiating, took a lock of her lovely auburn hair and cut it off, we all wept audibly.

The sight of her in a nun's habit, with the crown of white roses it is customary for the newly made *religieuses* to wear the day of their profession, made me feel that a barrier had risen between us and I have never overcome that impression.

Shortly afterward Maria left for the novitiate in Paris. We tried to make life at home go on as before but there had been a break.

I saw less and less of Juan and was kept busy looking after the household in my new role of eldest daughter. Our house was very large and it was the custom in Malaga to have a great many servants. Their salaries were very low. We had a cook and her help, two maids, the *ama* and another nurse, the washerwoman and her help, and two women to scrub the large marble-floored rooms and staircase.

I was overwhelmed by my new duties and divided in my own mind as to what I should do. Someone who had a nun for a sister could not, I felt, just give up her time to worldly affairs. I felt I must live up to our new standards and do something worth while.

Trini Alvarez, an old school friend I came across just then, helped me for a time. She was fond of visiting persons who needed help and took me along with her, but was soon disappointed at my lack of discipline. She was working in collaboration with an organization and was expected to make the people she helped promise they would go to confession and communion. I hated to make a barter with sick men and women who did not even have a mattress to lie on. One day we went to see a young man whose wife had died, leaving four little children. He lay on the ground. Bugs ran up and down the walls and there was not a single stick of furniture in the room. It had all been sold for bread. The neighbors tried to help but they were miserably poor, also.

I ran back home and piled mattresses and bedclothes and food into a cab and went back. Trini tried to extort a promise from the man that he would receive the priest. The man refused. She wanted me to take everything back. I paid no attention and, helped by the neighbors, we made him a little more comfortable. Two days later I was told I could not do things like that.

"You may take all you want from the house for anyone who needs it," my father said, "but you must take care not to encourage people who are undisciplined. That man is probably a socialist."

It was the first time I had ever heard the word "socialist" and I never forgot it.

That summer we found the children needed a change badly but as mother was not well enough to leave Malaga, I volunteered to take Anita and José Luis up to a village in the mountains called Yunquera.

Father wrote to the village priest and hired a house and after much deliberation we set out. There were the two children, the cook, whom we called Tata, a dark, one-eyed woman who was so passionately attached to Anita she decided she would not be left behind, the *ama*, and a strange assortment of trunks, round bathtubs — for no one ever dreamt of bathing in Yunquera — and kitchen utensils.

We went by rail to Alora, a little village famous for its fruit and flowers, where we were to be met by three muleteers and their mules, for the five-hour ride up into the mountains.

The muleteers were over an hour late so we spent the time

looking at the village women sorting out the raisins in boxes for shipping. There were hundreds of workers, most of them young and with flowers in their hair. They stood by twos facing each other. It was fascinating to see their slim hands push the layers of raisins on to the beautiful gold-edged paper after tying little bows of colored ribbon to the biggest bunches. A picture of a Spanish dancer covered each layer.

I felt it was work I should like to do but when they told me they earned only one peseta for a long day's work, and that the job only lasted two or three months, I came to the conclusion it would not be worth while.

We had some trouble settling on the backs of the mules and starting. I went first, sitting on the old-fashioned *jamuga*. It was supposed to be a woman's saddle but was exactly like Abuelita's armchair.

After me came Tata, sitting on the top of a very high mule and, on each side of her, in big esparto-grass baskets, Anita and José Luis. *Ama*, on another *jamuga*, brought up the rear. A string of small donkeys, carrying our luggage, followed closely. Yunquera is perched near the top of a high mountain range. The narrow mule track bordered a precipice most of the time. I dared not look down. The vegetation changed as we went along. Alora was surrounded with olive fields, vineyards, and orange trees, but, as we went on, chestnut and walnut trees and, later, the northern pine trees took their places.

We were met at the village by the priest and the doctor, who escorted us to our temporary home. They were very surprised to see I had no chaperone. Fortunately my conduct all the time was so exemplary they were quite won over. The doctor's mother and sisters were very friendly. The mother had a brother who was a canon in the Malaga cathedral and her youngest son was destined to go into the church. I do not think he had been consulted and he was not at all enthusiastic over the idea but, as he said, "With my brother a doctor and me a priest, mother can live in comfort."

As my ideas on science and priesthood went beyond such worldly considerations, I was rather shocked.

The doctor, one day, told me he had fallen in love with me, but I answered that his outlook on life was not mine. He looked quite worried when I asked him whether he did not think his profession was a "calling" and that doctors should be ready to sacrifice everything for the sake of humanity.

"Yes," he said rather humbly, "I suppose so, but I am not a hero." That finished it.

The desire to do something heroic myself began to grow. I went to church a great deal and tried to hear some special "call." It finally took the shape of just one little venture. There was a tiny, ill-clad, dirty-looking little girl of about three years old who attached herself to me in such a way we could not get rid of her. She had no mother and her father was always away, working on other men's land. Her aunt who looked after her had seven children of her own. We began by giving her two good meals a day. Then I thought we should celebrate the day of Our Lady of the Rosary by dressing her decently. We had to bathe her first, of course, and she was so frightened it nearly drove her into a fit. Her hair was so filthy it had to be cut, but she came through the ordeal looking quite a different being.

I began to worry about what the child would do when we went away and at last decided to take her home with me. The priest whom I consulted thought it would be a good idea and recommended me to send her to some orphanage in Malaga where she might be properly brought up. I said to myself that I would settle that later. Both Tata and *ama* remonstrated with me but I was deaf to their claims.

The whole village turned out to see the Malaga family taking the *huérfana* (orphan) as everybody called the child, into town.

I had not notified mother or father about the new arrival so their surprise may be easily imagined. Mother tried to explain that it was too great a responsibility for all of us.

As to the people of Malaga, they were positively outraged at the idea of one taking a strange and poor orphan child into the family.

I never discovered what really happened but suspect that the priest in Yunquera was told the child must go back to the village, for a few days later her father turned up and took her away. I have later thought that Malaga criticism was so biting it gave rise to a suspicion the poor child might be the consequence of some secret sin, and, in the face of it, my parents were forced to make a decision.

This disappointment, far from discouraging me, fanned my growing desire to rise above the common level, but nothing short of heroism moved me. The lives of saints who had been just simple humble servants of their convictions did not impress me at all. I wanted martyrs. That winter I tried to measure my own possibilities of resistance. I would walk up to Calvary with little stones inside my shoes and come back triumphantly when I actually got a small wound on one of my feet. *Ama*, who discovered what I was up to, tried to remonstrate but I won her over and tried to convince her that she should do the same. She refused to do that, however.

"My poor feet are painful enough running after you all these years," she said. I thought she was right.

The next move was to mortify my feelings of vanity and curiosity by walking down the streets of Malaga without once raising my eyes from the ground. The surprise of my friends can also be imagined. Sometimes they would stop me and try to speak, but I refused. I did not, of course, realize that there was nothing but vanity behind this show of apparent sacrifice and I really got great enjoyment out of the thought of my own superiority.

That winter I changed my confessor.   A Jesuit priest undertook to "direct" my spiritual life.   At first we got on quite well.   He began to hint at the possibility of my entering a religious order.   I feared it might be the great sacrifice I was called upon to make.   Still, it was flattering to think I was a "chosen soul."   However, one day all these dreams were destroyed, too.   My confessor had told me to go early to church as he had something important to tell me.   It turned out he had written to the Superior of the Sacred Heart Convent in Madrid about me and she had answered she was perfectly willing to try me out.

"We shall speak to your parents at once," he said, "and you can go to Madrid early next week."

I listened in amazement.   My idea, if I ever entered a convent, was to choose an order where real, visible self-denial was necessary.   I had visions of myself going down some African river in a canoe, a missionary among savage tribes, or following Father Damien's example and looking after the lepers.   To devote my time to teaching, as I had been taught, was too tame.

I got such a fright that I left the confessional and ran for home, with *ama* panting behind me.   I did not mention what had happened to anyone but I never went back to that confessor.

I suppose father and mother began to fear these exaggerated reactions for they decided to send me to England that winter. I stayed for several months with some dear friends, the Innes Thurns, whose mother had been one of the Miss MacCulloch my mother was visiting in Malaga when she met father.

This stay in England was at first very upsetting.   Everything was so different from Malaga. My first impression was

My friends were all being married and I could not fit into the plan. The lack of freedom and the constant gossip choked me.

I went back to England and Scotland the next two or three summers and came to know more interesting people. The great English actor, Sir Henry Irving — whose lectures on *The Theatre Such As It Is* and *The Art of Acting* I had translated — asked me to dine with him and a group of other friends. I was quaking with excitement when he seated me beside him. I had not expected him to be so small and fragile looking but it was marvelous to watch his face light up when he talked of the theatre. As on the stage, he seemed to grow taller and more strong. I still keep a letter he wrote to me in which he thanked me for the translation of the lectures "which," he said, "are I am sure much more interesting in their Spanish dress than in the original." This meeting with Irving awakened me to a new concept of the theatre. Until then I had considered it chiefly as a source of amusement. From then on I began to look upon it as a great art.

This impression became stronger when, some time after, I met the famous English actress, Ellen Terry, who was playing Shakespeare in London and would receive me in her little *camerino* after the show. She was still beautiful then. Her eyes would dance with fun when she spoke of her age.

"Years are nothing," she said, "if your life is interesting enough to make you forget them." When she talked of the difficulties of her profession she always added, "All the same, it is the finest in the world. I would not be anything but an actress if I were to begin life over again." The day I saw her for the last time, she gave me two photographs of herself.

Through mutual friends I came to know Anna Pavlova that same year. First, I saw her dance in one of the large London theatres and was fascinated. Her interpretation of *The Dying Swan* left an unforgettable memory.

Pavlova was anxious to know something about authent Spanish dancing and asked me to her house, somewhere ne: St. John's Wood, to talk it over with her. I showed her m castanets and played them for her.

Some mornings I would go down to see her give a dancir lesson to her class of some twelve or fifteen girls betwee eight and twelve years old. The children adored her ar brought bouquets to her every day.

Pavlova would stand facing her students in the long mi rored studio and teach them different steps, trying to commur cate some of her own inspiration to the girls. A few wou respond and, when this happened, she would turn her love head and dark eyes toward me and smile. She looked ve tiny herself in her white tunic, and slippered feet.

This world was so different from the Malaga one that sometimes felt as though I were not myself but someone el When I went home that year I made up my mind that I wou not go on living as I had done. I must be allowed to choose n own way and to find the means of expression I felt I neede It was obvious that I would never be allowed to do this Malaga.

One day I sounded my father on my wish to do somethir He did not disguise his dismay.

"What do you want to do?" he asked.

"I do not know. Just something." I dared not tell hir wanted to go on the stage. "I think I ought to earn my l ing." This shocked him still more.

"You don't need to," he said, "you can have all you want home."

I saw that it grieved him so much I did not press my point a was glad of it afterward, for that winter father fell, broke hip and died after six weeks of great suffering. He died my arms, calling for my sister Maria who would not have b allowed to come home even if she had been in the Malaga convent.

It was my first great sorrow and I rebelled against it openly. The sense of irretrievable loss nearly drove me to despair but fear for my mother brought me to my senses. During some weeks we feared that she might lose her reason. Father had meant so much to her that it was very difficult for her to face life without him.

It was thought imperative to get her out of Malaga for a time. Deep mourning in the town was so rigidly observed that we would not have been able to open our window shutters or leave the house, except to go to church, without provoking harsh criticism.

A house was found outside the town and we moved into it at once. The change did mother a world of good and she and I began to be closer to each other than we had been for years. So close that, after a few months, when I spoke to her of my wish to do something, she did not discourage me.

Time began to hang heavily on my hands for our household was now reduced to mother, Juan, who was trying to go ahead with father's business, and me.

Ricardo was in Scotland studying engineering. José Luis was in the Jesuit school and Anita and Inez had been sent to the convent.

Little by little, my old interest in the theatre revived. I began to learn bits out of our classical dramas by heart. Calderón de la Barca and Lope de Vega gave me a wide scope. Mother caught me one day when I was reciting to myself before a mirror, but I thought I would say nothing to her yet.

I also tried writing and found that I could forget myself in the characters I tried to portray. An attempt at a novel made me almost abandon the idea of the theatre. I made the hero of my story a socialist, I thought this justified my making him and his daughter do and say everything that I should have liked to do and say myself if I had dared.

No one knew what I was doing. I wrote at night and hid the manuscript in the secret drawer of an old Moorish cabinet, where my husband found it long afterward.

Through it all I felt I was doing what would finally estrange me from the people I knew. At times I was frightened and would ask myself if it would not be better and safer not to try to swim against the current. But the answer was always "No."

Suddenly I had a chance to begin to be economically independent. Someone who had a friend who knew the Im-Thurns said there was an English family with business in Buenos Aires, anxious to practice Spanish during the summer months. I was asked whether I would undertake the job. I was going to England anyway. Mother said, "Yes."

I was supposed to stay with the family in their country home in Sussex. I accepted the offer after long deliberation and, one day, I got off the train at the station of Haslemere, where I was expected. I felt rather like the heroine of an English novel and everybody at home thought I was very brave. My charming hostess and employer, Mrs. Juan Drysdale, met me. She had lost her husband two years before and was herself conducting his business in the Argentine but spent most of the time in England where her sons and daughter were being educated. She ; her unmarried sister, Nancy Carr, one of the rarest and most beautiful souls I have ever met ; the two sons, Ronald, who was at Oxford, and Gerald ; and the daughter, Dorothy, made up the family.

Very soon I quite became a member of the household and a friendship that still lasts sprang up between us. We have often laughed since, remembering how shy we all were of one another when I first arrived.

It was at their house that I met the British author, Sir Arthur

Pinero, who had taken a cottage for the summer near the Drysdales. He was a charming *causeur* and a great admirer of Spain.

I felt very proud when I went back to Malaga that year and showed mother the first money I had earned. It was not just pounds, shillings and pence to me, but something that meant much more. It was, I thought, the proof that I could earn my living, it was the key to my future.

CHAPTER V

"Isabel," said my cousin Rafael to me one day toward the end of our half mourning, "I am giving a small luncheon party for Maria Tubau in the Hernán Cortés gardens next Sunday and I want you to join us. I am sure you will like Maria and you have always been interested in the theatre."

"I should adore it," I answered.

Rafael, Aunt Maria's eldest son, was my godfather, having had the doubtful honor of actually holding me in his arms during my christening, thereby making himself partly responsible for my spiritual welfare. He lived in Madrid now, like the rest of the family, and was staying in Malaga with a political mission.

"Maria's husband, the author, Ceferino Palencia, and their two sons will also be there," he added.

It was enough for me that I was going to meet Spain's greatest actress. Mother did not feel up to going so Rafael said he would chaperone me. "What a chance, mother! What a chance!" I kept saying. Mother thought it was indeed very interesting for me to meet Maria Tubau but she did not guess the undercurrent of my thoughts.

I felt very shy the day of the luncheon party when I entered the garden of the Hernán Cortés Hotel, famous for its situation near the sea as well as for its excellent food.

Maria was coming close to the end of her brilliant career, though neither she nor her husband suspected it. She was still beautiful. One could see few grey threads mixed with the coils of light brown hair. The eyes of a curious blue-green color were full of light and fire. The expressive mouth and dazzling white teeth denied her years.

Her author husband, Ceferino Palencia, was standing close

68

to her when I went in and hurried up with Rafael to be introduced. His cordial smile and Maria's gracious words did not dispel my nervousness but I recovered somewhat when I found myself sitting between the two sons, Ceferino and Julio, who simply bubbled over with fun.

The table had been laid under a huge chestnut tree and one could hear the swish of the waves against the shore and snatches of song from the fishermen who were drawing in their nets close by. We did not begin the meal until a plate of fresh sardines, just brought out of the sea and grilled on the shore over the ashes of a wood fire, had been served. This typical Malaga dish was hailed with delight by everyone. A thin piece of cane, used as a skewer to turn the fish over on the fire, helped us to eat the sardines without soiling our fingers.

Soon the conversation became general. A great discussion arose over the two weeks' tour that was to begin the next day.

"I find this place very much changed," said Don Ceferino. "It used to be quite liberal and now, look at the papers !" He handed round cuttings from the Malaga journal in which regret was expressed that Maria Tubau should have included two of Alexandre Dumas' plays in her repertory.

"Dumas is disapproved of by the church," one paper said.

"Disapproved of by the church !" exclaimed Don Ceferino. "Did you ever hear of such a thing ? What can they find to disapprove of in *La Dame aux Camélias* or in *Francillon* ? But," he added bitterly, "these things keep the people away from the theatre."

I felt quite uncomfortable as I always did when anyone found fault with the church. It seemed to me that in some way I was responsible for her shortcomings. However, by the time the party broke up I had quite forgotten this. Maria Tubau's sons were so full of life and fun. One could not worry long over anything when in their company. They had both just graduated from the Madrid School of Law and spoke with buoyant faith of their plans for the future. I could not understand why, being the sons of artists, they should have chosen what seemed to me an uninteresting career. Lawyers were very numerous in Spain. As a matter of fact young men of wealthy families always chose this profession as an excuse to attend the university. This had given rise to Antonio Cánova's statement that "All Spaniards are lawyers unless they can prove the contrary." The conservative leader had evidently gathered that experience from his followers.

"I like my profession," said Julio, the younger brother.

"I have studied law simply to please my mother," said Ceferino.

I found them very different from the youths I knew, who could chatter endlessly about their love affairs but never dreamt of talking about books and art. Ceferino and Julio were already engaged in literary work of their own. They knew all the interesting people of the time and spoke about them in a familiar way that I found fascinating.

Both were fair-haired and blue-eyed and at first glance looked almost like twins. Maria Tubau simply doted on them. Every sally of Julio's, who was the more brilliant, was listened to with unbounded admiration by his mother. My cousin Rafael and the other guests assumed her attitude toward him. Evidently they knew nothing could please the great actress more than to show appreciation of her offspring.

Don Ceferino, on the other hand, thought of nothing but Maria. "We shall see which is the stronger," he said, referring again to the Malaga newspapers, "Maria's talent or fear of Dumas."

I did not dare announce that Dumas had been banned from our library. We sat in the garden until quite late that afternoon and I never knew time to pass so swiftly.

"Well, what are Maria Tubau's sons like?" inquired mother when at last I got home.

"They are both charming," I said, "but I think I like the older one the better."

During the next few days I saw a great deal of Maria and her family. I was asked to the theatre every night and grew more and more amazed at the flexibility of this great actress' genius. How did she manage to be so different in every role?

Toward the end of their stay my cousin Rafael, to whom I confided my wish to go on the stage, asked Don Ceferino Palencia whether he would take charge of my budding hopes and give me a trial during the next season in the theatre in Madrid. Both he and Maria said they would be delighted to do so.

When I heard what Rafael had done I felt I must tell my mother. To my great surprise she did not raise any serious objection.

"If you really think you want to do it," she said, "I do not see any reason for refusing. Only," she added, "I shall be with you all the time so that people cannot criticize you."

She did not know Malaga. No sooner had word gone round that she and I were leaving for Madrid and that I actually thought of appearing on the stage, than a wave of righteous indignation swept through our social circle. My brother Juan was so upset he refused to speak to us for days.

Matters were made much worse by a letter from my sister Maria who wrote to say that such a step on my part would bring disgrace upon the family. Mother was called upon to use her influence and to dissuade me from accepting Maria Tubau's offer. No one thought of giving me advice from an artistic point of view. The only argument brought forward, apart from the usual moral considerations, was that the stage was not the proper career for people of "our class." "Think of what her father would say," was a common remark, also "It is wrong to expose an innocent young girl to such danger."

Mother did not allow herself to be influenced. "My daughter Maria chose the life she thought best and Isabel can do the same," was her answer.

This shocked people more than ever. To compare Maria's choice with mine was little short of heresy. The good Malaga ladies shook their heads, fearing the worst.

We went up to Madrid the first week in October, mother fully as excited as I, and settled in a little pension. Our first care was to go and see Aunt Maria who was living with her married daughter and two grandchildren, besides her three single girls and her son Juan. Rafael and his family had an apartment close by.

Aunt Maria was sadly changed. It had been quite a struggle to make her leave Alhaurín after her husband's death and go up to Madrid where she continued to lead the same retired existence. She insisted that she was very sick but so far no doctor had been able to discover anything wrong with her health. I really got quite a shock when I saw her come into the drawing room, in a long black gown and with a white bandage over her forehead. At first she did nothing but sigh and groan but after a while some of her old fire would show itself in a witty sally or a sarcastic word.

"My idea is that everyone has a right to do as he likes," she said when we told her about the opposition of the other members of the family to my going on the stage.

Afterward I realized that this was the comfortable philosophical attitude that she had adopted toward all problems except those that concerned her own daughters who, although they were old enough to take care of themselves, were never allowed to go out alone. All three, Rosario, Isabel, and the youngest, Lola, who was quite a beauty, and, as I afterward found out, the hope of the family for a fine marriage, volunteered to take me about.

"We have a lady companion every morning and some afternoons," they said, "so we can go wherever you like."

The lady companion was an institution in Madrid. As a rule she was a genteel but impoverished middle-aged woman who was hired by the hour to accompany some young lady on her devotions and shopping in the morning and on her afternoon promenade or calls. It was a pathetic sight to see these unfortunate ladies following their young and often giddy charges along the streets and parks of Madrid, becoming an uncomfortable third person when a suitor appeared.

Mother and I did not avail ourselves of the offer. It was nicer to go out together and discover a Madrid unknown to us, away from the beaten track on the handsome Calle de Alcalá and the Puerta del Sol. This small-sized round plaza, the Puerta del Sol, proudly called "the heart of Madrid," was the meeting place for pedestrians and vehicles alike. There all the trolley lines converged. There cabs and taxis parked. There friends met and chatted, obstructing traffic, and people from the villages assembled to see the great clock of the Ministry of the Interior strike the midday and midnight hours while a golden ball ran down a chain with a rattling noise.

We had seen all that in our previous visits, also the Calle de Sevilla at one end of which bullfighters with an eye for a contract, and at the other end actors in search of a job, would meet their impresarios.

The well-furnished and much-ornamented cafés, with their imported foreign names *Lion d'Or, Maison Dorée, Savoy*, in the new sector of the town were less interesting than the typical ones in old Madrid with their long mirrors, plush-covered benches and marble-topped tables, where the newly married couples of the small bourgeoisie held their wedding receptions followed by a seven-course dinner, where old men played dominoes and pooled their money to buy a lottery ticket at the end of the month, where incipient genius found its first listeners, where talkative waiters volunteered information on every possible subject from the latest achievements of favorite bullfighters or primadonnas to the best way to grow tomatoes in a flower-pot.

The mornings we usually spent in the Prado Museum. I knew the famous picture galleries, of course, but had never done more than just glance at the best-known pictures. Now, armed with books on Velásquez, Greco and Goya, we tried to understand the different schools of Spanish painting.

"'Rubens, Titian, Rafael and the primitives can come later," said mother, following the advice of one of our friends, Gabriel, an amateur painter and, thanks to his large fortune, a man of leisure who was at the time paying me a great deal of attention.

"I don't see why we should have to obey Gabriel's instructions," I would sometimes say rebelliously.

But mother thought it was better to follow some sort of method.

In the afternoons we were usually asked to the house of some of our relatives. They did not agree with Aunt Maria on the subject of the stage and renewed their efforts to keep me away from it. In order to get arguments in favor of our point of view, I wrote to distinguished Catholics in England and mother consulted priests in Madrid. We invariably got the same answer, "It is not a sin to go on the stage but extremely dangerous."

I am afraid this increased rather than diminished my desire to take the plunge. It was almost heroic to go against opinion like that and for the sake of art !

Maria Tubau came back from her tour a month before Christmas. Her Madrid season was to open about the middle of January. I was delighted to see all her family again. The day after their arrival Don Ceferino heard me recite several pieces of poetry and prose. Then he made me very proud by saying he would give me a small role in one of his own plays that had been chosen for Maria's opening night. He did not seem to think I required any special training.

"You will learn as you go along," he said.

The day of my first rehearsal mother and I went down to the theatre in a state of intense excitement. I am sure she felt, as I did, that we were doing something quite meritorious in defying prejudice and convention.

The rehearsal had been set for two o'clock in the afternoon. It was the first time we had been inside a theatre in the daytime. The stage door was open and we glided in holding our breath. The only danger we encountered was the possibility of breaking our noses in the long dark passages that led to the stage.

My first experience in this supposedly dangerous profession turned out to be very tame. There were two semicircles of chairs on the poorly lighted stage and a table with an electric lamp in the centre. Maria and the other ladies of the company sat on one side, the actors on the other. Don Ceferino, with a man who turned out to be the prompter, was poring over a manuscript laid out on the table.

Maria rose to greet mother and me and Don Ceferino introduced us to the rest of the company. The men were very cordial but the women, with the exception of a fat old lady, looked down their noses at us.

We sat down and waited. A man handed me a paper with the part I was supposed to study. I could not make head or tail of it. In private theatricals our written lines were preceded by cues, but evidently in the theatre actors were given the script of only their own speeches. I read my lines nervously. The rehearsal also was different from what I had imagined. As we were merely going over a repertory play nobody did more than mumble the lines. When my turn came I was so flustered I could hardly speak. The prompter read the words ahead of me and increased my confusion. Don Ceferino tried to be encouraging.

"Take this home with you," he said when the rehearsal was over, handing me a manuscript. "Read it over very carefully until you know all the characters. It will help you."

Both he and Maria had been kind to me but quite aloof, I thought, and I was worried at their change of attitude. However, when we were about to leave, Don Ceferino called me aside and said :

"I am afraid you must have found Maria and me very unresponsive today, but it is better so. The people of the theatre are the best in the world but very jealous, and we do not want them to see that we make any difference between you and them."

I left the theatre with very mixed feelings. The rehearsal had proved anything but exciting. I felt sorry for mother sitting in the semidarkness all those hours. Besides, I began to feel doubtful of my own abilities. The way I had acted that afternoon did not look promising. Supposing I failed after all the talk and discussion ?

But as the days passed I grew more confident. I found I could say my lines without faltering and even make some adequate gestures. Don Ceferino was a splendid stage director. He would make an actor go over his lines twenty times if necessary, with such energy and knowledge that he positively galvanized the least endowed into intelligent action. He had a very quick temper but the actors put up with it because they realized he was right. I had been given a little dressing room all to myself and mother and I had great fun arranging it.

The opening night of the season and of my début the theatre

was filled. There was not the usual excitement of a first performance, but a great number of authors and artists flocked to Maria Tubau's salon to pay their respects to her. The play, *Pepita Tudó*, written by Don Ceferino several years before, dealt with the life of a Spanish actress in Goya's time. It was a great favorite with the Madrid public and was always well received so no one was nervous except myself. When I went on, my knees trembled and I had the sensation that the whole theatre was going to fall on my head. Don Ceferino watched me from the wings and when I made my first exit patted me encouragingly on the back, while Ceferino and Julio smiled their congratulations.

"Very good," Don Ceferino said, "you have done well. Go ahead and don't be frightened." He evidently was not worried about me for he went back to the salon and did not turn up again until the play was over.

My little dressing room was crowded also. None of my girl friends came near us but the men turned up in full force and I received many beautiful bouquets.

All the Madrid papers spoke of my début the next day. I was disappointed to find they gave more importance to my courage in defying convention than to my acting.

The play ran for several weeks while we rehearsed a new piece by an old-fashioned but well-known author. I thought it indescribably stupid and wondered why Don Ceferino wanted to produce it. My part was insignificant and even Maria could make little of her long and uninteresting role.

"I cannot understand what has led them to choose such a play," I said to one of the actors who had become quite friendly.

"There are very few good plays these days," he said, shaking his head, "and what decent ones there are the public does not like. Have you seen anything worth listening to in any of the other theatres ?"

That was true.   There seemed to be a blight on dramatic art. All the plays then running were either stupid or grossly farcical. Maria Tubau could not lower herself to accept farce.

"I do not understand why the taste of the public cannot be raised to a higher plane," I said.

"Too expensive," the actor answered, shrugging his shoulders.   "Managers must first be business men and then artists."

His words were as great a shock to me as those of the doctor and the priest of Yunquera.   Business men first ?   Well, Don Ceferino did not strike me as particularly endowed in that sense. I did not know the theatre was going badly just because of that. I thought if I were manager I would insist on having my way.

As time passed the situation grew worse.   Maria Tubau, who was very delicate, turned up only for the evening performances.   Don Ceferino was irritable.   His sons kept out of the way.   The actors grumbled all the time.   They were afraid our theatre would have to close as others were doing.

The new play did not help matters.   The first night the audience overlooked the stupidity of the piece, thanks to Maria Tubau's magnificent acting, but in the succeeding performances the box-office returns dwindled in an alarming manner, and one fine day we were met at the stage door with the news that Maria Tubau was down with pneumonia and that the theatre would be closed indefinitely.   Everybody rushed to try and make new contracts.   I hesitated about what I ought to do.   If I were to continue being an actress it was useless to join any other company.   I wanted the best that dramatic art could offer me in Spain and Maria Tubau was its best exponent.

So I decided that the only thing to do was to wait.   I was surprised to find I was not much disappointed.   Evidently the theatre had not turned out to be the all-absorbing passion I had expected.   Mother and I left the pension and took an apartment. We had part of our furniture sent up from Malaga. It was nice to have a home of our own again but I felt strangely unsettled and restless. My admirer Gabriel was pressing his suit very hard. From a worldly point of view he was a brilliant catch, with a title and a fortune not to be despised. At least so thought my friends, but I was not in love and marriage seemed more hateful than ever.

I began to write again just to pass the time. My room was littered with written sheets that I would not allow anyone to see. Little by little I grew so interested in my new work I could think of nothing else until a few months later Maria Tubau, who had almost recovered, asked me if I would care to play in the gala performance which was to take place in the palace of El Pardo to celebrate the wedding of King Alfonso to Princess Ena of Battenberg. I accepted and was given a small part in one of Don Ceferino's plays which had been chosen for the occasion.

The theatre of the royal residence was so small that the audience had to be limited. I do not think the rules of precedence and etiquette have ever been more discussed than they were during those days in Madrid. Everybody who was anybody thought he had a right to be invited. But it was no use. The petitions of Spanish grandees, high government officials and palace dignitaries were turned down with the implacable words, "There is no room." Very few people, apart from the members of all the European reigning dynasties who had arrived for the wedding, and the Spanish royal family, were able to squeeze in.

It was indeed a gala affair, but it might have ended in tragedy, for it was afterward discovered that the anarchist who threw a bomb at the bridal carriage on the wedding day, just missing the royal couple but killing several people, had been prowling round the Pardo grounds in the hope of getting into the theatre the night of the performance. The trend of European history might have been altered if he had carried out his plans.

Once the performance was over, Maria Tubau went back to the country and I moped around, not knowing quite what to do. I could not make up my mind to abandon the idea of the stage altogether, for I felt I had not given myself a fair chance. On the other hand, I could not disguise the fact that I was no longer so interested in it as I had been. "Is it worth while waiting for ?" I would ask mother over and over again. She told me I must do whatever I thought best. My pride rebelled at the thought of giving in. Two or three managers offered me contracts but their programs were so poor I could not bring myself to accept.

At last I made up my mind that I did not have a real vocation for the theatre and one more of my ambitions was laid to rest. Mother seemed relieved to see me place a final *Requiescat in pace* over these lost hopes. Although she never complained, she must have been pretty sick of the long rehearsals and the late hours.

That summer my sister Anita came home from school for good. She found me ready to go in for something new. This "something" took the shape of a woman's magazine. It would be the first of its kind to be published in Spain. I was sure there was great need for it. Women in our country read little news because they were not given any to read. With the exception of a limited number who could subscribe to English and French fashion journals, no one dreamt of even looking at the local papers. It was thought they only interested the men.

I realized, of course, that it would be necessary to use caution so as not to frighten our future readers or their censors. *La Dama* (*The Lady*), as we decided to call the magazine, must be frivolous enough to be attractive, deep enough to achieve its purpose, and subservient enough to custom not to provoke criticism.

I did not like to ask mother for money so I started with just a little sum of two thousand pesetas a woman friend, Raimunda Avecilla, and I managed to scrape together.

The first number of *La Dama* was published in the following month of December. It had twenty-eight pages of printed matter and — so it seemed to us — a beautiful cover of blue-green paper on which a reproduction of Sir Joshua Reynolds' picture of the English actress, Mrs. Siddons, looked most impressive.

Anita acted as general secretary and I did almost all the writing, but under different names. What fun we had! I have never been able to understand how we managed to make *La Dama* cover expenses for the next two years. No doubt the dearth of other magazines was at the root of our modest success.

But *La Dama* was not my only experiment that year. Shortly after the publication of the magazine a friend in England wrote to ask me whether I would be willing to be the Spanish correspondent for the Laffan News Bureau. This was a London agency which required information of all kinds. I did not hesitate and, with the daring born from ignorance, volunteered to cover every field for them from high politics to vulgar crime or picturesque events.

This was followed by a petition that I should also cover news for the London paper, *The Standard*. Thanks to our many friends and relatives in high places, I was able to send in reliable political information, but since then I have thought how funny those stories from my inexperienced hand must have seemed to the editor. I suppose he accepted them for their intrinsic worth as news.

Undoubtedly I owed much to this new work, for through it I

began to understand for the first time what Spain really was, how and where she stood in relation to the rest of the world and, above all, what new developments were taking place within her frontiers.

I discovered that small party politics, and the interjection of the church and army into public life, had kept the country in an abject state of poverty and ignorance. Over fifty-two per cent of the population was illiterate. The wages, especially for workers of the land, were disgracefully low. There was no limit to working hours, and living conditions even in the capital were a disgrace. Child mortality in Spain was among the highest in the countries of Europe, and as for an outside policy, it did not exist. Meanwhile in Madrid the conservative and liberal parties succeeded each other in a poor imitation of British Whigs and Tories. Every time there was a change of cabinet, a legion of civil employees lost their posts to the new arrivals and went home to twiddle their thumbs and hope for a prompt defeat of their political opponents.

The only hopeful sign was to be found in the labor movement. Under the guidance of Pablo Iglesias the workers were being organized into unions and were fighting corrupt politicians while they strove to better conditions for the people. The words "general suffrage" had until then meant nothing, but every new election brought a change, at least in the big cities where the seats were strongly contested and often won from nepotists in power.

Shortly after I had been promoted to the post of correspondent to *The Standard*, the birth of a son and heir to the Spanish throne revived world interest in Spain. Members of European reigning houses again flocked to Madrid, this time to be present at the christening of the new Prince of the Asturias, and most of the important newspapers sent out special correspondents to report on the ceremonies. I was kept extremely busy describing the official routine : how the members of the Spanish cabinet had to wait outside the queen's bedroom until King Alfonso brought out the new-born babe, lying naked on a silver salver, to be duly examined by the government ; how the minister of justice then had to qualify to the birth certificate of a male heir ; how the queen, before and during her delivery, had to wear a girdle belonging to an image of the Virgin that was supposed to protect women during labor.   In addition to all these historical accounts, I had to send in descriptions of attendant celebrations.

The announcement of the birth of his son was made by the king at the opening session of parliament which took place in the senate.   As special seats had to be reserved for the foreign representatives and their suites, only a small number of places were left for the press.   There was a scramble for tickets but many of the non-resident correspondents were unable to get them.   The night before the session the special correspondent of the *Illustrated London News* rang me up in despair.

"Oh, Miss Oyarzábal," he said, "I hear you have managed to secure an invitation for the session tomorrow and I want to know whether you can draw, because if so, I should like to ask a great favor of you."

"Draw ?   I can't draw a line," I answered.   "But what is it you want ?"   He explained he must have a plan of the senate with indications of where the king and the royal family and the British delegates were going to sit.   He actually persuaded me to do it, too.   And what a plan I drew !

It served its purpose, though, for within the next few weeks I received a copy of the *Illustrated London News* with a magnificent picture of the ceremony and a written message that said, "With many thanks to a friendly collaborator."

My work as a correspondent also upset all my conventional standards.   Among other things, I became accustomed to treat men on a basis of simple comradeship.   Up to that time they had always been somewhat mysterious beings with a lurking tendency to make love which I alternately hated, despised, or felt attracted to. Perhaps the order of feelings should be reversed.

Now I met my colleagues on a plane of absolute parity and gave or received help without feeling that I was putting them or myself under any obligation. There were no insistent and tender glances, no compliments, no subtle meanings attached to their remarks. They were just "good friends." It took a good deal of romance out of life, I suppose, but on the other hand, it enabled one to work serenely. Perhaps I did not miss it too much because I got as much attention as was good for me outside my work.

Our house in Madrid was now the meeting ground of many young and ambitious intellectuals, poets, writers and artists. I was the only woman. Ceferino and Julio Palencia were among the most assiduous visitors.

One day the group decided I should give a lecture at the Ateneo, which was the pivot of the intellectual life of Madrid. Its auditorium had been the scene of many debates and every well-known Spaniard as well as many famous foreigners had made themselves heard within its precincts.

"You will be the first young woman to speak there," said the secretary of the literary group and a great friend of ours, "and my section wishes to have the honor of organizing it."

I answered that I would never dare do such a thing. "What am I going to speak about ?" I asked them.

But they were determined. I received a formal invitation from the executive board and someone suggested that I should speak on Sir Henry Irving, whom they knew I had met, and his ideas on the art of the theatre.

After long deliberation I decided I would accept, but I said that I must read my speech if I were to deliver one. With a sinking heart I heard the date had been fixed.   Even if I read the lecture anything might happen.   I remembered how I had used to stumble reading the prayers at school out of sheer nervousness.

At last I sat down to write out a long and tedious study of Sir Henry Irving's influence on the British stage.   Once it was ready I gave it to a friend to look over and when he had passed a favorable dictum I read the painfully written sheets aloud to my mother several times in order to try my voice.   Mother was all sympathy and confident that I was going to do very well.

When the fateful day arrived I drove down to the Ateneo and was met at the door by two or three members of the board and all our group.   The auditorium was crammed.   I was introduced in a flowery speech by the president, Señor Moret, who was one of the leaders of the liberal party at that time.

When he had finished he asked me to step to the platform. My ears drummed and my heart beat violently as I sat down on the huge armchair before the table on which my speech had been previously laid.   I wondered why I had been such a fool as to appear.   The audience applauded, then settled down to listen.   For some awful moments I thought I was not going to manage to read.   The lines of the manuscript seemed to jump up and down, my tongue stuck to the roof of my mouth and my feet could not reach the floor, which gave me the sensation of being hung over empty space.   Suddenly I remembered that mother was sitting in the front row and that I could not fail her.

I swallowed hard and began.   I wished I could drink some water out of the glass that had been put temptingly before me. But I knew if I stopped I could not go on again, so I read and read and read.   Every sheet that I laid aside lifted a little of the awful burden from my mind and the last words were actually said with a flourish.   At least I thought so.

The end of the lecture was greeted with thundering applause. I am sure the relief of my friends was greater than their appreciation, but my heart felt very light.   It was over.

The next day the Madrid press paid me extravagant compliments, extolling the fact that a "young girl" should have "honored the Ateneo by consenting to sit on the time-honored platform of the auditorium," and so on.   Little mention was made of the speech itself except to say that Sir Henry Irving would most assuredly have been glad to be present.   A far-fetched compliment that certainly did not satisfy me.   One commentator said that with practice I would become a good speaker.   I was honest enough with myself to feel it was the only remark worth taking count of.

This lecture was followed by petitions for others in different places.   I proceeded slowly.   Experience developed awareness and then fear.   But I was not daunted.   Time simply flew past.

One evening in the early fall Anita and I went to the theatre with two young actresses and their mother who was an old friend of Maria Tubau's.   Ceferino and Julio Palencia were our escorts.   We sat in the box engrossed in the performance. All of a sudden I turned my head and met Ceferino's eyes. They had a strangely intent look.

I turned my head again and our eyes met once more.   A curious feeling swept over me.   I felt inclined to cry.   The play, a sensational melodrama, had evidently upset my nerves. I looked again.   Ceferino seemed in a trance, as though he were very near and yet unaccountably remote.   No man had ever looked at me that way.

We had seen a good deal of the two brothers during the past year, but more of Julio.   Ceferino was not shy but stood rather aloof.   I continued finding him the more attractive of the two.

He was tremendously interested in music and painting, never missing a concert if he could help it, even at the cost of giving up an invitation to our house. This had rather piqued me. That night we walked home after the play, Ceferino and I together in front of the others. We did not speak a word yet when I reached home I knew that he had told me something.

After that night Ceferino — Cefe, as we usually called him — never seemed aloof to me again. He came to see us oftener and every time after he left I had the same strange feeling that he had spoken of something without need of words. At intervals he would disappear for days.

If I remarked on it his answer was invariably the same, "I felt sad so why come ?" I did not dare ask why he had felt sad. What was the use of forcing him to say what I knew was in his mind : that he was afraid Gabriel, who had become tiresomely insistent, would make me accept him. He had so much to offer from a worldly point of view. However, I was not attracted by Gabriel and one day mother dispelled any fear I might have entertained regarding her opinion on the subject by saying :

"Darling, don't bother your little head thinking you ought to marry Gabriel. You would not be happy with him. If you were not what you are I might perhaps give you other advice but, as it is, you must marry for love or you will ruin your life."

She did not mention Cefe that day but a few weeks later she referred to the matter again, saying, "I am sure you are going to do what everyone will consider extremely unwise but, knowing you as I do, I believe you should be allowed to do as you think best. After all, love means a great deal."

It certainly had meant much to her. If only Cefe would realize how much it meant to me.

The nineteenth of November was my saint's day. After

mother had become a Roman Catholic we had almost given up
birthday celebrations and accepted the usual Spanish custom of
commemorating the day of one's saint.   Mine was Saint Isabel,
Queen of Hungary.   Quite early in the morning presents and
flowers began to pour into the house and by five o'clock in the
afternoon our apartment was filled with them.

"Is Cefe not coming to see us today?" Anita asked Julio
when she saw him come in alone.

"He said he was but that he had to be at the law-court for a
case at three o'clock, and will be late."

Time passed.   I watched the door.   Gabriel, rather annoyed at my absent-mindedness, left the house.   Still no Cefe.

We had partaken of refreshments long before and I was sitting in the drawing room trying to look interested in what
people were saying when I saw him come in.   I went forward
without waiting for him to speak and said :

"You must be very tired.   Come into the dining room and
have some tea."

I do not recollect what happened after that except that we
found ourselves in the dining room alone, that he was holding
both my hands, and that I was saying, "Yes . . . yes, I
know. . ."   I have never ceased being grateful that it should
have happened like that for I should not have liked a formal
proposal.   They are so silly.   I suppose Cefe must have said
something but I am certain it was not the usual thing.   Otherwise my reaction would have been entirely different.

We stood there looking at each other and smiling, Cefe murmuring the Spanish name of endearment, "Nena, Nena."   And
there Anita found us when she burst in to say that some of our
guests were going and wanted to say good-bye.

It was quite late by the time they all took their departure.
When Anita and I went into our room to get ready for bed I

surprised her by sitting down and covering my face with my hands.

"As though you were afraid of something," she told me afterward. It was true.

"Anita," I said after a little, "do you know what I have done ? I believe I have become engaged to Ceferino Palencia."

"Believe ?" she cried. "Surely you must know whether you have or have not."

"No," I said dejectedly, "no, because we have not said a word about an engagement. But I know now he cares for me and he thinks I love him."

"And you don't ?" asked Anita.

"Well, I am not at all sure."

Anita could not believe her ears. "You have been sure at other times that you did not care," she said.

That was true. Besides, I had been sure when Cefe had been near me. Then why was I so terribly, incomprehensibly afraid ? After thinking for a while I sat down and wrote him a long letter which was delivered to him next morning by special messenger.

CHAPTER VI

"I must see you. I must speak to you." The written words stood out from the white sheet of paper with what seemed to me accusing distinctness. They were Cefe's answer to the letter in which I had tried to make him see that we had been too precipitate, that I was not sure that I really loved him.

"Tell me if you are going out this afternoon and I shall meet you. If I do not hear I shall wait at the door of your house until you come down," it went on.

I sent another note telling him to meet me at the printer's, where I was going with Anita that afternoon on business connected with *La Dama*.

I would much rather not have seen him so soon after our interview of the day before. His note showed he was suffering and I hated the idea of hurting him more. But what could I do? Morning had brought me no relief from my own worries. Cefe interested me more than any man I had ever met. His sensitiveness and extraordinary response to beauty of all kinds appealed to me much more than the assertive strength and daring of others. But did I love him enough to marry him?

I left the house that afternoon feeling perfectly miserable. I wanted to be absolutely honest with him. This at least is what I told myself.

"Why should your saying you love him be dishonest?" asked Anita, in answer to my protests.

"Because I am not sure that I do."

"Don't you like to talk to him better than to anyone else?"

"Yes."

"Don't you miss him when he doesn't come to the house for a few days?"

"Yes."

"Wouldn't you be unhappy if you were never to see him
again ?"

"Yes, yes, yes," I answered impatiently. "I have answered
all those questions by myself long ago. The thing is, do I love
him enough ? E-n-o-u-g-h," I insisted, spelling the word to
give it more emphasis. "Am I sure that I shall go on thinking the same for years, all my life ? Fancy feeling the same
now and at forty, and at fifty and sixty, all one's life !" I ended
dramatically.

"I don't see why one should worry so far ahead. And, in
any case, if you are happy with Cefe, well, it just means years
and years of it," said Anita with practical good sense.

"Besides, I don't want to be tied down," I added after a little.
"When I think of marrying I get the same feeling I had in the
convent."

"Heavens ! Cefe won't tie you down."

"Oh ! Cefe ! Cefe ! Cefe !" I began, but Cefe himself cut
me short. There he was outside the printer's office, walking
up and down, the very image of dejection.

I greeted him too casually to be entirely natural and, asking
him to wait for a few minutes, I went in to see Señor Blas, the
great bearded German, who took as much interest in *La Dama*
as I did. Anita stayed outside, keeping Cefe company. She
had to go and see someone near home so we all walked back
together, talking of different things. That is, Anita and I
talked, Cefe did not say a word.

By the time we reached Anita's destination I was so nervous
I felt as though I could shake Cefe. His silence was so much
more accusing than words.

"Well, what did you want to say to me ?" I said rather defiantly as we directed our steps toward our house.

"Just one thing," he said after a pause, "that I love you with
all my heart and soul."

I had expected reproaches and had prepared for them, but I did not have an answer for those words.   It was already night and threatening rain.   I felt I should not remain out too long.

"You said you wanted to speak to me," I volunteered.

"Yes, I thought I had a great deal to say but now I find I only have this : that I love you with all my heart and soul."

He stood before me with his eyes fixed on mine and his whole attitude was so simple, so like his words, that I knew it would be useless to employ arguments.

"I love you, too," I blurted out almost unconsciously.

"Then . . . ?" and regardless of the fact that people were passing, he grasped my hand.

I began to walk forward and he took my arm, not in a masterly way but protectingly.   We passed the house and I never noticed it.   Cefe began to speak hurriedly :

"I know I have very little to offer you.   Times are bad for the theatre.   My parents have lost all they had saved and Julio and I must help them.   Mother has worked for us all so long ! Perhaps I should not have said anything to you under the circumstances but I could not help myself.   I might as well try not to breathe."

The rain began to fall.   We had no umbrellas but we continued to walk up and down a little avenue near our street. There were only a few houses surrounded by gardens so we were not bothered by people passing.

I dared not look at Cefe.   His words had touched me deeply and I felt my resistance was melting.

"I love you with all my heart and soul.   That is all I can say," he repeated.

"I know, I know, but we must try and be sensible," I said.

"Love and sense don't go together, but you must not think that I want to force you.   And I do not expect that you should love me out of gratitude, no, never that !"

He had given me my cue and I hurriedly took advantage of it. "Yes, I know, and that is the reason why I wrote to you," I said. "But, Cefe, I am not sure of my love. I must wait and see. I am afraid of being married and tied down to someone all my life. Even to you." I looked at him, afraid he might think I had been hard.

"Then let us wait," he answered suddenly. "Let us wait until you are sure that you cannot love me or until you can say, as I do, that you love me more than anyone on earth."

I wanted to cry out, to protest that I cared for him in the same way but I could not. As we walked home we discussed what we should do.

"If you prefer it I shall not come to the house," Cefe said.

"Of course you must come, but as a friend only. You can come whenever you feel like it and we shall go to the theatre some evenings together just as we have been doing. Give me time," I implored, feeling that I was cruel and unfair, not wishing to give in yet reluctant to lose him. Cefe agreed.

In the middle of December Maria Tubau went down to Seville to give a few performances. She had gathered a company together again and hoped to tour Andalusia while the cold weather lasted. Before she went I had a long conversation with her and Don Ceferino about my change of plans regarding the theatre. They quite understood my point of view.

"If you do not need the theatre as a means of livelihood there is no object in devoting your life to it at present," Maria said rather bitterly.

"Unless," argued Don Ceferino, "you have a large capital and want to spend it starting an art theatre."

"I should not advise it even in that case," interrupted Maria. Then, patting my hand, she said, "If you really loved the theatre you would not be able to give it up and I think, all things considered, it is fortunate you do not.   As matters are at present, the outlook is heartbreaking."

Ceferino and Julio joined their parents for Christmas.   I heard from Cefe almost every day.   His letters were like pages out of a diary.   His literary style, being excellent, made them most interesting reading.   At times I felt myself back in Seville through his descriptions of the life down there.   But what touched me most was the underlying feeling which at times refused to be kept down.   Breaking through his self-imposed restraint, he would tell me in a few short sentences all that I refused to listen to, yet wanted passionately to hear.

On Christmas Eve Aunt Maria was unable to leave her house and dine with us, so mother, Anita and I spent it alone in our little apartment.   We had been through the fair in the Plaza Santa Cruz two days before and had bought the funny little clay figures for our "Bethlehem" and a turkey for the Christmas supper, together with all the typical sweet things : marzipan from Toledo, almond paste from Alicante, cookies from Seville and raisins from Malaga.

"I am sure you would have loved to have Cefe here," said Anita, who was very fond of her "future brother" as she called him to me.

I did not confess that I was finding the time unbearably long without him.   Fortunately I had a great deal to do.   The news bureau required constant attention and *La Dama*, although less pressing, also took up a great deal of time.   Our special Christmas number had been quite a success, chiefly because the young intellectuals of our group had volunteered to help.   Thanks to them all, we were able to give away an almanac with a contribution from our twelve best-known writers for each of the twelve months of the year.   Julio also sent in a story and Cefe a drawing that I thought beautiful.   Mother and I could not understand why he had not taken up painting seriously.   It seemed his father and mother had opposed his wishes on the subject although they knew he loved art and had shown real talent when allowed to have a drawing master during one short season in Barcelona.

"Mother wanted us to have a profession and not depend just on art," Cefe had told me once in answer to my remonstrances. "As all professions are the same to me, and Julio liked studying law, I became a lawyer, too."

Just before my fateful name day he had been made an attorney in one of the municipal law-courts of Madrid and was hoping that the post would prove satisfactory at least from an economic point of view.

During the following months I went out a good deal. Now that I had given up the theatre my family and old friends were anxious to receive me again. Not that they approved of my writing. Any work would, of course, have been considered obnoxious for a woman who was not on the verge of starvation, but writing . . . and for the newspapers! If I had favored the Spanish press with my literary efforts perhaps they would not have felt so anxious. Aunt Amalia's daughter, Amalita, whose husband had by then scaled the heights of political power, said to me one day, "Women can do a great deal of harm working for foreign papers that are not under ecclesiastical censorship." Her words breathed disapproval of the unoffending Laffan Bureau.

In spite of these fears, we were asked out a great deal.

I hated the receptions and balls where the people we met did not have a single thing in common with us. The young men were very like those we knew in Malaga. Without a thought beyond their love affairs, bullfights, and horse racing.

I turned with relief to our special set and saw Cefe frequently. Apart from an occasional outburst when Gabriel was more attentive than usual, Cefe did not harass or press me in any way.

Little by little we established certain customs that brought us nearer to each other. Cefe would pass every morning down our street on his way to the law-court. It meant a long detour but that did not seem to matter. He invariably looked up at our windows and, if we were looking out, would smile delightedly. I got in the way of watching for him but did not show myself every day lest it encourage him too much.

One day matters came to a climax. It had been almost settled that I would not go to England that summer. I had much to do and did not wish to leave *La Dama* for long, but no sooner had we arrived at this decision than some old Malaga friends wrote, begging me to go with them to London for two or three weeks. They knew no English and had been looking forward to the trip with me for a long time.

Mother urged me to accept.

"You are working much too hard," she said, "and the change will do you good. Besides, you can see your correspondent for *La Dama* as you go through Paris."

When Cefe heard I was leaving he was terribly upset.

"You told me you would not be going this year," he insisted over and over again. I objected to his tone and we came very near having a quarrel.

"Forgive me," he said, "but I cannot bear the idea of being so long without seeing you, not knowing whether you are going to love me in the end."

He looked so unhappy I felt it was unfair to keep him in suspense much longer, so it was settled that on my return I would give him a definite answer. I was surprised to find that somehow our little tussle seemed to have brought us closer. I tried to make up for the coming separation by going out with him every afternoon under Anita's chaperonage. Even mother dared not let me be seen in public alone with a young man. As

a rule we chose Madrid's central park, El Retiro, for our tryst-
ing place. There was one special stone bench beside the lake
where we could sit and talk while Anita went round trying to
amuse herself, buying all kinds of indigestible eatables from the
old women who sat at the entrance of El Retiro, selling peanuts
and toasted chick-peas and the Moorish *altramuz* softened in
salt water to make it palatable. If the rumors concerning the
insalubrity of Madrid water had been true, my chaperone
would most certainly not have escaped typhoid that summer.

Before going to sleep the night before my departure I wrote
Cefe a long letter. The feeling that I was not going to see him
for so long drove me to be much less reserved than at other
times. At the end I said, "If all goes well you might perhaps
come and meet me in Paris on our way home." At the last
minute I slipped a photograph of myself into the envelope with
the Shakespearean quotation "to be or not to be" written on
the back of it.

There were a good many people at the station to see us off,
so our good-bye had to be quite conventional. However, I
had time to give him my letter and to whisper, "Read it in El
Retiro," before getting into the train.

No sooner had we started than I would have given anything
to go back.

"It's all my stupid pride," I kept on saying to myself. And
then, "Of course I love him. I love him with all my heart and
soul." How stupid and cruel not to have told him those words
he so longed to hear instead of repeating them like a parrot into
empty space. I cried myself to sleep.

I was delighted to hear we were only going to be away one
month, and wished July did not have thirty-one days.

Cefe's letters followed me to Bordeaux, where we stopped
for two days, to Paris, and to London. Two weeks after our

departure I wrote to him asking if he would be able to meet me in Paris on the twenty-ninth.   I received a telegram saying he would be there.

I do not know how I ever got over our stay in London.   And yet we had a funny time, too.   Our party was composed of a rather stupid but very rich spinster, a married couple with no children, another with one little girl of two and her *ama*.   She was an ignorant peasant woman from the mountains of Granada who had never left her native village before and who could see nothing to be surprised about in the biggest capitals of Europe. She insisted that St. Paul's Cathedral and Notre Dame were the same size as her village church and found it extremely stupid of the English and French not to know Spanish when, as she said, "People in Cuba can speak it perfectly, and I am told Cuba is farther away."

The morning on which Cefe was to arrive I went down to the station of the Quai d'Orsay to meet him, dressed in my prettiest frock.   It was his first visit to the French capital and I knew he would be very excited.   I had to use all my arts of persuasion to convince the station master that it was imperative for me to go down to the platform where the southern trains came in.

"It is forbidden, *mademoiselle*," he said, "unless you are expecting someone who is sick.   Do you really believe it is necessary in your case ?"

I nodded my head vigorously, thankful that I did not have to lie for I was ready to swear Cefe was dying, if by so doing I could get down to meet him.   I knew he would be bitterly disappointed not to see me the moment he got off the train.

There were very few people downstairs.   At sight of me Cefe dropped his valise and rushed forward crying :

"Nena !   Nena !"

In a state of mutual bliss, we somehow managed to reach the hotel.

"We shall see all the interesting things together, shan't we ?" he asked.

I told him that I had not wanted to go to any museum until he arrived. During all my previous fleeting visits to the town I had done little more than go shopping and to an occasional theatre if the play could be recommended, so I did not really know Paris.

I informed my friends that I intended to go about with Cefe alone as engaged couples in England were accustomed to do. They did not raise any objections. "You are half English," they said, shrugging their shoulders as though that made all discussion useless. Besides, they were too busy buying frocks to want to be bothered.

Cefe and I had one perfect week. In the mornings we wandered around the picture galleries and the second-hand book-shops near the Seine. And after lunching at some cheap little restaurant, where the food was always good, no matter what misgivings one might entertain as to the authenticity of the veal — which I suspect was often horse meat — and the pureness of the milk, we would go off to visit old Paris.

In the evenings we dined at the hotel and ended up the day at some café on the boulevards, making plans for the future. We now considered ourselves definitely and formally engaged.

We thought we would not be able to marry for some time. Cefe was making very little money but he was sure everything would come out right. One day he said he would like me to give up all my work after we were married. People in Spain still thought it was a reflection on the husband for a married woman to work. I was very indignant. "Give up everything that I have striven so long to have ? Never."

He consulted mother, being under the delusion that she would agree with him.

"I think it would be a terrible mistake," she said, "Isabel is too vital ever to be satisfied with doing nothing.   On the contrary, she must have something to do, and the ideal solution would be for you both to work together."

When the news of my engagement got round, people thought I must be crazy.   Everybody knew Cefe did not have a penny to his name and no one could understand why I should choose a man with no means when I might have made a good marriage.

Mother was not the least worried.   "If it were anybody else I might be anxious," she said, "but I know Isabel and am sure everything will be all right."

She was very conventional about our engagement and did not permit us to go out alone.

"There is no earthly use in your getting talked about," she said, "and Anita is delighted to go out with you."   So for months poor Anita had to "carry the basket" as chaperoning an engaged couple is called in Spain.

In the house we were allowed to see each other without being constantly watched, a freedom not the custom in Spain.

The months passed by very quickly.   We had not yet fixed a date for the wedding when mother suddenly made up her mind she would have to make a trip to the United States in order to take over my brother José who wanted to study chemistry and had been told he could do no better than follow the courses in America.   Mother, who loved traveling, jumped at the excuse and as Inez had finished her schooling at the convent, she decided to take her and Anita, too.

"It will be a nice experience for them," she said, and added rather wistfully, "why don't you come along with us ?"

But I refused to be separated from Cefe.

In view of the turn events had taken, we decided the best

thing we could do was to be married right away. At first there was a little opposition both on the part of his family and of mine. How could we marry with so little ?

"Why not wait ?" everybody said. We held firm and the wedding was fixed for the eighth of July.

I begged mother not to give me an expensive trousseau, Cefe and I would have to live very simply and cash was far more important to me than clothes. Mother agreed and, instead of buying the usual twelve dozen of every item that all self-respecting brides were supposed to receive, she handed me a substantial check and told me to spend it the way I thought best.

All my relatives over in England did likewise so I found I had quite a nice little nest egg with which to start my new life. It would have been just the same if I had not been given a penny, for Cefe and I had reached a point when nothing material mattered in the least. Life spread before us like some wonderful dream, and we resented being brought down to earth in order to settle unimportant questions such as who was to be asked to the wedding and what we were going to wear and where we were going to live when we came back from our honeymoon.

"I don't want any fuss," I said. "I shall be married in a simple tailor-made dress and we shall invite only our intimate friends."

Mother solved the house question by telling me we could stay in her apartment until she came back, in about a year or so. She advised me to keep our two servants. "It is better for you to do your work than to lose time looking after the house." This was true. Servants' wages were still very low, even in Madrid, and my own work would bring in far more than I could save by dismissing one or both the maids.

Everything was settled the way I wanted it except the wedding dress. When Maria Tubau, who had been away on tour, heard that I was not going to wear the conventional white bridal gown, she was dreadfully disappointed. I gave in. After all, it did not matter to me and, as Cefe had insisted that *Lohengrin's Wedding March* should be played during the ceremony, I thought the white dress might, after all, be more appropriate.

The eighth of July of that year was one of the hottest days Madrid had ever known, but I did not realize it.

We were married at twelve o'clock. Cefe and I knelt between our godparents, Maria Tubau and Don Ceferino, and the ten witnesses stood near us. Mother had refused to be the godmother. The coming separation was turning out to be very hard and she did not want me to know it if she broke down.

As a matter of fact, everybody except Cefe and me wept or looked as glum as though they were at a funeral. I could distinctly hear sobs just behind me and afterward learned it was Inez.

When the nuptial Mass with its attending ceremonies was over and we had signed our names in the register, we went to Cefe's house for a quiet wedding breakfast.

Mother, Anita and Inez were leaving at once for London, where they meant to take a liner for the United States. Our good-byes had been said in the house before going to church.

Cefe and I left by train that afternoon. We were bound for Paris and, if our money went far enough, intended going on to England. As the train moved slowly out of the station I remembered my departure of the year before. Then I had stupidly left everything behind me. A whole year had been wasted. . . I looked up and saw Cefe smiling at me.

We would make up for it now.

Book Two: In Harness

CHAPTER VII

Cefe and I came back from our honeymoon with exactly twelve pesetas left over from what had been put by for the trip. From Madrid we had gone to Valladolid where we stopped for two days. Cefe had studied in the university of that old Spanish town and wanted me to visit the haunts of his early youth with him and to see some of the art treasures in the church of San Pablo and the fine polychrome statues. Valladolid is on the main railway line to the frontier so we hopped on to the train again and spent a day and night at Hendaye to get a glimpse of the sea. Then we went on to Paris where we retraced our steps of the year before, and finally landed in England. I was quite anxious lest Cefe's admiration for Paris would lead him to belittle London. However, he did not do so, but to this day I have been unable to discover whether or not this was just politeness on his part. London had less to offer him as an artist than the French capital, though it might compensate in other ways.

We stayed with the Drysdales for a little while so he had at least an inkling of what country life in England was like.

The day we got back to London we found the streets lined with colored sheets of news. War had broken out in Spanish Morocco.

We decided to hurry home for the news bureau would require looking after. In Paris the papers were full of the disaster suffered by our troops in North Africa and dark rumors about happenings in Barcelona. Evidently serious disturbances were taking place there.

Once over the frontier and into Spain, we got a more definite picture of the state of affairs. We were told that great numbers of Spanish soldiers had been killed in action in Morocco. It was the same old story. Incompetence on the part of army chiefs, lack of adequate arms and ammunition, and indifference to all our colonial problems in Madrid had caused the sacrifice of hundreds of young lives in a strife that was unpopular with every single Spaniard, except those who used Morocco as they had used Cuba, simply as a means of promotion ; and of course those who were war profiteers. I could not forget the words I heard in Alhaurín from an old peasant whose son had been killed in another Moroccan campaign.

"Why do they take our sons from us ?" he said. "We don't want to fight the Moors. They are just men like us and their land is just like our land. Geraniums and cactus and vineyards are there ; I know, for I have been there. What right have we to take their land from them ? We shouldn't like it if other men came and took our land from us !"

This was the feeling throughout Spain. The people knew nothing about strategic positions and the problems of the Mediterranean. They had a suspicion that wars were waged in Morocco just to enrich a few men usually included, or supported by others, in the government, and they did not see why they, the people, should be sacrificed.

Exacerbated by the military disaster, the workers of Barcelona who had been organized for some time past, initiated a movement that might have turned into a nation-wide revolution. To the cry of "no more war" they went out into the Barcelona streets. The Catalonian separatists took advantage of the rising to further their own ends and gave the movement full support.

As in every revolutionary movement that has ever taken place in Spain, under the monarchy or under the republic, convents and churches were the chief object of the people's indignation. It is difficult for outsiders to realize why this should be. It is almost impossible for anybody in the twentieth century to understand that the church in Spain is again politically and economically all powerful, that its influence has been constantly directed against the people, and that its sacred mission has occupied only a secondary place. The people have risen against it as the people all the world over rise or try to rise against the abuse of power.

Many places of worship were burnt at that time but there were few casualties. However, stories of supposed atrocities were widely circulated and everyone was duly shocked on hearing that Alejandre Lerroux, leader of the republican party of Catalonia, had urged the rebels to "raise the veils of the sisters [meaning the nuns] and make them mothers." They little suspected that this was the man who, years later, would join the extreme reactionary groups and help to bring about the civil war, called by them a religious crusade, and the destruction of the republic.

Personally I was more frightened that Cefe should be called upon to go to Morocco than I was at the revolution. I could not help sympathizing with the women of Barcelona who were throwing themselves bodily against the lines of civil guards stationed round the transport ships that were taking human cargoes to Africa. However, there was such confusion in my mind about what "patriotism" demanded of me, and what I thought human and just, that I did not dare express my feelings openly, not even to Cefe.

Why should those women not try and keep their men at home? After all, Africa was not their country. This was my constant thought. To my relief, no more reserves were called up.

The war shattered some of our hopes in the economic field.

A position that had been offered to Cefe, legal adviser to a new business concern, was canceled with the excuse that the situation in Spain was too unstable for trade. We were just recovering from this blow when, a few weeks later, we received a letter from the Laffan News Bureau saying they were going to close it.

The day I got the letter I went down to the corner of the street where Cefe used to get off the trolley car when he came home to lunch. I always met him there if anything a little out of the common happened. I hoped he would not be too much upset with the bad news, for our income was now reduced to Cefe's salary of ninety pesetas a month from his small government job, and to whatever he might make as attorney in the municipal court. Unfortunately this had proved very unsatisfactory, for he was not given a fixed stipend, only a percentage of any fines imposed by the court on minor offenders and an occasional fee for special papers he might have to sign. Needless to say, such a method led to every imaginable abuse. Cefe soon found out that the municipal court in which he was supposed to administer justice was, like every other of its kind in Madrid, a nest of corruption and bribery.

Being the most unsuspicious as well as the most honest of men, he could not at first understand how it was that he got only thirty or forty pesetas a month, while the minor officials round him were living as though they had thousands. One day he discovered the reason. A poor worker who had been taken before the court for some alleged offense and whose case had been dismissed by my husband, came round to the house and complained that one of the employees had extorted twenty-five pesetas from him for a copy of the sentence he had a perfect right to have free. Cefe made a terrific row and threatened to have the employee discharged, but nothing was done. The official was the friend of a friend of a friend of some political boss and could not be removed. This case was followed by many others until we felt sick at heart over the whole business.

"What is the use of trying to be just ?" Cefe would say in despair. "Real offenders are rarely brought before the court because they bribe the officials and their papers disappear as if by magic. The only people who have to go through trial are, as a rule, poor workers caught in the mesh of some petty infraction."

It was not until several years later that this disgraceful state of affairs was changed, but by then Cefe was no longer an administrator of the law.

That morning had been unusually hard. All the cases he had had to deal with were people of the poorest class.

"I just can't bear it," he said as we walked home. "It is all so unfair. Those people have no money to pay the fines and if they are sent to prison they can't work and the family does not get anything to eat. I shouldn't mind it so much if the law was applied equally to all, but as it is . . ."

He looked so worried I hesitated about reading Laffan's letter to him. However, there was not much good keeping it back. At first he did not say a word, but as we were going up the stairs to our apartment, he stopped and looked at me with a dejected air.

"This is going to delay my giving up that horrible job in the law-court," he murmured.

I was dismayed. He usually made light of our money difficulties. We did not say anything more about it then but I made up my mind we would bring our wits together and find a way out of it for him. I was sure it could be done.

All that afternoon Cefe worked hard at a portrait of me he had just begun. His longing to paint was at last getting an outlet and it made me very happy to see him, brushes in hand, singing at the top of his voice or talking about the really wonderful things he might do if the portrait was a success.

Some days we were both very downcast for even to our hopeful minds the picture did not seem right.   Then I would propose that we go out for a turn and by the time we came home Cefe would have recovered his spirits.

"I am going to ask Aureliano Beruete to come in and see it," he said one day when it was finished.

I looked up anxiously.   Aureliano Beruete was the best art critic in Spain and, though an intimate friend of Cefe's, I was sure he would not spare him if he thought the picture a failure.

"Ask him to luncheon," I suggested with the vague hope that a good meal might lead to his being indulgent.

Our faithful little cook and I laid our heads together and prepared a really wonderful lunch.   Beruete and Cefe partook of it with relish but I could not swallow a bite.   My thoughts were with the picture, which we had placed on one of mother's finest consoles in the most advantageous light possible.

When we had finished our coffee Beruete walked up to the painting, laid his arms on the console and stared at the portrait. I stood beside him holding my breath.   "Why doesn't he speak ?   It is mean of him just to stare at the picture and try to find out everything that is wrong," I said to myself.   Then suddenly I realized that several things were wrong, though I had not noticed them before.

Cefe waited patiently, tearing away at his nails as he always does when he is nervous.

"Well ?" he asked at last, very humbly.

I felt inclined to cover up my ears.   I simply could not bear to hear anything disparaging.   Besides I dreaded the effect it might have on my husband.   He would be discouraged from painting forever.

"Do you know what I have to tell you ?" Beruete began very

slowly. "Do you know what I have to tell you ?" he repeated.

I wished he would go on.

"This picture has things in it that are simply grotesque."

I felt I wanted to hit him but Cefe merely acquiesced.

"They might have been done by a child. And yet there are other things that show very great talent."

I could have kissed him.

When Beruete left Cefe and I went into transports of joy.

"You must resign from your post in the law-court at once," I said to him. "It cannot do your art any good to be in that atmosphere." I felt very important.

"But, Nena, I do not think I ought to do that," remonstrated Cefe. "God knows we have little enough as it is." It was perfectly true. We had so very little that even the meagre sum from the law-court meant something. My small funds were almost exhausted. As for *La Dama*, it just managed to pay its own way. And I was expecting a child. However, we decided that Cefe must give up the hateful post and go in for painting.

"I shall first get another opinion on the picture," he said. "My friend, Eduardo Chicharro, who lives next door, will tell us what to do."

Chicharro was one of the most famous painters of Spain at that time.

Cefe went to see him the very next day and came back in a tremendous hurry to put the picture up on the console to be inspected once more.

Chicharro's verdict was even more favorable than Beruete's.

"Of course, I do not know what your husband will turn out to be in the end," he said to me in his slow drawl. "So many promising painters fail after a while."

Cefe was not daunted by these words, especially after Chicharro asked him to go and work with him in his studio. He looked radiant when he came back after escorting Chicharro to the door, and began work the very next day.

Chicharro was an exacting master. Several other young painters were working under his guidance.

"There is a Mexican studying with him, too," said Cefe to me one day. "His name is Diego de Rivera."

We had a pretty hard winter. My nest egg had entirely disappeared so we were obliged to cut down expenses to the utmost limit. I wrote a few articles for the London papers and was lucky enough to have them published, but we had to keep the money to buy clothes for the baby. We went without many things, fuel among others. For the first time in my life I realized that postage stamps, shoe polish and tramway fares were items that counted in the home budget. I had made Cefe promise that, except in the case of some severe illness, we would not allow the family to hear of our difficulties. After all, we had chosen to marry and it was up to us to find a way out. It was easy to keep things from mother, away in America, but Maria Tubau looked at us anxiously sometimes and inquired whether we were getting enough to eat.

In spite of these hardships we were perfectly happy. We went out very seldom except to see Maria and Don Ceferino.

One morning toward the end of May I was suddenly taken ill. The baby was coming! Cefe had already gone to the government job which kept him busy till lunchtime. I sent our little maid to Aunt Maria's house, asking her eldest married daughter to come to me.

I did not have the slightest idea when I should call the doctor. The physician who was going to look after me was one of the most famous Spanish specialists of the day. He was old and had been a great admirer of Maria Tubau's. He had kindly offered to attend the case without a fee. This made me shy about giving him too much trouble. Besides, I wanted to be alone as long as it was possible. For months I had dreamt of this moment. Ever since I had felt my baby stir within me it seemed as though I were living a little apart from everybody else, even from Cefe. I was not a bit scared, though, just awed.

The day wore on. I begged Cefe not to tell his parents anything yet. Perhaps the baby would arrive that night and we could surprise them the next morning with the news. When night came the doctor had to be called and soon I found myself driven into that abyss of pain from which there can be no turning back.

No woman in Spain in those years was given relief at such a time. None but the queen who, it was rumored, had insisted on being helped by some new-fangled method when the Prince of the Asturias and later, her second child, had been born. But such a proceeding had met with general disapproval.

My doctor was far too old-fashioned to give in on this point. For three days and nights he watched over me with unremitting care but, when I implored him to do something to ease the torture, he shook his head and murmured :

"Every woman is destined to bring her children into the world through pain."

I was too exhausted to protest. The agony of those long hours had sapped the last atom of strength in me. Everything was turning out so different from what I had expected. I knew there would be pain but not enough to break the intimate communion with the new life I carried. I had thought that communion would have ceased only with the entry of my child into the world.

No one had told me that I would feel like a hunted animal oblivious to everything except the gnawing pangs inside my tortured body. Only one thought was uppermost : "The child must not be a girl. It must not be condemned to go through this."

During one of my wanderings round the apartment, I came upon a sight which made me smile in spite of everything. On a chest which mother had left in an unused room, there was a lighted candle, a bottle of clear water, three pictures of the Virgin, and a strange-looking plant something like an artichoke. My cousin Maria and the two servants were on their knees, murmuring a prayer before the improvised altar.

"What are you doing?" I asked.

"Nothing, nothing. We are just saying the rosary," my cousin said, and then, with a confident smile, "everything is going to be all right."

It appeared that in view of my prolonged sufferings she had gone to the houses of different friends of hers who had had children lately, and had come back armed with all their pet devotions for times of travail. The bottle contained water from the River Jordan and was to be kept on hand lest the baby's life was in danger and it had to be christened at birth. The candle, burning before the pictures of the Blessed Virgin, was a votive offering for my safety but it must not be allowed to burn out before the end of my labor, otherwise it might bring bad luck. "I put it out now and then to make sure it will last," my cousin said to me with childlike simplicity. The plant was, she told me, a "rose of Jericho."

At the beginning of a woman's labor it was tightly closed, but as the moment of delivery drew near it gradually opened to its full size.

"Just look at it! Your baby will be here this very afternoon."

And so it was.

As I lay panting on my bed after the final sundering and

rending of my whole being, I smiled to myself again. The "rose of Jericho" had guessed right. My son had come.

A small bundle lay on my arm and Cefe was looking down at me in the same remote way he had done that night in the theatre when I had first known he loved me. From the folds of the shawl which enveloped the living proof of that love, two tiny hands emerged. The little nails were purple. My baby had fought for its life, too.

For one fleeting minute, I foresaw all the alternatives of joy and agony and hope and fear which I would go through in the future, because of that little bundle. He was called Ceferino after his father.

CHAPTER VIII

I had often wondered what I should do if one day I had to face the possibility of *La Dama's* discontinuance. When it happened I was surprised to find how little I seemed to care. I had struggled to keep it going for over three years and had enjoyed the experience but, somehow, I felt we had outgrown it. Life seemed so much bigger than we made out on those shiny, lustrous pages on which nothing new or progressive could be published. Sometimes we tried to introduce a different line but our young readers or their mammas immediately protested. They loved the pictures of charming society women and pretty brides and the descriptions of balls and parties and the sickeningly sentimental novels, generally translations from the British mid-Victorian period. We had introduced four pages of classical music and an occasional reproduction of a famous picture to leaven the mediocre material, but even these did not stimulate anyone's curiosity. Nudes, however famous, were of course carefully avoided.

At last a day came when we found it impossible to keep up with the rise in the cost of labor and paper. Had we had some capital we might have gone in for a total reorganization. There were now some groups of intelligent women who would have welcomed a magazine that was up to their standard. But such a step was out of the question. We then tried to sell the paper to another publishing house, but its editor had just started a woman's paper and was not interested in investing more capital. So I said farewell to still another venture and went ahead.

The translation of the fifth and sixth volumes of Havelock Ellis's work on sexual psychology kept me busy for several months and helped to keep the pot boiling at home. It did more to me than that. Like most women of that day in Spain,

I had been kept in total ignorance of the principal facts of life up to the time of my marriage. Even after I was a wife I was still kept in the dark about many things, such as specific diseases and aberrations of all kinds. Havelock Ellis opened my eyes so suddenly to these phenomena that for months I suffered from the shock. My responsibilities as a mother seemed to have increased a thousandfold and for a while I looked with horror upon the world. It seemed to me at times that everyone I met must be the victim of some hidden and terrible force. After a little I calmed down and was able to consider these questions with more common sense. The feelings of repugnance and intolerance faded and life seemed acceptable once more. I had gained in understanding.

We were still very badly off. Two years after our marriage we moved into a smaller apartment. I liked it better than the other one. The high ceilings and large windows reminded me of Andalusia ; and mother's furniture, some of which had belonged to my grandmother, looked much better in the new rooms than in the others. As we could not get it all in, we stored the bigger pieces.

Cefe had been going to Chicharro's studio regularly, but one day he came in rather crestfallen to tell me that Chicharro was going abroad.

"Some of the students intend keeping up the studio," he said. "They will share the expenses, but I don't see much good in spending the money when there will be no one there to correct our work." He did not say anything more that day but about a week later he announced that he had a plan. Instead of going to the studio, he would paint at home and begin with my portrait.

"It isn't going to be just a study this time," he said, "but a real life-sized portrait. Perhaps it will bring me fame."

I listened to him with mixed feelings. I wished he had chosen someone prettier, someone with fair hair and a decent complexion. My picture, I felt, would never attract anyone.

"Aren't you pleased?" he asked, looking at me anxiously.

"Pleased that you are going to paint something new and here at home with me? Why, of course I am. Only," I added a little shyly, "I wish you had a nicer model. I am not pretty enough."

"Darling," he said, coming round and kissing me, "you are far more than pretty. You are interesting. I would rather paint you than anyone else in the world."

But I was not really convinced. He evidently said this to please me. Well, I would make up for it by being a good model in other ways.

Cefe brought home a huge canvas, then fetched all his colors and brushes from the studio. We decided that our dining room would be the best place to paint as the light was very good. So we proceeded to haul the furniture out. Suddenly Cefe dropped the chair he was carrying.

"Nena," he cried, "I have forgotten the easel. I haven't an easel."

We sat down and considered the situation. We had just sufficient money to keep us going until the beginning of the next month. Cefe had bought the canvas on credit and felt he could not go and ask for anything else until he had paid at least part of that order. He did not know the other art stores well enough to ask a favor.

"I am afraid I shall not be able to begin until next month," he said despondently. "You see all Chicharro's easels are required by the students."

I looked around. We had several old-fashioned high-backed chairs.

"Couldn't you manage with one of these ?" I asked diffi-
dently.

I felt it was hard for an artist to work under such conditions.
On the other hand, I was anxious to see him go ahead when he
was so sure of himself and so full of hope.

Cefe looked at the chair and then at me.

"We can try," he said, smiling.

We pulled the canvas up and tied it to the back of the chair.
It stood up very well.

"Why, it is splendid !" he cried.   "Nena, you are a genius."

I was beside myself with joy.

The picture was begun that very afternoon.   Cefe made me
wear an ivory-colored silk dress and a black lace mantilla.
The pose was easy but rather tiring.   I stood with my arms
lightly crossed, the right hand holding an antique fan.

Cefe worked at the portrait for weeks during which we both
passed from black despair to triumphant hope.   I would stand
for hours not daring to say I was tired lest I cut short the stream
of inspiration I could almost see flowing from him.

When he remembered he would murmur, "Sit down, Nena,
you must be tired."   But I never let on that I was, though there
were times when my feet grew numb and my hand felt like a
dead fish.

Cefe painted until the light had gone, then he would go out
for a turn.   I always preferred to stay alone with the picture.
It was the only way to examine it at leisure, without the artist's
anxious eyes following me about and his anxious voice asking :

"What do you think of it ?"

Of course, I was no judge, but there were times when I could
detect things he had passed over in his anxiety to get on.   I
would untie the canvas from the chair and place it under the
light and examine it from every possible angle.   Then if I

found any little thing I thought was not quite right, I would tell him very carefully so as not to discourage him. Cefe was always inclined to think he had failed. At last one day he declared the portrait finished.

Aureliano Beruete was called in once more and declared he was amazed at Cefe's progress. Other friends and artists also came to see the picture. They all seemed to think he had a fine future before him.

Our little apartment became the centre of a new intellectual group. We always stayed in on Sundays and welcomed whoever felt like dropping in. There were many. A young girl friend of Cefe's, Maria Martos, used to help me with the tea. She was half Irish, a descendant, she said, of the royal Irish branch of the O'Neales. One day Cefe got an order to paint a portrait of King Alfonso for a government department.

The day he received the order he was quite overwhelmed.

"I do not know if I should accept it," he said.

I was ready to swear he would turn out something better than Goya's portrait of *The Family of Charles IV*.

"The subject is not inspiring," he added, after a little. "And I suppose they expect me to paint him in the usual way, wearing some gaudy uniform as captain general of the army with a hundred decorations, standing near a table with a book lying open on it and a red plush curtain for a background. This is the sort of thing those people like. But I am hanged if I will do it."

And he didn't.

After a long talk with the master of the king's household and the chief valet, Cefe's choice fell on the dark blue uniform of the *alabarderos*, or palace guard, and the white cape of the military orders of Santiago, Alcántara, Calatrava, and Montesa, of which the king was grand master. A white plumed hat was to be held in one hand, an ebony stick in the other. The background was to be a simple landscape. The king had offered to pose twice so the picture had to be done from photographs.

Cefe was so annoyed with all the difficulties that arose before things were settled that he very nearly canceled the order. At last he got started. The king's outfit, even down to the royal boots, was sent round to our apartment. A friend of Cefe's, Ricardo de la Vega, son of the famous author of the same name, had volunteered to pose in place of the king. He was exactly the same height and weight, the only difference was the length of the arms. Ricardo's were shorter than Don Alfonso's. This we settled by pinning up the sleeves of the uniform. Cefe began to work and the picture was getting on finely when one day we had a mishap. Ricardo had been posing all afternoon when suddenly he remembered he had an appointment. He took off the cape and began to tear off the uniform when . . . "crack, crack!" He had forgotten to take out the pins which held up the sleeve and the cloth had torn!

Cefe came in to tell me. He looked so glum I thought something terrible must have happened to the picture.

"It is awful," he said, after explaining what had happened. "Do you know what a uniform like that costs?"

I had visions of having to sell our furniture in order to pay for it. Cefe and I looked at the damage done, over and over again. It was in the back part of the sleeve, near the shoulder.

I hardly slept that night thinking out a plan which I put into practice the next morning while Cefe was away. I had learnt how to darn in the convent and the nun there had told me that delicate mending on dark materials should not be done with silk or thread but with hair. So I sat down near the window with the finest needle I could find, pulled out several wisps of my hair and began to darn. The result was excellent. It was almost impossible to detect the tear and then only on close inspection.

When Cefe saw it he was delighted.

"It's perfect," he said. "No one will notice."

But I was not quite happy. I had a growing conviction that some day it would be discovered and perhaps the valet would be blamed. I confided my fears to Cefe and at last persuaded him to go and see the master of the king's household again and explain what had happened. He did not like to do it but he went, and came back quite relieved.

"Do you know what he told me ?" he said as soon as he was in the house. "He is delighted it has happened because the uniform is very old and it is time to order a new one."

I was glad to hear it.

We had now been married four years and had not been able to get away for even a week-end. Fortunately baby Cefito was a healthy wee chap and did not seem to suffer from it.

That summer I had more translations to do and Cefe began a new portrait, not an order this time. His model was a very tall, very thin and very pale priest. His name was Don Felix.

"He looks exactly like a Greco," Cefe said, when he explained why he was anxious to paint him.

This time he worked in a friend's studio. The heat up there was appalling. The poor priest, who at first was rather flattered at being chosen for a model, nearly fainted under it. In the end he was disappointed with his picture. Cefe, however, was very pleased.

"Do you know what I am going to do ?" he said to me one day after he had brought the portrait home. "I am going to show it to Sorolla. I want to know what he thinks of my work."

"Will you ask him to come here ?" I asked excitedly.

"Well, I can hardly do that. I shall see what he wants to do." Cefe knew the great Spanish painter quite well, for he was an old friend of Maria's and Don Ceferino's, and was full of reverence for his talent.

. We had no telephone in the house, so one day after lunch Cefe rang up Sorolla from our neighbor's apartment.

"Quick, darling," he said, tearing into the house again in frantic excitement. "Help me to get the picture out. Sorolla is waiting for me. He wants to see it. Ask one of the maids to call a cab, an open one," he shouted as I left the room.

The canvas was enormous, long and narrow. We helped Cefe into a one-horse cab and I stood and watched him turn the corner holding on to the portrait. The last thing I saw was Don Felix's head swaying to and fro.

An hour later Cefe and his picture were home once more. At first he could hardly speak.

"Nena! Nena!" he blurted out at last, almost choking with excitement. "Do you know what Sorolla says?" I was listening with eyes and ears wide open.

"He says that the picture is very good. That I have the makings of a really great artist in me, that . . . that . . ." He could get no farther.

After a little I was able to gather that Sorolla had said Cefe must go on painting and that it was best he should do it alone. No master could teach him anything now. He had also advised him to do nothing else but paint.

This was easier said than done. Pictures were not sold every day. And what were we going to live on in the meantime? It is true Cefe had only his salary in the National Library, but if he gave that up he would have even less. We decided that he would go to the library in the morning and paint all afternoon.

Just about that time a new woman's magazine was started and I was asked to send in some articles. This meant an increase of funds. One day the editor suggested that it would be very good for the paper if we could get the queen to give her opinion on what she considered the best methods for the upbringing of children.

It was easy for me to request an audience. It was granted at once. My impression of the fair-haired Victoria of Battenberg was that she was extremely shy. She tried to be cordial but only succeeded in being stiff. I could see now what it was that made the Spaniards keep at such distance from her. As a people they are not given to pandering to the rich and powerful. They are too proud, too individualistic to render unconditional obeisance to any one person. That is why they have never been really sympathetic to the monarchical régime. I have not witnessed in Spain, as I have in other countries, for example, in Great Britain, great crowds assemble to see the royal family drive by. Neither do the events within the royal palace awaken any special interest except among a very few. Even the Pope is not granted in Spain that unquestioning obedience of other Catholic peoples.

Queen Victoria of Spain, with her rigid aloofness, was certainly not capable of breaking through the Spaniards' indifference, even supposing they had been willing to accept her from a political point of view.

I found her ready to help in every possible way within the limitations of her rank. She spoke with concern of the high mortality among the children in Madrid but, of course, could not see that the chief cause for it was the terrible poverty of the working classes brought about by social injustice. She put it all down to ignorance, not realizing that the monarchical régime was chiefly responsible for that ignorance. The tragedy of hereditary disease was already casting its shadow across her own path but at that time she seemed free from care.

My editor was delighted with the interview, which was illustrated with pictures of the queen and the royal babes and their private apartments. He considered it a great scoop and I suppose it was. One of the ladies-in-waiting, who was a friend of ours, said to me some days later, "This is the first time such a thing has been done," and I gathered from her manner that, if she had anything to say in the matter, it would be the last.

Just about that time a family event gave us plenty to talk about. Cefe's brother, Julio, who two years before had entered the diplomatic service and was acting consul in Salonika, announced his engagement to Zoe Dragoumis, the daughter of Stephan Dragoumis, Governor of Macedonia and one-time Greek premier and political opponent of Venizelos.

This marriage introduced a totally foreign element into the Palencia clan. I, after all, was Spanish, even if the Scottish side of me came to the surface at odd moments.

Zoe Dragoumis was half Greek and half Russian and could not then speak a single word of Spanish though she was of course proficient in English and French. The newly married couple came to Madrid for their honeymoon on their way to Julio's new post in Costa Rica. We had rather a funny time at first. Maria and Don Ceferino spoke nothing but Spanish so every word between them and their new daughter had to be interpreted. However, they were all coming to know each other when suddenly a bolt fell. Maria, or *mamita* as her sons called her, took to her bed with what seemed a slight attack of influenza, and unexpectedly passed away. Her heart had failed.

The great actress' death was a blow to dramatic art in general for, although she had not acted for several years, her name was a standard in the theatrical world. A standard for fine living and fervent dedication to art. To her family her death was an incalculable loss. Don Ceferino was simply heartbroken. She had been not only his star and inspiration as a dramatic author, but the great love of his life. To their two sons she had been the most devoted of mothers.

Her loss left a great void in my own life as we had been drawn very close to each other.

All Spain mourned for Maria Tubau and for nine days after her death I had to sit in her drawing room receiving the expressions of condolence from hundreds of mourners of all classes, high and low. It is customary in Spain for the rosary to be said in houses where someone has died, during nine consecutive afternoons after the death. When prayers are finished people sit around and talk. They are supposed to distract the minds of the bereaved family from their sorrow. I found it very trying.

Maria's death brought about a radical change in Cefe's and my life. Don Ceferino could not bear the idea of living alone and I found it impossible at such a time to refuse his wish that we should merge the two households into one. We left our beloved little home and moved into my father-in-law's huge straggling apartment of twenty-three rooms, located in the very heart of the town in a narrow twisting street, La Carrera de San Jerónimo.

The Spanish House of Commons and three or four old houses belonging to the aristocracy, crowned with their coats of arms, are the only survivals of the past glory of this thoroughfare which is now a fashionable shopping centre. Our two maids, Maria and Asunción, followed us there and, with the other two women who had looked after Maria, made up our household.

Zoe and Julio had already taken their departure by the time we were settled. Life was very different now. Don Ceferino was very kind but, of course, there were no more tête-à-tête meals for Cefe and me. No more quiet afternoons. People were coming and going constantly. I felt life was much more complicated.

One day, early in the spring, Cefe came into my sitting room. "Nena, do you know what I am going to do ?" he said. "I am going to try and get your portrait accepted for the national exhibition next month. Of course I know I shall not get any prize, but being an exhibitor, I can get in without paying anything at the door. You can, too, being a journalist. It is very necessary for me to see the exposition often. One learns a lot that way."

I hoped the picture would be well received and was greatly relieved to hear the jury had passed it as "acceptable."

The day of the opening Cefe and I dressed in our best, which was not saying much, and showed our "passes" proudly at the gate. There was a huge crowd. The royal family, the minister of education, and other high government officials went in first. When they left we were allowed to enter.

Holding on to Cefe's arm, I went from room to room looking for his picture. We searched in vain for quite a while. It was not among those hung in the first and second halls where the paintings of beginners or unimportant artists were exhibited, nor in the rooms where other better-known artists were showing their work.

"Where can it be ?" I asked Cefe.

A friend stopped us and said, "Congratulations, Palencia, your picture is well hung. I suppose you have seen it."

"No, where is it ?" we both asked at once.

"Over there with the bigwigs," he said and pointed to our right.

We came upon my portrait in a small room where there were only three other pictures. I felt very nervous. A great many people were looking at it. I hoped they really liked it.

In the days that followed very good notices about the picture appeared in the press and Cefe was happier than I had ever seen him. Every afternoon he would go to the exposition and meet people. I was finishing a translation and could not go. The day of the prize giving arrived. The jury had been meeting for several days. We were not much interested. It could not affect us.

One day we heard the medals and prizes had at last been awarded so we thought we would go to the exposition that afternoon and see if our favorites had been well treated.

Don Ceferino went on before us. It was a lovely day. Cefe and I walked along leisurely. As we drew near the gate of El Retiro where the exposition building was situated, I saw a man wave his arms at us and begin to throw his hat into the air.

"Cefe," I said, "that looks like your father, but if it is, he must have gone crazy. Why is he doing that?"

Don Ceferino kept on waving and calling us. When we were in earshot he cried:

"Son! Son! You have been awarded a medal!"

Don Ceferino, the trees and the ground whirled around me for a minute. When I had steadied myself I took Cefe's arm.

"Oh, Cefe, can it be true? Can it be true?" I said, shaking him.

"I can hardly believe it," he answered, bending down and kissing me before the astounded gaze of a group of nursemaids.

We went into the exposition building and were met as we entered by a large number of friends who congratulated us warmly, men like Pinázo, Mezquíta and Zuloaga, who had reached the summit of fame long before.

Holding Cefe's hand, I hurried to the room where his picture was hung and, sure enough, a piece of cardboard placed at the foot indicated that a medal had been awarded to it.

Isabel de Palencia
from a painting by her husband, Ceferino Palencia

That medal, with its accompanying prize in cash, helped us go through the next few months, if not in luxury, at least without fear for the next day's meal. I was expecting my second child so I felt relieved, but over and above every other feeling, was the certainty that my husband was now on the road to happiness.

That summer the war broke out in Europe. Public opinion in Spain awoke with a shock. What her own conflicts and losses had not achieved, the gigantic conflagration succeeded in bringing about. Before a month had gone by Spaniards were divided into two passionately interested groups : pro-allies and pro-Germans. In the cafés, in the streets and in the homes people argued with such violence that more than once they came to blows.

As a rule the clergy, especially the hierarchy of the church, the army and the aristocracy, sided with Germany, while the intellectuals and the working classes were for the allies. A great many writers and artists realized the necessity of helping anything that meant progress against tyranny. Those more alive to home requirements were also convinced that the victory of the allies over German militarism, with its caste prejudices and its feudal concept of a country's organization, would favor Spain. They thought that the victory of the allies would help to defeat the combined efforts of reaction to maintain Spain in its backward state.

France was particularly abhorred by most pro-Germans because it was the cradle of the revolution and the creator of that "pernicious doctrine," the rights of man. England was Protestant, therefore an enemy to Catholicism. They ignored Germany's religious denomination because German propaganda had insinuated that the kaiser was going to restore the temporal power of the Holy See.

The government managed to keep the country neutral and, on the whole, Spaniards might have derived great benefits from their position had they known how to manage. But the river of gold which came into Spain was not invested as it should have been in a total transformation of the old-fashioned industries and the development of the country's natural resources. It was hoarded in the banks and later used to buy up German marks. When the mark crashed, many Spanish firms crashed with it. Cefe and I were naturally on the side of the allies.

Early in the war three of my Scottish cousins were killed.

We were disgusted when Julio and Zoe wrote, to find that they were entirely pro-German. A few squabbles through the post merely served to show that we were miles apart spiritually as well as physically.

On the eighth of December of that year our second child was born. Once more pain followed love and torture flooded all consciousness as a new being was brought into the world. This time I was desperately anxious that it should be a girl. Since the war had begun I did not want to have a boy. I got my wish.

It was the day of the Immaculate Conception, a feast day in Spain, and the bells of all the churches in Madrid heralded the appearance of the tiniest baby imaginable.

Don Ceferino was overjoyed for this was the first baby girl to come to the Palencia family. Cefe had only boy cousins. She was christened in the parish of Saint Sebastian and we called her Maria Isabel.

"I want her to have the names of the two people I have loved best in the world : mother and you," said Cefe.

Maria Isabel's double name was, however, soon cut down by her young brother to one : "Marissa." And Marissa it has been ever since.

I used to look at the little cot with its small occupant and think that as a woman my baby would perhaps have to go through great trials.   She might have to suffer pain in order to give life, but she would not be obliged to lose her life giving death to others in war.

CHAPTER IX

During the year 1915 a group of women started a debate on women's suffrage in the auditorium of the Ateneo of Madrid. I was keeping very much to the house those days and none of my nearest friends were taking part so I did not hear very much about it. To judge from the accounts in the papers, however, everything seemed to be going admirably.

A great many men had seconded the women's demands and a question that would have been mercilessly ridiculed a short time before was now treated with the utmost respect. The war had made us all more politically conscious.

The first outcome of the debate was the setting up of a committee charged with calling on all the women of Spain to join and defend their rights. At that time, and in fact until the new constitution drafted by the republic was enforced, years later, the Spanish women not only had no political rights, but were treated almost all their lives like persons under age. If they were married they could not open a banking account or sell their property or be given a passport without the authorization of their husbands. They had no rights over their children. If they did not marry, or if they became widows, they rarely asserted their independence. The marriage laws of the time only allowed legal separation of husbands and wives, not divorce. The separation was granted in cases of flagrant adultery, of repeated ill treatment or desertion of the home : it was not difficult to obtain, especially by men. Remarriage was, of course, out of the question.

A few months after the appeal had been made the women grouped themselves into an association and started to work in earnest. I was asked to join but did not feel like it just then. Home life was too complicated or perhaps too absorbing.

The news of the war was terribly depressing. It made me bitter to see how Madrid was changing. Never had our capital been so gay. A great many people had taken refuge in Spain in order to escape the privations of war. They wanted to be amused. New cabarets were opened. War profiteers hastened to enjoy their newly acquired wealth.

The influx from abroad affected our group, too. Spanish writers who had been living in some of the countries at war, many of whom had married foreign wives, came back to the safe home land. A lasting friendship sprang up between some of these women and myself. Trudy Graa, wife of Luis Araquistain, and her sister Luisi, who was later to become Mrs. Alvarez del Vayo, were perhaps those who came closest to my heart. They were like two younger sisters to me.

The war had now been going on for three years. My youngest brother José had volunteered for the front, increasing my fears a hundredfold. Mother was still in America. She was anxious to come and see us but we begged her to wait for fear of the submarine warfare. Besides, Anita and Inez were studying and hoping to graduate from a university and Ricardo, now a civil engineer, was in Cuba. I felt they were safe on the other side of the ocean.

By that time we ourselves had moved out of the centre of the town to an apartment near the principal promenade of Madrid, la Castellana. As there was no room for Cefe to paint in, we took a studio a few streets away and arranged it nicely with part of the furniture from our own house.

Some of the happiest hours of those anxious months were spent in that big comfortable room looking over the housetops, surrounded by our friends. Andrés Segovia, the musician, would drop in some days with his guitar and play for hours at a time while we sat around dreamily listening and trying to forget the tragedy of the war. He was very young then and inexperienced.

"I don't know what I am going to do," he said to me one day. "I am told that no one can be a really great artist unless he suffers. I am trying my best to be unhappy but I cannot manage it."

I reassured him. Suffering, I said, would come to him in good time without having to be summoned. I wonder whether this has been the case with him. Another habitué was the conductor of the Madrid symphonic orchestra, Enrique Arbós, who was a marvelous story teller.

While Cefe worked hard at a picture he was painting for the next exhibition, I was writing a daily article for the new journal, *El Sol*. A liberal pro-allied paper that was creating quite a sensation on account of its high standard. The staff had been chosen with the utmost care. There were writers like Luis Araquistain, thickset and combative, whose relentless pen struck terror into the hearts of his opponents; Ramón Pérez de Ayala, the novelist, whose book *A.M.D.G.* (*Ad Majorem Dei Gloriam*) written in the days of youthful ardor and hotly condemned by the Jesuits, was being followed up by bland attempts to hide a growing scepticism which was to be very useful, years after, when events in Spain demanded self-sacrifice from the men who had been her leaders in the field of independent thought; Salvador de Madariaga, agile minded and critical, who was amusing himself by sending rapier thrusts into Spanish reaction from his retreat in a British university; Gregorio Marañón, the beloved doctor of an aristocratic clientele that smiled indulgently at his progressive views, guessing perhaps that a time would come when he would achieve great feats in the art of sitting on the fence.

José Ortega y Gasset, the Spanish philosopher, also used the paper as a trying-out ground for his views. He spoke as a spectator looking at Spain. Unfortunately he remained a spectator, never an actor, all the rest of his life.

The Countess Emilia Pardo Bazán, one of the finest writers of the end of the nineteenth century, had joined the staff as an occasional contributor. She was getting on in years and was still smarting under the curt refusal of the Royal Academy of the Spanish Language to have her elected to its sacred circle under the pretext that she was a woman. One would have thought that so intelligent a person as she undoubtedly was would have taken this decision of the old fossilized academi-cians as a joke. She did not, however. The day before the paper came out little Cefito, barely four years old at the time, had the honor of being taken around the building by Doña Emilia who tried to instil into his young mind the importance of the press in our age.

Last but not least was Bagaria, the clever Catalonian car-toonist whose anti-German caricatures were the despair of the German embassy in Madrid.

Among the contributors there were other well-known names of men in the advance guard of the new Spain. Some failed in the end, but others proved faithful.

One of the tasks assigned to me on the new paper was that of sending in a write-up on the costumes and scenic decorations of every new play of a certain category, produced in Madrid during the season. As there was a large number of theatres, and producers were constantly renewing their programs, my job was by no means a light one. The theatres in Madrid give two performances a day. What is called the matinée takes place at six p.m. The second one, at ten forty-five at night, is rarely over before one o'clock in the morning. The new productions almost invariably took place then at the second performance and, as all reports on the new plays are supposed to be published in the morning edition, I had to write my story immediately after we left the theatre. I often did not go to bed before three or four a.m.

Generally I wrote my "stuff" in a café while enjoying a belated cup of chocolate with a crowd of our friends who sat around the table, chatting and discussing the play we had just seen. Manuel Azaña, who some years later was to be President of the Spanish Republic, would sometimes be there ; also the great poet, Don Ramón del Valle-Inclán, who would stroke his long beard while giving utterance to the wildest vagaries, poetical, philosophical or literary.

It was not always easy for me to be sincere, for the actors as well as the author, who were almost all personal friends, would take the slightest criticism very much to heart. They thought, wrongly I believe, that it affected the success of the play. However, I do not think I ever allowed my personal feelings to lead me away from the path of justice. Not even when Don Ceferino would intercede in favor of some colleague like Jacinto Benavente who was a great friend of us all. I thought a man who was in possession of the Nobel Prize did not need to worry over my little efforts in favor of historical accuracy or light effects on the stage. And of course he didn't.

Gregorio Martínez Sierra — co-author with his wife of *The Cradle Song* and at the time manager of one of the principal theatres in Madrid — was perhaps the most appreciative of all, but then, he was wonderfully careful of his *mise en scène* and looked personally after the smallest details.

I thoroughly enjoyed this work at first. For one thing, it brought me back into the atmosphere I loved, and, although a good play was still the exception, a first-night performance in Madrid was always exciting. People voiced their approval or disapproval in the most open manner and the discussions about a new production would sometimes last for days.

Writing for *El Sol* was not, however, my only task. I

would give an occasional lecture and it was on account of my speaking that I went to one of the oldest and loveliest cities of Spain.

I had never been in Salamanca and was delighted when an invitation to speak there provided me with the chance not only of seeing the wondrous city and its university, but also of getting away with Cefe for a short rest and holiday. Salamanca was the birthplace of Beatriz Galíndo, the governess of the Catholic Queen Isabella and a great Latin scholar. I had used her name as a pseudonym for some of my articles and the members of the Ateneo of Salamanca thought it would be interesting for me to give a lecture from the very chair in the university that the real Beatriz Galíndo had been wont to occupy.

We left Madrid early one beautiful spring morning. I felt as if we were starting for another honeymoon. The distance should have been covered in three or four hours but at that time there was no direct railway line between Madrid and Salamanca. One had to go halfway up to Burgos and then come back again and it took almost the whole day. But we did not mind it in the least and amused ourselves watching the people in the villages at which we stopped : there were Castilians with their sombre-hued capes ; there were peasants from the province of Avila dressed in their picturesque costumes ; the women wearing gaudy fancy straw hats, trimmed with artificial flowers and bits of looking-glass, and bright-colored petticoats and kerchiefs ; the men with their black velvet knee breeches and embroidered white shirts. Passengers were constantly getting on or off the train. They were mostly talkative so we got plenty of impressions as to the state of affairs in these regions and plenty of complaints about the government.

The rector of the university, Don Miguel de Unamuno, and the members of the executive committee of the Ateneo met us

at the station of Salamanca.   I had met the famous author of
The Tragic Sense of Life and other not less interesting works
in Madrid two or three years before, but I had never had the
chance of speaking to him at length as we were able to do during the time of our stay in the city.

I delivered my lecture the night after our arrival in the large
university auditorium.   I spoke on *Women in the Past*.   Unamuno and most of the faculty were there and a large number
of students and outsiders.   I felt very nervous but everyone
was charming so I passed through the ordeal without a break.

"Do you think women should be given the rights they are
asking for?" Unamuno asked me the next morning when he
came to fetch us at the hotel for a tour of the town.   We had
been talking of women's influence in general.

"Why, yes," I answered.

"Don't you believe it," he said, shaking his head.   "My
experience is that women without rights get their own way
much better than we men who are supposed to have all of them.
In my family at least that has always been the case.   My grandmother ruled my grandfather.   My mother ruled my father
and her sons, and my wife rules our whole family.   If you give
them 'rights' you will find they lose their privileges."

I could not help laughing.   I did not know Mrs. Unamuno
but had often heard that she was one of the most prudent and
retiring of women.

Unamuno took us personally all round the university.   We
lingered in the class where he gave his Greek course.   His
private workroom and library fascinated me with its long walls
lined with books, its rounded ceiling and deep windows.

"Do you know what women excel in?" he said suddenly,
while we were there.   "Do you know one of the things in
which they are superior to men?"

"In several," I answered, laughing.

"Yes, I admit it. But where they really surpass the masculine mind is in writing novels. There is no greater novelist in the world than Emily Brontë, at least in my opinion. I would rather have written this book," he said, taking a copy of *Wuthering Heights* from a shelf, "than any other book of fiction in the world."

"Which shows that women are capable of creating though men always deny it," I retorted.

"They are capable of everything," Unamuno said, smiling.

Cefe and I spent quite a while in what had been Fray Luis de León's classroom in the university where, the day he renewed his classes after seven years' imprisonment by orders of the Holy Inquisition, it is said he addressed his students with the simple words, "As we were saying yesterday," thus ignoring the wrong done to him and the passing of time. The words are characteristic of the man and of Spain. The classroom is preserved as it was in Fray Luis de León's time. It is a long, narrow and very dark room. In the wooden desks generations of students have carved their names. The lecturer's chair, empty now, stands in solitary state at the head of the room.

Unamuno took us all over the city. We went to monasteries and churches where he was admired for his knowledge of art and feared because of his liberal spirit, into old palaces where his knowledge helped to endow history with a sense of reality, down the old streets at night not to dream of the past but to listen to the voice of Spain moving up to the present.

While we stayed in Salamanca, Unamuno used to come and sit with us when we were having lunch. He partook of his meal earlier and kept the afternoon free for walking and writing. He told me he had divided the twenty-four hours of the day into three parts, eight hours for work, eight for meals and recreation and eight for sleep. He certainly looked as if this division of time agreed with him, a fine upright healthy Basque.

The long restless fingers of the rector were constantly occupied with something. When they did not hold a pen they would be busy folding pieces of paper into unbelievably clever shapes of frogs, birds, little chairs and tables. He gave this amusement of his the name *cacotología*. Needless to say, Cefe and I brought away quite a collection of his creations. When he did not have paper near at hand he would pinch a bit of bread off the soft part of a loaf, soak it in water and work it with his fingers while he talked.

Once our sightseeing was over for the day, we would spend an hour or two wandering along Unamuno's favorite walk, a long highway between Zamora and Salamanca. Once there, history and art forgotten, Unamuno would launch into long discussions on the subject that was always uppermost in his mind, a subject that was an obsession with him : the after life.

Contrary to what the church said Unamuno was far from being an agnostic. He was a speculator, a non-conformist, but an ardent believer and, like most Spaniards, a mystic.

I was as much interested in the question as he and we two would remain far behind Cefe and our other friends, analyzing possibilities of a future existence. In several letters written to my husband Unamuno refers to our talks and expresses a desire to renew them.

The next time I went to Salamanca, however, we did not get a chance to talk. I was there only for a few hours and the time I spent in Unamuno's company he insisted on reading aloud his translation of *Phèdre*. The play was produced after the advent of the republic, several years later, in the most wonderful of settings : the Roman amphitheatre of Mérida. I was interested in hearing his adaptation of the work but I very nearly missed my train on account of its length.

Cefe and I went back to Madrid with renewed strength and

settled down to work. It was the first time I had been separated from the children and I was glad to be with them again.

One day the group of women who had started the movement
for woman suffrage came to see me. They wanted me to join
them. At first I demurred. I was too busy. Besides, I was
personally not yet interested. However, they seemed really
anxious for me to help out and felt that I could be specially useful in getting them in touch with other groups abroad, so I
accepted and a few weeks later found, to my surprise, that I
had been elected vice-chairman of the association. That winter I did some public speaking. I gave another lecture in the
Ateneo and two more in different societies. Cefe encouraged
me but never dared come and listen to me. He said it made
him nervous. I found the only way to forget about the war
was to be busy the whole time and just as I was beginning to
think that I had succeeded, something happened that drove all
my thoughts into one channel and paralyzed all my energies
for a time. It changed my whole life.

CHAPTER X

It is strange that after all these years I should still shrink from forcing my way into the hidden recesses of my own heart.

Does the wound still bleed ? No, there is only a scar. But memory has a terrible power of awakening pain, even after the cause of that pain has been removed. I fear it ; and would fain avoid it, yet believe it is not right to skip a chapter in my life even if in accounting for it I shall be hurt.

She was beautiful. . .

During the war she and her husband had come to Madrid from abroad and joined our group. They were both Spanish. I looked on her with a sympathy born of pity. It was said that she was not happy with her husband.

Cefe asked me one day whether I did not think it would be interesting for him to paint her portrait. I was delighted. She was, too. Cefe began to work. Soon he seemed immersed in his task. He would rush from the house as soon as luncheon was over and would come home full of plans as to what the portrait was to be. Twice he asked me to go up and see the first studies he had made. They were not good. He tried again but was still not pleased.

Little by little a great change came over him. He, usually so happy, so good-natured, became morose and irritable.

"Is the portrait not going well ?" I would ask, thinking that was what was upsetting him. He scarcely answered.

One day as I was pondering over things, worrying over Cefe's strange manner, a vague suspicion surged within me. How I hated myself. For days I struggled against what I thought was my disloyalty. To have doubt of him . . . of Cefe ! I tried to make it up to him by asking her repeatedly to come to the house, to share our meals. Cefe grew more and more irritable. Soon I hardly saw him. The afternoon he would spend in his studio. At night he left the moment dinner was over, saying he was too nervous to read, that he must walk . . . must get out in the open. He never asked me to go with him and was cross if he found me awake when he came in. Often I made believe to be asleep.

Now he never mentioned the portrait. . .

I fought desperately against myself, against the horrible thoughts that clouded my brain. After some time I began to think that people were looking at me pityingly.

And at last one day I just knew. Cefe had not needed words to tell me of his love. He did not need them now. But we had always promised each other that, if the almost impossible were to happen — if the love of one of us failed — we would never deceive one another. We would speak openly and tell the truth. I hoped now that he would keep his word.

It was dreary work : waiting. My fight now was to prevent myself from watching him. I swore that our love would not be demeaned by contemptible little tricks. I did not wish just to "find out." I ceased asking him questions as to what he had done, where he had been.

One night he told me. He came in late and found me still up. He was too worn out to protest. I asked him to sit down beside me. Before five minutes had gone by he had laid his head on my knees and was blurting out his story. Every word he said left a mark.

We sat there almost all night. The house was very quiet. Everyone was asleep. Cefe talked unceasingly as though by talking he could get rid of a burden. At times he would begin to accuse her, then he would turn against himself.

"Nena! Nena! I hate myself! I hate myself, and yet I cannot give her up." Suddenly he took hold of my hands.

"You will forgive me, won't you, Nena ?"

Forgive ?   What was there to forgive ?   It was not a matter for forgiveness.   I could not see that he had done wrong.   It simply was that he no longer cared for me.   He could not help that.   I told him so.

Cefe reacted at once.   He swore that I did not understand. Of course he cared.   He loved only me.   This was a passing madness. . .

"I might believe that in anyone but you," I said, "but you are not the kind of man to be led just by passion.   You always put something of your innermost self into everything you do. You give something of your spirit and . . . that is love."

"Then ?" he inquired anxiously.

"Then we shall arrange matters in the best possible way.   I shall think of something," I answered.

"You must not think of leaving me, not that."   There was a note of terror in his voice.   "Nena, promise me that you will never go from me.   I shall be a lost soul if you do."

I persuaded him to go to bed.   We would say no more about it for the moment.   He was too exhausted to reply.   While he slept I walked up and down my room, from the door to the window at the other end, like a caged animal.   I was going to do little more than that for weeks to come.   Up and down, down and up, for hours, thinking. . .

Cefe and I did not speak again of what had happened until a few days later.   He looked for me of his own accord when he came in one night.   I was exhausted and feigned sleep, but he insisted on speaking to me.

"Nena," he said, "we cannot go on like this."

I looked up in surprise.   So far there had been no change. Our life had gone on as before.

"Everything seems different and I cannot stand it," he said.

Again we talked at length.   I tried to make him see that the only dignified thing for us to do was to separate.   We could do it without provoking any talk. He could go away to Paris. A new journal was going to be published shortly in Madrid and he had been invited to go on the staff as art critic to the paper.

"Ask them to make you their correspondent in Paris," I said. Cefe would not listen. He refused to leave me. I tried to make him see that it was not fair to make me stand and look on while he "recovered his senses," as he termed it.

That night he told me that she wanted to see me. She had left off coming to the house for some time. I hesitated, then agreed to see her the next day.

We met in the park. I managed to keep calm but from the first I saw there was nothing to do. I told her I could not blame her for falling in love as I had done. But I expected one of two positions. Either a point-blank refusal to give Cefe up — and I would have understood it if she had refused — or total renunciation. She took neither one. She merely said something vague about not wanting to hurt me. I proposed that they go abroad together and try to begin life again. She did not seem to wish to do that either. She thought it was too great a responsibility. We said nothing more. I left her, feeling very much discouraged. I was sure that it was useless to try and rely on a promise she had made not to deceive me.

"It is the only thing I ask of you both," I had said. But they kept on deceiving me all the time.

It took me a long time to obtain complete mastery over myself. Fortunately, I did not give in to the temptation of telling anyone what had happened, not even my dearest and closest friends. I felt that talking to someone would make me bitter and I did not want that. Besides, I did not wish to do her harm. So long as I appeared not to know anything, no one would go openly against her. There was nothing specially noble in this, for what should I gain by making her suffer?

Pacing up and down my room, one day after another, I came to the conclusion I could stand it no longer. If Cefe did not go away, I would. I knew that it would be the breaking up of the home, that if once I went I would never come back. But I was breaking down under the strain. The children would go with me, of course. I was making enough money to keep them and me ; Don Ceferino, too, if he wanted to go with us. Perhaps he did not know what was going on but sometimes I caught him looking at me suspiciously. I had nearly come to the conclusion that I would leave the house when one day I received the visit of a young Frenchman whose father lived now in Madrid. The father had been divorced from a first wife and had married again. The son got on quite well with his father's new wife and spent six months of the year with them and the other six with his mother.

We got to talking about his childhood and he surprised me by saying, "I love my parents dearly, but I shall never forgive them for having been divorced. I did not ask to come into the world and it was their duty since they brought me here at least to give me a home. People who have children are not free to do as they like. They need not live as husband and wife if they don't want to, but they should keep up appearances for their children's sake. I am sure there is not a single child of divorced parents that does not feel as I do."

"There are cases," I ventured to say.

"Very exceptional ones," he answered, smiling.

What he had said made me think a great deal. It made me impatient at times. I had made up my mind to go and felt that by doing so I would somehow be liberated, that I would get rid of this awful burden. The suffering was so acute that sometimes I could feel it physically. And now a sense of duty arose to keep me back.

"I must go, I must go," I said to myself. I did not care

where, I just wanted to get away from the torture I was going through. There were moments when I felt that I should like to open a hole in the ground and bury myself in it, a sheer animal desire to hide.

Up and down, down and up, the length of my room. Cefe had told me that in spite of everything it was I he loved. But how could I believe him ? His mind, his thoughts, even his art, were no longer mine.

Cefe would sometimes try to bring the conversation round to her again. He did not realize that, like everyone in love, he did it just to be able to speak of his obsession. But I did. Other times he was frightened, thinking I might leave him, and he tried to deceive me. That was worse than anything else. I begged him not to do it.

Months went by, I saw him pass alternately from intense artificial excitement to the blackest of moods. Suddenly a friend, who did not know what was going on, unconsciously gave me a clue to something the woman was doing that might have damned her utterly in Cefe's eyes.

I was at once engaged in another fierce struggle with myself. To be able to take revenge. . . The idea was terribly attractive, but I could not stoop to that. Our love had been too great to drag it down to such a level.

Up and down, down and up. Little by little the turmoil within me subsided somewhat. The spiritual travail reminded me of those awful hours in which I had given birth to new lives. But then there was something wonderful to look forward to, now there was nothing but emptiness.

My whole life had been ruled by my faith in Cefe. I had looked up to him in everything, counted on him for even the slightest things, and now there seemed to be an abyss between us.

I felt I owed much to our love and to him. He had opened

up so many ways to an understanding of beauty and of passion, too. Life had been complete : the perfect merging of our two selves physically and spiritually into one.

Now I must stand alone, think alone, and live alone, with this gnawing despair in my heart. I rebelled. I said to myself that I would not stand it.

Up and down, down and up. There were moments when I was so exhausted I thought that everything was over, that I was free from pain, cured at last. But a note of music, a line in a book, a simple memory would bring it all back and the fight would begin again. Little by little, however, the intervals between those moments became longer and at last, one day, I found that the worst of the struggle was over.

I was still wondering at the strange numbness that had come upon me when one day Cefe asked me to go up to the studio.

"I have finished the portrait," he said to me, hesitatingly. "Won't you come and tell me what you think of it ?"

To my surprise I was able to answer him naturally. "Yes, of course, I shall go with you to-morrow."

When we entered the studio I thought the past was going to rise up again. The room with all its recollections was almost more than I could stand.

We had loved each other there. Sometimes in the days gone by we would play at being lovers and make an appointment like a runaway couple. It was lovely to feel that we were alone, totally and completely alone, looking over the rooftops. Cefe would order wine and candy and flowers to be brought up. I would arrive dressed in my prettiest frock, and would ring just like any visitor. He would open the door and take me into his arms.

Now it was all over. Perhaps those very scenes had been enacted there with her.

I nearly turned away. But the feeling of numbness overcame me again and I walked to the end of the room. Cefe waited a little, then turned the canvas to face the sofa where I sat. I hardly dared look at it for a time. When I did I almost cried out. It was not her portrait. It was mine! Not a perfect likeness by any means, but much more me than her.

"What do you think of it?" Cefe asked humbly.

"Cefe," I said, "it is not a good likeness."

"I know," he said. "Do you . . . do you . . . think it is like anyone else?"

"Yes," I answered, "it is like me."

Cefe sat down beside me and buried his face in his hands. "I was afraid you might see it," he said. "She hates it but I could not help it. I could not drive your face out of my head." Those words some weeks ago . . . But they had come too late.

I do not remember much about the days that followed. Everything around me seemed dead. I had wanted to be liberated from pain and now I would have given anything to be going through it again. All the past suffering was better than this awful void, this unfeelingness.

One day Cefe announced that everything was over, really and truly over. I saw by his manner and the tone of his voice that it was true this time. I did not care. He spoke tender words, wrote me passionate letters that he would slip under my pillow. I knew they were sincere but they said nothing to me now. It was too late!

I thought of the words I had written on the back of the photograph I had given him long ago, "to be or not to be." Why should love be denied us? Sorrow of another kind invaded me now. It seemed all wrong. One was born to feel, to suffer and to enjoy. To live as I was doing was not worth while.

I thought it was not fair that after all Cefe should be the

happier of the two. He could see there was a change in me. Although he dreaded what it might mean, he was still able to love.

He was alive.

CHAPTER XI

I threw myself feverishly into my work. It was the only way to forget or at least not to think. Events all round helped me. Just about that time my dear brother Juan lost his wife. They had had five ideal years of married life. Two tiny children, Maria Teresa and little Juan, were left motherless. I could not do much to help them in their loneliness but the moment mother heard the news she gave up her house in America, war or no war, and started for Spain with Inez who, by this time, had been graduated as a nurse from Carney Hospital in Boston. José was still at the front. Anita remained in America.

I had not seen mother for over eight years. The day she and Inez reached Madrid I was beside myself. The relief of knowing she had come safely over the ocean intensified the feeling of thankfulness. They stayed with us for a few days before going on to Malaga. Mother did not ask if I was happy. She evidently surmised from our cheerful household that we all were. I did not breathe a word of what had happened.

She was greatly interested to hear about the development of the woman's movement in which I was now taking an active part. Speakers were in great demand and I was quite over my nervousness. But I was so busy studying the problems of women of the educated classes of the higher bourgeoisie that I had completely overlooked what was going on in other quarters. I did not realize that Spain was being pushed up from beneath. That the people's hunger, their despair of ever getting justice, was breeding a fire which would some day break out.

One day two members of the executive committee of the

women's group within the socialist party called on me to ask whether I would be willing to speak for them in the Casa del Pueblo (the Trade Unions' Headquarters) on the anniversary of one of their unions' constitution. They chose as their subject *Women's Education*. I was delighted to accept. It was the first time I had ever set foot in that house and soon I realized that I had gone in a different spirit from that which should have prompted me. The "people" were still to me a class that was badly treated. One should be sorry for them and try to help them, but I did not have the slightest idea of their problems nor of their solution. I looked upon the whole situation from the old point of view of charity rather than from that of justice. They were still "the poor." I knew nothing of the relations between capital and labor or of the contribution of the workers to the country's economy. To me they were employees who were miserably paid and housed and fed, and to try to convince their employers to be more humane was our duty.

My first visit and succeeding ones to the Casa del Pueblo opened my eyes to many things. There I met earnest, intelligent, devoted men and women, with a knowledge of home and world affairs very superior to mine.

When my cousins heard that I had gone to the Casa del Pueblo they were horrified. One of them expressed the pious hope that one day it would be burnt down with everyone in it. She probably included me in the general holocaust and her wish was nearly granted years later when German bombers attacked Madrid during the Spanish war.

Toward the end of the summer, we all woke up one morning to find that there was no bread, no milk, no shops open and no trolley cars running. A general strike had broken out.

I was tremendously excited. I knew enough of the workers' struggle now to feel in sympathy with their cause, but I had not grasped the real meaning of what was going on.

That morning I went down with the children to the promenade and found the Castellana almost deserted. No *amas*, no governesses, no young ladies with their *dames de compagnie* and their elegant escorts. Soon armed police began to pass down the silent sidewalks. The moment they saw a group of two or three men stop and talk to each other the police charged them. "No groups are allowed," they said.

I thought it would be better to go home.

Cefe came in to luncheon in a state of wild excitement. There were rumors that the strike was the prelude to a revolutionary and very serious movement to overthrow the monarchy. The government was taking severe measures to maintain order. Don Ceferino grew nervous.

"What is it the workers want?" he kept asking.

"All that they lack," I said rather impatiently.

"Well, can't they ask for it quietly?"

The words made me react. I felt how unfair he was. Quietly? What had they always been but quiet? And had they gained anything by it? No, nothing.

During the afternoon some neighbors dropped in to see us. The strike was spreading to other cities. There had been disturbances.

The answer of the government did not take long to make itself felt. In the days that followed, Madrid was placed under military control. Machine guns were set up in several streets. A number of persons, among them a little deaf and dumb child, were killed in the savage charges of the civil guards. A massacre of workers took place in the prison. At last they succeeded in arresting the revolutionary committee formed by socialist and trade union leaders, among them Don Julián Besteiro, a professor of Madrid University, who was to join General Casádo in the surrender of Madrid in 1939, and Don Francisco Largo Caballero, Spanish premier in 1937.

A general débâcle followed. Houses were searched and many people of progressive ideas had to flee. Luis Araquistain, who was up north at the beginning of the outbreak, was arrested in his home some days later. This brought the movement very near us. I felt quite worried about Trudy. Her house was constantly watched and all the food she sent her husband was cut up in case any papers were hidden in it.

The trial of the principal persons involved in the movement kept us in suspense for days. Everyone was sure they would be condemned to death but the death sentence was commuted to life imprisonment. Yet they had only desired the good of the people that were in want. It seemed terribly unfair. At the next general elections all the men convicted in that trial were returned for Madrid and freed. At last the people had begun to impose their will.

In 1921 I went down to Malaga with Cefito and Marissa. We had decided to spend the summer with mother and Inez and Juan's children in Alhaurín. The old family home in the village had been sold long ago but Juan had an attractive two-story house up on the hillside near a spring of delicious mountain water.

It was extraordinary to watch the village folk and see how little they had been affected by the passing of time. The old customs still prevailed. Young girls were kept behind the latticed windows and not allowed to meet their sweethearts alone. The old rivalry between the inhabitants of the high part of the village and those of the low still survived. The cause of their dissensions was futile. Up in the church near us there was a sacred image dressed in a green tunic that was greatly reverenced by the villagers in that parish. In the church below there was a similar image in a purple mantle, also an object of ardent devotion on the part of its parishioners.

The villagers from above said that their image was more powerful and heard prayers more efficiently than the other image and this opinion was contested by the group from below. Thus the village had been divided for years. The feud had become so acute at times that the two groups, each wearing its own color to show on what side its sympathies lay, would on occasion come to blows.

I had taken a green dress along with me that year and had to give up wearing it when we went down in the village because people looked upon me with such disapproval. It made me quite uncomfortable.

I found that Alhaurín with its ten thousand inhabitants still had no school. I spoke to the mayor and the priest about it but they both shrugged their shoulders. "It is the fault of the government in Madrid," was all the answer I got. My impression was that neither of them was particularly anxious for the people to be educated, such fine people, too.

While we were there Spain suffered another terrible disaster in Morocco, a disaster that cost thousands of lives. Many officers of the Moroccan forces had come over to Malaga to see a bullfight and left their subordinates in charge of important positions. Some of these were taken by the enemy in a few hours. The head of the expeditionary forces, General Silvestre, who had been aide-de-camp to King Alfonso, disappeared. It was never known whether he had been made prisoner or killed.

Malaga is so near Africa that on fine days one can see the coast of Morocco. The faraway booming of the guns those days was plainly distinguishable in Alhaurín. The villagers began to fear the Moroccans might come over the strait to Malaga. Juan, who used to spend the week-ends with us, brought us news. He said everyone was overwhelmed. The government tried to stem the advance of the Moors by sending

reinforcements. The people were furious. The upkeep of
our Moroccan protectorate was costing Spain millions of
pesetas a year. Everything, schools, public health, child welfare, had year after year been sacrificed to the needs of the
army in Africa. Now it turned out that there was nothing
to show for it. No guns, no ammunition, not even proper food
for the men, nor fodder for the horses.

Again there was an outcry all over the country. There were
rumors that the king was responsible for the senseless operation
that had ended in defeat. In many ports the women tried to
prevent the men from going on board the ships that were to
take them to Africa.

At night, when the stagecoach had brought in the post and
it was known that we had received the daily news from Malaga,
the villagers would steal up to our house and beg for news of
the war and of their sons out in the midst of it.

"Please see if the paper says anything about my Antonio,"
one would say, and, taking courage, others would implore me
to read and tell them if José or Blas or Francisco were mentioned. It was heartbreaking to listen to their remarks. One
day I had to go in to Malaga and took the little local train that
stopped at several villages on the way.

At every station we picked up groups of lads suddenly called
to the front. As we were leaving one of these tiny depots the
train that had just started up suddenly stopped. Heads popped
out of the windows to see what was the matter. I looked, too.
An anxious young face appeared in the window next to mine.
We heard a sudden shriek and saw people running toward the
engine. I got off and ran, too. On her knees between the
rails I saw a small dark-skinned woman in a black dress, her
body bent back. Her hands were holding to the rails so tightly
that the tendons in her thin arms stood out like cords. Two or
three men were trying to lift her by force. The conductor of

the train whistled. The engine puffed. The station master hustled us all back to our compartments.

The train began to move and I covered my face with my hands. Could they be passing over that small tense body? Suddenly we saw a group of men carrying a dark bundle in their arms, the air was rent with a penetrating, almost unearthly wail.

"Son . . . son of my womb!" In the window next to mine the lad with the anxious face was leaning out. "Mother . . . mother!" he cried as we passed the group. Then the train rushed on.

I felt I could not stand it. All the way to Malaga my brain whirled. I felt the hate of war, the hate of all those who brought about war, surging up from within me.

This time the Moroccan war did not create just a passing impression. The people were thoroughly aroused. There was a general demand for an investigation. "We want to know who has been responsible," was the general outcry. The government tried to quiet them by promising that the moment peace was totally restored in the protectorate the matter would be looked into.

The Association of Spanish Women was really coming to be of some importance. It had quite a large membership and women from all over Spain were trying to set up auxiliary groups.

One day our chairman, a woman of fine capacity for organizing, asked me whether I would be ready to act as delegate for the association at the Congress of the International Suffrage Alliance to be held in Geneva the next month.

We had already requested an affiliation with the alliance. I said that I thought our chairman should be the one to represent us.

"No," she said, "I don't speak English or French properly. You are the vice-chairman and will do the work beautifully." Her motion was supported at the general meeting so there was nothing more to be said.

Two other members of the association volunteered to pay their expenses and go with me. We arrived in Geneva the night before the opening of the conference just in time to be present at the meeting of the women of all the countries that had taken part in the European war. This was the first congress to be held since the world conflict. I had expected to be interested, but not to be as impressed as I was throughout the meeting of the alliance.

Mrs. Carrie Chapman Catt was the chairman, an admirable one, too. Under her wise guidance the women of over fifty countries worked in a fine businesslike way.

I met all the women prominent in the world-suffrage movement : Mrs. Corbett Ashby, Chrystal Macmillan and Kathleen Courtney from Great Britain, Dr. Jacob from Holland, Madame Malaterre Sellier from France, Frau Adele Schreiber from Germany, Fröken Kerstin Hesselgren from Sweden, Emilie Gourd from Switzerland, Rosa Manus from Belgium and ever so many others from all Europe, from China, Japan, British India, and South America.

The main objective at that conference was the maintenance of peace. We were registering so many victories in the movement that we felt sure it would be possible. The women of the United States, Great Britain, the Scandinavian countries, Germany and Holland had not only been granted the right to vote but were being elected to their respective parliaments and occupying high posts in the administration. We were sure the other countries would soon follow suit and with those arms in our hands we thought we were invincible.

In the sermon she delivered from Calvin's chair in the Cathedral of Geneva, Maude Royden, the English divine, bade us strain every nerve to prevent war. Unfortunately at the next congress, held in Rome two years later, we realized that many of our hopes had already been dashed to the ground. Germany and Austria were facing problems impossible to solve without the aid of the other European powers and that aid, much to the surprise of true democrats, was being withheld. In Italy, Benito Mussolini was making life unbearable for all liberty-loving Italians.

The dictator made the opening speech at our conference that year after presenting Mrs. Catt with a huge photograph of himself. It was curious to watch the square-jawed, squat little figure of "The man of Italy" and the open-mouthed admiration with which the Italian delegates listened to his flowery speech delivered in a sharp, staccato voice.

One of the items on our program was an audience with the Pope. The delegates prepared their black frocks and lace mantillas in good time, but the representative of one of the South American republics had not realized that short-sleeved dresses cannot be worn for a visit to the Vatican. She and I had arranged to go in together and when I saw her arms showing through the lace of her mantilla, I warned her that she would not be allowed to pass. She did not believe it and was very much upset when, just as we were about to enter the first reception room, a young priest stopped us and barred the way, pointing to her arms. "What shall I do?" she asked me as we turned back. "It is too late now to get another dress and the members of my organization will never forgive me if I tell them I did not see His Holiness while I was here."

I thought for a moment then, taking her by the hand, I dragged her down to the bottom of the big staircase, past the Swiss Guards who looked at us in some surprise.

"Where are we going?" she kept whispering. The other

delegates were already coming up in groups of three and four, all properly garbed in long, high-necked, black dresses.

"Stand as close to me as you can," I said to her when we had reached the last steps. She obeyed. Quickly unfastening my dress from the side, I tore off the shoulder straps of my black satin slip, let it fall to the ground and stepped out of it. Then I folded it, laid it over her shoulders under the mantilla and pinned it tightly over her arms. The result was perfect modesty. Not an atom of white flesh could be seen above the wrists. We rushed up the stairs again and were met by the same young priest who looked at her carefully and with an approving, "*Bene . . . bene . . .*" motioned to us to go in.

When the Rome conference came to an end we all felt rather depressed. The elation of two years before had evaporated. However, we went our ways, hoping that the victories obtained after so long a struggle would not be lost. Alas! Where are they now?

Cefe and I had been very anxious to spend some time in Paris. We felt we needed the change and the stimulating influence of the French capital, so we suggested to our respective editors that it would be a good plan for us to go to France and obtain interviews with the most interesting people there. Our employers agreed and we lost no time in starting.

The first part of the journey was a repetition of our honeymoon trip. It brought back the memory of those lovely days so forcibly I could hardly bear it.

Outside everything was the same, within . . . what a change!

Cefe must have guessed my thoughts. He got up from the seat opposite, took the place beside me and held my hand. We were alone in the compartment. After a little he laid his head on my shoulder and dozed. The train dashed into Valladolid.

Cefe did not move. As we sped out of the station again I made up my mind I would not look back on the past. Better to sacrifice the memories of the first years of my married life than to allow myself to be embittered by pondering over the events that followed them.

The terrible parched feeling that had possessed me was beginning to disappear, giving way to a strange new tenderness that was taking the place of all that had gone before. I would respond, whatever it might be. I could not doubt that Cefe loved me. The "madness" over, I was everything to him. It was for me to be generous, to give him something in return. Something that would be less exalted than my first absorbing love but perhaps deeper and more understanding. Lost in my thoughts, I did not feel Cefe's weight on my shoulder until he stirred. Then I realized that my arm was quite numb. I smiled, remembering how my feet used to "go to sleep" when he was painting my portrait. Cefe opened his eyes and smiled back at me with the confidence of a child.

I felt years older.

We had been offered very little more than our usual salary for the trip, so we knew we would have to be careful, but that was half the fun. After long deliberation, we landed at a small hotel on the left bank of the Seine where, for a moderate sum, we were given a good double room and bathroom.

Cefe and I had a number of letters of introduction to different well-known people and it did not take us a week to find our place in that charmed circle of writers and artists, which was for us one of the chief attractions of Parisian life.

France was still suffering from the effects of the war and, although prices in general were not so high as we had feared, there were some items we made up our minds we could go without. One of them was the use of taxis. During the dav it was possible to find a driver who would charge a reasonable fare, but in the evening one might be asked to pay anything between one hundred and fifty and two hundred francs for a lift home. More than once we were left stranded and had to walk long distances in our evening clothes. We did not mind. It was such fun living in Bohemian style, free from care and making the most of everything.

In order to save our pennies, we always had some meals in the hotel. It was forbidden to cook in one's room but we managed breakfast, with coffee and milk, warmed up *au bain-marie* with hot water from the bathroom, and buttered fresh rolls. Canned meat and fruit sufficed for dinner at night.

Our greatest difficulty lay in getting rid of the empty cans. We could not throw them into the wastebasket because we did not wish the hotel manager to know what we were up to. He might have made a row just to force us to order our food from the stuffy little dining room downstairs.

The first night we waited till it was late and threw the cans, which we had made into a parcel, as far as we could out of the window. But they came down on the pavement with such a bang we were afraid someone might hear it. After that we took the parcel with us when we sallied forth in all our finery to spend the evening at some elegant reception, concert or theatre. Cefe would hide the cans under the folds of the Spanish cape he always wore until he found a safe place to drop them. I had never before realized how difficult it is to get rid of anything without attracting attention. Sometimes we had to walk several blocks before we dared let them fall.

There was one particularly good corner we picked out but a loving couple decided to meet there so we had to give it up.

One of the first persons we called on in Paris was André Suarès. He loved Spain and insisted that our seventeenth-century author, Francisco de Quevedo, was the best writer the world has ever produced, not even excepting Shakespeare. What amused us was that he tried to make himself look like Queveda by wearing the same small pointed beard and a cape of identical style.

André Suarès is not only a fine writer but an excellent pianist. One day at his house we got into a tremendous discussion as to the superiority of one art over another. Cefe gave precedence to music, but Suarès and I voted for writing. Suarès said music appealed to people more than the other arts because it is much the more sensual. He hated the extreme modernism in art and when we told him about an evening spent in a friend's house, hearing Darius Milhaud's music, he said he wondered at our patience.

"Well, Cocteau is a tremendous admirer of it," Cefe volunteered.

"*Ah!*   *Ce pauvre Cocteau,*" Suarès said with a shrug of his shoulders, "*il aura toujours quatorze ans.*"

We had, however, found Cocteau and the whole advanced clique very interesting and we thoroughly enjoyed taking part in their discussions rather to the disappointment of our dear Camille Mauclair who was just then in the black books of the young generation. They could not forgive his disdain of the futurists.

"They think because I believed in the impressionist school I must accept any nonsense they choose to champion," Mauclair said to us with a smile.

We also had the pleasure of meeting Henri Barbusse.

One of the things we enjoyed most during our stay was the Vieux Colombier theatre. It was so fine, so truly art. Jacques Copeau, however, told me he was greatly discouraged.

"Tourists come to see us," he said, "but I don't wish the theatre to be a show piece. I want it to permeate through the actual bad taste and frivolity to the very heart of the people."

The great actor, Gemier, was equally disconsolate over his own efforts to lift the taste of the people through fine drama. I thought of my own small experience in Madrid. Evidently it was the same everywhere. Could it be that the theatre was definitely doomed ?

"The novel is going to disappear, too," said Colette to me one day when I was talking with her, "at least for a time. This is the age of speed and people are not going to be bothered wading through pages and pages of printed matter when they can get everything they want in ten sheets of a daily paper — everything : emotion, news, stories of all kinds." She tossed back her hair from her high and powerful forehead. "I have never been so excited, so interested in my work as I am now." And she looked around her room in the offices of Le Matin, where she was then editor, with a proud smile.

When I told our other friends, Francis de Miomandre, Rachilde, Lucie Delarue-Mardrus and the Comtesse de Noailles what Colette had said, they threw up their hands in horror. "She herself does not believe a word of that," said the charming, exquisite comtesse, whose poems were the only thing I did not hear criticized all the time we were in Paris.

Miomandre wasn't quite so sure. This pale, delicate-looking little man was one of the straws fighting against the overpowering current that delighted Colette. His frilled shirts and marvelous dressing-gowns were entirely out of place in a world of noise, hurry and general sans gêne.

Before we left Paris we made arrangements for Cefe to hold a one-man exhibition there whenever he had sufficient pictures for the show.

"And you must come and lecture for us, too," said Lucie Delarue-Mardrus as she waved a last good-bye.

CHAPTER XII

When Cefe and I reached home we found Spain in a turmoil. The disaster of 1921 was not and could not be forgotten. The whole country had made up its mind that it must know the truth of what had happened and punish those who had been responsible. During the last few years, ever since the Spanish officers, against all rules of military discipline, had organized themselves into committees or *juntas*, with the apparent pretext of defending their special interests but with the real intention of influencing politics, any allusion to the army, if not flattering, was taboo. The prestige and honor of the armed forces could not, it appeared, be affected by continued disaster in the field but was liable to suffer if the slightest honest criticism touched it. This allowed for indirect intervention in the nation's politics. Strange inexplicable crises in different cabinets had invariably turned out to be the result of underground activities of the *juntas*.

Instead of looking to the people for support King Alfonso petted and spoilt the officers. The country had stood it for a long time in almost absolute silence but now the cup of bitterness was full. For the first time in Spanish history the whole nation united to ask for light and justice. Huge demonstrations in which every social class was represented : business men, workers, women, students, priests, and even officers — believing it was of the utmost importance that the confidence in the army should be restored by showing who had been in the right and who in the wrong in the campaign — paraded through the streets of Madrid and presented petition after petition to the government for an investigation of the Moroccan defeat.

At last a small military committee was formed and sent to

163

Africa to investigate. Its first results were kept secret. Enough news got through, however, for strong suspicion to fall upon high army officers and the king. Greater pressure was then laid on the liberal government in office by the socialists and more progressive members of parliament and it was finally decided that an interparliamentary committee should be set up in order to carry out a complete investigation. The socialist deputies at first demurred, alleging that they were certain the committee would not be given real facilities and that the matter would never be allowed to come before parliament if facts compromising certain individuals should be discovered.

The prime minister allayed their fears by promising complete freedom of action and sincere collaboration. He ended by saying that parliament would go into recess for the summer but that as soon as the committee had finished its work it could meet again.

The summer went by. The committee worked with a will. Many important documents were collected and, when parliament was about to meet, Spain woke up one fine morning to find that a *coup d'état* by General Primo de Rivera had placed the whole country under military control. There is not the slightest doubt that the Spanish dictator took such action with the exclusive intention of saving the king. Had it been otherwise, had he been sincere in his affirmations that he wanted only the good of the people and their liberation from the "petty rule of corrupt politicians," his first care would have been to have the question of the responsibility for the Moroccan defeat thoroughly investigated.

Instead of that, the very first measure adopted by the group of generals, who under his chairmanship were going to "save Spain," was to dissolve parliament and destroy all the documentary evidence that had been accumulated. King Alfonso's throne was saved for the time being but the seeds of a new régime were sown in those days.

The happy-go-lucky Primo de Rivera found himself suddenly converted into the supreme master of Spain, thanks to the acquiescence of the crowned sovereign, the co-operation of the army and the support of the big industrial firms of Barcelona which were afraid that the liberal government was going to develop a tax policy inimical to their interests.

The dictator general was by no means an exceptional man. His ignorance of international affairs was colossal and his knowledge of home problems almost as poor. But he had "nerve" and when the moment came to slap Spanish democracy in the face he did not hesitate. Even his brother officers, who would have given their ears to take his place and who were to amuse themselves later by laying all kinds of obstacles across his path, had not the courage to oppose him at the critical moment.

As for the people of Spain, the blow was so unexpected, so sudden, they did not have time to return it. Without a particle of independent public opinion behind him, without any solid personal experience to help him, Primo de Rivera proceeded to govern the country, assisted by other generals whose knowledge of the administration was as limited as his own. The appointment of General Martínez Anido as minister of the interior or home secretary struck terror into the hearts of the working population. They knew what his "methods of persuasion" had been in Barcelona when he was military governor of that city.

There was a group of people, however, who, although they did not approve of dictatorship, were so sick of the weakness and incompetence of the old politicians that they accepted the new situation with the best grace possible.

Primo de Rivera was clever enough to flatter the army in general, with the exception of the artillery corps which has always been the aristocracy of the army in Spain and into which he had failed to pass as a young man. He also flattered the women, paying them flowery compliments and assuring them that he would grant them their rights.

As a matter of fact, he did grant them rights, but with limitations. One fine day a decree was published conferring the right of suffrage to all unmarried women and widows but not to women who lived in wedlock. His excuse was that in order to grant suffrage to married women he would have to change the Spanish marital law. As he had already suppressed the whole constitution of the country, this should not have worried him much. In any case, there was little the women could do with those rights for Primo had suppressed all voting.

Very soon the people began to show their discontent. The aristocracy disliked the dictator because he took precedence over them ; the monarchists because he overshadowed the king. The intellectuals and the workers had, of course, been opposed to him from the first. There remained then only big business and part of the army on his side, together with a group of people whom he favored with high posts which they would never have succeeded in getting on their own merits.

A strict censorship was at once laid on the press, so it was not much fun writing for it. In view of this Cefe and I thought we could do no better than to carry out our plan of returning to Paris and holding an exhibition of his pictures. He had been working very hard so we were able to collect altogether fifteen canvases and some drawings. Night after night we pored over our accounts, balancing actual expenses against potential benefits. We calculated that, at the very worst, we would come back home economically no worse off than we had been before starting. I also prepared a lecture on Spanish popular art that I had been invited to deliver under the auspices of the old Duchesse de Rohan.

I hated leaving the children again. They were very close to me, but we felt that since it was going to be difficult for intellectuals and artists to get on in Spain, it was wise to take up work abroad.

Cefe's show turned out to be a success. A great many people went to see it, the press notices were very good, and he sold several pictures, so we were much relieved, especially after hearing that the Madrid paper he was on had been indefinitely suspended. While I waited to give my lecture, the committee of an Anglo-Hispanic Association wrote and asked me to go over to England and speak after I had finished in Paris.

A good deal of my time those days was taken up in posing for Leonetto Cappiello, the Italian painter, who had seen some of the costumes I intended showing to illustrate my talk and had raved about them. He asked to paint my portrait in the wedding dress of the women of Segovia. While I posed, Cefe amused himself going about with the Spanish writer, Vicente Blasco Ibáñez, who lived in Paris. He had refused to go back to Spain as long as it was under the sway of a dictator. We had known the author of the *Four Horsemen of the Apocalypse* for many years. In fact, Cefe had done a great deal of translating for his publishing house.

In the evening we usually went to see Argentina dance. She was at the height of her fame but success had not gone to her head.

The day of my lecture Cefe was so nervous he refused to sit in the hall where I was going to speak. A great many people from the literary and artistic world of Paris were present but I was quite calm ; I loved the subject of my talk. Those dresses I was going to show were part of the Spain I loved, the Spain of the people, of the unspoilt children of a beautiful land.

Before I went on to the platform someone played the *Danzas de Granados*. Edmond Jaloux, one of the French writers who has loved Spain best, came up afterward to say, "It was just the proper introduction to your lecture, Madame Palencia."

The next day we left for London. I had been told that the Spanish ambassador, Señor Merry del Val, had asked to be patron of the lecture which was to be delivered in Leighton House. I had never met him.

We reached London in the thickest fog I have ever seen. Our train was two hours late and at Victoria Station we found it extremely difficult to get a cab. It was a nuisance, for my lecture had been set for three o'clock that afternoon and it was past one when we reached the house of our friend, Beatrice Erskine, who was to introduce me. We had a hurried luncheon. Beatrice was very nervous, fearing that the fog might keep people away. Fortunately it lifted a little toward the hour of my talk and the hall of Leighton House was crowded.

The ambassador spoke a few words after Mrs. Erskine's introduction and then sat down in a reserved seat in the front row. At first he looked so worried it almost upset me but, little by little, he relaxed, and when I showed the costumes he kept applauding and talking to a big man seated behind him whom he introduced to me after the show. It was the American painter, John Singer Sargent.

"I cannot tell you, Madame Palencia," the great artist said, "what your lecture has meant to me. I love Spain and you have brought back all the memories of your beautiful country so forcibly that I feel as though I had just been there." Then, rather wistfully, he added, "I wish I had."

When I asked the ambassador what made him look so anxious he laughed. "I have had to be present at so many talks by people who have said they could speak English and whom nobody could understand that I was terrified this might be the case with you."

The notices of my lecture in the London press were extremely good and I was asked to return to England in the spring for talks at the Æolian Hall and the Victoria and Albert Museum.

Before we went back to Spain we spent a few days in Sussex with the Drysdales. The two sons were away in the Argentine and the daughter, Dorothy, had married a Canadian and was in her husband's country, so we were a small party.

Cefe liked London this time enormously. He loved dawdling about the West End streets and told me that he found it more distinguished than Paris. H. G. Wells, whom we had met in Spain a short time before, asked us to his house and so did Sir John Lavery, who was supposed to be the most fashionable portrait painter at that time.

We returned to Spain just before Christmas and had a grand time unpacking our load of presents for the children. It seemed wonderful to be able to indulge in this. I felt the power of a full pocketbook as I had never done before.

Spain struck us both as very depressing. The dictator had begun to persecute people who were opposed to his régime and there were legions of them. Fortunately for the Spaniards they have a keen sense of humor and it was not long before every possible chance was taken to poke fun at him through clandestine pamphlets and sheets. Primo de Rivera was at that time anxious to change the trend of Spanish international policy. His plan was to shake off the traditional French and British influence and strengthen his bonds with Fascist Italy, so he accompanied the king on his official visit to the Italian monarch.

It was said that Alfonso, who never thought of others, however much he might owe them, had introduced the dictator to King Umberto by saying, "This is my Mussolini."

The joke went round Spain and henceforth Primo was called "General Percalini," an Italianized version of percale, one of the poorest, flimsiest textile materials available in Spain, out of which cheap decorations and scenic costumes are made.

During our second visit to England I had realized that my talks were not only a very real success but something unique. One of the London papers said that I had discovered a new form of lecturing. What had happened is that my love of acting had found expression in those talks, and they had become interpretations, in a very simple form, of different types of Spanish women. It certainly helped to make my work more interesting and evidently my audience enjoyed them. As I did not read my speeches nor learn them by heart, I was able to improvise and introduce changes whenever I thought fit and this made it all the more exciting.

The satisfactory results of Cefe's show and my little lecture tour led us to think it would be a good idea to extend our field of action outside of Spain even further than Europe so I gladly followed up the suggestion made by a friend that I should try to arrange a tour in the United States. It seemed a very big job but I wrote to the Institute of International Education in New York and much to my delight found that my offer to go to the United States and give some lectures on Spain under the auspices of the institute was favorably received.

The moment I found that sufficient engagements had been signed up to cover all my expenses, I went ahead. The trip had an additional attraction besides the visit to a new country. Mother and Inez had gone back to the United States and I would see them, as well as Anita and José. The latter I had not seen since my marriage fifteen years before.

When I told Cefe that I had made up my mind to go he was greatly distressed. It had seemed to him quite a good arrangement before but, when the separation appeared inevitable, he was so depressed I very nearly gave up the journey. I hated leaving the children also, although I knew Maria and Asunción would look after them and the house perfectly.

Cefe went to the passport office to authorize my passage as though he were going to be hung. I packed my precious costumes and my personal apparel at night so as not to make the children unhappy with the sight of my trunks, and I finally slipped out of the house feeling almost as if I had committed a crime.

By the time I went on board the steamer at Le Havre after a lonely trip from Madrid to Paris, I was exhausted. I have often thought death when it comes will not be worse to meet than that parting. As in death, I had left a weeping and disconsolate family behind and was being swept away into the unknown.

I was so seasick all the way out that my sister Inez, who was waiting for me on the New York pier, hardly knew me when I got off the boat. I felt very strange to be in the great city with its snow-covered streets and gay crowds. Rather too noisy I thought it for anyone wishing to work.

After a two days' rest I began my tour with a lecture at Vassar College. The success there was followed up through all my travels. I was specially glad because Doctor Stephen Duggan and Miss Waite, chairman and secretary of the institute, had taken great pains to get me started and I would have hated to disappoint them.

Had I not changed the lecture about at will I should have been bored to death. As it was, I enjoyed it. I loved my work and was delighted to be seeing a new country, but I was terribly homesick at times. Besides, I did not feel altogether at one with the people I met.   Their ideas on many things were in such conflict with mine that it was almost as though we belonged to different planets.

One night I remember having a long discussion with a large group of people.   We were talking about sorrow and someone said, "You are always talking about sorrow as though it were something everybody had to endure."

"And so it is," I answered.

There was a general outcry.   They tried to make it clear to me that such a thing might be the case in Europe but that in America they were going to stamp out sorrow.   They could not understand what I meant when I said that it hurts to grow spiritually just as it does to develop physically.   No one agreed.

"Everyone has to suffer," I insisted, "and the important thing is to suffer for what is worth while."

In spite of these small dissensions I found my American friends inexpressibly dear, the most generous people in the world.   I went back home on a Spanish liner with a nice little parcel of checks sewn into the inside of my bodice.

Cefe came down to Cadiz to meet me.   I felt faint with the sheer delight of being back in Andalusia.   The lovely white-washed houses and the vivid human interest of every person one met in the street gave me a feeling of warmth that was very comforting.   In the huge American cities one often felt quite lost, as if nobody cared if one lived or died.

In that small southern Spanish town the workers standing round the dock, the little bootblack who hung about waiting for a job, the waiter in the little café who served us a bottle of delicious sherry and asked us to jot down on the marble-topped table the number of glasses we took so he would know what he had to charge, and then walked away and sat down to read the paper, were all our friends.

On the way up to Madrid, Cefe told me that the situation in Spain was growing more and more tense. There had been several attempts to overthrow the dictatorship but so far without success. Primo de Rivera had changed the military directory for something approaching a cabinet. Several civilians were included in the government. One of them, the Marqués de Guadalhorce, was married to one of my cousins, a granddaughter of Aunt Amalia. He was supposed to be the only competent person of the lot.

"Affairs are going from bad to worse for us," Cefe said. "The dictator hates the intellectuals more than all the rest of his enemies put together." It was true. Like many men of limited mental capacity he was suspicious of persons with brains, and certainly the Spanish intelligentsia did not disguise the disdain they felt for the régime and, above all, for the ridiculous official notes with which Primo was wont to enliven his decrees.

I returned to America for another lecture tour a few months later. This time the family took the news even more tragically than before. Cefe, after again agreeing with me that it was the only thing for us to do if we were to refill our depleted stock of funds, took the matter so seriously that he refused to speak about it. Except for helping me to get my passport, he did not take one single step.

I knew it was childish of him but realized he was moved by terror lest something happen to me. Again I packed my trunks at night when everyone in the house was sleeping and took out my ticket as though I were fleeing somewhere. And I was : fleeing from Don Ceferino who looked as glum as if I were on my deathbed, from my dear servants, Maria and Asunción, who would be found weeping in corners. As for the children, they protested all the time, Cefito violently, Marissa quietly. It upset all the pleasure I had been deriving at the time from the appearance of my first book, a study on child psychology which was just out and had been favorably reviewed.

This trip, however, was not quite so bad in a way. I knew where I was going, and that I would see my mother and many beloved friends. Travel was hectic : from Montreal to Miami and from New York to San Francisco, from icy-cold North Dakota to sunny New Orleans. I felt sometimes as though it were not I who was moving but the towns and the fields and the great open spaces, as though I were looking upon a film in which I was actor and spectator at the same time. One day I would speak in the luxurious drawing room of a woman's club, another day in an art gallery as I did in St. Louis, at other times in a college auditorium or even in a church. I never knew where the lecture would be held but every place seemed appropriate.

My message was one of beauty : the beauty of a people that had instinctively given expression to their feelings for color and line and rhythm in their homespun textiles, in their embroideries, in their gorgeous dresses and wonderful dances.

Anita was now Professor of Spanish in Wellesley College and we had two or three nice quiet days together in that lovely spot. These days, with the three weeks that I spent in Baltimore with mother, and a week-end with the very dear Berta and Elmer Hader were the only moments of rest that I enjoyed in the hard-pressed months of my schedule.

Berta and Elmer were building their house in Nyack then and often gathered their many friends around them. There I met Norma and Herschel Brickell, Jean May, and Bertha Gunterman, all of whom had been or were going to Spain, and Betty Beatty who was always ready for a discussion on any and every subject and "Bill," as we called her husband, William Sauter, the actor, and many others. Berta in her bright-colored cotton frocks and quaint humor and Elmer with his quizzical smile and courteous manner have always seemed to me the most ideal of hosts.

I remember telling them that year I would make a "wish" for anything that they might be needing in their new house. They told me that their water supply was rather low that year. Requesting silence, I mounted a big stone near by and recited a Spanish poem. Then three times I called on the water fairies to grant the gift of *agua, agua, agua* (water, water, water). How we laughed when they told me the next time we met that I must never ask for water again as their basement had been nearly flooded after my departure.

Although I felt happy in many ways, I was in a hurry to get back to Spain. I longed for the dear ones there: Besides, Don Ceferino was not well. He had been ailing with kidney trouble for several months and the last news from home was not reassuring.

This time I took the Spanish line to Coruña. Cefe met me there. The joy of our reunion was spoilt by a conviction that his father could not live much longer. We stayed two days in Coruña and ran down to see the old university town of Santiago.

The wonderful cathedral dedicated to the Apostle Saint James is one of the best-known sanctuaries of the Catholic world. Pilgrims from every corner of the earth have been to Santiago, among them the tender and pure-hearted Saint Francis of Assisi.

It was not a happy home coming. When we reached Madrid the doctor advised us to let Julio and Zoe know that there was no hope for Don Ceferino. Julio was at the time acting-consul in Tetuan, in Spanish Morocco, so they were able to join us at once. Cefe's father passed away a month after my return. I missed the kindly old man who, in spite of many disappointments, had never swerved in his devotion to the art of the theatre and had kept on steadily writing good dramas to the very end.

His death affected my husband even more than his mother's loss had done.   Life was telling on Cefe.   Sadness born from disillusion was beginning to embitter his happy childlike open nature.   The disillusions were inevitable.   They were the result of contact with the outside world.

That winter my second book was published, a novel called *The Sower Sowed his Seed*.   It dealt with the problem of heredity.   It was well received and I got quite a number of encouraging letters from physicians besides good press notices.

Shortly after my return we had bought our first motor car and spent that summer making excursions into the very heart of the Pyrenees.   The valley of Ansó with its twisted narrow streets and its inhabitants dressed in fifteenth-century costumes delighted us, but Cefito nearly came to blows with the young lads there.   He had tried to take some snapshots of the women sitting at their sewing and they were incensed.   We returned to Madrid by way of Jaca and Huesca and reached home to find that the dictator general had arrested several of our friends and sent them to jail.   The breach between Primo de Rivera and the Spanish intellectuals was growing wider every day.   University professors, men of science, and writers of all sorts were being constantly persecuted.   Poets were his pet aversion. The number of clandestine sheets that were circulated increased every day.   Many of them were written in verse and, as the author had never been discovered, Primo was suspicious of anyone who could hold a pen in his hand and make two words rhyme.

Cefe and I had been so busy the last few years over our own work that we had not worried much about politics.   We hated the dictatorship, of course, out of principle, but had taken no active part in any movement against it. However, the ever-growing injustice could not fail to awaken response in our hearts and we could not help feeling glad that the king was losing ground every day while the republican party grew in strength.

That winter a group of democrats, Cefe among them, signed a manifesto against the dictatorship. One could clearly see that the whole country was seething. Primo was leading Spain into economic ruin. The new roads built in his time were greatly admired by tourists, but the Spaniards wanted other things, too : schools and health centres and, above all, that beautiful gift called liberty. The censorship was galling. The press was government controlled and the whole atmosphere was so charged with suspicion and distrust it made life hardly worth living.

Two or three years after Primo's *coup d'état* we had started the first Spanish woman's club in Madrid. All the intelligent and progressive women, as well as the wives of the best-known men of science, writers and artists, belonged to it. It was the only place in Madrid where one could breathe but it received a bad name in consequence. The club had six divisions : literature, fine arts, music, science, and international and social sections. During the first years there wasn't a distinguished foreigner coming through Spain who did not visit the club or deliver a lecture in our little hall.

The social-service section found so many enthusiastic workers among the members and such generous supporters outside that it was very soon able to start a day nursery for the children of working mothers. Under the direction of Mrs. Bástos, the wife of one of the leading Spanish surgeons, a perfect little house was built on ground lent by the municipality. The tiny tots were as happy as they could be and well cared for. Unfortunately the reactionary elements of Madrid attacked it at once. They declared that no lay institutions of the kind should be supported, that the church alone could be the source of all philanthropic movements. It was alleged that the club was an anti-religious organization, an accusation based on the fact that one of its rules forbade religious and political controversy, as if that was not one of the fundamental rules of any club ! In spite of the opposition, however, the children's home flourished. I was chairman of the club for several years and shall never forget the whole-hearted support given to the work by many devout Catholics.

All this time the political situation was growing more and more unsettled. In the month of January we heard that the conservative ex-premier, Señor Sánchez Guerra, had landed in Valencia in order to lead a movement against the dictator. Part of the army was supposed to be implicated in this attempt. However, the movement failed. Sánchez Guerra was arrested and confined in a man-of-war.

Shortly after this event Cefe, the two children and I were just sitting down to luncheon one day when Asunción came into the dining room to say that two men were outside asking to speak to my husband. "Tell them, please, to wait a few minutes," I said to her.

Cefe, however, would not hear of it. He was at that time literary director of a theatrical company and thought our callers might be actors anxious to get a contract or perhaps authors with a new play.

"I shall be back in a moment," he said to me.

We had barely begun our luncheon when the door opened and back came Cefe, followed by two strange men. I thought he looked rather queer.

"Nena, I must go with these two gentlemen," he began, but was interrupted by one of them.

George Guthrie
Scottish grandfather
of Isabel de Palencia

Ceferino Palencia
at the time of his engagement
to Isabel Oyarzábal

Isabel de Palencia
and her daughter Marissa

Ceferino Palencia
in his studio

"We are members of the police force," he said, folding back the lapel of his coat and showing us his badge. "Señor Palencia must go down with us to police headquarters."

Cefito started up from his seat. Marissa looked frightened. I got up, too, and went toward my husband.

"Why should he go there?" I inquired.

"Do not worry, señora," said the other policeman in kinder tones. "He will probably come back in an hour or so. It is simply that they wish to ask him something down there," and he jerked his thumb in the direction of the street.

"But who has ordered this?" I asked. The two men shrugged their shoulders.

"Never mind, Nena," interrupted Cefe. "Don't worry. It is sure to be a mistake." Then turning to Cefito, he told him to go round to the house of the poet, Enrique de Mesa, who was Cefe's chief in the National Library and his best friend. They had been together all morning. "Tell him what has happened to me."

On hearing this, the more agreeable of the two men stepped forward again. "Do not trouble to go," he said. "Don Enrique de Mesa has been sent for also," and, touching Cefe lightly on the shoulder, he added, "let's go."

I stepped forward and stood beside them. "I am going, too," I said. The two policemen tried to push me back but I insisted. "My husband has done nothing," I began, but Cefe put me gently aside with his hand.

"Don't, Nena, please," he said imploringly.

I tried to keep calm. There was nothing to be gained by irritating the men, but it was terrible to let Cefe go with them alone. Cefito began to walk about the room impatiently. I feared an outburst that might endanger him, too.

"Good-bye, Nena," Cefe said, kissing Marissa and me.

"Son," he added, turning to Cefito, "take care of your

mother." Then as he was leaving he waved his hand and said in a loud voice, "And remember we don't want any favor from this government."

I knew what he meant. If he were sent to jail as he feared he would be, he did not want me to go and see my cousin and beg for his freedom. He should have known I wouldn't do that. Ever since her husband had accepted a position in the dictatorship cabinet I had ceased seeing her.

When Cefe and the two policemen had left our apartment I rushed to the window. Were they going to make him walk through the streets like a criminal? No, there was a taxi waiting before the door. The neighbors had evidently gathered that something was up and were peeping out of their windows. I waited a while, then finally Cefe appeared, one man on either side and two more behind him. These had apparently been watching the back door. Cefe got into the cab. Three of the men followed. The fourth got up beside the driver.

The taxi started. I felt as if I must cry out. Just as they turned the corner a hand appeared behind the little window at the back of the car. Cefe was trying to wave to me. I turned to run out of the room but my boy caught me in his arms. Poor little Marissa was sobbing bitterly in a chair near by. The sight of her made me break down. I tried to control myself. There were other things to do than cry.

The first thing was to find out where they were taking Cefe. I rang up some of our friends who had acquaintances in high places. No one knew anything. I did not intend to beg for favors. My husband had been taken away without a warrant, without even a written order. What I wanted to know was why this had been done and where they had taken him.

Staunch friends, many of them now long dead, gathered round us with offers of help. Among the first was the great writer, Don Ramón del Valle-Inclán, fearless in his opinions and ready to do anything for his friends. The warm interest shown was comforting, but it could not drown the agonizing anxiety.

In the course of the afternoon my son drove me round to Enrique de Mesa's house. I found his wife, Carmen, in the same state of despair. The police had searched her home. They had done nothing in ours. If Cefe had been a suspicious character, if they really believed he was mixed up in some plot, they would surely have tried to find some proofs. I then drove to police headquarters. No one would give me any information.

"I have the right to know what has been done to my husband. Where he has been taken," I said to one man after another in the different departments. The place was crowded, impatient policemen and officials and anxious men and women asking . . . begging for news. The answer was always the same, "We know nothing."

I had been told that there were hundreds of persons waiting to go to prison in the dungeons of police headquarters. Could my Cefe be there ? I wished that I could beat down the heavy doors which led to the corridor where I had been told the dungeons were. The guard pushed us back when we came near.

"Let's go home now, mother," begged Cefito. "We can do nothing here and someone may be bringing us news to the house." I let him lead me to the car. It was a comfort to feel his young arms holding me up.

We reached home to find Marissa still sobbing her heart out on Maria's shoulder. A great many friends were waiting for us but no one had been able to find out where Cefe was.

They stayed till quite late. I began to wish they would leave me alone. I wanted to think. It was impossible to do so with the noise all round. Cefito and Marissa tried to persuade me to go to bed. They refused to go unless I did. At last I lay down without undressing, thinking that I might get news at any moment that Cefe needed me. Marissa slipped in beside me and was soon fast asleep. So was Cefito.

At last I could not bear the stillness any more. I jumped out of bed and went to the library window. It was bitterly cold. The streets were empty. A big clock belonging to the building of a right-wing paper, the *A.B.C.*, struck three o'clock in the morning. In spite of its reactionary tendencies and its high-class readers this journal was anti-Primo Rivera. After a while I found the silence around me unbearably oppressive. I looked up at the blinking stars, down to the grey pavement, nothing but silence, emptiness. Where was Cefe? What had they done to him? I recalled with anguish all the things that were said : things that we knew were true about the minister of the interior. It was his police, the men under his orders, who had taken away my husband. I cried out Cefe's name into the night. There was no answer. The stars kept on blinking. I began to walk up and down the library as I had done years before when I had felt utterly desolate. I began to wonder whether Cefe was also walking up and down the narrow precincts of a prison cell. The thought was unbearable.

Then I remembered that hundreds of other women in Spain were probably crying out into the night, too, calling for their husbands, their fathers or their sons. I wished that I knew who they were and where they were. We could form an army and break open the prisons and take out our men. I wondered what I would say to the children in the morning. What plan could I tell them I had prepared? How they would laugh at all that I had taught them in the past. We had always said that no man had anything to fear if he were true and honest and faithful to his principles. Now it turned out

that it was the men who were true and honest and law-abiding
who had everything to fear from those who had done away
with legality and the constitutional rights of the people.

Day dawned at last. Cefito's first question was, "What
news?" It seems to me those were the only words I was to
hear for days. The morning's press brought a notice to the
effect that Don Enrique de Mesa and Don Ceferino Palencia
had been dismissed from their posts in the National Library for
having spoken against the government, "calumnied," the paper
said. So they had not only taken them away but they also intended to starve us.

The news, however, did not worry me overmuch. I knew
I would manage somehow. What I wanted was to know
where Cefe was now. I rang up some men who were on the
staffs of different papers. I had given up writing for *El Sol*
some time before. They all said the same thing. They had
done their best to obtain information as to the whereabouts of
Cefe and Enrique but it had been impossible to find out. The
press had been forbidden to say a word about their "arrest."
It all seemed very serious to me. The hours passed by, Cefito
and Marissa were at school. The house was full of our friends
but I could not keep still, just waiting. Whenever I could
give some decent excuse I would rush out and walk stupidly
along the streets. A vision of Cefe being hurt or in prison or
even worse pursued me everywhere. It was maddening.

At last one day, I forget which one, I received a short note
from my husband saying he was going to be taken away. He
did not say where but asked me to send down to the police department in the railway station some clothes and a little money.
I got a few things together, put a hundred pesetas into an envelope and asked Cefito to drive me down to the depot. My
heart beat wildly when we were near the police bureau.
Would Cefe be there? At least they would tell me where

they were taking him.   But the only answer I got was, "We know nothing."   I left the parcel and went back home, feeling desperate.   Afterward I learnt from Cefe that he was in a room close by all the time and had heard my voice and my request.

Several days went by before I knew that my husband had been confined in the town of Logroño, not far from San Sebastián.   When his letters began to come in I was relieved to find that he had made friends there at once.   The hatred against the dictatorship was such that everyone persecuted by the government was sure to find help and support wherever he went.

I now had to turn my attention to other problems.   The economic one was not easy to solve.   Cefe had been promoted to a higher post in the National Library and his salary had become quite a respectable one.   Its suppression was a serious loss.   I had only my books and the checks I had brought over from America to cover all our expenses and all of Cefe's.   I was therefore greatly relieved to be offered the post of correspondent for the London *Daily Herald* and I set to work with a lighter heart than I had had since Cefe's arrest.   Not that this kind of job was easy, as everyone who has tried writing under strict censorship knows to his cost.

I felt as though the clock of my life had been put back and I were again living through the years of my youth when I worked for the Laffan News Bureau.   Now it was easier because I had more knowledge, but it was more difficult, too, because I had developed a sense of responsibility.   Anyway it was going to help me to meet expenses and that was enough for the moment.

Just when I was beginning to recover from my anxiety over Cefe, I received another heavy blow.   In the month of May mother came back from America with my sister Inez who had been asked by the Rockefeller Institute to help start district nursing in the new public health centre opened in Cáceres. The job was interesting if not remunerative. Cáceres is one of the towns of Spain where child mortality is highest. The population, like that of all Extremadura, was at the time very ignorant. Moreover, there is a great deal of malaria throughout the whole province. Inez, who always had longed to come over and help Spain, jumped at the chance and she and mother set up housekeeping in the lovely, if backward, city of Cáceres, thinking that they had come to stay for good.

They had not been there three months when mother fell ill. The doctors, suspecting the existence of a malignant tumor, urged her to go to Madrid for further advice. Inez saw to it that not a moment was lost. The fears of the Cáceres physicians were confirmed by the Madrid specialists, and after all the long years of absence mother had come back to Spain only to die.

We made her as comfortable as possible in our apartment and I took upon myself the task of letting all her children know the truth. A letter flew over to Maria in her quiet convent in Belgium, another to Cuba to call Ricardo, one to the United States to let Anita and José know, and one to Malaga for Juan to hold himself in readiness.

One month later all of them except Maria, who could not leave her convent, and José, who was unable to come from the United States, had joined us in Madrid. Juan and his two children came up from Malaga almost at the same time. Christmas was very near. We had all made up our minds that mother must not know from what she was suffering. Fortunately she had no pain. We invented all kinds of excuses to explain the presence of almost the whole family and thought we had managed to deceive her.

It was not long, however, before she said to me one day,

"Child, I know what is the matter with me, but don't let the other children know yet." We kept up the farce for two months, and had a right royal Christmas with presents for everyone, the most for mother, of course. And on the tenth of January, the anniversary of father's death, she went away from us.

Death certainly held no terrors for her. She received the last sacraments, settled all her affairs and then, smiling, took her leave, her spirit being triumphant. We all tried to be worthy of the privilege of being near her at such a time.

The day before she died mother kissed Marissa, who had come into her room to say good-bye. I was sending her to stay with some friends until everything was over. Then, turning to me, she said as my little girl took her leave, "Marissa will be your consolation," adding after a moment's silence, "and you will look after my baby, too. Won't you ?" — meaning Inez — "and after Anita ?"

Her children dispersed almost immediately after she had gone. Anita went back to Wellesley, Inez resumed her duties at Cáceres, Ricardo went down to Malaga and settled there. Business was bad in Cuba so he thought he would go in for chicken farming near the old home.

At the time of mother's death Cefe was in Paris. After some months in Logroño he had been allowed to come home, but under supervision. Our letters were all opened and one never knew when he might be taken up again, especially if there was any disturbance. Our economic situation was still very difficult for Cefe had not been taken back on his job and he could get no other work. People were always afraid of employing political suspects.

His great friend, the poet Enrique de Mesa, who had come back to Madrid under the same conditions as Cefe, did not survive the difficulties of his position. A reserved nature, an aristocrat by birth, and as magnificent a Spaniard as he was fine as a writer, he died suddenly shortly after he came back to his home. Spain lost one of her picked men with his death and Cefe lost his best companion and mentor.

After some time, feeling he could not bear the situation any longer, Cefe made up his mind to go to France. Some friends helped him to get over the frontier and up to Paris. He had not been there very long when someone he knew introduced him to the manager of the Paramount Film Company in Paris. The post of Spanish translator was then vacant and it was offered to him. Needless to say, Cefe jumped at the chance. He found the work — which consisted in translating American stories into Spanish with a view to pleasing the usual moving-picture audience — of a sentimental type, rather absurd, but at least he had something to do.

Early in the summer he insisted that I go and spend a few days with him. He was drawing a very good salary and wanted to give me a good time after our long separation and all we had been through. It was almost like old times. Cefe took me to his rooms and pointed to a new suitcase placed on the table. "Look what has come for you!" I opened the case and found quite a collection of gloves and silk stockings and delicate lacy underwear. There was also an order for a new dress and hat that had been set aside for me but must be tried on.

I turned to Cefe with tears in my eyes. He held me close. "Nena, I am so glad to be able to do this for you," he said. I stayed in Paris as many days as I thought prudent. Then I hurried back to Spain. The students were always getting into trouble those days and I was afraid for Cefito who was now studying with the Faculty of Medicine. Anything might happen, for although Primo de Rivera had already been ignominiously dismissed by the king, his successor, General Berenguer, was, if anything, more of a dictator, and certainly a harder and more implacable man than Primo. Besides, I felt that it was my duty to the *Herald* to be on the spot. A sudden change might take place. I was not far wrong. In December there was another rising against dictatorship. This time it was quite serious. I had great difficulty in getting my story over to London before all communications with the outside world were cut off.

This new movement was led by a group of civilians, constitutionalists, belonging to different parties, who were determined to bring about a total change of régime. It was supported by part of the army. The uprising was quelled, of course, but it left a mark. Some of the civilian leaders managed to escape. Others, like Señor Alcalá Zamora, who was to become president of the republic ; Largo Caballero, general secretary of the Spanish Trade Unions ; Professor Fernando de los Ríos ; Miguel Maura, son of the great conservative statesman, Don Antonio Maura ; Alvaro de Albornoz, were arrested and sent to jail. In Jaca two young officers led their troops out as they had promised and marched down to Huesca along the same road we had traveled in our car a year and a half before. These troops were held up after a short struggle and the two officers, Galán, and García Hernández, were courtmartialed and shot. The new republic had now two more martyrs.

In Madrid several army officers also gave their support to the movement, among them General Queipo de Llano ; Ramón Franco, brother of the rebel general who was to drive the country into a civil war and allow it to be invaded by two foreign powers ; Ignacio Hidalgo de Cisneros ; and others. They all managed to escape to Paris, and there Cefe met them.

The failure of the movement was a great disappointment to the majority of Spaniards. It had caused the death of several persons and had ended in jail or exile for some of the finest men in Spain. Everyone felt that all hope of liberation from dictatorship would be long deferred. It came as a great shock to me, also. I had been so immersed in my own work that I had not realized how much the success of the liberal movement would mean to Spain.

My lectures, my books, had been claiming all my attention. I had even been able to do some acting, not as a professional but in a little art theatre in the house of the writer, Pío Baroja, and his brother and sister-in-law. We were all amateurs and the theatre had been called *El Mirlo Blanco* (*The White Blackbird*) to show how exceptional it was going to be. Everyone who could was supposed to contribute a one-act play and to act in it unless the stage manager thought he was too impossible. A little piece from my collection, *Dialogues with Sorrow*, was accepted and produced the same night with plays by Pío Baroja and our great Valle-Inclán. Both of them insisted that I take part in their pieces, also.

It was great fun, the rehearsals especially. Pío Baroja, who had to play the role of an apothecary in his piece, took it so seriously that he used to appear in a flowered-silk waistcoat, which his mother had made for him, several days before the first performance. He said he had to get accustomed to wearing it. He would be so tickled over his own jokes in the play that it was all I could do to keep him from laughing out while we waited for our call at the back of the stage.

At times I almost felt tempted to close my eyes to what was going on outside, to live my own life. But I found it impossible. I could not ignore the call for freedom nor forget the hardships that I had seen the people endure. Neither could I submit to the indignity of being ruled by an irresponsible and arbitrary power. Life without liberty was not worth living. All Spain was awakening to that fact. It was our duty to help her.

CHAPTER XIII

"Leaving tomorrow." I stared at the slip of paper that Asunción handed me as I came into the apartment after scouring the town in search of someone who was to see somebody else who had offered us two cases of Valencia and Murcia oranges for our exiles in Paris. Indalecio Prieto, the socialist leader, had been ordered by his doctor to eat fruit and the price of oranges in Paris was beyond the purse of political refugees. "Leaving tomorrow." The telegram was from Cefe. He was coming home. Two years' absence, even with an occasional meeting, had been very trying. The children were developing fast and I had many responsibilities, not merely on the economic side. Cefe's contacts with the Paramount Film Company had helped enormously, had even allowed us to put by a little. But in all other respects I had been forced to make all the decisions and to bear the brunt of all the anxiety, a considerable responsibility when one is surrounded by ardent generous youth that will not be careful. This was the case with Cefito's friends, students of medicine like him, ready to risk everything for the future they dreamed of, a future with liberty.

Many students had been arrested and beaten up during the past two years so I was consumed with anxiety when my son was late or when he and his friends assumed an innocent air, a sure proof that they had been up to some of their tricks : pasting slogans on lampposts or walls or distributing sheets. Pastimes that were innocent enough in themselves but dangerous even then. Even little Marissa would do her part, sticking bits of paper on the trees of the promenade when she took her dog, Brujo, out for a turn before supper. She would be very pleased the next morning, when I took her to school, to see policemen scraping off the paper with their penknives. Those little pieces of paper with *Viva la República* written on them were the guileless expression of Spain's desires. It has been often said that youth should not mix in politics. But how could they, those intelligent young minds, not be alive to what was going on when even the most conservative and balanced of men, the professors whom they loved and admired, had been forced to take up positions against ignorant brutality, the brutality of machine guns against reason and of force against justice, when the fundamental laws of the country were being trodden under by those in authority ?

Our lives had indeed been turned upside down. The sword was given precedence over culture, the uniform over the academic robe. Bluff had been substituted for truth. Decent people were in jail and the usurpers and violators of the law enjoyed freedom.

I would have found it very difficult to keep up the morale of the young ones round me had it not been for their own indestructible faith in right.

The *Herald* was keeping me very busy. I had made another good scoop by being the first foreign correspondent that managed to get into the Madrid jail to see the political prisoners after the December uprising. I joined the daughters of Señor Alcalá Zamora who had been allowed a permit to see their father, and was taken for one of them. Someone had been able to sneak in a vest-pocket camera and to take some snapshots. This made it possible for the *Herald* to publish a front-page story with a photograph of the future president of the republic looking out from behind the bars of his prison cell. The first time I went into the prison, which soon after became the meeting place of the most distinguished people of Madrid, I was more depressed by the look of the place than I thought I should be. The heavy iron doors guarded by armed sentries, the long bare corridors swept by an icy January wind, the sensation of doors being locked behind one, were certainly not attractive. A vision of our convent door came back to me when the warder led the way to the department for political prisoners. These are never supposed to be mixed up with what are called "common offenders."

Inside the gallery where the cells of the prisoners were situated, the scene was gayer. People were chatting and making plans as though they were quite sure of the future.

I said something in that vein to Alcalá Zamora.

"But of course we must make plans," he answered, "they cannot do anything to us. We have risen not against the law but on behalf of the law and every Spaniard knows it."

The prisoners in fact spent most of their time drawing up programs so as to be ready to meet events and perhaps rule the country after their release and when the people of Spain had been duly consulted.

That morning my mind kept turning round the immediate present : Cefe was coming home.

The king, realizing at last that he was endangering his throne beyond recall, had got rid of the second dictatorship and appointed a provisional government charged with the task of restoring normality. Many persons who had been dismissed from their jobs and sent into exile without reason were called back and reinstated, among them Cefe. Justice could not be done to his great friend, Enrique de Mesa. The poet had died four months after his arrest.

My husband was in wonderful spirits when he reached home. The outlook was so much brighter that one felt life was going to be worth living again. The first thing we did was to put a long-cherished plan into practice. We began to build.

It had been one of Cefe's dreams in the past to have a house of his own. Cefito and Marissa wanted it, also. I was not so keen.   I thought it would tie me down.   Besides I hated houses built in series, standard types that are set up in rows and are exactly alike.   But they were the only ones that came within our means.   Fate willed it that we should just then come across a company that was building the way we liked.   Five kilometres out of Madrid, near a lovely wood of pine trees, in funny twining lanes, every house was different from its neighbor, from the height of its walls to the number and shape of its doors and windows.   They were well-built houses, too, solid in structure, not the usual pretentious, flimsy dwellings.

We made out the plans with the help of the architect.   It would have been much more expensive if we had chosen a house along the road as most people would have preferred.   A Spaniard is never happier than when he can command a good view of the street or the highway from his window.   The busier the thoroughfare the happier the inmates of the house will be.   The highest compliment Aunt Maria or her mother could pay a house was to say it was like "a cab waiting in its stand."   Fortunately we were all agreed about having a quiet location for our own home.

Mother had left me some money at her death and this, together with what Cefe had saved in Paris, allowed us to pay the first installment which was of course far and away the heaviest.

Like most people who build, we went almost every day to see how the house was getting on.   I laid out the plan for the garden at once and busied myself getting the trees planted so that we could have some shade when we were settled.   There were varieties from the different provinces of Spain.   Like all new garden owners in hot countries, I planted far too many, but so long as they were small it did not much matter.

The day I first saw the workers laying down the foundations of our future home, I felt a queer thrill go down my spine. The deep cut in the ground, the stones and mortar opening out like great veins — my whole being responded to the ancestral call of the earth, its resting place.

While the walls grew and the timber was laid across them to form the roof, we drove to the villages round about, looking out for plates and jars and vases of popular pottery with which to increase the collection we had begun some time before, a collection of simple ceramics at little cost yet beautiful with their bright coloring and naive designs.

That winter my translation of Eugene O'Neill's play *Anna Christie* was produced in Madrid, and it was a success.

Soon, however, we were again carried away by the wave of political agitation that permeated the country. The king had ordered the government to call municipal elections, and everyone was getting ready for them. The object was to feel the pulse of public opinion and, if these elections turned out well, that is, with a substantial majority for the king's interests, to call a general election later. The trial of the political prisoners was also giving rise to speculation. They were to be brought before a military tribunal. Its president, General Burguéte, was, it appeared, sympathetic to the prisoners. The lawyers charged with the defense, among them a woman, Señorita Victoria Kent, were all persons of prestige. They intended making use of an irrefutable argument : the arrested men had only sought the restoration of legality.

I was present at all the sessions of the trial. Great precautionary measures had been adopted. Evidently the government was afraid of demonstrations, perhaps even of attempts to liberate the prisoners. This was another proof of their lack of vision. The people of Madrid were convinced that the case of the leaders of the uprising would be dismissed without need of pressure from without. If they lined the streets from the prison to the court and stood by hundreds round the entrance it was merely to express their regard for the prisoners. The demonstrations, however, took place inside the hall, especially on the last day of the trial. The people who had been admitted to the court, and who with rare exceptions were republicans, stood on their seats. It was more like a political meeting than a military tribunal. The case was dismissed. The prisoners were driven back to the jail, midst the enthusiastic cheers of the crowd, to wait until the sentence had been signed by the authorities.

The moment they were freed they set about perfecting their plans. Either in the coming or in the next elections the monarchy must be overthrown. No one doubted that so long as the king was in Spain a more or less disguised dictatorship would subsist.

The electioneering campaign went ahead. We were all confident that many republican candidates would be returned.

It felt strange to be able to speak freely even in public after nearly seven years' oppression and to send one's stories abroad without first having them passed by the censor. The rightist and leftist parties vied with each other in their efforts to secure the votes of their supporters. The means of persuasion used by the right were different from those of the left : offers of presents of all kinds in the shape of clothing, food or cash ; promises of schools and roads, of fountains, too, in villages where water was scarce, were made freely by those who, for hundreds of years, had kept the people without clothing, food, cash or water. Instead of promises, the left appealed to the villagers' conscience. It tried to make them see that their liberation depended on unity and co-operation.

At times the opponents came to blows. Sometimes a rich proprietor would receive a haughty answer such as a Spanish peasant is capable of giving when his pride is hurt. The case of a certain downtrodden Andalusian worker of the land is not uncommon. This man was being pressed by the bailiff of a large property to vote for "the master." The bailiff's arguments were always the same :

"Don't be a fool. Vote for us. What can the others give you ? Nothing. They have nothing themselves. We can help you. Give you work. You are hungry. We can provide you with food. Don't be a fool. You are hungry. . ."

"And what is that to you ?" interrupted the peasant. "I am master of my hunger."

A magnificent answer ! He might be, he was, empty of aught else but hunger. His eyes were sunken, his skin shriveled, but his hunger was his to do with as he liked. He could sell it or not. He was the master of his hunger and like many others he chose not to sell.

A race of men that nothing will defeat in the long run, they have proved it many a time. Spaniards are called individualists, rather, one should say, they are a people one cannot drive.

It did not take long to discover that in most places the coalition of republicans and socialists was going to be very hard to beat. Contrary to what might have been expected, the electioneering campaign was in several places carried on without noise, in a serious dignified way. The rightists also worked in earnest. From the very first it was obvious that these municipal elections were going to be different from the others. There would be no squabbling. One side at least wanted to keep things on a high plane. More than an election, this was going to be a plebiscite.

I was kept very busy with my paper. I had good friends everywhere who kept me informed of how things were going. Sunday, April the twelfth, the polling began very early in the morning. Great crowds swarmed to the booths. Before sunset, the closing time in Spanish elections, every voter had done his duty. The impression early in the afternoon was that in Madrid the monarchists and rightists had been seriously defeated.

We sat at home with a large group of friends, waiting. Every now and again I would be called up over the telephone and, with rare exceptions, every call was to announce a new victory for the republic. At nine o'clock that night I received a copy of the list, with the results of the polling, that had been taken to the king. Alfonso had been relying on the assurances of his government. They had said that the throne was safe, but by the time the king went to bed he knew it was doomed.

Count Romanones, the lame and wily but loyal monarchist premier, had been forced to speak the truth to his sovereign. He could not understand what had happened. None of the other members of the cabinet understood it, nor the generals, nor the bishops, nor the big business men, nor the high palace dignitaries. But the fact was there. Spain was republican. The people, making use of their legitimate and constitutional rights, had said what they wanted. And what they wanted was not a king but a republic.

By Monday morning everyone knew that the monarchy was defeated. While the people of Spain prepared themselves for the great task that lay before them, many of the courtiers and their wives packed their belongings and disappeared. The people of Spain waited calmly. The men who had stood for trial before the military court and a few others, representing the republican and socialist parties, issued a manifesto declaring that they had decided to constitute themselves into a provisional government and expressing their determination to carry out the people's wishes. The king still tried to parley. Count Romanones advised him to give in. The powerful civil guard and a large majority of the army declined to fight for him.

That night the people began to express their joy at the turn events were taking. Groups met and sang. There was a collision with the police and two casualties. The groups dissolved.

April the fourteenth dawned bright and sunny. I left the house early with the intention of going to the headquarters of one of the big journals for news.

A member of the staff met me on the stairs. His face was beaming.

"The republic has been proclaimed in Eibar up in northern Spain," he cried out. While we were talking another man came out of the telephone booth. "The republic has been proclaimed in Barcelona and Zaragoza. *Viva la República!*" he cried.

As I turned to leave I came across the editor who was also beaming. He gave me the latest news. The provisional government had met in the house of Miguel Maura. The king had been advised to leave. I rushed down to the post, sent a long cable to the *Herald* and flew home. When I burst in with the news, Cefe was talking over the telephone to Marcelino Domingo, one of the exiled republican leaders who was in Paris. He was giving him an account of the results of the elections. I snatched the receiver out of his hand and told Domingo what I had just heard. Cefe thought at first that I had gone crazy.

While we were having luncheon Alcalá Zamora himself telephoned and asked us to give a message to the exiles. "As you have been with them all this time," he said to Cefe, "I wish you to have the pleasure of informing them that the king is leaving tonight, that the cabinet is meeting today, and that Prieto and Domingo, who are members of our government, are to come to Madrid at once. If possible, they are to leave tonight."

I could hear every word he said and realized the importance of finding out by what frontier the king was going to leave. I took up the receiver and asked him.

"We have counseled Romanones not to let him go by Irún. The people are very much excited down there. I think the best plan would be for him to go to Portugal, but he prefers leaving by sea from Cartagena."

I rang up London. Then dashed off some copy for the *Herald* while Cefe got in touch with Paris.

Prieto and Domingo were not at their hotel but we were able to get hold of Commander Hidalgo de Cisneros who volunteered to forward the message.

After that, Cefe and I and Cefito and Marissa started out. All Madrid was in the streets and everyone had somehow or other provided himself with a flag of the republican colors — purple, red and gold. Those colors were already flying from the post office, from all the government departments and from many houses. The republican flag that we had dreamt would one day be ours and that we had been forbidden to use was now openly and freely displayed. It gleamed in the tender light of the glorious spring afternoon. Where had the people hidden it all this time?

We walked along the Castellana to the broad Alcalá trying to reach the Puerta del Sol. Every moment we were stopped by someone we knew and embraced. I have never been so hugged in my life.

There was no rowdiness, no noise, no vulgar demonstration, no misbehavior. There were no civil guards, no police that one could see. The churches were wide open, so were shops of all kinds. There was not one single attempt at looting or petty theft. I did not see any drunkenness. The people had come into their own and felt no hatred. After the king left and the queen with her six children had been left alone in the palace with just a handful of aristocrats to keep her company instead of the stately retinue of other times, word was sent to the provisional government that she desired the guard to be reinforced. It would have been a ghastly mistake. Two young socialists volunteered to keep order. They tied a bit of rope between two trees before the palace door. It was meant as a sign that no one should trespass. And no one did.

The next day the queen left Madrid by car for the Escorial. She took all her jewels with her. Under the shadow of the great monastery where the Spanish royal family is buried, she boarded the train and, with a few members of her suite, left for Irún and Hendaye on the French border. No one molested her.

At about six that afternoon, from a window in the Puerta del Sol, we saw the members of the new government arrive at the home office. Their cars found it difficult to break through the great seething mass that cheered itself hoarse.

One of the first decisions of the provisional government was to declare the following day a national holiday. We went home quite late but the streets were still packed with people too happy to go home. Deep, confident joy was everywhere. I think that sunny April day in 1931 was the most unselfishly happy moment of my life. I told Cefe so before we fell asleep.

With the hopeful confidence of the convalescent after a long and serious illness, Spain rose to face life with almost unbeliev-able energy. For years and years she had tried to rid herself of the lethargic weight of ignorance and poverty and now of a sudden every possibility of redemption from both ills was be-fore her.

That Spain had not been unconscious of the reasons which had caused her decadence is obvious in the fact that her first clamor was directed toward education. The republic that was to restore her to health was petitioned for schools. According to the latest statistics of the time, over fifty-two per cent of the Spanish population was illiterate. The percentage was not evenly distributed. In some regions, as in Catalonia, where a large industrial population fought illiteracy, and in the Basque country and in the Asturias where Spanish emigrants would build schools with the first fruits of their labor in America, the proportion was much smaller. In Andalusia, Extremadura and Castile, the figure was as high as eighty per cent.

"Schools! We want schools!" was the cry from every part of the country. Before water or food or a rise in wages, what Spaniards wanted was knowledge.

The Minister for Education, Don Marcelino Domingo, said it was the most touching thing to see the ill-spelt little letters that came into his department from thousands with that one request: "Schools." And the republic answered by setting up a five-year plan in order to endow Spain with all the schools it needed. In the first two years of the republican régime twelve thousand five hundred new schools were opened. This allowance not only covered the more pressing needs but also absorbed the twenty-eight thousand teachers, men and women, that had passed through the normal schools and were out of jobs because the preceding governments had not worried about giving the people of Spain the schools they were asking for.

The measures adopted by the government of the Spanish republic in the first two years of its existence were in themselves sufficient to justify the change of régime. Step by step, but unremittingly, measures were adopted for the extension, diffusion and conservation of the Spanish culture. A few more years of such care and the plan would have been completed. Unfortunately the brake was put on this plan the moment the government changed.

Life was really worth living then. Every day the *Official Gazette* would bring us proof of the feverish activity with which all government departments were working for the good of Spain. Plans were elaborated for the irrigation of hitherto sterile lands, others for the setting up of public-health centres, more for the development of the industrial possibilities of the country and for the preservation of our art. Meanwhile, behind the thick walls of the labor department, an earnest self-contained man sat day after day, poring over papers that were going to crystallize into the finest labor legislation of the world.

Its author was the Minister of Labor, Don Francisco Largo Caballero. He knew what the problems and the sufferings of the workers were. He had endured them in person ever since, as a small boy of eleven, he had been forced to work for his living. Yes, he knew the needs of the workers, their qualities and their failings. He would do everything possible to improve the conditions of their lives.

But he would be as severe with them as he had been with himself, would pass over no treachery, no meanness. No one knew better than he what it was to fight with every odd against him. He had been persecuted, put in jail, condemned to death more than once. All his life had been one long struggle against want and for a cause. The luxurious furniture of his new office, the fine car waiting at the door, were to him just part of his post. What mattered to him was his work. He was essentially a man of the people and, like a true Spaniard, every bit as dignified as the highest born of the land.

Cefe and I were on pins to do something for our country, too. Soon I was appointed member of several boards. A board to draw up the rules for a new national school for the deaf and dumb, another to control and superintend the hospital for mutilated workers. One more to look after old donations that had been lying idle and must be duly applied to the end held in view by the donors. And still another to direct the activities of the Society for the Protection of Plants and Animals.

A few days after the republic's installation Luis Araquistain rang me up over the telephone.

"I have been asked to head the government delegation to the International Labor Conference next month and should like you to form part of it," he said. "Please accept."

I told him I was ready to do anything they thought useful. From that day until the time for our departure I worked hard, studying the different questions that were going to be brought before the conference and those that interested Spain particularly.

"I want you to take care of everything concerned with the work of women and children," Luis Araquistain said to me when we met to discuss the matter.

The republic could have offered me no post that I could have accepted with more pleasure than this one. The League of Nations was still the hope of all pacifists. Its need as a means of bringing about a better understanding between nations had been foreseen and felt as long ago as the first half of the sixteenth century by the Dominican friar, Francisco de Vitória, from Salamanca, the founder of International Right, whose teachings are considered as the most progressive and uplifting of the time. He was entirely opposed to any war except in legitimate self-defense. The point having first been well proven and maintained that a conqueror may be a judge, never a prosecutor, and that a defeated people should not be made to suffer the consequences of wars that have been undertaken without their consent by their rulers.

I approached the great municipal hall of Geneva, where the Conference of the International Labor Offices as well as the

Assemblies of the League of Nations were then held, with a feeling of deep reverence. Spain had been absent from the Geneva meeting the last few years because Primo de Rivera did not approve of it. Italian influence was evidently already exerting its influence on the Spanish dictator.

Although there were a few signs of the final crumbling away of the institution, the league was still strong enough to make people hold on to the idea that it was going to create a new international order. Its prestige had been increased by the peaceful solution of the Corfu incident and the avoidance of war between Bulgaria and Greece, but little cracks were beginning to appear which one felt might easily develop into a sundering of the whole structure. The International Labor Office was the most vital and therefore the most interesting part of the league ; the conflicts between capital and labor are world conflicts. It was like a huge laboratory in which experts of every nation tried, and tried with good results at Geneva, to find a way for the solution of all the difficulties and the abuses which the economic system that governs the world brings in its wake.

Our arrival created quite a sensation. The three delegations from the young Spanish Republic : government, employers and workers, all walked in together. The democratic representatives hailed us with sympathy, the others with ill-disguised irritation. A new feeling of respect was evident among the delegates of the Spanish American republics. They had fought for their independence against the Spanish monarchy. It was natural that the change of régime should bring them closer to the old country.

We set to work at once. I took part in the deliberations of the commission that was preparing a new convention for the defense of child workers. I am afraid I rather scandalized my colleagues by bringing up a proposal to limit the hours of acolytes under a certain age. No one advanced any convincing arguments against the motion but it was not accepted.

However, I was not discouraged, on the contrary, this first real World Parliament impressed me considerably. It was sincere. At least two of its groups were. Employers and workers defended their mutual interests in the open. If the governments were not always at the level of their high mission it was not the fault of the office. Under the masterly mind of Albert Thomas it could not be otherwise. He was, of course, the soul of the organization. Men and women delegates could stress their points to the utmost, throw all the weight of their influence — the wealth and power of the employers and the support of the masses of the workers — into the fray. At the end of the conference Albert Thomas' ardent eloquence, his good-will, his human understanding, had convinced them that the work must be carried on. They would separate with little or no bitterness, ready to begin the struggle anew the next year. Even Léon Jouhaux, after letting loose the torrent of his words, "his thunder," as the employers' group called the speeches of the French workers' delegate, would be ready to discuss things quietly with Albert Thomas.

The staff of the director of the office collaborated magnificently. I have often been amused by the supercilious attitude adopted by some of the employees of the league *vis-à-vis* those of the labor office. The superiority as far as the work achieved was concerned and the intelligent interest developed was certainly not just on one side. The league's staff perhaps unconsciously has, with very rare exceptions, imitated the ways and the manners that are usual among diplomats. Evidently the presence of so many secretaries for foreign affairs and of delegates who are also members of the diplomatic corps has been responsible.

In the labor office there was nothing of this. I have had occasion to meet many of the staff and have always been struck by the simple direct way in which they tackled all problems. My work brought me more frequently into contact with Madame Marguerite Thibert who was in charge of the department interested in the work of women and children, and I have certainly never co-operated with anyone more intelligent and devoted.

While I was still in Geneva, Cefe rang me up over the telephone one day to say that the government had appointed him Civil Governor of the Province of Almería and that he must leave Madrid at once. A civil governor in Spain is what the *préfet* is in France and it is difficult to imagine a more complicated and difficult position for any man to fill, especially at that time and in a province like Almería : one of the most backward, ignorant and downtrodden of Spain.

At first I thought Cefe would not be able to stand the strain. The workers were naturally in a hurry to better their condition and strike followed strike until my husband was in despair. However, in all the time he stayed in Almería he never came up against a conflict that he did not manage to solve peacefully. It was the first time the people of that province had been treated fairly, without the intervention of the civil guards, and they came to love Cefe because he knew how to treat them.

After my return from Geneva he had thought of coming up to Madrid to see us. He was getting ready to leave when the workers of the port — usually the most difficult to deal with — suddenly announced their intention of going on strike. Cefe, who knew their leader well, turned to him with an aggrieved air.

"You are nice fellows," he told him. "I was just going up to Madrid to see my wife for two or three days and now you are going to do this."

The man — a tall, thin, brown-skinned Andalusian, with magnificent grey-green eyes, who was always dropping into Cefe's
office to discuss some problem — looked quite concerned.

"And is it long since you saw the señora ?" he asked.

"Three months."

"Well, I shall tell you what we can do, señor *gobernador*,"
he said, putting out his hand to take back the paper on which
strikes had to be announced to the authorities. "We shall
change our plans and have the strike after you come back."

Cefe laughed and assured him it had been a joke.

"No," said the dock worker, "it is only right that you should
see the señora. We are in no hurry." And to Cefe's amazement he walked out of the room with his usual dignified air.

My husband did not know what to do but finally came up
to see me. "If they say they won't go on strike, they won't,"
his private secretary had assured him. And they didn't.

The day after he got back to Almería the dock worker called
on Cefe again, asked how he had found the family and presented his paper. I am glad to think that they got a rise in
wages as a result of the strike.

In the month of September I was again called upon to form
part of the government delegation in Geneva. This time for
the yearly assembly of the league.

It was an interesting meeting but I was disappointed in the
way business was carried on. On the surface, everything was
admirable. There were some excellent speeches, a great deal
of talk about good-will and neighborly feelings and faith in
democracy, loud clapping of hands and then a rush for the
refreshment hall. But the real work consisted in lobbying or
intriguing — the old political methods on a world scale.

Still there were moments that year and for several others in
which the spirit of the league, the spirit with which it had been
founded, would flare up unexpectedly.

I was proud to feel that Spain always responded — Don Quixote perhaps. Who knows? But we need not feel ashamed that she always stood up for what was right, for China against Japan, for Ethiopia against Italy, and with all the oppressed and downtrodden against the oppressors. That she was afterward betrayed herself does not matter. I would gaze at the delegates and listen to them and wish that all they said in so eloquent a fashion could bring better results. I met many famous men. Beneš of Czechoslovakia, able and agile ; Edouard Herriot and Paul Boncour of France, who were always charmingly polite ; Minister Rickard Sandler from Sweden ; Sir John Simon and Mr. Anthony Eden from Great Britain ; Baron Aloisi from Italy ; Engelbert Dollfuss, the pocket dictator of Austria ; clever Mr. Litvinoff, Soviet Commissar of Foreign Affairs ; and Mr. Wellington Koo, the great upholder of China's rights. Some countries always sent women delegates. Sweden never failed, so I got a chance to renew my acquaintance with Fröken Kerstin Hesselgren who has undoubtedly been one of the best collaborators that the league has ever had, Madame Malaterre Sellier, always up in arms to defend women's rights, Helene Vacarescu whom I had met in Paris long before and whose speeches sounded like poems.

When I went back to Spain I decided to give as much of my time as possible to the study of international law and labor legislation. I managed to do it while covering news for the *Herald*, looking after the house and attending the meetings of the different boards, but I went out socially as little as possible. Week-ends we always spent with Cefe in Guadalajara, where he had been appointed after Almería.

In the month of January a decree from the labor ministry announced the setting up of a board of factory inspectors who were to be selected by a tribunal after very hard competitive examinations. The moment I heard of it I made up my mind

I would have a try. I wanted to do something useful for the republic and this was a good chance. Some of my friends tried to dissuade me. "It is going to be very hard and you are not strong enough," they would say. But I kept on. For months I could scarcely sleep or rest yet I really believe nothing I have ever done has pleased me more than passing those examinations. I was the only woman who succeeded and I was at once put in charge of everything connected with women's and children's labor. This was much more interesting, I thought, than the plan of sending me as plenipotentiary minister to Holland as they wanted to do.

Shortly afterward we moved into the new house. It was really lovely. The old cabinets and chairs and tables that had been part of my background as a child seemed quite at home in the large rooms.

One of the most wonderful sensations I have ever experienced, which is mixed up with my impressions of the republic because both belong to the same period, was meeting in Madrid the great woman scientist, Madame Marie Curie. The tiny, feeble body, the pale face, the magnificent forehead, the deep eyes, the nervous hands are fixed indelibly in my memory. When I was introduced I could not say a single word at first, so overawed was I to think that I was face to face with this extraordinary woman, one of the very greatest minds of the world, and with it, or rather, because of it, an ardent upholder of all noble causes, primarily the cause of peace.

The new chart of Spain drawn up by the constituent parliament was now in force. The women had been granted all their rights without a single restriction. The labor legislation was a fact, not a myth. The workers were being raised to a decent level. They were no longer downtrodden, underpaid hirelings, but men in possession of their rights.

A great deal has been said about abuses that were supposed

to have followed. There may have been some but I can vouch for the fact that the government, and especially the minister of labor, took the necessary measures to prevent their repetition. The workers' organizations were not allowed to interpret the law as they chose and, as far as the U.G.T. is concerned, there is no doubt but that they kept the workers in hand and were opposed to any overstepping of the limits that the cortes, with the approval of the whole country, had laid down.

The army was also reorganized in a sensible way. Don Manuel Azaña, who was then minister of war, was trying to turn the army into a really efficient force. There would no longer be eight hundred generals and over twenty thousand officers as in the days of the monarchy, and those in the service would be decently paid. He would make these changes slowly so as not to prejudice anyone. The large landholders who had never bothered about their property except as a source of income were going to be asked to sell their holdings to the nation. The Catholic Church would be separated from the state but would enjoy total freedom and the use of all the beautiful cathedrals and temples that had been built for those of the Catholic faith. Followers of other creeds would be granted liberty of worship, too, as in all civilized countries.

One would have thought that the Spaniards would have been content, that they would have been grateful to a régime that had not persecuted even those who were responsible for the country's backward state. Some of them lost certain privileges but they were granted the highest of all privileges : that of being free men in a free country with no limitations other than those imposed by the laws. If some religious orders were banned, just as they had been in the time of the king, still their members were allowed to go on living in the country as citizens.

However, the régime was not considered satisfactory by certain groups and, before the republic was many months old, part of the old autocratic forces in the army, the church, and the aristocracy were already plotting against it. One could easily sense it in the sabotage directed not only against new measures and institutions, but also against many an old-established business. The idea was to breed distrust and discontent and let the blame fall on the republic.

The Spanish middle class, which has always tried to ape the aristocracy instead of standing on its own feet, was at first a useful tool. Small shopkeepers, afraid of losing their rich clientele, lent willing ears to the complaints that "The republic is going to do away with religion ; the army is going to be so reduced it won't be able to defend the country ; the land is going to be given to the peasants and they won't allow their products to be brought to the big cities," and so on and on. Some of the church hierarchy, disregarding the orders of the Pope that they should respect the orders of the republic, encouraged part of the clergy to rebel. Together they sowed the seeds of future disaster. But the great majority of the country would not allow itself to be led away by reactionary influences that appealed to treason and force.

In 1933 those elements of disorder headed by Alejandro Lerroux, the leader of one of the republican parties who had entered into a monstrous alliance with Señor Gil Robles, representative of the extreme reactionary groups and supported by the Jesuits, persuaded Señor Alcalá Zamora, President of the Republic, that the constituent cortes should be dissolved or in any case that the government of Señor Azaña should be dismissed. It was all done politely, in view of the fact that Señor Azaña could not be thrown out because of a lack of confidence of the cortes since its members proved they were entirely with him — the president deprived him of his own support, after showering compliments on the works achieved by the First Government of the Republic. Señor Azaña naturally resigned at once and Lerroux formed a one-party cabinet with his own group.

The day before the new cabinet was to go before the cortes, Manuel Azaña, Largo Caballero and Marcelino Domingo met at our house in order to discuss the speech Don Manuel intended making the next day. We all kept the meeting secret but the press of the opposition found it out, and it gave rise to a great deal of talk. Azaña's speech made such an impression in the cortes that Lerroux was completely routed and had to resign.

In order to carry out their plans the reactionaries then persuaded President Alcalá Zamora to dissolve the cortes. A weak man and jealous, too, of Azaña's popularity, the president gave in, and general elections were called for the month of November, 1933. I was just back from the Assembly of the League of Nations and had been able to gauge to their full extent the repercussions that the changes in Spanish policy were having abroad. Salvador Madariaga had been the head of the Spanish delegation that year. He was sure the change in home politics would be for the better. Could he not see how all the countries that were enemies of progress were rejoicing?

It had been a difficult assembly. The German delegation, headed by Goebbels, adopted a defiant attitude that heralded trouble. It was the same as had been taken in the labor conference by Dr. Fey, head of the German delegation, who was recalled because in an interview with the press he complained of the league procedures and said something about Germany having to submit to being on a parity with other nations like the Latin American republics which were inhabited by monkeys. Even Hitler found this too hard to swallow. There was quite a scandal at first. The Italian delegation led by astute De Michelis was upset at the lack of tact on the part of the Germans, but it was hushed up and the excitement subsided.

Goebbels was too intelligent to commit any such errors. He kept himself surrounded by a young menacing Nazi guard and tried to put a spoke in everybody's wheel while a young lady in his delegation, who was very *nouveau riche* and absolutely ignorant of what was happening in the world outside Germany, plied the other women delegates with invitations to dinner at the most expensive hotel in Geneva in order to explain to them the wonders of the Nazi system.

She did not succeed in getting hold of me. I was feeling tired. My vanity was flattered by my having been authorized to sign a convention in the name of my government. The first convention of the league, I was told, to be signed by a woman as plenipotentiary minister, but that did not make up for other things. The assembly seemed to be half asleep. The failure of the disarmament committee — Sir Arthur Henderson's sad face was expressive enough to indicate what this meant — and the growing fear that Fascism and Nazism would end by plunging the world into war, weighed heavily on us all. Yet it made one angry, too. Why didn't England and France exert themselves in the face of danger?

A large mass meeting in favor of disarmament had been arranged to take place after the assembly finished its labors. Lord Robert Cecil was to be one of the orators and I was asked to speak, too. That morning I went down to the league offices. They were still in the old building. At the entrance I met one of the members of the staff. He looked very serious.

"Madame Palencia, have you heard? Germany is leaving the league."

I was struck dumb. What a calamity! Was this the prelude to war? Just then Sir John Simon came out of one of the committee rooms. He came forward to congratulate me on my election to the Committee of Experts on Slavery in which he took a deep interest.

"Have you heard about Germany ?" he asked.

"Yes," I answered, "and what is going to happen ?"

"Oh, we are not going to allow anything to happen," he said firmly. "The league will continue its work as it has always done. . ."

The arrival of some members of the press, eager for news, stopped him. I pondered. . . One would really have thought he had spoken sincerely and of course his first words came true. The British cabinet he belonged to did not allow *anything* to happen. Spain soon learnt that to her cost. In spite of Germany's decision we held the meeting.

The refusal of socialists and republicans to join forces in the Spanish elections that winter was responsible for many evils. It allowed Lerroux, together with the extreme right, to obtain a large majority. It made it possible for reactionary Gil Robles, who had refused to give allegiance to the republic and openly declared he would destroy it, to be successfully maneuvred into a cabinet of which the republican leader was the head only in name.

When in the face of it Lerroux's party broke up and its most decent supporters followed Martínez Barrios and joined the other republican groups, we all felt that we were going to have very heavy ordeals to face.

The Asturian miners and the Catalonian republican parties of the left, with the support of the general trade unions in Madrid, Bilbao and other big cities, considering that Gil Robles' appointment as minister was illegal and unconstitutional, rose in rebellion against Lerroux and his cabinet. Had they not done so, Spain would have been laid under the heel of a dictator then. They managed to delay the evil day. The struggle was so violent, and the Asturians held out so valiantly that Lerroux was afraid to go further.

The Moorish troops were brought over to Spain for the first time by the very Catholic minister of war in order to quell the uprising. The infidels were commissioned to kill Christians. One wondered what Santiago, the Patron Saint of Spain, whose chief glory had until then resided — according to the Spanish Catholics — in his victories over the Moors, must have thought of this strange turning of tables. Santiago has always been portrayed riding a white steed, with bleeding heads of Moors hanging from his saddle. It appears that Franco has had to suppress the Moors' heads in the modern pictures of Santiago.

The Pope issued a declaration forbidding Catholics to join the movement against the government. The Sovereign Pontiff declared no Catholic had a right to rise against a legally constituted authority. It was this statement that perplexed so many Catholics when they saw the Spanish Church hierarchy give their support to rebel Franco.

The repression was brutal. Luis Companys, head of the Catalonian autonomous state, and his cabinet and Señor Azaña, who happened to be in Barcelona at the time but had taken absolutely no part in the movement, were arrested. In Asturias every conceivable cruelty was inflicted on the unfortunate working population. Men and women were shot, beaten and submitted to torture. A demoniacal spirit seemed to have taken possession of the organizers of the repression. In Madrid, Largo Caballero, General Secretary of the U.G.T. (General Trade Unions), was put into jail with hundreds of others.

The homes of well-known republicans and socialists were searched. I received a surprise visit from fourteen civil guards, six members of the secret police force and two lorries full of assault troops one morning. I was alone in the house with Maria and Asunción and, hearing a noise, came down the stairs to be met by two civil guards pointing their guns and six policemen leveling their revolvers at my not very large person and at the even smaller maid and cook who followed at my heels. It was as grotesque as an Italian operetta.

They searched all the rooms. My husband's studio they found very intriguing after they discovered the overalls Cefe used to wear when painting tucked away under a bookshelf. They evidently surmised this meant there was another person — a worker — in the house. I was intrigued, too, when I saw the two civil guards advance very cautiously with fixed bayonets toward a large canvas on which Cefe had been painting a life-sized nude figure. At first I thought their modesty had been outraged but when they suddenly turned and looked behind the picture I gathered it was that they had feared some dangerous republican had taken refuge there. Although they did not find a single thing at which they might have taken offense, the secret police continued searching the house periodically for about three months.

Meanwhile life in Madrid had become impossible. No free speech was allowed. Everyone was watched and the press severely controlled. The foreign correspondents were at their wits' end. News of the repression was leaking out to the world outside and the papers were asking for details. These were difficult to send, the government being anxious to hide what was going on. We were forced to submit all our stories to the censor but this did not exclude possible reprisals. The censor might approve and the police disapprove.

One day a British correspondent was arrested. Thanks to the efforts of his embassy, he was not kept in jail but forced to leave the country. In reply to some questions of the Spanish reporters regarding the case, Premier Lerroux answered :

"He has been let off so easily because I hear he did not write the article we have objected to himself. It was taken from another London paper, the *Daily Herald.*" I wondered what would happen to me. I was the author of that article. For several days, every time the dogs barked I imagined it would be the police. However, nothing came of it. Perhaps they thought it was not worth while to follow up the matter.

During these days I was called upon to help with the unfortunate women and children in Asturias. It was very difficult for the government had declared that all aid given to the rebels was a punishable offense. The children and women were evidently supposed to be rebels, too.

In spite of it, every leftist party set up a committee and worked hard to collect funds and, what was much more difficult, to get in touch with those in need. The workers' organizations and liberal societies abroad helped a good deal and the Spanish republicans were most generous. We had to meet in a clandestine way for months. The danger of detention affected not only us but also the recipients of aid.

Julio Alvarez del Vayo, Maria Martínez Sierra, the young lawyer, Rufilanchas, Cazorla and Andrés Manso and myself worked on the same committee. The last three have since been shot by Franco. It was natural that the mutual suffering should bring about the much desired union between the leftist groups. Sorrow creates very strong bonds and every party now had its martyrs.

Day after day we could see those bonds drawing closer. The unity of all parties was indispensable if the republic was to come into its own again. The spirits of the people began to rise. Hope in the future was once more the moving force and, by the end of 1935, no one doubted that the president would be forced to dissolve a parliament that was already disunited and call another general elections. We all began to prepare for them.

At home Cefito, Marissa and their friends employed their spare time trying to get up a company for a little art theatre they hoped to take on the road some day as a channel for culture. We were only able to have two performances. Political events interrupted our plans. The cast was made up by Victoria Cásares Quiroga, daughter of the minister of the interior in the First Republican Government ; Paz, Sara, and Maria Luisa Vilches, the three daughters of the well-known Spanish actor ; Carmina Llópis, the niece of the Under Secretary of Education ; and Cefito and Marissa.

It was such a success that we had to give a special evening performance and, by a strange coincidence, some of the men who were to be most prominent in the future governments of Spain were present. Azaña, Cásares Quiroga, Marcelino Domingo, Fernando de los Ríos and others.

The curtain fell on our little theatre. We did not know that soon it would rise on another scene, this time a most tragic one. The prelude to that tragedy was the coming general elections.

Book Three
Acceptance Not Resignation

CHAPTER XIV

That year of 1936 the people had a better slogan than ever before to lead their parliamentary campaign. One that would find an echo in everybody's heart. It was "Save the political prisoners." Those who were better prepared knew that besides this great humanitarian cause there were other things at stake. The whole republican system was in danger. The prisons were crammed. Around forty thousand men and women had been held in jail for nearly two years, their only crime being that they had given support to the republican cause. Hundreds of children had been transferred from Asturias to the eastern coast of Spain because they were literally dying of hunger. The rest of Spain was throttled.

Strict censorship prevented all circulation of news. That is, it tried to, but no one could ignore the fact that the enemies of the new constitution were all meeting, and abetting a revolt against the political system that had been freely chosen by the enormous majority of the Spanish people. The enemies of the new constitution included the large landowners who had been illegally holding land, lent their ancestors by the crown, centuries back, in payment for some service, which the republic had obliged them to return ; officers of the army who could not bear to keep their fingers out of the political pie ; hierarchs of the church who were now obliged to rely for their income only on the generosity of the faithful ; and a group of aristocrats to whom a title with no royal palace to grant prerogatives was an empty honor.

To the aid of these political discontents came what is the backbone of every revolt that hasn't an ideal for its banner, every revolt that is based purely on personal motives ; to their aid came money. It came forward in the person of the Mallorcan, Juan March, whom the republic had put in jail for shipping contraband. With him were the private bankers and some of their wealthy clientele ; business men and big industrialists hurt in their pride more than in their pockets by a labor legislation that had redeemed the worker ; finally, a small crowd of people suffering from an inferiority complex. It was composed of women of the middle class who had never been able to shine in society and resented it ; men unable to stand on their own feet who were accustomed to hold jobs only through favoritism or nepotism ; and finally, those who were afraid. Strange creatures these, afraid of the leveling of class differences though they belonged to a nondescript class, afraid of agricultural reforms though they did not own a single acre of land, afraid of the disappearance of titles though they had nothing to go by except their modest and unknown names, afraid of everything. Such was the army of Franco, an army ready to fill his coffers with large sums made up from the miserable contributions of these people.

Franco is himself a *parvenu.* The leader elected for the revolt was old General José Sanjurjo whom the republic had reprieved after the revolt of 1932, an old man who had been a gay dog with women and was now invested with one great mark of distinction : he had been to Germany and seen Hitler and had gone to sleep, they say, during a speech by the dictator. This appears natural since he could not understand a word of German. General Sanjurjo was unable to lead the revolt because his plane crashed as it was leaving the Lisbon airdrome and he was killed.

Franco benefited by the accident.

The general elections took place on February 16th, 1936, under the auspices and control of a right-wing republican government. Two coalition groups stood face to face. On one side the rightists led by Gil Robles whose taste for power had been sharpened by his two years and a half in office. His party's slogan was pasted all over the country under grotesque giant-sized colored pictures of the leader : "For the three hundred." Its meaning was that their campaign was a bid for three hundred seats in parliament. The remaining one hundred and seventy-three they were generously leaving to be divided between republicans of all tendencies, monarchists, socialists and communists.

Sunday morning, all Madrid turned out to vote. Cefe, Cefito, who was voting for the first time, and I stood in the long queue before the booth of one of the most aristocratic quarters of the town.

I looked around me. The line formed by haughty grey-haired matrons, carefully watching over giggling daughters, old women with unearthly white faces and trembling hands. One could guess they were nuns because of their nervousness. An order from the bishop had forced them from their quiet secluded convents, an order to vote. Cloister or no cloister, vows or no vows, they must vote so as to increase the numbers of those who were fighting the republic.

There were many other types of men and women : quiet determined people who looked like teachers, doctors, artists, students, funny little shopkeepers and a large crowd of over-alled workers.

No one showed impatience, not even when a bustling red-faced man whom we knew to be a leader of the local branch of the rightist party ran frantically up and down, offering advice that was not wanted, slapping a friend on the back, scowling viciously when the workers talked among themselves and smiling blandly at the owners of luxurious cars that drove up to discharge load after load of the blind and sick brought out of their humble homes by rich ladies who had given them money or a mattress in exchange for a vote. Many of them voted against the rightists and for the Popular Front in spite of these favors.

We drove about Madrid until lunch time, looking around us. The order was perfect. Already one could sense that the leftists would win many seats, enough to make it very difficult for the right to govern if they won. The words "Save the Prisoners" had worked miracles.

Everyone was at his post. The women's votes, which in 1933 had contributed to the loss of the elections, were now turning the tide in favor of the republic. Not in vain had they seen their liberty threatened by reaction in the past two years. Not in vain had the suffering of all those thousands of children, victims of a brutal repression, clamored for justice.

By evening we knew that the republic had triumphed in Madrid, by midnight, that it was almost certainly a general victory. Our telephone did not cease ringing all day : "Have you heard ?" "Were you told ?" "We have won," and always "*Viva la República !*"

As in 1931, on Monday the whole town was quiet but tense. Those in the secret knew that pressure was being brought to bear by the rightists on the government for it to allow a dictatorship to be installed with its collaboration.

"That would be fascism," the premier, a centre-wing republican, Señor Portela Valladares had answered.

"Anything rather than communism," was the retort.

"What communism ?" There was no reason for that fear of communism, but the word was a good one, a useful and efficient instrument to frighten the shopkeepers and the haughty middle-class bourgeois women and the poor little nuns and the bankers and the large landowners.

The cabinet wisely resisted temptation and, two days later, after testifying to the victory of the Popular Front, resigned. The leader of the leftist coalition, Don Manuel Azaña, was asked to take office and, under his premiership, an entirely republican cabinet was formed. No social democrats were in it, and no communists.

The latter had obtained fifteen seats, thanks to the coalition, only fifteen out of four hundred and seventy-three. Yet communism was the excuse given for the revolt of the army. The movement was not anti-republican its leaders said. Oh dear, no! It was simply anti-communist. So the whole of Spain was to be drenched in blood and sold to the totalitarian powers because fifteen communists had been returned to parliament.

The new cabinet at once set to work. The political prisoners were granted amnesty. The plans for school-building went ahead but there was something in the air that seemed to prophesy trouble.

Strange strikes broke out, led by the C.N.T. which was under no organized discipline. Undoubtedly there were *agents provocateurs* at work. Army officers known for their republican sympathies were shot down in the street. Officials belonging to the republican administration or to educational centres suffered the same fate.

Suddenly a rumor was circulated to the effect that General Franco and two other of his colleagues were meeting in secret and plotting against the republic. Feeling among the population ran very high. It was insistently said that Franco and General Mola had been called by the military authorities and questioned on the subject, that they both had denied having any intention of revolting against the republic and that the said authorities had been naive enough to believe them. In any case, General Mola was kept at Pamplona, the most reactionary anti-republican zone of Spain, and Franco in the Canary Islands, both with the category of supreme chiefs of the respective forces.

I had been extremely busy for the past few weeks. There was a binding promise on the part of the republican party to issue a decree the moment it came into power to re-employ all workers who had been thrown out of work for seconding the strike in 1934, or for their political opinions. In the month of March special boards were set up to study each individual case. Like the mixed boards of trade, they had a president, a secretary, and two representatives each from the employers' and the workers' organizations. I was appointed president of one of the Madrid boards dealing with all the cases affecting women's work, especially those relating to the garment makers' union.

In Madrid alone there were thousands of men and women who had been without work for nearly two years. We lost no time in setting to our task. For weeks my board would sit from eight o'clock in the morning until ten or eleven at night. I could not bear to lose a minute, knowing those people were starving while they waited.

Toward the middle of June I had finished with the last case. Most of them had been satisfactorily settled but I was being continually threatened by the employers and their legal advisers — not that they could do anything, since the law was clear.

"You must get ready for the International Labor Conference," said the labor minister to me the day I sent in my report on the persons re-admitted to work.

I accepted gladly. The year before, not wishing to represent the reactionary government then in office, I had refused to be included in the delegation and had attended the conference as a member of the workers' group. While we were in Geneva disquieting rumors reached us from Spain. The journal *El Socialista,* the organ of the socialist party and generally very reliable in its news, kept on advising the government to beware.

Something was undoubtedly brewing. Signs of disloyalty among army officers and some members of the diplomatic corps were singled out by the paper. The conference that year was less interesting than at other times. The forty-hour-week convention was not accepted in spite of the efforts of France, the United States and Spain to get it through. We Spaniards were all impatient to be back. We felt that our place now was at home, and yet the government did not appear to be very much concerned over the rumors afloat. In the International Labor Office all my friends had been delighted to see me turn up with the government delegation.

"When you come as a government delegate," they said, "we know that things are going well in Spain."

I left Geneva toward the end of June. My husband, with Cefito and Marissa, was waiting for me at the Madrid airport. They seemed quite happy, only rather puzzled at seeing a German Swiss who, with his wife, had taken my sister Inez' house next to ours, talking confidentially to an aviator whom we knew to be a Fascist.

"Why does he always say he does not know anybody in Madrid if he knows that one?" Marissa said.

"Why is he flying all over the place in our planes," inquired Cefito. "Foreigners should not be allowed to use our planes and our airport unless they are officials," he insisted.

The night after my arrival a group of Falangists was discovered holding a secret meeting in the church of San Jerónimo. They had a large number of firearms with them. The church was closed for a few days and then reopened. The authorities seemed to think the parish priest had not known what was going on.

On the seventeenth of July I had been asked to make the closing speech at a congress of hospital nurses which was being held in Madrid. There were several speakers. Just before I went on the platform someone came up behind me and whispered :

"Have you heard the news ?" I turned my head. "There has been a rising in Morocco. Part of the army against the republic."

So it had come !

I made my speech and hurried out to meet my husband and son who were waiting with the car in the Recoletos Promenade. I found them sitting with a group of excited friends. They, too, had heard.

"Let us go to the *Libertad* and get the latest news," said Cefe.

The offices of the *Libertad*, one of the principal republican papers, were crowded. Cefe, who belonged to the staff, managed to squeeze into the editor's room. He came out looking very grave.

"It is true," he said as we drove through the Puerta del Sol, which was full at that hour of people rushing home to dinner. "General Franco has flown from the Canary Islands to Morocco and is at the head of the movement there."

None of us slept that night. I was kept busy until one o'clock in the morning telephoning to London. Cefe, Cefito and Marissa sat beside the radio and passed on the news to me.

The press next morning gave an account of the measures that were being taken by the government to strangle the movement. The revolt, however, was spreading. During the afternoon large groups of men assembled in the principal streets clamoring for arms, for the defense of the town. Sunday we heard that several other generals had risen. Fighting was going on in different cities, between rebel forces and the population. In almost every garrison town the army itself was divided.

"Hot fighting in Catalonia," "Malaga on fire," "San Sebastián defends itself against Navarre," said the headlines.

The whole world seemed to be whirling round us. The government in office fell. Another was set up in order to parley with the rebels. It was too late ! Too late !

The new government did not last over a few hours and at last Don Manuel Azaña, who had been elected President of the Republic in the place of Señor Alcalá Zamora who had authorized unconstitutional measures and been impeached in consequence, set up an all-republican government with full authority to quell the rebellion.

Saturday, shooting began in Madrid. Cefito left the house after lunch. In the evening he rang up to say he would not be home until next morning. A great deal of sniping was being carried on by the Fascists from the windows and roofs of the houses and several persons had been killed and wounded. He was rushing about with an ambulance, doing what he could.

"Don't worry about me, mother," he said, "but I beg you and Marissa not to leave the house. It is really very dangerous."

It was impossible for me to promise that. The government had set up a severe censorship and I could no longer telephone to London from our own house. I had to go to the telephone company building in the Gran Vía, in the very heart of Madrid. As for Marissa, her fiancé was sick with typhoid fever and she insisted that she must go to see him. Fortunately he lived at a good distance from the most dangerous spots. Meanwhile the radio advised us to keep listening in and we would know all that was going on.

By the next morning we knew that the rebel officers of Madrid, with General Fanjul at their head, had concentrated in the Montaña barracks. The people, realizing the danger of a march on the capital, were massing together to prevent it. With the help of some loyal officers they got hold of two old discarded cannon. A few rifles, hunting guns, pistols, sticks and stones were the only other arms they had. Inside the barracks the rebels had accumulated a large quantity of armaments of all kinds.

Thanks to the loyalty of the aviation corps there was nothing to fear from that quarter. It was rumored that the artillery school of Segovia, with the best officers of the corps and good guns, was going to shell the capital from the Guadarrama Mountains. Rumor after rumor! Call after call!

All the political leaders addressed the members of their parties over the radio. The sniping grew worse.

I drove to and from Madrid three times that day. Cars were rushing all about the town. Sometimes people fired from them. Snipers were growing more and more audacious. I managed to get my stories off to the *Herald*. All the foreign correspondents were at the telephone centre awaiting their turn.

Cefe tried frantically to get in touch with me from his paper but we somehow missed each other every time. Since it was Sunday, he came home for dinner and stayed with us. We could not use our car since Cefito was not there to drive. So when we had to go into town we did like everybody else. We stood in the road and hailed passers-by. I always got my ride.

At last, utterly exhausted, and having prevailed upon Marissa to go to bed, I made up my mind to lie down, too, and to try to sleep. Impossible. We would shut off the radio and two minutes later we would open it again, just to learn if anything new had happened.

In the middle of the night a woman's voice came to us over the air. She was calling on the people to defend themselves.

It was Pasionaria. Her voice haunted me for months afterward. I had just lain down again when the telephone near my bed woke me with a start.

"Look out," said a friendly newspaper man whose news I was sure I could trust. "At four o'clock in the morning the attack against the Montaña barracks is going to begin."

I jumped up in wild excitement. Should I tell Cefe ? He was fast asleep on the sofa near the radio. Better let him rest, I thought, so I went back to bed, wondering where my boy could be. Perhaps he was with his ambulance near those barracks ! It was impossible to keep one's eyes closed. Half an hour later Constancia de la Mora rang me up and confirmed the report. She had been able to get in touch with her husband who was commander of the air force, so she knew of the raid. It was past two o'clock. I looked out of my window into the great open space behind our house. A dog was barking. The lights of Madrid twinkled merrily. No one could have imagined what was going on behind that peaceful scene.

Another telephone call, this time a foreign correspondent who wanted to know if there was anything going on. I cautioned him not to go to sleep. Something might happen.

Three o'clock, four. . . I shivered though the night was hot and sultry. Four o'clock and not a sound. . . I started to go downstairs and met Cefe coming up to his room. I told him what we were to expect and we both stood at the window, listening. . . Nothing.

He decided to go to bed and I promised I would call him if I heard anything. I stole down to the garden and paced up and down the walk at the back of the house. It seemed a long time. Could it be that the attack was not going to take place ? We could not afford to lose time. . . Perhaps the fighting was on and we were too far off to hear.

Suddenly there was a noise like that of thunder far away.

Cannon . . . I held my breath. Again came the long-drawn-
out rumbling sound followed by a great many more. Firing
was going on without intermission. My mouth felt very
parched.

"Where can my boy be ?" I asked myself. And then,
"What can be happening to those men who had only sticks
and stones ?" I had seen them that very afternoon ready to
fight with every odd against them.

"They will be killed ! They will be killed !" I repeated
to myself while I held my hands to my throat as if by doing so
I could shut out the vision of the people shelled, bleeding,
dying. . .

Two figures appeared round the corner. They were bathed
in the light of the rising sun, their hands crossed over their
bosoms, their heads lifted toward heaven. There was tragedy
in their drawn features, in the dark shadows of their eyes.
They were my two faithful maids, Maria and Asunción.

"Ay . . . señora . . . señora . . . ! Where is the boy ?"
The boy was Cefito, the child of the house to them who had
seen him come into the world, who had showered on him and
on Marissa all the unbounded mother love that a Spanish
woman's heart is capable of hoarding up for any child under
her care.

"Where is the boy ?" they asked in agonized whispers as
though they were afraid that someone might hear.

"He is safe, don't worry," I said, trying to convince myself
that I spoke the truth.

Marissa's anxious little face looked out of a window. "What
is it, mother ? Where is Cefito ?" She and her brother had
always been great chums.

The rumbling continued for a while, then ceased.

The sun was quite high when a telephone call set my heart
beating. It was my boy.

"Mother," came his gay young voice, "are you all right ? Is father home ?"

"Yes . . . yes . . . where are you and when are you coming back ?"

"I can't come. I am going up to the sierra with an ambulance. We are just getting ready."

"But, darling, I must see you."

"Well, why don't you come round to the Casa del Pueblo ? We shall be leaving before midday. But look out. There is a lot of sniping."

The telephone rang off, only to begin a few minutes later with the announcement of good news. The Montaña barracks had been taken. There was now no more danger from that quarter.

I dressed hurriedly and with Marissa caught the bus that was still running occasionally into town. We reached the Casa del Pueblo just in time to see an unforgettable scene. The place was alive with men going up and down, in and out in streams, disheveled, unshaven, with sunken, deep-set eyes. They had not slept for three nights and had been fighting all morning. They spoke of the action of the Montaña barracks without swagger. They just mentioned it as though it were the most natural thing in the world. Now they were going on to the sierra to stop the rebels from coming over the mountains. Some were bareheaded, others had handkerchiefs tied round their heads, but the most amazing thing about this army going to war was the armament. Apart from a few, very few, rifles, every imaginable gun, pistol, axe, or blade, had been requisitioned and was being carried with as much care as though it were the latest model of war engine. And they were all volunteers, offering their lives of their own free will for liberty.

I found Cefito in one of the halls surrounded by a group of

women to whom he was giving a few hasty instructions. They were the wives or sisters of some of the combatants, and had volunteered as nurses.

My boy was every bit as disheveled and grimy looking as the others. He had just come in with his ambulance which had been riddled by bullets, the work of snipers. He was happy and excited.

"Don't worry, mother," when I asked him if he had had any food. "We shall be all right and you will hear from me often." Then, he went out to get a car. The street was full of every kind of vehicle requisitioned for transportation, buses, private cars, lorries.

The din and noise increased every minute. I wished I had the brush of Goya to preserve the scene on canvas as similar scenes of that other Spanish war of independence against Napoleon were captured for us by the great painter.

That evening more good news came over the air. Barcelona had reduced the rebel officers after fierce fighting. The Catalonian capital as well as the other three provinces were safe for the republic. A little later we heard that Valencia had also beaten down the revolt.

Great excitement had been created during the day by two airplanes – loyal ones – flying over the city. The people were overjoyed. They thought everything would be all right if the air force was with them. How could they know that Franco, who began the revolt without a single plane, would crush loyal Spain, temporarily at least, thanks to the heavy bombers that Germany and Italy poured into the country? Franco. . . It was logical that he should have acted as he did. He had felt no scruples about sending native troops to murder the Asturian miners. Why should he feel any about letting German and Italian pilots massacre other Spaniards?

During the days that followed, all loyal Spain was in a frenzy. The government had, through the treason of the rebels, been deprived of all means of maintaining order. The "atrocities" that we have been accused of were the result of the rebellion and should be laid at the door of the insurgents by all fair-minded persons.

What about the other side ? Why was nothing said of the assassinations committed not by an uncontrolled mob but by order of the leaders — "Christians," they called themselves and "defenders of religion" — in all the zone that from the first moment of the revolt was under their "protection"?

The loyalist government did its best to prevent these regrettable incidents and was very soon able to put an end to them entirely. Another point that commentators on the Spanish war forget when speaking of the attacks against nuns and priests — attacks that were grossly exaggerated — is that many convents and churches had been used as depots for arms. They forget that the people were fired on from some of them and that the reaction, though much to be lamented, was natural. What people of what country would not have burnt down churches if they had been attacked first from them ?

All the week we kept the radio open day and night. Besides the news there were speeches by members of the cabinet and leaders of the different political parties and organizations, also by the President, Señor Azaña. The elation in Madrid was extraordinary. No one doubted for a moment but that Right would win.

The government had at last made up its mind that the only salvation for democracy was to let the people defend it. Very slowly, impatient youth and earnest middle age were armed. Very slowly because of the scarcity of rifles. In the outskirts of the town large groups of men of all classes and ages were training for the front. Lorries full of ill-equipped youngsters

dashed along the thoroughfares of Madrid. Large placards
were pasted on the side boards : "To the front to defend
World Democracy."

They sang as they passed us, and waved their hands.

How many . . . how very many never came back. There
was no depression, no regret. Those who went did so because
they wanted to go, because they had taken to heart Pasionaria's
cry, "We would rather die on our feet than spend all the rest
of our lives on our knees."

The women were all trying to help, too. The convents
from which the nuns had fled, some of them before the rebellion broke out, evidently advised of what was coming, were
being used as schools. They were brightened up to make real
homes for the little ones. No children were allowed to wander
about the streets.

Marissa joined the group in the Calle del Fúcar which had
been put under the care of the wives of some aviators. Among
them were Constancia de la Mora and Teresa, the wife of
González Gill who was among the first to fall in action on the
Guadarrama front. Concha Prieto, daughter of the socialist
leader, was also with them.

I hardly saw Marissa during those days. She would come
home dog tired. Besides, I had been appointed member of a
committee charged with organizing all the social welfare and
this kept me very busy. I also had to attend to the *Herald*. It
would have been madness to miss the chance of letting the
world know the truth of what was going on in Spain through
one of the very few British papers that did us some justice. But
it entailed a sad loss of time.

There were days when I had to stay in the telephone building from midday until two o'clock in the morning waiting for
my call. My blood used to boil sometimes to hear the remarks
of some of the foreign correspondents who were waiting there

with me. It was still more amazing to see that their stories were actually influencing world opinion, an opinion that I afterward found out, unfortunately, was only too anxious to be thus influenced. It was much more comfortable to try and convince their own consciences and those of others that the loyalists were all dangerous assassins who were getting what they deserved rather than to have to acknowledge that they themselves were going back on their most sacred traditions.

The Fifth Column — which the world has come to know, and at what cost — was already doing its work within our cities but wanted to keep in the dark. Many days the streets were not safe. Members of the Fifth Column kept up their deadly task from the safe retreat of foreign missions, too. I was more than once dragged for protection into the shelter of a shop or house by some young worker on the watch for snipers.

The day we heard that the governments of democratic countries had actually refused to sell arms to the legitimate government of the Spanish Republic our people were furious. They might have been dismayed. They were only indignant. It seemed so unspeakably mean. The news, however, did not discourage anyone.

It was the same thing when they heard that Italian and German planes were transporting the Moroccan troops into rebel Spain. So there was not even going to be parity ? The Spanish people squared their shoulders and decided to fight the democratic world's battle alone. Every day that passed increased their determination.

We could see, however, that the situation was daily growing more serious. The government would have not only to build up an army in the middle of a war, but to solve innumerable problems such as looking after the children, the old and the sick, working out plans for the care of the refugees, and defending itself from the treacherous elements inside its own institutions.

We were cheered by the news that the greater part of the navy had also kept loyal, that is, the crews and some of the officers. The days passed by with lightning speed. We had no time to be bored or dull. Every minute was full. I had no time for thinking except at night when I reached home and sat up waiting for Cefe to come in from his paper. Often it was almost daylight. Dear old Maria kept watch, too. She was always expecting Cefito to drive down with a serious case that could not be well looked after at the front and to peep in for a bath and change of clothes. She sat with her head bowed, just waiting, until I ordered her off to bed.

Every day Germany and Italy sent more help to Franco and every day the campaign of lies and slander against loyal Spain was carried further and further, giving the so-called democratic governments an excuse for their betrayal of democracy, of decent conduct and international law. Spain was being slowly strangled but we did not quite realize it at the time. Even if we had, the defense of our principles would not have been weakened.

We rarely saw our friends now. Occasionally someone would telephone and ask if he could drop in for a few hours' rest in the garden. Friends just came and went as they chose. The British chargé d'affaires called two or three times, too.

"Señora Palencia," he would say, "will you be home this afternoon, and if so may I come and have a chat?"

"Yes, come to tea, but bring your own sugar," I would suggest. Sir George Ogilvie Forbes was a charming man and a most able diplomat. He really wanted to know what was happening and he judged events impartially.

Our neighbors, the German-Swiss couple, we did not see

for several days after the revolt had broken out. They kept their windows closed in spite of the heat and did not even come out to the garden as had been their wont. The day our planes began to fly over the city, however, I was surprised to see them both rush forth, look up at the sky and go in again. This was repeated every time that the drone of an air engine was heard. I remembered what Cefito had said the day of my arrival and at last I could not help remarking on it.

"I see you are very much interested in planes," I said to the man.

"Yes," he answered hesitatingly. "Why do you think so?"

"I see you rush out every time you hear one coming."

"Well, I can fly. So, of course, I am interested."

But after that he never came out.

A few days later we were able to observe that there was someone up in the house all night and that their radio was kept going all the time. We began to watch them. Very early one morning a man came and helped them take down some wires from the roof. Evidently they had set up a clandestine station. We thought it was time we notified the authorities. An hour later they had gone from the house, leaving most of their furniture behind them. It was not long before we heard that the man was flying for Franco.

Toward the middle of August the United States embassy began to make arrangements for all North American citizens to leave Spain. This meant that means of transportation to the United States would be less every day. I began to feel anxious about Anita who was spending the summer with us but who was due at Wellesley College, where she is professor of Spanish, by September. I asked her whether she did not think she ought to leave. There was no object in her failing to be at her post. Besides, she was not strong enough to help in Spain, then. It was very difficult to persuade her.

"I cannot leave you now," she said, over and over again. "I shall be miserable so far away." But in the end she agreed.

The separation was hard on us both.

Life went on with but little change for some days. I had lost sight of many of our friends and was amused to see some of rightist sympathies turn up without hats or ties, adopting a proletarian appearance that was as false as it was unnecessary. They would show membership cards of the anarchist party and swagger round trying to impress us with their anti-bourgeois ideas. We heard later that some were doing work for the Fifth Column.

My cousins, Rosario and Isabelita, would also drop in to spend an afternoon in our garden and would give me news of their two nieces who had married wealthy men and had left Madrid and gone to the Franco zone. I wondered what Aunt Maria would have done under the circumstances. How far away we were from the days of her political influence ! One thing was sure, she and Aunt Amalia would have been on opposite sides in our present conflict, also.

CHAPTER XV

"The government wants to send you to a diplomatic post in one of the Scandinavian countries."

"I think I could be more useful in Spain now."

"That is not for you to decide."

The government in office when the war broke out had been replaced by a Popular Front cabinet with republicans of different tendencies, a Catholic Basque representative, some socialists and two communists. The premier was Don Francisco Largo Caballero, one-time labor minister of the republic. The Minister of Foreign Affairs was Julio Alvarez del Vayo. It was with him that I had been holding the above conversation.

The government wanted to send me to a Scandinavian country. It meant giving up my work for the *Herald* and my place on the welfare committee.

"We won't talk any more about it now," he said, "because I want you first to come to Geneva for the assembly. It will be a very important one for Spain."

There were still a few weeks ahead. I worked day and night trying to do as much as possible before leaving. Marissa had been sick and was needing a change badly so I thought I would take her with me. We threw a few things into two suitcases and left Madrid. Isabel García Lorca, sister to our great poet who had been assassinated by the rebels in Granada, and Laurita de los Ríos came with us. They were going to join Laurita's father who had been appointed Spanish ambassador in Washington and had gone to Geneva to receive instructions from the minister.

It was evening when our train steamed slowly out of the Madrid station. There was a number of wounded on board bound for Valencia. The lights on the train were kept low and covered with green shades. Bombardments had taken place all along that line the day before.

I did not feel nervous but greatly depressed at leaving Spain. Leaving her even for a few days in this her hour of need hurt deeply. I have often thought that men do not feel the same as women do about their country. Men show a sort of filial affection for it. To women, at least it has always been so in my case, the land is our child, the land and the people. Tears rolled down my cheeks as we went through the sun-baked fields near the city. I had been told we could come back as soon as the assembly was over but I had a feeling that it would be long before I saw Madrid again. I have never been back there since. . .

The stations as we passed them were full of men in overalls. Those overalls were the uniform of the republican army during the first months of the war. I strained my eyes looking out for them in the darkness. They were Spaniards, my people.

In normal times express trains take twelve hours to cover the distance between Madrid and Barcelona. We were taken first down to Valencia and from there sped up to the Catalonian capital.

At the Valencia station we were met by friends armed with huge bouquets. "Tell them in Geneva that democracy will win in Spain," they cried. Those words enveloped in the fragrance of the flowers were the last impression we carried away with us. The blossoms survived until we reached Geneva.

Don Fernando de los Ríos was at the station to meet his daughter and Isabelita. His first words to me were :

"It has just been settled that before going to Stockholm, you are to make a tour through the United States and Canada. It is extremely important that they should know the truth about Spain over there."

Marissa looked at me in dismay but I smiled at her reassuringly. "We shall go to Spain first," I said.

Geneva gave us the first taste of what the world thought of our war and of what the attitude of the democratic governments was going to be. The real friends were, of course, much concerned and crowded round us, but the others did their best to destroy any illusions we might have entertained regarding the solidarity of official democracy. To come from Spain to Geneva at that time was like falling into a strange planet. From the exaltation we all had in Spain, born from a conviction that we were doing the right thing not only toward Spain but toward the whole world at the cost of incalculable sacrifices, we plunged into an atmosphere of indifference not to say hostility. The hostility, I think now, was chiefly the outcome of a feeling of inferiority. We were doing what they knew they ought to do but did not want to do when their turn came along.

As we sat in the assembly hall in the places assigned to the Spanish delegation, I surprised furtive glances turned in our direction, glances that revealed hidden thoughts. Some showed admiration, others pity, others anger. But they were seldom followed by words.

Señor Alvarez del Vayo made an impressive concrete statement in his speech before the Assembly of the League of Nations. He had accumulated all kinds of proofs in support of his contention that Spain was not fighting a civil war but that she was laboring to free herself from a foreign invasion. He was listened to with respect but met with no real response. It was evident that everybody was afraid of the Spanish conflict. Everybody except Mexico who openly maintained the legal position by stating that : "The legally constituted Government of the Spanish Republic has every right under international law to receive arms for its defense and we Mexicans intend to abide by that law."

Russia spoke along the same lines and Mr. Anthony Eden, handsome and nonchalant as usual, hummed and hawed and spoke a great deal, but said next to nothing. Believing him to be a man of good faith, I felt he must be ashamed of the position he was now obliged to take toward Spain, but after all, had it not been worse in Ethiopia's case?

France was in appearance more sympathetic but in reality as empty of good intentions as was England.

The smaller countries obediently followed suit, yet one could not refrain from thinking that in their heart of hearts many delegates must have hated the situation into which they were forced. However, no one seemed able to act in any other way.

We were very soon given to understand that the Spanish question could not be mentioned because it made other countries uncomfortable. Of course, everyone knew that the *thing* was there, just as sickness and death are in one's household at times, but it is considered indiscreet to speak about them.

It was terrible, of course, to think of the unequal struggle, to hear about Moroccan troops being taken over to Spain in Italian airplanes, of German tanks and guns reinforcing the insurgents' possibilities of attack. Many of the rebels must have cursed Germany and Italy for being so careless as to allow the Spanish government and the foreign press to find out what they were doing. But no one on the other hand ignored the fact that Great Britain and France did not wish to be dragged into an armed conflict just yet. And the tension in all Europe was such that the slightest move in what was thought to be the wrong direction might cause a general flare-up that would involve every country. And so Great Britain, well seconded by

France, had been able to concoct that marvelous panacea for
universal peace called the "Committee of Non-Intervention."
This was forced down people's throats well sugared with arguments such as that "Spain must be allowed to decide for herself
what is best for her people," that "All risks of annoying Hitler
or provoking Mussolini must be avoided." Thus the intervention of the two dictators in the Spanish war was openly
acknowledged with the other well-known excuse, "Who
knows, perhaps it is true that Franco is leading an anti-communist movement," and so on and on.

As in other years, the women's international organizations
represented in Geneva gave a reception in honor of the women
delegates to the assembly. The day before, one of its promoters
said to me, "We should love to ask you to be one of the speakers, señora, but it has been decided that this year only the
women who are here for the first time are to speak." I instinctively felt that they were afraid a speech by me might
create trouble. There were a great many people at the reception. Mademoiselle Gourd was chairman during the short
session at the beginning of the evening. As we sat round her,
I looked at the familiar faces near and said to myself that no
woman there could possibly approve of the way Spain was
being treated.

Kerstin Hesselgren and Kathleen Courtney did not disguise their sympathy, neither did Madame Alexandra Kollontay, Soviet Minister to Stockholm and Delegate for Russia that
year, who was sitting close to them. The Portuguese delegate
was the last to speak. To everyone's amazement she took advantage of the situation to make a violent attack upon Spain
and also upon Russia. It was so unprecedented and ill-bred
that it provoked immediate reaction. People hissed and there
were cries of "shame." Mademoiselle Gourd stood up and
energetically requested her to keep within the limits of what

her speech should be. The delegate was very much annoyed but had no alternative than to submit or sit down. She chose the former and spoke to us about "international understanding and love."

Every person there except the delegate from Hungary, and a haughty princess, a member of the Austrian group, came up to me when it was all over and expressed their indignation. I did not care. Spain was so immeasurably above the attack. I could only regret that a woman should have been guilty of such smallness. Before many months were over Austria had been taken over by Hitler and the princess' son was being persecuted in his turn by the totalitarian authorities.

The assembly had not been meeting for more than a week when Alvarez del Vayo said to me one day, "I believe you know that the government has been asked to allow you to go on a speaking tour to the United States and, much as I need you in Stockholm, I cannot refuse."

"I am ready to do whatever is best," I answered, and sat down to discuss the matter with him again.

"You can leave on the *Queen Mary* on October the fifteenth. Who do you think might be asked to make up the delegation ?"

After some discussion we agreed that Don Marcelino Domingo, leader of the left-wing republican government, and Father Sarasola, a Franciscan friar who was at that time in Paris, would, together with myself, be a good all-round combination. I knew Marcelino Domingo quite well but I had never met Father Sarasola though I remembered Cefe's telling me he was an authority on Saint Francis, his study of the Saint of Assisi being considered a standard work. Cefe himself has always been interested in this saint and has written a dramatic poem based on his life.

It was no sooner arranged that I was to go to the United States than I received orders from the government to leave at once for Edinburgh in order to inform the British Labor Conference, meeting at the time, about the Spanish situation. The question of the Non-Intervention Pact that had been accepted by the executive of the party was to be laid before the conference for discussion and it was extremely important that Spain should be heard on the subject. I left Geneva that night and was joined in Paris by Señor Jiménez de Asua, deputy speaker of the Spanish parliament, and a member of the Spanish socialist party. We flew from Paris to London with the intention of hiring a taxi-plane there in order to reach Edinburgh in time for the discussion of the matter in hand. To our great surprise the immigration authorities at Croydon airport, after examining our diplomatic passports and asking us where we were bound for in the British Isles, said we would have to wait for a little while. They politely suggested that we lunch at the airport station so as to while away the time and assured us that the delay would be merely a question of one hour at the most. That one hour was increased to five. I paced up and down the station, trying in vain to control my indignation.

"Why do you not telephone to your paper?" inquired Jiménez de Asua, but nothing would induce me to do such a thing. If the press got wind of what had happened and published a single line on it, we ran the risk of having other governments follow England's example and of having them hold up all Spaniards trying to enter their country. At last we were released, but we reached Edinburgh after the Non-Intervention Pact had been discussed and the British government's decision approved of.

I was desperate. The attitude adopted by the British labor party would, we knew, be extremely damaging to our cause. Señor Jiménez de Asua could not speak a word of English but I insisted that we must explain the situation fully to the party. The executive would not hear of it at first. A vote had been taken and the matter could not, therefore, be brought up again. Thanks to Lord Strabolgi, Miss Wilkinson, Philip Noel Baker and a few others, we gained our point and were authorized to go before the conference next morning.

Loud applause greeted us as we went onto the platform and I felt my heart swell with pride to think that at last the cause of our people was going to meet with some recognition. Jiménez de Asua spoke first. He explained how the Blum government had been so intimidated by the British ambassador in Paris that the arms Spain had ordered from France long before the war, and which had been paid for, were not allowed to be shipped. In order to avoid trouble for the French Popular Front cabinet, Spain took back her check and the arms which might have saved my country were allowed to remain idle on French soil. His speech, which was delivered in French and translated, created quite a sensation and by the time I spoke the conference was shouting like mad.

I explained everything again. I gave an outline of all that was happening and, remembering the way mother had often spoken to us when we were children, I ended my speech by saying, "You had the excuse that you did not know before but 'ye ken noo.' " Rarely have I seen such excitement. The people rose to their feet and shouted against the Non-Intervention Pact, called for "arms for the Spanish people" and forced the council to meet and discuss the matter over again in view of the information we had given them. As a result Mr. Attlee, leader of the party, and Mr. Greenwood, deputy leader, left that very afternoon for London in order to interview the government, place before it the information we had given them and urge that some action be taken. The next day the whole of the British press spoke of our visit to Edinburgh. I was amused by a very conservative London daily stating that I, "like a new Duse," had aroused the feelings of the people to frenzy. Evidently my short training for the stage had been of some use after all. At least we had succeeded in making the British labor party know what was really going on. It was up to it to do the rest.

These short hours in Scotland brought back many things to my memory. The places where I had played as a child and that I had visited with my mother, the softness of the air, the scent coming up from the earth and the quaint accent of the people brought back my childhood very vividly.

Before I left I rang up my cousins, the Murrays, but I could not manage even a short stay with them. I was needed in Geneva those last days of the assembly. A surprise was awaiting me there. During my absence from Madrid, Cefe had been appointed Minister for Spain in Latvia and he and Cefito, on their way to the Baltic, came to Geneva to see us. We had four days together. Cefito had been forced to comply with his father's request that he go and help him to settle in Riga.

"But I am going back to Spain as soon as I can, mother," he said to me the moment we were alone. "I am sorry not to stay with father as he wants me to do, but my place is in Spain."

I knew there could be no turning him back, besides I did not believe I should even try to do so. Cefe was miserable at having to leave Spain himself and at the idea of my going to America. Marissa, too, was heartbroken, as now that her father and brother had left Spain, she would have to go to the United States with me. I could not very well leave her alone in Madrid and worse than anything else was the realization that we could not go home before our trip to say good-bye to her fiancé.

The last drop, and a bitter one, was a letter I got from my youngest sister Inez telling me she had gone to Belgium to see Maria and had made up her mind to remain in the convent as a nun. The news quite stunned me. Inez was like a daughter

to me. She had been away in the United States on a Rockefeller scholarship. It was on her way back that she had come
to this strange decision. I have never been able to find out
what induced her to take such a step, but suspect that terror of
the war must have frightened her into it.

The very day the assembly finished its session, Marissa and
I left for Paris. We stayed one day at the Spanish embassy
with Trudy Araquistain, whose husband was then ambassador
to France. Early the next morning I met Marcelino Domingo
at the boat express and we started for Cherbourg to board the
Queen Mary. Father Sarasola turned out to be a very pale,
reserved man. He did his part nobly all through our tour but
was often very homesick and unhappy at the heartless way in
which he was treated by Catholics in America who, through
ignorance of the situation, have never been able to grasp the real
significance of the Spanish cause. I am glad to know that this
faithful servant of the Franciscan order is now safely back in
his convent once more.

Our arrival in the United States gave rise to much talk. The
day we landed a number of press reporters boarded the *Queen
Mary* at six o'clock in the morning and thousands of questions
were put to us before we could get off the boat. Among other
things, we were repeatedly asked whether it was true that we
intended persuading the United States to go into war on our
side.

When we walked into the Commodore Hotel where we were
to stay that day, the first thing that met our eyes were the headlines in the papers saying that President Azaña had had to leave
Madrid. It was implied that the Spanish capital was in imminent danger of falling into the hands of the rebels. My heart
literally went down to my heels. But after a moment's reflection I looked up again. The men I had seen fighting with sticks
and stones would never give up Madrid.

Our first meeting was held in Toronto, Canada. Marissa left New York a few hours ahead of me. She was going to stay with her friend Laurita de los Ríos in the Spanish embassy during the first part of my trip.

The feeling at the meeting was wonderful. It was stimulating to see the enthusiasm of the mass in its excitement before the platform we were speaking from. The meetings in Ottawa and Quebec, though less important, were good, too, so we left for Montreal thinking the way was clear and people quite alert. But we were very much mistaken. In this big Canadian city the Catholics had moved heaven and earth to get our meeting called off and they succeeded. While we were there the Franciscan fathers wrote Father Sarasola a very kind letter inviting him up to the convent during his stay in town. This cordiality was contrary to the rumors circulating about his being an unfrocked priest. Of course, subsequent events showed these rumors were not true.

The morning after our arrival in the city the hotel porter came up to me and said I was wanted on the telephone. At the moment I was talking to a group of newspaper men, being "grilled" with queries on the "Spanish question." I was amazed to find how much misunderstanding there was even at that late date. I forgot the porter's message. "It is a long distance call, madame," he said reproachfully, coming back again and evidently thinking the delay was a terrible waste of good money. I hurried to the telephone booth. "Hello," I said, anxious to get back to my conference.

"Oh, hello !" answered a man's voice at the other end. "This is New York speaking. Is that Madame Palencia ?"

"Yes . . . yes . . . who is it ?"

"Oh, Madame Palencia, this is . . ." and he gave me the name of a well-known New York reporter. "Listen, I have a

most interesting piece of news for you." My mind instantly
flew over to Spain. An interesting piece of news to me at that
time could only refer . . . to the war . . . to the Spanish
cause. . .

"Most interesting," the voice repeated. My thoughts centred on Madrid. Could it be that they had succeeded ? But
no, impossible. . . Madrid could not fall. . . Perhaps, on the
contrary, *we* had succeeded. . .

"Well, what is it ?" I asked in an agony of suspense.

After what seemed an eternity the voice went on. "The
Spanish Official Gazette has just published your appointment
as Plenipotentiary Minister for Spain in Sweden."

"Oh ! Is that all ?" I answered, depression in every syllable.

"Why, yes . . . aren't you excited about it ? . . . Did you
know you were going to be appointed ?"

"Yes, of course."

"Have you anything to say about your mission ?"

"Nothing."

"Well, the news is in the papers but we thought perhaps you
would like to give us something more."

"No."

"Good-bye then, and congratulations to you."

"Thanks, good-bye."

I turned and rejoined Marcelino Domingo, Father Sarasola
and our interviewers and found them trying to understand one
another by means of an intricate system of combined English,
French and Spanish words which certainly did not work.

The press conference over, I went up to my room to rest
before getting ready for a luncheon given in honor of our
delegation by some distinguished members of the faculty of
McGill University. I sat down and thought over the tele-

phone message I had just received. So the order had been definitely given. . . "The news is in the papers," the New York reporter had said, as though that made it final.

That night we left Montreal and as the train thundered through the darkness my thoughts turned again toward home and I marveled at the curious turns and tricks that Destiny plays with nations as with individuals. Here was Spain, long forgotten by the world, suddenly in the front pages of all the papers, making the foreign departments of state and diplomatic circles shudder with apprehension and, at the same time, moving to their depths the hearts of all men loyal to democracy.

The train rushed on. The engine throbbed like a gigantic pulse. My thoughts reverted over and over again to the truth that we were trying to make people see and to the recurring torturing memories that neither time nor distance can ever efface, memories of mutilated bodies and devastated towns. Then, like wheels turning incessantly around in my mind, ran these words :

"What use justice ? What use right ? And, alas for me . . . what use diplomacy ?" And on the heels of these thoughts sprang up the idea that became almost an obsession : "Should I accept the appointment ? Was I qualified for such a job ?"

I knew enough about diplomacy to realize that my job would not be an easy one, that many factors would be at play to make it a failure. I probed into my conscience. Was I afraid of this for Spain or for myself ? In any case, there was no alternative but to obey and meanwhile to do my best to neutralize the effects of the rebel propaganda in America.

Our next stop was New York. The meeting in Madison Square Garden has left an unforgettable memory. It was held under the chairmanship of Dr. Harry F. Ward. The vast hall was filled to overflowing and, as I looked down on it, twenty to twenty-five thousand persons seemed to stretch out their hands to us offering support for our cause. Twenty-five thousand hearts beat in unison under the spell of the word Spain. When my speech was over, Roger Baldwin rose to ask for funds. It was not necessary to ask. The crowd was rushing up to the platform to give : silver, banknotes and pledges amounting in all to thirty thousand dollars. We had only requested help for the women and children but I am sure that in their hearts that audience believed the money should have been used for arms.

That very night we left for Canada again. I found myself being driven to the station in a car with three unknown persons, one of whom turned out to be a detective who could speak Spanish and who had evidently been told to look after me. I have wondered who my protectors were and of what they could have been afraid.

Our Canadian tour took us through the whole country from the east to the west. In some cities like Saskatoon, Edmonton and Port Arthur we just stopped a few hours for a meeting. Sometimes one day was full of engagements as in Winnipeg where I spoke at a breakfast given by the women's organizations, a luncheon offered by the mayor of the town, at a meeting held in the theatre at three o'clock in the afternoon, at a dinner given me by the Royal Institute of International Affairs, and at another meeting at night before boarding the train for another city.

The press in all these towns was friendly. As were our audiences, the reporters were impressed by the dramatic situation in Spain. News of the bombardments helped our task by provoking general indignation and bringing the problem home to people whose only idea of Spain before had been that of a country where people spent their time dancing to the music of guitars and the sound of castanets. A Spain invaded by foreign troops and unable to defend herself, thanks to the Non-Intervention Pact, was a tragic reality that no sensitive person could look upon with indifference. In every paper the legitimacy of the loyalist cause was constantly stressed.

Vancouver impressed me as a lovely city and Victoria, sedate and old-fashioned, soothed our strained nerves and gave us a much needed rest of twenty-four hours before our mad rush down the American western coast.

I can say I have been in Seattle but not that I have seen it for we only stopped long enough to hold our meeting ; the same thing can be said of Portland. San Francisco on the contrary has left a lasting impression on my mind, probably on account of the reminiscences of Spain that strike the eye as soon as one enters the city or its surroundings.

We arrived on a beautiful evening. Marcelino Domingo, who had been immersed in a book all day, suddenly caught hold of my arm and pointed to the view.

"Look, we are in Andalusia," he said. It was not quite Andalusia, but enough like my native land to give me a pang.

In San Francisco we were kept very busy. I was asked to speak at the Western Writers' Congress which was being held just then and where I had the pleasure of meeting Upton Sinclair, John Steinbeck, Humphrey Cobb, Dorothy Parker, Haakon Chevalier among many others. I was hailed as the representative of democratic Spain with thunderous applause and eager questions.

Thomas Mann had sent a message that was already a strong plea for awareness. "The humanist's tolerance," it said, "must end when the most sacred and dearly won values are to be defended against the encroachments of irresponsible brutality." If in that year 1936 his advice, as well as that of many others, had been followed, the world would not find itself in the plight it is in today.

Besides the great meeting held in the evening of our second day in San Francisco, we addressed several groups of Spaniards in our own language. It was a touching experience in moments like those.

In Los Angeles good friends of Spain – the movie stars – gave us a splendid welcome. I should have loved to loiter a little in the beautiful gardens of this city but I was obliged to fly to Denver just after the meeting for a lecture in Colorado University and another in the city of Denver. From Denver I flew to Florida and shall never forget the night meeting held in Tampa in the huge football field. As I spoke from a small raised platform and looked up at the stars in the dark velvety background of an almost tropical sky, I felt that I was back in my native land of Andalusia and very nearly broke down. That night seems to stand out more vividly than others in my memory. After the meeting I saw many friends, some of whom had come to Tampa for the Congress of the A. F. of L. which was in full swing and over which there was a good deal of excitement because of the difficulties with the C.I.O. which were being discussed just then.

I had been asked by the Spanish trade unions to represent them at the Tampa congress as a fraternal delegate and it had been suggested that I deliver their message to the conference, but the executives decided otherwise and the members of the A. F. of L. would have been prevented from hearing about their comrades in Spain who were laying down their lives to save democracy, if they had not gone to my lecture. Almost all of them went. Miss Mary Anderson, whom I had met in Geneva two years before, was in Tampa and gave a luncheon in my honor at which many of the women attending the congress

were present. That night I asked for a long distance call to
Riga. Sherwood Anderson and his wife and some other
friends waited up with me until it was time for my call. It was
not put through till about four o'clock in the morning. I hate
talking over the telephone and much more when it is a long
distance call, but that day I was greatly comforted to hear
Cefe's familiar, "Nena, Nena . . ." finding its way over those
thousands of miles and Cefito's eager, "Mother, when are you
coming back?" I knew what this meant. My boy was anxious to return to Spain. I realized suddenly that I had not
been thinking about them. During all of my trip I had been
but vaguely conscious of anything except our cause. Like a
straw driven by a mighty current I had gone from one place
to another, bending under the will of something stronger than
myself ; never for a moment feeling physically tired, although
the strain on one's strength was enormous. Besides, it would
have been difficult for me to picture Cefe and my son in the
unfamiliar background of Latvia.

The first time I was brought sharply back into the orbit of
our private life was when the news of my brother Ricardo's
death was passed on to me by Anita over the telephone. He
had been helping our people in Malaga. He had been carrying food to the men at the front when an attack of pneumonia
brought his life to a sudden end. I felt his death terribly.
Ricardo had been brother and pal in one. During the reactionary movement in 1934 he had been put in jail, accused of the
terrible crime of giving the peasants who passed through his
little farm money and food when they were in need. The
experience had not daunted him, on the contrary he had continued to be a staunch republican. I little dreamt a day would
come when I would feel glad that he had been taken from us.
Three months after his death Malaga fell into the hands of the

rebels. If Ricardo had been alive he would have most assuredly been shot by them. At least we were all spared that tragedy, but for several days I found it hard to meet my audience. However, I kept on. Was not everyone in Spain keeping on, too ?

From Florida we went to the Middle West. In St. Louis I was presented with a photograph of myself in Spanish costume which someone had taken eight years before when I gave a lecture on Spanish art in the art gallery of that city. In Wisconsin we were met at the station by a group of Swedish women who, having heard of my appointment to their country, gave me a bouquet tied with the Swedish and Spanish colors and welcomed me in their native tongue. In Chicago where I had not been since Jane Addams' death, we were also given a fine reception. At the meeting that night huge baskets of food for the Spanish children were brought up to the platform, together with substantial checks. In Boston the meeting held at the Symphonic Hall was one of the most impressive.

Certainly we could not harbor any doubt that in the United States Spain had many friends of all classes of society from distinguished men and women of letters and science, university professors and leaders of religious thought, down to the lowly, unknown worker who, when the time came for giving, was often among the most generous. It sometimes hurt me to see women taking off their only jewel, a little gold wedding ring, to give to Spain. Cents and dollars hoarded carefully for a Christmas tree would go the same way but the children of our country needed the gold and the cents even more than the generous donors. Negroes in all the towns in which we spoke were well to the front in their desire to give.

In Washington, which was the last place on our itinerary, we could stay only one day, in the course of which I had the honor of being received by Mrs. Franklin Delano Roosevelt who was anxious to hear about the Spanish children and who was most sympathetic.

From the White House I was taken to a party given by the Society of Women Geographers of which I am a member and that night spoke, for the last time in that tour.

On the fifteenth of December, and again sailing on the *Queen Mary*, we finally left New York for Europe. We got a hearty send-off by many friends and by A. A. Macleod, secretary to the Canadian committee, whose understanding and careful piloting had greatly contributed to the success of our tour.

As the British liner sailed majestically down the New York harbor and I looked at the unique background formed by the towering skyscrapers which, from the distance, gave the impression of being the spires of some gigantic cathedral, I braced myself for the new task before me.

The past weeks had shown that abroad Spain had only just begun to cover the great distance between incomprehension, fear, distrust and full understanding, that millions of people all the world over still ignored the chief facts of the struggle our country was engaged in, that a persistent and ingenious propaganda had led many to believe the Spanish conflict, the revolt, was an effort to put down "communism." On the other hand, I had also been able to see the other side of the picture, to perceive the wonderful enveloping feeling of universal brotherhood in the warm clasp of hands ready to give or to fight for Spain, in the sight of tears shed for Spain. It would not be long before we would realize that the "Spanish question" as our cause was usually called, was one on which with rare unanimity the people of the whole world would take a stand that was in open opposition to their governments. People, like children, have an ingrained sense of justice and they were not slow in finding out that Spain was the victim of one of the most flagrant cases of injustice that we have ever been called upon to witness. The injustice of being deprived of her rights to obtain means for her defense, the injustice of being bound hand and foot while her enemies were allowed freedom of action to destroy her.

In the United States the great majority of the people wanted the arms embargo to be lifted. In France, in Great Britain, in Belgium and Holland and the Scandinavian countries, the people were against the Non-Intervention Pact set up by their governments. The torrents of gifts of food and cash and medical supplies that poured into Spain during the war were not only the expression of a feeling of compassion for human suffering, they were also an outlet for the troubled conscience of the world — a reparation of the sins of omission against democracy, the democracy that Spain was dying to uphold and to defend. The International Brigades themselves, what were they but a protest against official indifference and a desire to show that men of over fifty countries were with Spain and loyal until death ?

CHAPTER XVI

Both Marissa and I were sick on the trip home. The weather was very rough and our tour had not been exactly a health-building feat. I had spoken in forty-two cities in fifty-three days. Quite a record, but a happy one, for large crowds had been awakened to the sufferings of Spain and over two hundred thousand dollars, they told me, had been collected for our people.

Paris was surrounded by a sticky fog when we reached it a whole day late, due to the terrific gales we encountered in crossing. Instructions from the government were waiting for me at the Spanish embassy. I had been asked to go over to London to speak, at least once, on my way to Sweden, but my orders were to go straight to Stockholm. This meant giving up our visit to Madrid. Marissa was naturally very disappointed. She had not heard from Germán Somolinos, her fiancé, for several weeks, and was sure something must have happened to him. A fear that turned out to be justified for we afterward learned that he had been severely wounded in one of the bombardments of Madrid.

I barely had time to get my papers together and indulge in the choosing of two new frocks, a doubtful pleasure since I was worn out and there was the drawn-out process of "trying on" to go through, before we had to set off again.

There were many reasons for my reaching Stockholm as soon as possible. First and foremost, the fact that Señor Fiscowich y Gullón, who had been my predecessor in Sweden until the rebellion broke out, had taken possession of the Spanish legation building, which is the property of the Spanish government, and had announced his intention of remaining on the field until Franco won the war.

The curious thing was that Señor Fiscowich had at first made a statement declaring his loyalty toward the republican government, whereupon he had been granted the desire of his heart, that of being appointed ambassador to Berlin. He had, thereupon, resigned from his post in Stockholm and left for Germany. It is difficult to know exactly what happened there. It seems probable that, since his wife was German and a member of the Zeppelin family, some kind friend or relative advised him of Germany's intention to intervene in Spain on Franco's side and counseled him to transfer his allegiance to the rebel general who, with the aid of Hitler, would be sure to win in the end. A change of front became imperative. Señor Fiscowich resigned once more, openly announced himself a fervent partisan of the rebel *generalísimo*. The Spanish residents in Stockholm, having been thereby placed in a most awkward position, had requested the Minister of Foreign Affairs to send his legal representative over as soon as possible. This was the reason for my hurried departure from Paris.

On December the twenty-fourth I left for Brussels where I was to get more instructions and found that I would have to remain there over Christmas Day because the plane service to Sweden was not running. It was impossible for us to go overland by Germany, for Hitler had by then recognized Franco and we could not get the necessary visas. Besides, the plan was not tempting. I was not sorry for the short delay. My two sisters, Maria and Inez, were at the time in the convent of their order near Liége, and we were able to have a glimpse of them. I had not seen Maria for eight years and wondered what she thought about our war. I was not left long in doubt. The moment she saw Marissa and me appear, she broke into lamentations over the sins of the republican government. Inez, I could see, was not of the same opinion but then, she had only just entered the convent and knew much more about the situation. In any case, she would never have condemned what I approved of. On the whole, it was a sad meeting and yet I was glad we had gone. We had renewed the family bonds and in time, I felt sure, Maria would be brought to see things differently.

Early the next morning Marissa and I left Brussels for Amsterdam where we were assured we could get a direct plane for Copenhagen and Malmö. We had been carefully instructed not to take the airship between Brussels and Copenhagen because it had to make a stop at Hamburg and we would have run the risk of being arrested by the German police and of being sent back to Franco. Several Spaniards had suffered that fate and, of course, it meant death. So Marissa and I carefully selected a plane in the Amsterdam airport bound for a non-stop flight to Denmark.

There seemed to be no passengers that day except ourselves and a group of young pilots in uniform who boarded the airship just as we were leaving. I settled down in my seat, hoping as I always did that I would not be sick. The attendant handed me a map and I laid it out carefully on my knees. We had to fly over Germany for a while and I wanted to know when this would happen.

As a matter of fact, it was impossible to see anything for we were skimming over great masses of milky clouds and land was invisible. Time passed, I had finished reading my papers when suddenly it seemed to me that we had begun to descend. A slight lurch and the plane began to lean heavily to one side as it always does when it is going to land. I looked out of the window. One could see trees and houses just under us. My ears were throbbing. Almost immediately we touched the ground with the usual thump and began moving smoothly. Where could we be ? It was much too early for us to have

reached Copenhagen and there was no other stop on our schedule. Fear suddenly gripped my heart. I looked at Marissa
and saw my own doubts reflected on her face.

Had there been an accident ? Some mishap to the engine ?
A sudden running out of fuel ? Could we possibly have made
a mistake and boarded the airship going to Hamburg ? Few
times in my life has my brain worked at such lightning speed.
Nothing could be seen from the window now except patches
of dry grass with a light covering of snow.

The young pilots began to take their coats down from the
rack. They were laughing and talking among themselves but
the noise of the engine prevented my hearing what language
they spoke.

The plane was running very smoothly now so we must be
at an airport and they evidently had the intention of getting
off there. We slowed down. I looked out and to my horror
saw there was a number of other planes all around bearing the
swastika. In the distance one could see the station house decorated with the same sinister insignia. I looked at Marissa
again. She was very pale but bravely tried to smile. I could
see that the same thought about each other was running through
our minds : "What will become of her ? What will they do
to her ?"

The plane stopped. The pilots jumped down. I turned to
Marissa again. "If anyone comes and speaks to you," I said,
"make believe you are not with me." I knew that were the
German authorities to question us and discover our relation-
ship, it would increase the dangers of her position enormously.
"If they tell you to get down from the plane, just make signs
that you do not understand . . . speak in French," I hurriedly
whispered. Then, anxious to make her mind more easy, I said,
"This is a Dutch plane. They have no earthly right to touch

us if we don't get off." I saw a little skeptical smile lurking in the corners of her closed mouth. Right? Whoever thought of such a thing as that now?

Marissa was not my only anxiety. I was carrying important papers with me that must not fall into the hands of our enemies. I tried to think of some way by which I could, if necessary, destroy them. By one of those absurd back somersaults in which one's mind indulges in moments of stress, I remembered the days of my childhood in the convent and the way my friend Maria Luisa had there disposed of her letters. But I could not swallow those papers, they were much too bulky.

I heard someone walking up the plane behind us. Was it the police? I held my breath. No, it was our own pilot. He passed us slowly and walked into the cabin. The door of the ship banged. The second pilot came in and took his place beside the other one. The motor hummed and we began to move, to glide, to rise. Soon we were soaring high up beyond the clouds and beyond all danger.

A sob of relief caught my throat. Marissa leant forward and pressed my shoulder with her small gloved hand. She is the tiniest of creatures, like a little girl. . . When I had gained control of myself again I turned and looked at her. She was gazing out at the great empty space. Evidently she had forgotten the incident ; her thoughts were in Spain. . . After a time I, too, ceased to think of the swastika, to wonder why we had come down on German soil. Probably it was just to allow the young aviators, who were evidently Germans, to get to their post after the Christmas holiday.

We reached Copenhagen on schedule time. It was already dark and the town seemed to stretch out indefinitely under the plane, its many lights twinkling a cheerful welcome.

A short halt there, then a flight of just fifteen minutes and we were in Malmö, our first stopping place in Sweden. The airship swooped down to what was to be its nest for the night and we got off a little dazed, as one usually is after a long trip through the clouds, but happy to have reached the end of our journey, at least the part by air. I had not informed the Spanish vice-consul at Malmö of our arrival so there was no one at the airport to meet us. However, the courtesy of the customs and passport officials was such that we did not require any assistance.

As we went toward the car which was to take us into town, Marissa held my arm and looked up into my face with a smile. I felt it was good to have someone so dear close to me at such a moment. The future was as impenetrable as the dark northern night which enfolded us. Would Sweden be friendly or hostile ? So far, she had shown great sympathy toward Spain's sufferings. She had not hesitated to accept the new republican minister and had sent her agreement to my appointment at once. The socialist party was strongly represented in the coalition government that was then in office, and who could be more in duty bound to be our friends ? But Spain had had many disappointments. My thoughts were dispelled by the noise and light of the streets near the railway station where the car was to leave us. A nice clean-looking porter took charge of us and our luggage. He found someone who could speak English, helped us with our tickets and showed us where we could send off some cables.

The train for Stockholm was not due to leave until about eleven o'clock so, after telephoning to the Spanish commercial attaché there that we would be in Stockholm early next morning, Marissa and I went to the dining room in the station to have some supper.

It was our first experience of Swedish customs. In the centre of the room the famous *smörgåsbord*, laden with delicacies of all kinds, tempted the hungry diner to partake of its rich collection of dishes : stuffed pig's head ; roast fowl ; cold meat ; pies of every description ; omelet ; salted, smoked and cooked fish ; potato, Russian and vegetable salad. There were plates of the famous Swedish "hard bread," both brown and white, butter, cheese and ever so much more food, impossible to remember.

The table was ornamented with glittering ribbons of gold and silver tinsel and bright-colored candles to show that it was Christmas. Little Swedish flags were placed on most of the dishes.

People came up to the table, picked up a plate and a fork and knife, helped themselves to whatever took their fancy and retired to one of the little side tables to eat in peace. Marissa and I did likewise. The food was good, so was the warmth and comfort of the room and its gay decorations, but they brought into sharp relief the memory of our men and women for whom Christmas that year would be just an empty word, and the message, "Goodwill to all men," a cruel sarcasm. People came and went and spoke to each other in soft voices in a language we could not understand, though we seemed to be able to catch a word here and there. It was my first experience with the Swedish language, a tantalizing one for those who can speak English and German, and who are apt at first to think that they can easily follow the conversation but who suddenly realize they are quite at sea.

Some time before the train was due to start, Marissa and I thought we should try and settle down. We were directed to a huge man, with the benevolent expression that big men often have, who was just standing around. He was dressed in a fine uniform and wore a steel badge on his chest to indicate that he was the general source of information for all travelers.

He could speak English so we explained what we wanted and, with a protecting gesture, he escorted us to our train which was made up and ready, and left us to the man in charge of our carriage, who was also big and stout, but spoke only Swedish. The cleanliness of the trains in Sweden is proverbial and we observed the very small difference there was between first, second and third class. As a matter of fact, there is just one class. People going "first" have only one berth in their compartment, those traveling "second" have two, and those in the "third" class have to press a little closer to allow space for three berths : a lower and two upper. Otherwise all the compartments are exactly alike and are fitted into the same carriages.

The silence about the train was intense. We had seen deep snow on the streets when driving from the airport to the station and thought it the reason for the utter lack of noise. I had still to learn what winter in the north can be. My recent experiences of cold weather in the United States and Canada had been rapidly and confusedly acquired. In Sweden I was going to know what it felt like to be in a land literally smothered in a soft white fleecy shroud for months at a time.

During the night I tried to see something of the country as we tore through it, but it was too dark. Marissa was sleeping peacefully in her compartment next to mine. We had opened the door between us so as to be together. At times the train would stop for just a little, but only muffled sounds filtered through to my ears. Daylight found me still awake. I thought we must be quite near Stockholm. At last I was able to see a little of the landscape : miles and miles of white land, towering fir trees and an occasional little wooden house painted bright red, no large villages nor towns.

A rap at our door startled me out of my contemplation. It was followed by a stentorian voice. I opened the door and found a stout man bearing cups of steaming coffee.

"*Goddag, goddag, goddag,*" he said, beaming and bowing in the approved Swedish fashion after each "good day."

We were just finishing the generous portions he had served us when the train began to follow a decided curve. Houses appeared on either side of us. We were going through streets, over bridges, and in a few minutes we stopped. A little group of Spaniards rushed up to meet us. It seemed strange to be addressed in my own language by men enveloped in fur-lined caps and coats, more like arctic explorers than people from the "sunny south." They were Señor Ugarte, newly appointed commercial attaché ; the secretary of this department and the translator of the Spanish legation, Ernesto Dethorey — a Spaniard who has lived for many years in Sweden and is married to a charming Swedish girl — also the son of the Mexican minister to Sweden who had very kindly sent his car and chauffeur to meet me. I felt as though a ray of warm light had enveloped us.

Over the telephone the night before I had warned Ugarte not to inform anyone of my arrival ; I wanted to gain time and find out exactly how matters stood before the press began asking questions about the legation and its actual occupants. He and Dethorey gave me a short outline of the latest events and of the general expectation.

As we drove up to the Grand Hotel where I had decided to stay until we had freed the legation from the intruders, I was told that, in spite of our precautions, reporters of the Stockholm papers had found out that I was due to arrive that day or the next and had been calling up Ernesto Dethorey the evening before to try and find out when we would be in Stockholm. Although Dethorey had been guarded in his answer, he believed they would be arriving at the hotel at any moment.

The occupation of the legation by the rebel Señor Fiscowich and his declarations in favor of Franco had naturally given rise to a great deal of talk. It appeared that everyone was wondering what I would do to get the legation back. How long would Señor Fiscowich, who it seemed had no intention of leaving peacefully, be able to hold out ? What measures would the Swedish government be ready to take ? All these questions and ever so many more. The situation was of course a joy for keen reporters to handle. Whole columns would be filled and the slightest indiscretion on anyone's part would certainly be most welcome, for the Swedish press, with but few exceptions, delights in sensation more than any other European press I know.

We could, therefore, be sure that, until the unusual situation in which I found myself was definitely solved — that is, until I managed to eject Señor Fiscowich from the legation — my every movement, my every word and every gesture would be carefully watched, reported on and discussed. On the part of the Swedish government, of course, there was nothing to fear. The very promptitude with which they had accepted my appointment was proof that they intended giving full support to the legal government of Spain and its representative for the time being. During the afternoon, call after call from all the Stockholm papers showed that our arrival had been discovered but it was arranged that I should hold a press conference the next day and everyone seemed satisfied to wait.

Meanwhile, although it was a Sunday and many people were as usual out of town for the day, sympathizers with the Spanish cause hastened to welcome us. Dear Sonja Branting and her brother Georg were among the first to greet me. The son and daughter of Hjalmar Branting, the great Swedish statesman — champion of every humanitarian cause and one of the finest leaders the Europe of his time could boast of — would not have failed Spain at such a time. Soon my rooms were turned into a garden. A beautiful azalea and a note from Madame Kollontay were there to bid me welcome. The Russian minister to Sweden was out of town but her cordial mes-

sage showed she had thought of us.   A lovely bouquet from
Doctor Pérez Gil, the Mexican minister, had been sent with the
car.   Many other and beautiful blossoms were brought by
people I did not know.   They were simply presented as gifts
from "friends of Spain" and gave me a foretaste of what Sweden felt for us, making me forget, for a little while at least, the
strangeness and the cold outside.

For some time after everyone had left I remained thinking
over the situation with which I was confronted, thanks to
Fiscowich's sudden admiration for the little general who wanted
to be Spain's Mussolini or Hitler and who in his own opinion
was both.   It is amazing how people are able to throw beliefs
and prejudices overboard when something material is to be
gained by it.   I began to think out some plan for the ejection
of my predecessor from his point of vantage.   It was best to
move cautiously but with determination.   In spite of the
"realistic" doctrines that are so much in vogue today, to know
one is right is still the best of backings.   It may fail for a little
but it is the strongest of incentives to keep on going and in the
long run it wins.   What else was making the Spanish people
hold out as they were doing ?   What was turning plain men
and women into heroes ?   What was making them all so superior to others ?

At this point I could not help smiling over the last scene in
which I had taken part on the great stage of the League of Nations just three months before.   For some time one of Spain's
best-known artists, José Maria Sert, had been painting some
murals in the council chamber of the new building of the league.
They were to be the gift of the Spanish government to the
Geneva institution.   In the past month of September, Sert's
work being finished, it was decided that the Spanish delegate
would make the solemn presentation of its gift to the council

on the evening of one of the last days of the assembly. The delegations of all the other countries were asked to the simple ceremony. Everybody who has seen the paintings considers them one of the finest contributions offered to the league.

I sat looking at the powerful masterpiece while Señor Osorio y Gallardo, who was head of our group, made a short speech. It was followed by a concert from Manuel de Falla's works and then we all sallied out to the big hall near by. I had found it hard to keep my equanimity before the calm indifference of the members of the league to our tragedy, and when, later on in the evening, the delegate of a great European power came up to speak to me and remarked on my paleness, asking if I was tired, I almost jumped down his throat.

"Tired? Not a bit. Do you know how I feel?" I turned round to include the other delegates who had joined our group. "I feel more proud than I have ever been before, proud of the enormous superiority of the Spanish people. Here we are in the League of Nations in which we say we lay such faith. Well, such an organization for world peace was first thought of by the Dominican friar, Francisco de Vitória from Salamanca. Its *sanctum sanctorum* — the chamber of the council — has been embellished by a Spaniard and its principles are being defended, at the cost of their lives, by Spaniards, while all the other countries just look on and wait. . . Don't you think I have every reason to feel proud?"

With polite bows and a mumbled, "Of course, of course," they melted away, and like Spain I remained alone on the field.

Now I must brace myself for what I had on hand. So far I seemed to have done very little. Yet the urge to help was very strong. That night I again asked myself whether it would not have been better to remain in Spain or even in America. Governments in democratic countries are supposed not to move unless they are propelled by the will of the people. And the people must first know what they want. In the United States I had been able to get to the hearts of thousands and their interest in Spain had been awakened. But in cold diplomatic spheres there would be no chance for this. Already I was beginning to feel irked, tied down. The roundabout way has never been pleasing to me. Besides, I hate all the paraphernalia surrounding such posts ; the restraint and the make-believe. The latter is not necessary, of course. Silence can be substituted, the long deep silence in which the soul at least is free.

The clock struck eleven. It was the hour in which I was accustomed to get the latest news about Spain. I looked around. There was no wireless set in the room. Perhaps the hotel management . . . No, they were extremely sorry but had none to offer me. I wished I had not sent Dethorey away. He might have had some suggestion to make. We should have to order a wireless set the first thing in the morning. I opened my window and looked out. It was bitterly cold. "Stockholm . . . this is Stockholm . . ." I found myself repeating, "the setting of the new life that has begun for me. . ."

The lights from the hotel entrance spread a soft brilliance over the snow-covered pavement. A little further away high lampposts shed their rays over the boats that winter had kept icebound in the waters of the Mälar. On the other side of the canal two large buildings rose up into the darkness. They had been pointed out to me on the way to the Grand Hotel that morning. The one on my left was the Royal Palace, an imposing edifice, elegant in spite of its size. Seen in profile from my point of vision, there was nothing to hide its pure sweeping lines as they emerged almost from the water's edge. A little more to my right was the other building, a grandiose pile, heavily ornamented according to the German taste. This is the Riksdag, the home of the First and Second Chambers which constitute the Swedish Parliament. The life of Sweden, the future of Sweden, the well-being of Sweden are under the care and the control of those institutions.

A great quietness prevailed. . . Was it the peaceful muteness of the Sabbath, the quietude of sleep, or the impossibility of action ? Were all the inhabitants of Stockholm icebound like those boats in the calm white canal spreading out almost to my feet ? A queer feeling of inertia began to enfold me, too. It must be pretty late. . .

I closed the window in order to shut out the oppressive stillness and entered our bedroom. Marissa was sitting up in bed reading quietly. The light from one of the lamps fell on the evening papers which someone had left on my table. Big headlines again. . .

Madrid Minister härmed Dotter *

Minister Palencia har anlänt till Stockholm †

Spaniens nya Stockholmsminister,‡ and so on and on.

Then, there on the same front page, was the sharp reminder which again sent the blood pounding through my veins :

Spanska kriget, the Spanish war !

Suddenly the telephone rang, a sharp penetrating ring that startled us both. A voice at the other end said something I did not understand and then the word "Riga." It was Cefe ! Cefe and Cefito both wishing to speak at the same time, both asking how we were, both giving me the latest news about the war and telling me finally that they would be in Stockholm the next week. Cefe had been given leave to come to see us and Cefito would be on his way back to Spain.

* The Madrid Minister is here with her daughter
† Minister Palencia has arrived in Stockholm
‡ Spain's new Minister in Stockholm

CHAPTER XVII

"I hope that our inquisitive press has not been annoying you too much." These were the first words that His Excellency Rickard Sandler, Swedish Minister of Foreign Affairs, addressed to me after most cordially and kindly bidding me welcome to his native land.

"Oh, I manage to defend myself," I answered laughing, "although I have discovered that there is a car full of reporters on constant watch at the door of the hotel and that it follows me wherever I go." I did not say that evidently those reporters were laboring under the delusion that I was going to force an entrance into the legation.

"Well, we must not allow them to bother you," he answered with his ready smile, "but you are an object of great interest at this moment and they are naturally anxious to inform their readers."

Certainly the write-up on the press conference I had held the day before was voluminous. Before leaving the hotel I had seen columns of it, all headed by the words :

"Spain is fighting an invasion, not a civil war, says Madame Palencia !" An invasion, yes, of course . . . that *is* what Spain is up against.

We talked at length on the Spanish situation. The Non-Intervention Pact — into which Sweden, like other neutral countries, had been inveigled under the pretense that it would keep Europe out of war — was our chief topic. Sweden is one of the seven countries that were chosen for the permanent commission or subcommittee, a sorry distinction. Minister Sandler tentatively referred to the Spanish Government's evident disapproval of the pact.

"Naturally my government cannot approve of being deprived of its rights and, with them, of all possibility of obtaining arms for its defense," I answered. "But that is not the only reason for its rejection of the intervention arrangement, were it at least efficacious and fair. What the government fears — and everything points that way — is that the insurgents will go on receiving all and more than they want, and that the constitutional and legal government of the country will receive no parity. No one in all Spain doubts that it will favor our enemies."

Minister Sandler did not answer.

"In any case," I added, "investigations as to violations of the pact could be much more thorough." Then as a sudden thought struck me, "It would be a good idea to choose Palma de Mallorca for the permanent seat of the Committee of Non-Intervention. All movements in the Mediterranean could then be controlled from the Balearic Islands. They would make excellent observation posts. Don't you think so ?" I inquired ; and then I said with not a little malice, "I am sure the Spanish Government would not object to Menorca being used for that purpose."

"Ah, Menorca . . . yes," he replied with conviction. Then closing his eyes he kept a guarded silence. Much as he should like to, perhaps he could not give the same assurance in the case of Mallorca, for through Franco's courtesy it had been occupied by Count Rossi, in the name of Italy, three months before, although Mussolini still insisted that he had nothing to do in the Spanish affair.

I realized how difficult it must have been for Minister Sandler as well as for other members of the Swedish cabinet, to have had to accept the Non-Intervention Pact, which put the Spanish people in such a disadvantageous position in her struggle against the totalitarian powers. They undoubtedly had to give in to British pressure, but it is one of those cases in which loyalty to principle would have been the best policy in the end. The Swedish nation naturally wanted to keep out of the war with which Great Britain had made them believe all Europe would be menaced if her advice was not followed. One of the disadvantages of prosperity is that it makes people afraid, and Sweden was naturally unwilling to lose the fruits of many hard-earned battles in the social field, in a world catastrophe. Besides, the Mediterranean is so very much outside the orbit of Swedish interests, that she — like many others, including her sister and neighbor, Norway — was led astray from the path of democratic duty. It was easier to accept German and Italian statements than to annoy Great Britain when she declared that she had no official confirmation of the landing of German and Italian troops and armaments and of the thousand violations of the pact that all the other countries were observing so faithfully.

I am sure Minister Sandler never doubted that Italy would derive every possible benefit from her position in the Island of Mallorca, while hoping with his whole heart that the Spanish tragedy would not end in a victory for Franco. He was too clear-sighted not to be fully conscious that the Spanish war was the first act of aggression, just as Ethiopia had been the prelude to the tragic farce in which Austria and Czechoslovakia were so soon to play a role, for of course the destruction of democracy in Spain meant a big advance to the dictators, but she accepted the Non-Intervention Pact in spite of it.

Another stratagem in which Sweden had become involved against her own better judgment was that of harboring rebels in her legation at Madrid. As in many other cases this was done in the absence and without the permission of the heads of mission, but it does not alter the fact that part of the army of spies and Fascists that was threatening the life of Madrid was under the protection of the Swedish flag. This departure from the usual diplomatic relations is typical of the new methods employed in modern war.

The republican government would have overlooked foreign representatives giving refuge to leaders of a subversive movement who were in danger of losing their lives, within the limits set by tradition, but it could not possibly ignore the indiscriminate harboring of spies and armed men ready at any moment to join Franco's besieging forces. And with the exception of Great Britain and the United States there was not a single embassy or legation in the Spanish capital that did not prejudice the legitimate interests of the republic in this way. There were foreign missions even that leased large numbers of apartments as annexes and filled them with rebels. Underlings of those missions often made a thriving business out of it, charging high prices for the up-keep of their guests. It is to the credit of republican Spain that the matter was treated in a highly humanitarian spirit, and to the discredit of some governments that, when they were allowed to take their protégés out on parole, they helped those in their charge to betray their word.

Minister Sandler and I also talked about the situation in the Spanish legation. His excellency assured me that my rights would be upheld, and I responded by assuring him that the wish of my government was that the question be settled as harmoniously as possible. We agreed that the first steps for the evacuation of the legation which was the property of the Spanish government should be taken by the Ministry of Foreign Affairs. The undersecretary, who was a personal friend of Señor Fiscowich, volunteered to speak to the rebel diplomat.

I had met Rickard Sandler before that morning, at a League Assembly in Geneva. His excellency is a distinguished member of the Swedish social democratic party, the translator of Karl Marx's famous work *Das Kapital*. He has always been one of the few really active men who have represented their

country at the League of Nations.   It is true that Sweden, like
the other Scandinavian countries and Spain and Czechoslovakia
— Beneš will always be remembered in that connection — believed in the Geneva institution and helped it with a fine spirit
of co-operation and good-will.   Outwardly, Rickard Sandler
had changed but little since I first met him, but I was looking
at him from a different point of view now.   Within the Geneva
precincts, in spite of his boundless admiration for Mr. Anthony
Eden, Spain and Sweden had as a rule agreed on most subjects.
Here in Stockholm it might be different, not from an idealistic
point of view — Sweden claimed to be a democratic country —
but because of the more sweeping forces of material interests,
and these certainly were not in favor of the Spain I represented.
Rather one should say that the governments of other nations,
especially the government of Great Britain, had not realized or
had not wished to realize that those interests would have been
better protected in a Spain free from German and Italian intervention.   But it had not been so, and now Sweden with all the
other Genevites was being dragged into the fatal cataclysm
initiated and led up to by the big European powers that had
simulated an interest in peace.

Small, alert, and extremely courteous, his excellency is in
the habit of suddenly retiring within himself in the middle of
a conversation, as though pondering over his own words, lest
his very politeness should have led him too far.   I have heard
some foreign representatives say that Rickard Sandler is the
Minister of Foreign Affairs they have found it most difficult to
deal with, just because he is so urbane.   Whatever incentive
to good behavior this might be it was not, of course, meant as
a reflection on anybody else's conduct in particular.   We exchanged a few more cordial greetings before I left the minister's
study and passed out through the ante-chamber where other
foreign colleagues were waiting to see his excellency.

My coat was laid over my shoulders, with intense respect, by the same tall, thin individual who had relieved me of it before, and escorted by an official of the foreign department I went up to call on that most exquisite Foreign Affairs Chief of Protocol, Baron Barnekow. He seemed very stately and beautifully groomed as he graciously asked me to sit down after taking charge of the copy of my credentials as Spanish Envoy Extraordinary and Minister Plenipotentiary to Sweden. He then undertook to explain the intricate rules of etiquette by which the Swedish court is governed.

As everyone knows there are general rules which cover most aspects of world diplomacy, but each country has its own little peculiarities besides, and the chiefs of protocol of all Foreign Departments are responsible for their strict fulfilment.

The press, since my arrival two days before, had been asking when I should be called upon to present my credentials to His Majesty, King Gustav V of Sweden. His majesty was at the time out of Stockholm, having spent Christmas, as in other years, in the beautiful royal residence of Drottningholm, so it was believed a good many days would elapse before the ceremony took place. However, Baron Barnekow, without mentioning the exact date, insinuated that it was near at hand by presenting me with a list of official engagements for the immediate future, all of which must be preceded by the all important observance.

"On the fifth of January there is a dinner offered to the diplomatic corps by His Excellency the Minister of Foreign Affairs in his residence," he said.

Then, after consulting some papers, he announced, "On the eleventh, the solemn opening of the Parliamentary Sessions, which will take place as usual in the Royal Palace. On the fifteenth of January, the dinner offered by His Majesty the King to the diplomats accredited to the Court of Sweden. The formal invitation for all these functions will be sent at once to your excellency."

"And now, Madame Palencia," he added with a courtly bow, "I should like to give you a few suggestions regarding the ceremonial that is customary in Sweden for the presentation of credentials to his majesty. Notice of the day and hour will be sent to you very shortly, but there are a few particulars connected with this. . ."

Baron Barnekow looked at me with an apologetic smile, then coughed discreetly.

"Other particulars?" I repeated to myself. "He must mean the costume I should wear for the ceremony." I could not help feeling amused when I remembered a story told me in this connection about Madame Kollontay, Minister for the Soviet Republic in Sweden, who was, I believe, the first woman in the world ever to be charged with such a mission.

It was said that on her arrival in Stockholm nine or ten years ago, during her first interview with Baron Barnekow, the chief of protocol, whose duty, among others, is to advise the new foreign representatives what they should wear for the different palace ceremonies, had been rather perplexed as to the kind of dress he ought to recommend to a lady. Men diplomats often wear uniforms and in the case of representatives of countries with a republican régime, the evening suit is *de rigueur*. But a woman? Madame Kollontay had set Baron Barnekow's mind at ease by suggesting that she had thought of wearing a plain black dress. The chief of protocol thought this was quite appropriate.

"And I shall also wear a little hat," the Soviet minister had added confidently. But this addition to her costume had quite upset Baron Barnekow, who was not at all sure that a hat would be the right thing.

However, after discussing the matter at length, and taking

into consideration that the function was to take place about midday and that it might be a windy morning and her hair become disordered, Madame Kollontay won the day.

Instinctively I had thought of wearing the same sort of thing.

Baron Barnekow looked at me again and turned the papers he was holding over and over again in his hands. I hastened to relieve his anxiety by saying, "I do not know if there is any special custom regarding what a woman should wear at a ceremony of this kind, but I had thought that a long and simple black dress and a small hat or toque would be proper."

The chief of protocol beamed on me. "Perfect . . . perfect," he answered, evidently much reassured.

We went on to discuss other details. I heard with relief that in Sweden there is no exchange of those usually empty and noncommittal speeches which are common between the heads of state and new foreign representatives on occasions like these.

Then I was told that the ceremony would take place at midday and that *Monsieur l'Introducteur* would be at the hotel in order to escort me to the Royal Palace in good time. Finally I was presented with a list of the persons on whom I was supposed to call on the day of the presentation or soon after as in the case of members of the royal family and the speakers of the Swedish parliament. This interview ended, I had a short talk with Minister Christian Günther, Under-secretary of Foreign Affairs, on the subject of the Spanish legation. Herr Günther, an affable and highly intellectual gentleman, told me that he had been informed, and part of the press had echoed this rumor, that Madame Alfonso Fiscowich had not yet quite recovered from a recent serious illness.

"If that is the case," I interrupted, "they must not think of moving her until she is completely out of danger. I am not in a hurry to occupy the residential part of the legation, but I insist that I must have immediate access to the chancellery, and that all the papers and ciphers and other material be handed over to me without loss of time. Apart from this, Madame Fiscowich can take all the time she needs to leave the house."

"I am sure that your courteous consideration for Madame Fiscowich will be appreciated," said Minister Günther.

Our conversation ended, I crossed the ante-chamber again and found Dethorey waiting for me.

"A large crowd has assembled in the street in order to get a glimpse of you," he said, "and the reporters with their cameras are waiting for you to leave."

Considering that several snapshots had already been taken that morning, one of them while I was having breakfast in the hotel dining room, I could not help but feel a little bit impatient.

"Perhaps it would be better to wait . . ." he began. But his words were cut short by his excellency himself who, coming forward, said graciously, "Oh, Madame Palencia, you really must not be bothered any more, today at least. Would you like to use my own staircase ? Then you can leave the ministry unobserved."

"I think I should, for I really am in a hurry, and would not like to be detained," I replied.

Two minutes later, accompanied by Dethorey, I left the ministry. As the car went rapidly round the corner, I caught sight of a large group of people surrounding Minister Sandler, who had evidently left by the door I should have used. His excellency was smiling blandly and seemed quite satisfied to think we had outwitted them.

As I entered the hotel I was struck by the thought that events were changing fast. In a few days now I should have to set myself seriously to the new task before me. The Non-Intervention Pact had barred all possibility of my buying arms for Spain, even those required to save the civilian population from ruthless Fascist bombings.

It was heart-breaking to think how many women and children were being massacred in our cities for lack of adequate air defense. And Swedish Bofors cannon were among the best in the world for that purpose. . .

I would have to operate along other lines. The commercial connections needed serious attention.

Spain was beginning to feel the lack of certain foods : milk, butter, cheese and preserved meat. There was also a great demand for wood and pulp. On the other hand, Spanish products, above all the fresh fruit from Barcelona, Valencia, and Almería, must not be allowed to lose their place in the Swedish market. There were many competitors for the favors of honest Swedish buyers and consumers. Spain had hitherto always held her own against Turkish, Italian and Californian exporters, but the war had upset everything. Steamers were being sunk every day by the Italian and German air force, and insurance rates on shipped goods had consequently risen in proportion to the new risks. However, the Swedish buyers were willing to pay the price if only the fruit could reach them.

The afternoon and evening of that day went by peacefully. The diplomatic representatives of friendly countries had not waited, as is the rule, for me to present my credentials to his majesty, in order to bid me welcome. The Mexican Minister, heralded by beautiful flowers, had been the first to call. He had insisted on my using his car until the one belonging to the Spanish legation was given to me. Later on in the day other friends gathered round to express their sympathy for Spain.

Fröken Kerstin Hesselgren, Member of the Riksdag, and once President of the Swedish National Council of Women, spent quite a while with me. I always enjoyed talking to this white-haired, blue-eyed woman, whose softness of heart is never affected by her humorous sallies. Senator Branting, Chairman of the National Swedish Committee to Aid Spain, called to say he would be glad to accept my request that he act as my legal adviser in the legation matter. Barbro Alving, the clever reporter for the liberal paper *Dagens Nyheter*, also dropped in for a few minutes. She was just back from Spain and said that she had been very much impressed with all she saw there.

During the evening a new reason for anxiety cropped up, this time of a personal nature. Marissa came down with a severe attack of appendicitis.

A woman physician, Doctor Ruby Lind, who came to see her, said an operation should be performed at once. I looked at her in dismay.

"Is it absolutely necessary ?" I asked. Doctor Lind's kind blue eyes looked down into what must have been a very troubled face.

"Well," she said, "I shall try to help her and perhaps we can wait for a few days."

"To help" — what splendid words for a physician to use ! Yes, that is what medicine and surgery should do, not dominate, not force, but "help." Together we watched Marissa that night, and I was relieved after some time to see that the pain had diminished. If it were necessary, of course, she would have to be operated upon, but I wanted to consult my husband first.

On the bleak grey morning of the fourth of January, I was bidden to the Royal Palace to present my credentials to His Majesty, Gustav V, King of Sweden of the Goths and the Wends, for such is his title according to the Swedish *Year Book*.

The insurgent ex-minister, Señor Fiscowich, was still holding the legation, and some of his supporters in the Fascist press had been circulating the rumor that the presentation ceremony would be long delayed. One paper had insinuated that it might never take place.

"Madame Palencia may never ride in the carriage of the

seven windows," it stated, meaning the state coach used on such occasions.

The etiquette of diplomacy has no set and fast rules regarding the time that should elapse between the arrival of a foreign representative and his reception by the head of the state. Sometimes it is just a week or two, often very much longer. As it happened, His Majesty the King of Sweden thought fit to receive the representative of the Spanish republic just six days after her arrival in Stockholm.

It was a compliment that I knew would be duly appreciated in Spain. The ceremony was to take place at noon, and I had been asked to be ready punctually at eleven-thirty, because, as the chief of protocol said, when referring to this point, "His majesty cannot be kept waiting and neither should you."

Baron de Geer, *l'Introducteur des Ambassadeurs*, would, it appeared, be at the Grand Hotel on the stroke of that hour in order to escort me to the Royal Palace. There was a great deal of correspondence to look over that morning, and I was kept busy up to the moment of leaving. Fortunately the close-fitting black velvet dress I had had made in Paris and my little toque did not take much time to don. As the clock struck the half hour there was a discreet rap at the door of my little salon. Ugarte and Dethorey had come up to announce the arrival of Baron de Geer. This member of a very old and distinguished family, a perfect courtier, entered almost immediately afterward. He was dressed in court uniform. He bowed, I bowed. We sat down for a few minutes and exchanged some polite words in French. The baron asked for leave to look at his watch.

"You will pardon me, madame, I hope, but . . ." repeating the same argument the chief of protocol had used, "his majesty cannot wait and neither should you." A few more words . . . another look at his timepiece. "The distance from here to the palace is short," he volunteered. Then suddenly, he said, "Now we can go."

The hotel elevator rushed us down to the hall which was full of people. The press had already made me an object of curiosity in Stockholm. Besides a ceremonial of this kind always attracts attention. Marissa was still suffering from the after-effects of her attack. Ugarte and Dethorey said they would stay with her until I returned.

The state coach with its six horses and postillions was at the door. Its folding steps had been let down. I shuddered as I looked out at the expanse of snow and ice between us and the Royal Palace. Outside the crowd was larger. I was told afterward that two members of Fiscowich's staff were there. They must have been disappointed at the inoffensive appearance of one they wanted to convince the world was a dangerous "red." Very gingerly I picked my way over the pavement and mounted the three steps into the luxurious old-fashioned quilted-satin vehicle. The baron took the seat beside me. As the wheels turned round the coach swayed slightly on its high springs.

Very slowly we drove over the streets and the wide bridge which lead to the Royal Palace. Baron de Geer and I exchanged a few more amiable platitudes. Passers-by stopped to stare at the little procession. A great many hats and humble caps were lifted — friends of our Spain.

The swaying coach went past the palace courtyard and the outside guard. It stopped before the large glass doors that give access to the principal staircase which was lined on both sides by the palace guard in full uniform. I stepped down from the coach and, escorted by Baron de Geer, began the ascent, while acknowledging the salutes. Remembering this scene, I realize I did not experience the slightest feeling of nervousness nor even of shyness, which my Scotch ancestry might justify.

Baron de Geer accompanying Isabel de Palencia to the
Royal Palace, Stockholm

My brain just grasped the one all-important question : Spain, Spain fighting, bleeding, for democracy, for Swedish democracy, too.

Halfway up the stairs, liveried footmen took my coat. "We are in good time," said Baron de Geer, with his eyes fixed on his wrist-watch.

Up . . . up . . . very slowly between the two rows of uniformed men, beside the courtly *Introducteur*. Then of a sudden the vigilant baron's voice that had lost its calm and had become more hurried, exclaimed, "Now we had better go a little faster !" And in one minute more we were on the high landing thronged with palace officials, dignitaries, and courtiers.

Count von Rosen, Master of the King's Household, came forward to meet us. "Be so good as to come, madame," he said, and I was ushered into the presence of the Swedish monarch, who stood in the center of the room, dressed in full uniform and wearing many glittering decorations.

I curtsied low, in the approved manner of the court. How tall and slim he seemed, and how vital in spite of his seventy-nine years ! His majesty bade me sit down and graciously accepted my credentials. He asked me whether I preferred speaking in English or French.

"I leave the choice to your majesty," I said. "Both languages are equally familiar to me." His majesty smiled and we conversed in a mixture of both tongues.

Very kindly the king inquired about Spain and conditions there. "Yours is a beautiful country," he said several times, and then, "What a pity ! What a pity !" He must have been thinking of the destruction caused by modern warfare for he asked many questions about our artistic treasures and about the bombardment of open towns and villages. I gave him details of the awful massacre of helpless women and children.

His majesty then referred to the presence of foreign troops

in Spain.   I respectfully gave an account of the situation, adding that everything connected with this question could be
found in the report presented by Alvarez del Vayo, our Minister of Foreign Affairs, to the League Assembly last September,
in which testimonies of the most convincing quality had been
accumulated.

The king very discreetly wondered whether there were no
foreign troops fighting on our side, too.   I answered that men
from over fifty nations had, of their own free will, and without
arms, gone to help Spain and defend world democracy.   But
that those men had not been sent by the order of any foreign
government, nor had they been armed and equipped by their
countries like the troops Germany and Italy had sent to Franco.

"If Spain had received one third of the foreign aid that the
insurgents had," I said, "your majesty may be sure that the rebellion would have been quelled long ago," and then I added,
"if Spain were at least allowed to exercise her rights."

His majesty looked as though he were about to answer, but
stopped, and passed on to speak of something else.   Did I like
Sweden ?   Had I seen much of Stockholm yet ?   Was my
daughter any better ?   He had heard she was sick.

I looked up at the face that was still so young looking.   It
was tanned from constant exposure to the air and I asked myself whether he was really interested in having an answer to
those questions.   He must have asked the same things so often.
And my answers must have been repeated so often, too.

After a while the king rose.   My visit was at an end.   I left
the room with another deep curtsy and found myself once
more in the ante-chamber where I was again greeted by the
uniformed courtiers.   Count von Rosen accompanied me to
the head of the stairs and, escorted by Baron de Geer, I went
down the broad low steps, still lined with the troops of the

palace guard. Slowly we drove back to the hotel where the baron took his departure and I went up to our rooms to find Marissa up and dressed and, to my intense relief, feeling a little better.

After lunch I had to finish my crowded schedule for that day. It had all been clearly put down in black and white by the chief of protocol. It is comforting to think that one cannot make mistakes in matters connected with a royal palace as long as one does not take the initiative. Everything is planned out carefully. Nothing is just left to chance, and in order to be right, one has only to obey. I found it quite restful for a time.

Wearing the same gown I had used for the morning's ceremony, I launched forth again. My first duty now was to pay my respects to His Royal Highness Gustav Adolf, Crown Prince of Sweden, and to Her Royal Highness, the Crown Princess Louise Alexandra, born Princess of Battenberg, and therefore cousin to the Spanish ex-Queen Victoria, and afterward to their Royal Highnesses Gustav Adolf and Sibylla, Hereditary Prince and Princess of Sweden.

The first of these calls took me back again to the Royal Palace. This time to the ground floor. I had to pass through several salons full of courtiers and ladies in waiting, in full dress, before I found myself in the presence of their royal highnesses. The rules of etiquette relaxed as the afternoon wore on. The crown prince and princess are charmingly simple. We talked in English about many things, Spain first, of course. The prince is almost boyish in his enthusiasm for all matters both cultural and social. The safety of the priceless pictures of our Prado Museum was evidently a matter of concern to him.

I was glad to be able to give every assurance that no harm would come to them, and explained how all Spaniards from the

290290290

highest officials to the lowest peasants had contributed to their safety. The League of Nations is another subject of interest to his highness.

"I am sure I would like them a lot," he said, when speaking about the League Assemblies and their usefulness as a meeting ground for men of all nationalities.

The Hereditary Prince and Princess of Sweden have made their home in a small castle just outside Stockholm. I felt, as I was shown in, that it might be the residence of a simple country gentleman. Emblems of sport were to be seen all over the place. Stags' heads hang from the walls. Merry flames spring up from the large open fireplaces. The prince and princess chatted pleasantly for a little while and when they rose, I took my leave. With this, my official day was ended.

I was just on the point of falling asleep that night when a telephone ring woke me up with a start, and a friendly voice from the other end exclaimed, "Oh, Madame Palencia, I hear you have made a wonderful impression in the Palace !"

I smiled to myself. "This terrible red !"

Early the next day I called on the Norwegian minister who was then dean of the diplomatic corps, and Mrs. Wollebaek. They struck me as simple, kind-hearted folk. The minister asked me about the situation with Fiscowich, and told me he had been very much impressed by the dignified way in which I was conducting the affair. I also paid my duty calls to Speakers of the Two Chambers in the House of Parliament. They, too, were very cordial, especially the Speaker for the Chamber of Deputies. Then I passed on to see the Prime Minister, Per Albin Hansson. The moment I set eyes on him, my mind flew to Spain. There was something in the tanned face and the twinkling, clear eyes, that reminded me of our Largo

Caballero, also a man of the people. Per Albin Hansson was very sympathetic about Spain, and very anxious about the future of the Spanish workers. But I saw at once that he had been misinformed as to the true nature of the war.

Some of the arguments used by pseudo democrats and pseudo socialists had colored his own personal opinions. Above all, I could see, he was not optimistic about the final results of our struggle. He could not believe it was possible for us to win. I was to find many who shared that opinion. They were always people who had not been in our country and did not know the Spanish people well. But it troubled me because pessimism of that kind leads even those who are most sympathetic to a cause to let things slide, because, as they say, "What is the good?"

Scandinavia having been a sort of trying-out ground for women diplomats, my appointment in Sweden could not create much excitement, and if anyone felt curiosity regarding my personal appearance, they had a chance to satisfy it the evening after my reception by the king, at the dinner given by the Minister of Foreign Affairs. It was my first meeting with the other members of the diplomatic corps and I, too, felt a certain interest in seeing them and finding out who was friendly and who unfriendly to Spain. However efficient diplomatic reserve might be, I felt I could make a near guess as to each one's position on this question, even in so short a time. By each one's position I mean his government's, of course.

The invitation card for the dinner mentioned that decorations were to be worn, so I pinned the medal of the *Order of the White Lion*, which President Masaryk had granted me two years before, for my studies and work on Czechoslovakian popular art, on the bodice of my evening dress. It is the only distinction of the kind that I possess, and I appreciate it because it really seems to mean something. Therefore I felt gratified when the minister for Czechoslovakia noticed it and said, as he advanced to greet me, "Thank you for wearing that."

Mr. and Mrs. Wollebaek were specially kind that evening in making things easy for me, helped by Madame Kollontay and the Mexican and Chinese ministers, with their wives, who went out of their way to make me feel at home among them. The French and Turkish representatives were also friendly.

As is usual in functions of this kind, the women spent their time looking over each other's gowns while the men formed little groups or sidled up to some colleague from whom they hoped to extract information. One cannot say that in diplomatic circles "smartness" is the outstanding note in feminine apparel, rather the contrary. As for the men, most of them seemed to have outgrown their uniforms ; they looked stiff and uncomfortable.

Madame Kollontay smiled approval at my simple black décolleté dress, and nodded vigorous acquiescence when someone murmured, "Madame Palencia, you look like a picture by Goya."

The Soviet minister is popular even in this *milieu*. She is charmingly bright and her knowledge of languages is, of course, a great help. That night I had heard her speak in perfect English, French, German and Swedish. Little Madame Wang King-Ky, wife of the Chinese minister, looking very attractive in her plain purple high-necked dress, came up to inquire after Marissa. She had heard about her illness and, having a daughter of about the same age, was naturally interested.

The residence of the Minister of Foreign Affairs in Sweden is a beautiful old house. It is furnished with exquisite taste and makes a charming setting for diplomatic gatherings, for the bowing and the assenting, the restrained conversation and the courteous half tones that are characteristic of these circles.

Even the quaint old-fashioned bobbing of the female servants, which is one of the most deep-rooted customs of the country, seems natural. His excellency and Mrs. Sandler did the honors of the house in a charming simple manner.

Once these first official functions were over I could consider that the introduction into this new chapter of my life was complete. I was now invested with full authority as minister for Spain. This, in Sweden, means that the word "minister" will remain with me until I go down to my grave. In this most formal of countries, a title once acquired is yours for life, not to be lost unless it is superseded by another of a higher grade. That is why a Swedish directory simply overflows with ministers, consuls, directors, professors and, above all, with the word *direktör*, a title which is conferred on all those who haven't any other.

But I was a minister without a legation, for Señor Fiscowich was still barricaded in the Spanish government's property and refused to listen to the request of the Foreign Affairs Ministry to give it up. He had also denied that his wife was sick and maintained his refusal to leave on the ground that Franco, being the head of the new Spanish state, he, as representative of the rebel general, was the only person entitled to make use of the legation. The Swedish press continued to serve up whole columns on the situation with great gusto. But even the most reactionary journals were beginning to disapprove of the ex-minister's pugnacious attitude.

"Madame Palencia," said one, "is ready to accept a harmonious solution, but declares that, being the representative of the legal government of Spain, she alone has a right to occupy the legation. Everyone is interested in seeing how she manages to conquer the property and if she does so without provoking an open conflict she will have given a proof of fine diplomatic tact."

Fun was also being poked at Señor Fiscowich. "The nervousness of the inmates of the Spanish legation is increasing," said one reporter. "We have not been able to see Mr. Fiscowich," he added. "He spent all day Tuesday in the legation, well protected by a force composed of two policemen and two ferocious terriers." Finally one paper alluded to the rebel ex-minister as "Mr. *Fiasco*wich."

All the same, the delay in occupying the legation building was hampering our work seriously, so I was glad to hear from Advokat Georg Branting that everything would be satisfactorily settled within the next few days.

CHAPTER XVIII

"Cefe !" Not one more word could I manage to speak through my sobs as I fell into my husband's arms on the icy cold Stockholm dock when he and Cefito got off the Latvia boat at seven o'clock in the morning a few days after his telephone call. Fortunately there was no one there except Dethorey and a few unknown passengers who had come over with them. I have never understood what it was that set me off in that absurd way. Probably a case of long pent-up tears that the slightest emotion sets free unexpectedly. Whatever it was, Cefe was terrified by the sight of them. He thought that we must have lost the war during the night.

With his and Cefito's arrival my mind was partially relieved about Marissa, it was so good to be able to share responsibility. She was physically better but in a state of constant anxiety over Germán who had written her about his having been wounded a month after it had happened. This had been the reason for his silence, but she would have preferred to know at once.

Cefe could only stay four days after which he would return to Latvia while Cefito went to London for a glimpse of his fiancée, Mary Morgan, a young Irish girl with whom he had fallen in love in Biarritz at the age of sixteen and to whom he had only recently become engaged.

"I shall be in London a fortnight or three weeks and then I shall go to Spain," my boy said as we drove back to the hotel. My husband looked at me.

That evening after dinner Cefe asked, "Do you think the boy need go back ? He was among the first to volunteer for the front and I really need him in Riga ; I have no one there to help me that I can trust. Besides," he added, "he can go the moment they call him up for military service. I hear they are going to set up conscription again."

I waited for a few minutes. It was easy to understand Cefe's desire to keep our son with him. The anxiety of knowing he was in Spain would make it difficult for us to concentrate on our work properly. On the other hand . . .

"I think he should be allowed to make his own choice," I said.

Later that night I had a talk with Cefito. I had waited up for him and he came straight in when he saw the light in my room.

"Do you really think you ought to go, darling?" I said, broaching the subject at once and preparing myself for that eternal struggle of mothers, who from the moment they see their children trying to stand alone have to let them do so, even at the cost of bumps, until the day when they face two paths and must make the choice for themselves, whatever pain it may bring to them and to us.

"Of course I must, mother." He put his arms round me. "It isn't that I particularly want to go. I don't like the war. I hate it and . . ." he laughed shyly, "I am just as much frightened of it as most of us. I am no hero but . . ." he looked grave, "I simply can't stand not being in Spain now."

The simple words almost made me break down. They were so natural, so devoid of all affectation. They implied it was his duty to go without the need of high-sounding phraseology. It was the way all our boys spoke then.

When I told Cefe, he agreed with me that nothing more should be said to Cefito and I tried to lay aside our permanent anxiety about Spain for a little and to make the most of the days we had together.

"Why don't we do something tonight?" Cefe said the next evening. "Can't we go to a theatre?"

I thought it would be dull to sit through a play without understanding a word of it however fine the acting might be.

"Well, let's go to a revue," he insisted. I understood his wish to avoid a *tête-à-tête*. He went down to consult the hotel manager and Dethorey about the best thing to see. After a little he came up with tickets for seats in a fashionable theatre for Cefito, himself and me. Marissa did not feel well enough to go.

At the theatre we found our seats were in the front row. The house was well filled. The revue was good and the first actor and manager of the show, Karl Gerhard, was a great favorite in Stockholm.

We arrived after the piece had begun, having been detained at the door of the theatre by the press, anxious to take some family snapshots. Although we did not understand a word of what was being said or sung on the stage, it was easy enough to discover that Karl Gerhard was making some political allusions. Names of dictators and members of the Swedish cabinet provoked shouts of laughter. It was soon clear that Gerhard had recognized us and I feared, for a moment, that he might make some remark about the legation affair. Instead, at the end of the first act, he came forward with a bouquet of flowers in his hand and, giving them to the leader of the orchestra who was just in front of us, he motioned in my direction, saying in a loud voice and in French, "Madame Palencia, please accept them."

I thought it was not only gracious but courageous of him to take sides so openly with us before his smart and probably reactionary audience. It was not the only time. During the whole of my stay in Sweden Karl Gerhard never lost an opportunity of showing his admiration for democratic Spain and of helping our little victims of the war with performances that he himself would give for the Spanish children. He even spoke in public to the same end.

Cefe went back to Riga at the end of his leave. The parting

with Cefito was very hard for him.   A few days later my turn
came.   It is amazing how one can go through these ordeals
over and over again without one's strength failing.   The morning of his departure I looked out of the window to see my boy's
taxi go round the corner.   He had begged me not to go to the
station.

Cefito leant out and waved his hand.   Marissa and I were
alone once more.

Like all the other members of the diplomatic corps I had been
notified that the opening session of the Swedish Riksdag for
1936 would take place on January the eleventh instead of the
tenth which is the usual date but that year happened to fall on
a Sunday.   The ceremony would, as always, be held in the
Royal Palace.

Someone had told me to be sure to go as it would be interesting, different from such functions in other countries.   To
begin with, instead of the head of the state going to the House
of Parliament, the Swedish senators and deputies go to the
residence of the head of the state.   The Mexican minister and
his wife said they would call for me.

The ceremony begins with divine service in a church near
the Royal Palace at which the members of both chambers and
the king are present.   When the service is over they all walk
in procession to the royal residence.

Meanwhile, the ladies of the royal family, the high court
dignitaries, and the representatives of foreign powers assemble
in the palace, ready to occupy the seats that are assigned to
them in the great Hall of State.

One is supposed to be at the palace not later than a quarter
to twelve and in full dress.   I thought the ladies looked very
cold in their low-necked, long-trained evening gowns which,
in spite of the lighted chandeliers, seemed out of place at that

time of the day. The men, too, were dressed for the occasion, wearing their finest bands and decorations.

When we arrived we found Count von Rosen and Baron Barnekow trying to persuade the foreign representatives to get into line. Being the last comer to Sweden, I was also the last of the ministers in the queue. When they were all in their places in the double file — each man with his wife — we went down the few steps leading to the hall. Madame Kollontay and I, having no partners, had to march in alone.

Once inside the spacious Hall of State, we were directed to the diplomatic stand. The ladies pass in first and occupy the seats in the front row, the men sit behind them.

A little confusion arose on Madame Kollontay's and my account. It seems to happen almost every year. Someone, not well versed in diplomatic etiquette but true to the axiom "ladies first," wanted us to go in before the gentlemen. Baron Barnekow hastened to the rescue and, as "ministers in our own right," we were placed with our colleagues behind their wives.

I looked around curiously. To our left, between two huge statues and under a canopy of blue silk, was the king's throne with the royal mantle of ermine gracefully draped over it. On a table near by were the two other emblems of royalty : the sceptre and the crown.

Suddenly a tall slim figure in full court dress appeared on the hanging balcony facing us. There was a stir in the hall. Everybody rose to his feet. The Crown Princess of Sweden, for it was she, curtsied deeply to the foreign representatives, all of whom curtsied and bowed to her. Immediately afterward a second figure, the Hereditary Princess of Sweden ; and a third, the Crown Princess of Denmark — who was on a visit to her parents and is said to be the favorite grandchild of his majesty — and a fourth, Princess Ingeborg, came forward. They curtsied and took their seats. The balcony sparkled with the light of jewels. The faces looked ethereal framed by white lace veils. There was another stand opposite ours for the ladies in waiting. They wore the conventional court dress of black velvet with white satin puffed sleeves, slashed with black, old lace bordering the low-necked bodices.

A blast of trumpets announced the arrival of the members of parliament who took their seats on benches placed down the length of the hall, facing the throne. The two speakers were in the front row. His Excellency, Per Albin Hansson, Premier of Sweden, and Minister Sandler sat near the royal dais. The other members of the cabinet were grouped below our stand. Every one of them was attired in sombre hues. The sparkle and color and light were at the other end of the room, round the throne.

The four princesses rose again and curtsied, first to the members of one chamber and then to the members of the other, who answered with automatic lowering of their heads. More sounds of music and the tramping of feet. It was the palace guard, followed by courtiers, who preceded the crown prince and the hereditary prince, and finally, King Gustav himself came into view.

The Swedish sovereign stood before his throne and bowed low to the royal family, to the foreign representatives, and to the two chambers. This bow seemed to me significant: an obeisance of hereditary royalty to the elected representatives of the nation, and it gave one food for thought. In some countries it would have been nothing but an empty formality. In Sweden surely it must mean more. I had seen little of the country, yet enough, however, to feel that at least there was an honest desire for the people's welfare. A clean administration, a progressive spirit, all based on the principles of democracy. The king sat down on his throne. Everybody else took his seat. One after the other the two speakers read his short speech. I could not distinguish a single word. My eyes strayed over the room.

A queer sensation overcame me. On my left hand was the throne, the king, the princess, the balcony, the princesses. About them all the paraphernalia of court life : the radiance of lighted candles, the glitter of precious stones, satin, velvet and lace. On my right a mass of severe black and over it lines of fair heads and white-skinned faces : the people.

The first was like a fairy tale : something I might be reading about. The second was reality : life, something I could see.

When the speakers had finished, King Gustav unrolled a sheet of paper and in a strong voice read *The Speech from the Throne*. I could not understand it but I gathered it was the usual thing, a program of the questions to be discussed by parliament during the coming session. *The Speech from the Throne* probably marked the limit of the work to be done, stressed what was most needed in the country's legislation and made an appeal for good sense and hard work.

The guard trooped out. The king rose and bowed. The princesses curtsied and retired. The courtiers and the senators and the deputies filed out. We followed their example.

Two days later I happened to meet Mr. Sandler.

"What did you think of our opening session of parliament ?" he asked.

The socialist minister was, I felt, really anxious to know what impression I had received. Perhaps he thought I, a republican, had been shocked at the idea of a parliamentary session being held in the Royal Palace.

"I think you are a fortunate people," I answered, "to see the tree of democracy grow with its roots fresh and strong though springing from the past. Other countries have had to cut the roots."

Four days after the opening of parliament his majesty offered his annual dinner to the diplomatic corps. In spite of the strong leavening of democracy, the rules of etiquette observed in the court of Sweden are among the stiffest and most rigid of the monarchist world. This is probably due to the formal nature of the Swedish customs themselves more than to the influence of the régime. Be it what it may, a court function in Stockholm has always a savor of olden times because of its spectacular display.

The heads of mission were supposed to be in the palace fifteen minutes or so before the hour fixed for the dinner. It always took a little time for the guests to rid themselves of coats and furs and to congregate in the round salon and occupy their places, according to a precedence ruled as elsewhere by the years of permanence in the mission.

Sharply on the hour King Gustav made his appearance and stopped before each one of his guests in order to shake hands and say a few words. Following him came the crown prince and princess, the hereditary prince and princess, and the king's brother, tall and stately Prince Carl, with Princess Ingeborg. The diplomats and their wives bowed and curtsied over the extended royal hands and answered the courteous remarks of each member of the royal family. Kind inquiries were made of me regarding Marissa's health.

Then the company, led by the king, went into the large banqueting hall hung with beautiful tapestries and sat down to dine off the fine service, carefully served by a large number of liveried footmen. The chief butler and cupbearer, wearing a turban adorned with a straight peacock's feather, supervised the service. The music played. The guests talked or exchanged smiles across the long table.

After dinner coffee was served in the salon while the king

again went the round of his guests before retiring. The dinners and receptions at the palace were always over early.

Prince Eugen, the other younger brother of the king, was rarely present at the palace functions. A very good painter indeed, he spends his time working in his studio or going to concerts, lectures and exhibitions of various sorts. A true artist, Prince Eugen is also a liberal and interested in all just causes. I know he felt great sympathy for our Spain. He spoke to me on several occasions of his admiration for Spanish art and for the natural beauties of the country, which he knows well for he has painted landscapes in Catalonia and other provinces and motored through some of our most beautiful regions.

Soon after the palace dinner Georg Branting told me that the question of the legation would very soon be settled. He had held several interviews with Fiscowich's legal adviser. The case of the rebel minister was so weak it could no longer be supported. Following the advice of the Foreign Affairs Department and in view of the fact that Fiscowich would not listen to reason, we decided to hand in a formal appeal to the Civil Governor of Stockholm, who would then give the orders for the ejection of the intruders.

The appeal was written and sent to the authorities and a rumor began to circulate to the effect that the ex-minister was going to leave. While we waited I had time to look around and learn something about the country where I was now to live.

Stockholm is a delightful city to roam about in, even with almost arctic weather, and many afternoons during the following weeks, I left the hotel immediately after luncheon and wandered in and out of the streets of the town which is, one might say, carved out of the living rock.

You see those rocks holding the houses on their dark solid surface and even at times encircling part of a street protectingly. A fountain or a seat may perhaps be cut into the mass more for ornamentation than for usefulness.

It is said that to know a people well one must know their capital, a remark that can only with deep misgiving be applied to some countries, for whoever would dream of passing judgment on Spain after seeing only Madrid, or on the United States after a visit only to Washington? But it can be said of Sweden, for Stockholm is not only the loveliest town of the realm, the centre of the political life of the Swedes and the seat of their executive and legislative institutions, it is also the headquarters of almost all their industrial and commercial activities, the rallying field of their social movement. In one word, it is the very heart of Sweden. All the emotional reactions of the people, the new currents of thought, the plans and hopes and orders that have made and are making Sweden what it is, appear to have been born and developed and issued in Stockholm.

The capital has a serious rival in that other Swedish town of Gothenburg which is more progressive in a way and is endowed with many fine institutions, among them the Art Gallery which is quite as important as that of Stockholm. But Gothenburg itself is not so original nor has it the balance and the finished air of Stockholm.

One often hears the Swedish capital compared to Venice. I suppose the alleged similarity is based on the fact that there are many canals and bridges and houses that rise out of the water, but I can see nothing else. No, Stockholm is Stockholm. And that is enough to say for it. Its great charm is that as one walks about the streets it is possible to hear and feel the heartbeats of the country of which it is the capital.

Those heartbeats are not easy to discern perhaps in the rich new sectors of the town where there is much to attract one's attention and the "still small voice" is drowned by the noise on the surface, but they are plainly audible in the narrow streets and the old, old houses, the unexpected twists and turns of the water, and the isolated little groups of buildings held in the town's embrace. And one can feel them, too, in the quaint dining houses where the workers assemble for their midday meal and where every possible question is solemnly discussed. But one cannot overlook the beauty of that other Stockholm that one sees in the fine avenues and streets and, above all, in buildings like the Town Hall, standing out from its surroundings in all the perfection of its stately grace. The red brick it is made of is toned down to a warm russet color that makes a lovely background for the mosaics and the polychromed marble and the three golden crowns, emblem of the Kingdom of Sweden, that scintillate like jewels on the high tower. The beautiful terrace on the water front is one of the most decorative spots in the whole city.

Ragnar Östberg, the creator of this really fine piece of architecture, had not allowed himself to be carried away, as so many other Swedish architects have been, by the French and Italian influences which, since the sixteenth century, had dominated Swedish taste. The Royal Palace and other buildings are an example of this. Östberg has looked for inspiration in the old Swedish buildings, specially keeping in mind the ancient castle of the Three Crowns one often sees reproduced in engravings.

The interior of the Town Hall is as Swedish as the exterior. The "blue hall" — which is really red, for after it was finished the architect could not bear the idea of painting the walls and destroying the fine effect of the naked brick, as was done to the Princess Hall — is endowed with the same proud dignity one admires in other relics of Swedish architecture. The richness of the materials employed in the decoration naturally increases the impressive beauty of the whole ensemble.

Another beautiful modern building is the Concert Hall designed by Ivar Tengbom and one of the sights of the Swedish capital. It can hold two thousand persons and contains another smaller hall seating six hundred. Located in one of the biggest markets of the town, it rises proudly from among stacks of fruits, flowers and fresh vegetables that look at times like offerings laid at the feet of the Orpheus Fountain, one of the finest of Carl Milles' works, that is placed just in front of the steps leading up to the Concert Hall.

Liljevalck's art gallery by Bergsten, the Högalid Church by Tengbom and the City Library by Asplund are other fine examples of modern Swedish architecture. But there are many smaller buildings that also help to make Stockholm what it is : a town of harmony, a city of beautiful profiles, as clean-cut as the features of a Greek goddess, set in a background that never interferes with the graceful outlines. As one roams about the carefully kept streets, one realizes that good taste in every form is one of the most important and defined characteristics of this northern race.

The clothes worn by the people, even the humblest, the goods exhibited in the shop windows, the furniture inside the houses, the trimmings and patterns, the moldings and trappings of everything, are almost always beautiful. At their worst they may be uninteresting, perhaps a trifle drab, but never ugly, ostentatious or vulgar.

Stockholm is not a noisy city. Perhaps to some of us, accustomed to the clamor and din of the cities of the south, it is almost too silent. The motor cars glide through the streets without making a sound, for hooting is strictly forbidden. People talk in hushed tones and street vendors offer their wares without a word. Even dogs are careful not to bark.

The total silence is as impressive as the exquisite cleanliness. Not a scrap of paper lies upon the ground, not a cigarette stub soils the pavements. No weeds mar the beauty of the city parterres. At times one cannot help feeling a childlike desire to spoil this perfect order in some little way, to throw a bit of something on the ground to see if it will create a disturbance. But I suppose one would be crushed by the general disapproval such behavior would be sure to provoke.

In any case, the silence and cleanliness, the order and beauty were very restful to me after the hard grind of the past weeks, with the rush of hurried traveling and the strain that a sense of responsibility entails. Whatever changes the future may bring to Sweden or to me, I feel sure that the first impression I received of that country's capital will not change.

I may be able to see it in a different light, in a way that would awaken other impressions and reactions to the extent of making me believe that I was in another city. But the Stockholm that I saw in 1936 will always be something that cannot be altered. It is unchangeable and unforgettable.

CHAPTER XIX

On the beautiful island occupied by the Djurgården, which is surrounded by calm waters and bound to another larger island by a handsome bridge, there stands a stately mansion to which many people still give the name of Prins Carl Palats. That house has for several years now been the Spanish legation. It was bought by order of the Primo de Rivera government so that King Alfonso, who was contemplating a two or three days' visit to Stockholm, should have a place to stay worthy of his rank. This would not have been so easy to arrange under a democratic régime when expenses are discussed in a parliament, but in a dictatorship a mere stroke of the pen is enough. The house is in truth much too large and rich for a legation. Most foreign missions in Stockholm occupy only apartments, more or less luxurious. Great Britain, Germany, France, Italy and the Soviet Republic are excepted, but the Spanish legation is larger than any of them.

Our appeal to the civil governor of Stockholm had been favorably answered to the effect that I alone, being the legal representative of the only Spanish government recognized by Sweden, had a right to occupy the legation. Fiscowich was, therefore, forced to choose between two alternatives : either to stay where he was until the police obliged him to get out, or to take his departure at once with as good grace as possible. He chose the latter course. That is, he did what he should have done at the beginning and avoided the bother of the past few weeks. But evidently his resistance was due to a desire to offer some reparation to Franco for his desertion at the beginning of the war and thus to hope for compensation in the future. Whatever his reasons may have been, he had lost.

"I have just been notified that Señor Fiscowich's legal adviser will hand over the keys of the legation to me tomorrow morning," said Advokat Branting to me one afternoon.

"When is he leaving ?" I asked.

"Tonight."

"Then ?" I inquired.

"Then you are free to take possession whenever you choose. Would you like me to go with you, Madame Palencia ?"

"No."

"Do you prefer me to go first alone ?"

"No," I said, "we shall ask the notary public to go and make a new inventory."

And that is what was done. Three days later Branting, Ugarte, Dethorey and I drove up to the legation building. It was bitterly cold. The trees in the garden bent under the weight of newly fallen snow but the house had been warmed for our benefit. I went through the ground floor with its enormous hall and sumptuous reception rooms and study. The furniture was in place. Pictures hung from the walls. It was all most appropriate from an official point of view but not exactly what one would call homelike. It was only when we inspected the second floor that I began to entertain the hope that Marissa and I might find some corner where our private life could be spent in peace and retirement. My bedroom, with its two canopied beds, and the other rooms near it were all right, but it was a small sitting room on the same floor that really made me feel at home. It had two windows looking out on the garden and an open fireplace. When I was looking around, Dethorey, who had been staring at the view, suddenly called my attention to something that he had discovered written on one of the windowpanes.

"Look, señora," he said, "what I have found."

I came near. There were names and dates scratched on the glass by means of a diamond probably. Lower down there were some lines in Swedish, in the corner two more words : "Carl" and "Ingeborg."

Dethorey bent down to read them and then translated the lines. They ran something like this :

"We hope that those who come to live in this house after we have gone will be as happy in it as we have been."

"The names are those of Prince Carl and Princess Ingeborg and their children," Dethorey went on, "and these are the dates of their births and of someone's silver wedding."

I knew that the legation building had belonged to the brother of the king and that he and Princess Ingeborg with their young family had lived there until economic difficulties had forced them to leave their beautiful home and live modestly in an apartment in the town. One of the girls, Princess Astrid, afterward the Queen of the Belgians, had met a tragic death when motoring through Switzerland with her husband.

It must have been a blow to break up the home that had echoed for years with the sound of children's cheerful voices and the laughter and conversation of devoted friends, for both Prince Carl and the Danish princess he had wed were great favorites.

It must have been hard especially after the terrible accident that had cost their daughter Astrid her life, to feel that they would never again live in the rooms where she had played. I felt it required real nobility of character to be able to write kind words of welcome to those who might follow and wish them to enjoy what they themselves had lost. No woman with a mean possessive spirit could have done it and, as a new inmate of the house, I felt that the words written on the windowpane were good to see and was grateful for the message of human kindness they contained.

The next day Marissa and I settled into the legation. A cook ; two maids, Anna and Marie ; a fair-haired giant, Nils, who was to be chauffeur and general helper in the house, were already at their posts. My first care was to inspect the chancellery. I was quite well prepared, after seeing the notary public's report and inventory, for what awaited me.

I knew that I would find : no code, no files, an empty cashbox, and the republican flag cut to pieces on the floor of the salon, a silly bit of malice. After all, Señor Fiscowich had once given his allegiance to that flag, he had served under it for six years. He might have changed his mind but that was no excuse for the attempted insult to what it represented. As in Geneva after the intended slight of the Portuguese woman delegate, I only felt sorry for the smallness of soul such an act revealed.

Perhaps it had not been done by order of the ex-minister. Perhaps it was carried out without his knowledge by some minor and overzealous official. The blame then rests upon him or her. It is not that one lays such store upon the bit of cloth that flags are made of, but the fact that they are loved by people because of what they symbolize makes them worthy of all respect. Above all, Señor Fiscowich and his retainers should have thought that at that very moment thousands of their countrymen were dying in Spain to defend what they had democratically given themselves, a régime represented by the red, yellow and purple flag his officials had defiled.

We lost no time in setting things in order and getting to work. There was much to do, for, although the Non-Intervention Pact had limited the possibilities of buying arms in Sweden, we sometimes came into contact with people from other lands who were anxious to trade in every kind of offensive and defensive armament, a strange business this. Few things lead to more commercial brigandage than the traffic of the distributors of death.   Few things are so often managed by unscrupulous dealers and, although I had nothing to do with their actual buying, there were many questions indirectly connected with the trade that I was called upon to settle.   Several attempts to double-cross the Spanish republic were discovered by friends and denounced.

I remember one night when a distinguished-looking man called at the legation to inform me that a cargo, on its way to loyal Spain and paid for, was going to be "allowed" to fall into Franco's hands.   That time we managed to stop their little game, but similar cases were constantly cropping up.   Often there were victims.   Captains who were faithful to their trust and refused to give up their cargoes disappeared mysteriously.   Others were assassinated.

The real plagues, however, in time of war, are inventors. There is much more lunacy in the world than one believes and in moments of upheaval it comes to the surface in an alarming manner.   We have heard that war is a case of collective madness and to judge from the inventors one comes across at such times, the definition is quite convincing.   During my stay in Sweden and particularly during the first year, almost no day passed without our having one or two mysterious callers who asked to be received alone and then handed us drawings, plans, or written data about some wonderful device for annihilating mankind.   The creative faculty of these people finds constant, if distorted, inspiration in the destructiveness of war.

Other things kept me busy, too.   Connections interrupted during six months, through the absence of a legal representative, had to be renewed ; commercial bonds strengthened by means of special agreements and markets opened up to our products ; information about the latest developments carried out by the republic had to be distributed ; and the real situation of Spain explained in order to counteract the effects of the insidious propaganda from the Fascist side. The press had to be closely watched so that if false news were published it could be rectified at an early date.

In truth, during the whole of my stay, I had but few complaints to make on this subject. One of them was due to an absurd notice published in a conservative enemy paper to which my attention had been called by some of our friends. It took the shape of an advertisement for books. On one side of the space devoted to this publicity they had put my photograph and beside it the title of a book, *The Truth about Spain*. Underneath were several subtitles such as *Free Love, Our Churches Burnt*, and others. Although the name of the author was not given it looked exactly as though the work had been written by me. We were certainly surprised when we discovered that the author was no less a person than the Nazi, Goebbels. I have never been able to understand how anyone could have thought of such a stupid way of trying to annoy me. As I said to Mr. Sandler, I ought to feel flattered that, in order to sell a book by Goebbels, they have had to make believe its author was the representative of loyalist Spain.

Another most important task we had was that of keeping in touch with the Swedish Help Committee which, since the beginning of the war, had done so much to alleviate the sufferings of women and children. The support of the people of Sweden during the war and long afterward will live long in the hearts of those of us who were able to measure the full extent of the sacrifices it entailed. It was not only the remarkable generosity with which money was contributed, but also the time and trouble given to the organizing of groups to carry on the work in Sweden itself, in Spain and in France. Georg Branting, Chairman of the Central Committee, was in constant touch with the local branches established not only in the big cities but in many small towns and villages. Even in the tiniest hamlet one could find a little band of people always ready to send money or clothes or food to the devastated regions of Spain.

When I arrived in Stockholm the interest of the committee was for the time centred in organizing a complete hospital outfit that was to be presented to the Spanish government and set up in Alicante under the direction of that fine Swedish physician, Doctor Silversköld, helped by two or three other young surgeons and some well-trained nurses. Norway was sharing both in the expenses and in the carrying out of the plan. Spanish physicians were to be on the staff also and after a year or two the whole outfit would be handed over to Spain.

In view of the bombardments of open cities and the victims of this barbarous method of modern warfare, there was talk of taking a large number of children over to Sweden and settling them there in special homes with a mixed staff of Spanish and Swedish teachers and nurses to look after them. The Gothenburg Committee immediately set to work and prepared a house for the first group. However, after long discussion, it was thought best to leave the children in specially prepared homes in France, where the climatic conditions would not be so severe and the little refugees would feel themselves less far from home.

I knew we could count upon that wonderful Swedish Help Committee at any time. One day I got a frantic cable from Bilbao asking for food for the little Basque children, and a huge load of supplies of all kinds was sent at once. Another time a Spanish boat had brought a cargo of fruit into port at Stockholm and was going back for more. In two days the committee raised one hundred thousand crowns that were spent on food to be sent on that boat for the women and children in Spain.

A women's committee under the chairmanship of Fru Anna Lenah Elgström was also formed in Stockholm to help children on both sides. They called themselves neutral and worked very hard to raise money. Every facility was given them for the distribution of food and clothes within loyal Spain, but they found it difficult to carry on their work in the rebel zone. Their intention was good and although neutrality in a case like the Spanish war is inconceivable, there is no doubt that they did their best to help.

Another task I undertook at once was that of learning Swedish. I should not have been so diligent but for the despair I felt when the morning papers were brought into my room and I could not read the Spanish news. Dethorey, who was our press attaché and translator, usually arrived at the chancellery at half past nine or ten. That meant waiting for two whole hours to know what had happened in Spain. I could not understand the speakers on the wireless, and foreign stations were not easy to find with our set. So the urge to learn was strong and virtue was its own reward. Before I had been in Sweden many weeks I was able to get at least an idea of what the papers said, and before I came away I made a short speech to the people, thanking them in their native tongue for their help.

Little by little Marissa and I overcame the strange feeling that one always has when settling in a new country, that is, if the word settling can be used when one is only bodily in a place and the spirit is absent most of the time. It was only through my work that I could occasionally forget the terrible longing to be in Spain and the even more urgent need to be free. A diplomat can rarely say what his heart prompts and there are times when keeping the heart in the bondage of silence is more difficult to endure than the loss of physical liberty. My body seemed to be tied up in a knot. Even my capacity for admiring nature had disappeared. The only thing that touched me deeply was what affected Spain. It had become an obsession.

Not the land of Spain alone, though at times I felt as if I could have given anything just to touch its earth and feel it crumble under the pressure of my fingers, but the people, the men fighting and dying there, the women waiting and weeping, the children being born and being killed. Then every sigh and tear and groan tore at my being. There were moments when I felt I must get rid of the pain or cry out, that I must do something to get away from the memory of what I had seen and from what I knew was going on.

At first it seemed queer to be living through this torture in snow-clad tranquil Sweden. But it did not take me long to discover that, like those volcanoes that are also snow-tipped, Sweden is often calm just on the surface. Underneath there is a smoldering fire that might break out at any moment.

The people have been taught self-control and practice it to such a degree that one is apt to be led astray by it. Their language itself has trained them that way. There is a sentence of three words that is a good example of this: Var så god. Everyone, old and young, rich or poor, wise or ignorant, uses it constantly. It is difficult to translate because it means so many things: gratitude, desire to serve, courteous greetings. It is equivalent to If you please, By your leave, Please don't mention it, At your service, Thank you, and several other polite expressions all in one.

I have sometimes wondered whether this limitation in the use of words is not a brake put upon feeling. The formality of Swedish manners is also a cloak to hide emotion. Little boys bend their heads solemnly and little girls bob graciously when they would probably prefer to fling out their arms to the newcomer. But underneath this rigid demeanor there is great passion, a longing to find expression, a fulness of heart, that is revealed only after prolonged communion with some other soul and sometimes never reaches the surface.

The women are less reserved than the men who, in general, are helplessly secretive about their inner selves. This makes them appear indifferent, cold, disinterested or *gauche* whenever the real self tries to push its way through the outer crust.

As is often the case, a common anxiety and a common objective led the way to a quick understanding between the Swedish people and me. The glamour of a country like Spain held a special charm for this northern people, and the heroic fight of the Spaniards for what the Swedes prize most highly, broke down all the barriers and opened up deep currents of feelings. As the representative of the Spain they had learned to admire and love, I was made the object of constant attention. When I walked down the streets the words *Spanska ministern* followed me like the echo of footsteps. Footsteps of a people that, mentally at least, followed in the wake of Spain, and whom our tragedy had touched to the very heart. Many a Swedish volunteer fallen, or maimed for life, on Spanish soil, will bear witness to this.

Perhaps they needed this strong revulsion, perhaps their own achievements in the struggle for a higher standard of life had made them overcomplacent, smugly indifferent, to the needs of others. I have often seen a look of amazement come over the faces of those not yet awakened when I have answered their question : "Do you not think we are a most fortunate people ?" with "You are the most fortunate and with it the most unhappy people I know." And it was true. The Swedes who strove for other people's happiness, and there were many, had the mystical strength, the warmth and glow that comes from "loving one's neighbor like oneself," but there were many, too, who tried to shut out the cries from outside and were being morally drowned in their own comfort.

No bread hunger could be seen throughout the land, but there was hunger and thirst for higher things than food, which the Spanish tragedy gave many people the chance of satisfying.

I have often been asked whether I think the Swedes are like the Germans. I have no special taste for racial research so I could not answer from a scientific point of view, but there is, to my mind, one great difference between the two peoples. The Swedes have been born and bred under the rule of democracy and the Germans have not. Whether this goes deep enough into the human soul to make a permanent disparity is difficult to say. In other respects, in their understanding of culture, in their love of music, even in their outward appearance, Swedish people sometimes resemble the best type of Germans, but the Swedes are not sentimental like the Germans. They also have always shown good taste, a quality one cannot always find among the "chosen people" of the Reich.

Marissa came into my study one morning, perfectly radiant. "Look," she said, laying an open telegram on my desk, and then in a happy voice, "Germán is coming."

Germán, who was barely convalescent after his wound, had made up his mind to come to see her. They had been engaged now for months but had been separated from each other most of the time. This reunion was the best way for them to know each other, not with the *insouciance* of carefree youth, but with the maturity of mind born from danger and pain.

In spite of her liberal upbringing, Marissa had lost none of the traditional characteristics of her race. In her these things were not skin-deep. Life was a serious business. Love was not a passing phase to be adjusted at pleasure but something permanent. The idea of Germán in peril was constant torture that she would not have laid aside even had she had the will. The long intervals without letters had been such a source of anxiety that she was worn to a shadow. I was glad to think

Isabel de Palencia and Baron de Geer in the state coach on the way to present her credentials as Minister to Sweden

Madame de Palencia and her daughter Marissa
in the big salon of the Spanish Legation

that now she might have a small respite from all the worry and misery of the past months.

"I shall never be happy while Spain is suffering even if I were never to be separated again from Germán," she said to me when I told her something to that effect.

Like so many other Spaniards outside Spain, there was no peace for her so long as the war went on.

Marissa was a great favorite with the employees and servants of the legation. Accustomed to being petted and made much of by our own Maria and Asunción in Madrid, she instinctively looked for affection in the people round her, and she got it. Nils was specially devoted. He was so huge and she so small that I think, at times, he had the feeling she was a little girl and while he addressed her with the greatest respect as Fröken Palencia there was also something protective in his manner.

Often when he brought our tea to the sitting room upstairs, he would try to induce me to go out, hoping that Marissa would go out, too. It was seldom that I had the time and then I just longed to be back. Not even a run in the car through the great snow-white forests, with the fir trees singing their ageless hymns and the subconscious feeling that fairies and elves might lie waiting for the night in the empty cones on the ground, could awaken my heart from its deadly torpor for anything outside Spain's troubles. Nils tried hard to interest us. A fervent lover of nature like all Swedes, he would turn round constantly to point out some specially lovely corner in the forest or a view from a bend in the road.

"*Det är vackert, Madame Minister*," ("That is pretty, Madam Minister"), he would say hopefully and then, a little discouraged, would repeat as though to comfort himself, "*Så vackert.*"

And the forest was more than pretty. It was impressively

magnificent in the white quiet silence that was like a pall for the stately dead. Sometimes Nils would try another way. Marissa was in need of new shoes but we had left the United States in such hurry she had not made the necessary provision, and in all Paris we had not found any to fit her small feet. In Stockholm the shops we had so far tried had nothing in her size.

Nils made it a point of honor to take us to every shoeshop in Stockholm. He thought it was a good excuse to make us go out. Once the big stores had been searched through in vain, he insisted on driving up to the most hidden-away little corners where as a matter of fact there were just a few models.

The scene was the same everywhere. He would stop as near the pavement as he could, looking haughtily at the drivers of other cars if they tried to pass us. Then he would throw open the door of our car as though it were a state coach and ceremoniously help us out. After which he would escort us into the store, explain what it was we wanted to an employee and then retire to wait for us outside. As a rule it took only a few minutes for us to be told that our quest there had been useless. The moment Nils saw us coming he would hurry to the car, fling the door open again, and looking at our empty hands would say with a sorrowful air, *"Inte, Madame Minister?"* ("Nothing, Madam Minister?")

"Inte, Nils," was our invariable answer.

While he wrapped us up carefully we could hear him chuckle to himself and then as he took his place he would turn, with his face beaming, his two huge forefingers almost meeting in an effort to show what Marissa's foot was like, *so små.*

After which he would drive on to some other place, shaking his head over the shortcomings of Stockholm's shoemakers but secretly delighted over their discomfiture. I truly believe that if by chance one day Marissa had been fitted in a Swedish shoe-shop, Nils would have been bitterly disappointed. Even by having the shoes made to order we did not obtain very satisfactory results and in the end we made up our minds to have them sent over from the United States.

CHAPTER XX

We had not been in the legation long before the radio first and then the press gave us bad news of the war in the Malaga sector. I had been hearing from my brother Juan quite regularly and it was almost settled that he and his wife and daughter would come and pay me a visit, when the town was taken.

The Italian aviation and the Italian fleet encircled the city, partly supported in their task by a few groups under the command of General Queipo de Llano, the "Radio General" as he was called on account of his talks over the radio, talks of such blatant vulgarity and coarseness that Franco had to put a stop to them. General Queipo de Llano would have liked to take upon himself all the responsibility of the attack and the laurels of the victory. The Italian military command, however, was not going to be cheated out of a single particle of glory and it very soon made clear that Malaga fell under the pressure of the "glorious Italian fleet" and the "heroic Italian aviators."

In truth, heroism was entirely superfluous in that action, considering the town was not defended and the only attacks were those carried out against the civilian population which was shelled from the sea and machine-gunned from the air while fleeing from the city in search of shelter. The bodies of defenseless old men, women and children literally covered large portions of the road between Malaga and Almería which winds in and out of the coast in a beautiful undulating line.

Marissa and I were in our sitting room when the news came over the air. We were dismayed by it. Malaga in the hands of the invaders ? Malaga, famous for its strong liberalism, giving up without a struggle ?

The republican generals that were in charge of Malaga's defense were made the object of bitter criticism. Their intervention has never been clearly explained. Largo Caballero, who was then prime minister and minister of war, was also attacked. Whatever the reasons for the fall of the lovely Mediterranean city, one thing is certain, there were no arms. Could arms have been sent down in time ? In any case, there would never have been enough to save the city against the overwhelming strength that the Italian forces had accumulated.

I spent a sleepless night thinking of Juan and thanking Heaven that Ricardo was no longer there. Juan I knew would be safe. He was not a Fascist by any means but his extreme Catholicism made him lean always to the right. His only son, Juan, had left his home at the outbreak of the war. He was just out of the naval school and did not hesitate to stand beside what he considered the only legitimate government of Spain. At the time of Malaga's fall he was on board one of the destroyers of our fleet, a commander at the age of twenty-four !

I thought of the gay streets and of the lovely gardens of my home town, where I had played as a child and where I had first met Cefe ; of the happy days in the large high-ceilinged home when the idea of leaving my little goat, Morenita, alone on the terraced roof while I went to church, was almost unbearable. How remote were those days and how small my sorrows. The radio speaker had explained how the people had been mowed down as they fled and I could almost see the slender dark-eyed women and their babies lying on the road at the foot of the olive trees looking out toward a sea that had become their enemy. The beautiful blue Mediterranean in whose calm depths these very women must often have bathed and on whose shores their children must have played. How they must have wondered that it should have become an instrument of death !

A few days after Malaga's fall, the Swedish Riksdag passed a law forbidding volunteers to go to Spain. The measure came too late. The lovers of democracy and liberty and justice in

Sweden were already in my country. All the same, it was another sign of the times. Even in democratic countries the people were going to be prevented from defending their principles. Those men who went to Spain should have been looked upon as heroes but it was the reverse. And one more of our moral values was, for the time being, destroyed.

Germán was on his way to Stockholm. He was coming over with the new secretary of the legation, a young volunteer who had lost an eye in the war ; Aurelio Romeo and his newly wedded wife. They did not, however, reach Sweden together. The young couple had remained for a few days in Paris while Germán hurried on. Marissa and I were just discussing what train he would come by and how we would arrange to meet him, when a loud peal of the door bell sent us both flying to the staircase. It was only seven o'clock in the morning. Germán came up two steps at a time and caught Marissa in his arms as he reached the top one. I felt a queer little dismayed feeling ; there was something possessive in the way he tucked her arm under his and dragged her away to the sitting room.

Romeo arrived a few days later and he and his wife were having luncheon with us when I was called to the telephone. "Riga," said Nils to me with a pleased look on his face. He thought a call from Cefe would be sure to make me happy and that one most certainly did.

"Nena, Nena," my husband said, "have you heard the news ?"

"No . . . what news ?"

"We have had a great victory in Guadalajara." Cefe was so excited he could hardly speak. "The Italians have been routed by our army. They have abandoned large quantities of arms and are fleeing before our people."

It was true. Cefe had had to call up our embassy in Paris for something and they had told him all about it. I could hardly wait to get back to the dining room to tell the others. The world was amazed. There were long faces among some of my colleagues and delighted handshakes from others. From the very first moment I had been made to see the difference between those who were with my Spain and those who sympathized with Franco. Not always out of personal motives perhaps, rather from a combination of both. That was the case with the ministers of Great Britain, Belgium and Rumania, all three good friends of Señor Fiscowich and fervent Catholics whose minds had been poisoned by the rebel propaganda on the subject of our supposedly anti-religious tendencies, and by anti-communists in the political field. The Franco campaign of calumnies and lies had also reached them here. I could make no complaint as to their attitude toward me personally. It was courteous like that of their respective governments.

Others went out of their way to be cordial like charming Dr. Wang King-Ky and his wife and daughter. They were prompted not only by a personal liking and sympathy but also through the bond of a common cause. China and republican Spain were struggling for their liberty in the midst of the official indifference of the world. The French, Norwegian and Danish ministers, like those of the South American republics who had representatives in Stockholm, were always friendly, Mexico particularly so. Chile was represented only by a chargé d'affaires at the time and he was recalled after the advent of the popular front government in his country. The United States changed its representatives three times during the years I was in Stockholm : Mr. Laurence A. Steinhardt, who was transferred almost at once to Moscow ; Mr. Fred Morris Dearing who with his wife I found to be perfect examples of the

most charming American type, cultured, refined and unaffected ; and finally, Mr. Frederick A. Sterling who was still
in Stockholm when I left. The Finnish minister, Mr. Paasi-
kivi, I saw a good deal of, naturally, and found him to be a
good collaborator and endowed with an intelligent statesman-
like spirit.

Last but not least, Madame Kollontay. Rather than a colleague, I like to think of her as a friend, a woman of extraordinary intelligence, keen vision and unconquerable will, together with a warm heart. It is no wonder that in the face of
all opposition she should have managed to make a place for
herself even in such antagonistic circles. I felt drawn to her
from the moment we first met in Geneva. Alexandra Kollontay is above all things an idealist. Her political creed may not
be to everyone's taste, but one is forced to respect her for her
absolute loyalty to what she judges best for the world's happiness. We very rarely touched on these subjects. She knew
I was not a communist but there were many other ties to bind
us together without that one. First and foremost, the sufferings of Spain which she, being a woman, felt as I did. Endowed with an alert mind, a fine sense of humor and an extraordinary background, she would at times take me completely out
of myself with her interesting conversation. At times, too,
she would try to amuse me by taking me out for a drive. She
loved the snow and the forest but she never succeeded in breaking up the feeling of apathy that prevented me from enjoying
nature emotionally, not just with a purely intellectual appreciation.

Madame Kollontay's sympathy for the suffering Spaniards
was shared by all the members of the legation staff. Every
five or six weeks they would bring me the results of a collection taken among themselves. The money would be spent on
small but urgent needs such as bandages, medical utensils, food

and clothes for the children or sewing material for the women.

The victory of the republican troops over the Italian army of occupation, in Guadalajara, was hailed by the friends of loyal Spain as a proof that the republic had at last and in the face of almost insurmountable difficulties succeeded in forming a new army ; an army in which people knew what they were fighting for, an army for the defense of their country against a foreign invader. What mattered it that Franco or some other man with some other Spanish name should be the figurehead on the other side ? It was foreigners that led.

Those who had believed and hoped that Madrid would fall when the republicans had to fight with the queer assortment of arms they were able to muster, and had been astonished witnesses of loyalist resistance, were naturally greatly disturbed now that technical means were added to the moral strength which had won the day for the republic in many towns during the first days of the rebellion. Fascists above all were in despair to think that the representatives of Mussolini's "mighty power" had received such a blow from the "ragged militiamen" they so despised. The militiamen were as a matter of fact no longer ragged. The blue overalls with which the loyalists had carried out many an heroic deed had been superseded by military uniforms, conventional in shape and color. The sticks and stones had been supplanted by rifles and bullets but the spirit was the same indomitable spirit of independent Spain that has always in God's good time succeeded in shaking off foreign bondage, be it Roman or Goth or Arab or French.

Italy realized that the effort made so far was not enough. She knew that if Germany was to have the control of Spain's mines and centres of production to alleviate the dearth of metals and wheat that she suffered from, if Italy was to occupy the strategic spots she wanted for the control of the Mediterranean, and if, above all, the military prestige of both countries was not going to suffer other serious setbacks, they would have to make an even greater effort than they had done and pour into our country many more thousands of men and thousands of tons of war material with which to kill the "despicable reds" and destroy the beautiful Spanish cities. It would have been folly for Germany and Italy not to take advantage of Franco's complicity and above all of the fine understanding of the well-bred British and French governments who were so polite as to allow Germany and Italy to do as they liked and who were, on the contrary, so ready to uphold the rules of the Non-Intervention Pact when these were in danger of being violated by any other country wishing to help the "reds." Germany and Italy knew that any denouncement of totalitarian infractions would never provoke more than a delicate raising of the eyebrows on the part of England.

Loyalist Spain knew that her victory was going to cost her dear, that it would awaken such anxiety in Italy that Mussolini would redouble his efforts to help the rebels. If only the victory obtained could have been followed up ! But the loyalists did not have the necessary war means to keep on harassing the Italians, so part of the success of that brilliant action was lost.

It was good enough, however, to send the foreign chancelleries into hysterics again and the "home" impressions were faithfully reflected in their representatives abroad. Stockholm was no exception. Those of my colleagues who had not shown any interest in our struggle before were suddenly anxious to hear all about the republican army and its possibilities and asked for details regarding the extension of Italian and German intervention. The Swedish people themselves, and other friendly representatives, were overjoyed at the turn things seemed to have taken and hurried to offer their congratulations.

Democracy was lifting its head. Would it be long before it was given another blow ?

In the month of April I found I had to go to Geneva for the meeting of the Committee of the Experts on Slavery. I liked that committee because it worked so well. Mr. Haller from the league staff was most competent and always ready to help. Gouverneur Marchand, the French representative, kept the balance as chairman between the more conservatively inclined members like the Italian, Dutch and Belgian, and Sir George Maxwell who represented Great Britain, and myself.

Our task was, of course, non-political, but it is impossible to eliminate feeling even from the most neutral fields. As a matter of fact, the Italian member was the only one who tried to introduce disturbing elements into our peaceful midst. Italy was at that moment doing her utmost to persuade the world that her conquest of Ethiopia was due to the purest of humanitarian motives : that of redeeming a people from slavery and of exposing conditions in the fallen empire. This, from the Italian point of view, would have been most welcome, especially if that exposure was set up in accordance with the Italian concept of propaganda. But the committee was not taken in. The next time we met the representative of Italy's government did not come.

I had asked our Minister of Foreign Affairs for leave to go to Spain for a few days and see Cefito before returning to Stockholm. It was granted at once so I lost no time in catching the train for Toulouse and the plane on to Valencia from there. It was my first visit since I had left Spain for the league assembly seven months before and my heart took to jumping up and down or pounding my sides in the most extraordinary fashion.

It was a beautiful spring day. The perfume of the orange

trees in full bloom was intoxicating. Cefito had told me he would be waiting for me at the town depot so I was not disappointed at not seeing him when I got off. The airport looked very strange with the camouflaged cars and planes, and strict rules posted upon all the walls bidding people beware of spies. But everybody seemed to ignore the possibility of an attack by air and went about his business, singing cheerfully.

When my boy rushed up to the bus and lifted me out bodily I could have cried for pure joy. It was so good to see him and he was so full of fun and faith in the future that no wonder I felt optimistic. Not that time alone, but on every occasion on which I had been to Spain during the war, and sometimes conditions were very hard, I have experienced the same confidence and the same security, much more so than in the comfort and abundance of the Stockholm legation. We spent four very happy days together, making the most of every minute, meeting all his friends, new and old, and being greeted by my own. He was never tired of speaking of the marvelous feats of heroism of the republican army. The town was very crowded and precautions against air raids were being taken. I saw some shelters but thought them very small for Valencia's population.

Life in the loyalist zone had changed very much during those months. In an almost superhuman effort the government had formed an efficient, disciplined army. All disorder had disappeared. People were readjusting their lives to circumstances and with it all the exalted conviction in the cause had not diminished in the slightest.

On April the fourteenth, the anniversary of the republic and a national holiday, all Valencia came out to look at the waving flags and floral decorations. I went to President Azaña's reception for the diplomatic corps and had a talk with him. He was looking well and asked me to dine with him and Mrs.

Azaña the next day. The popular fervor for the republican cause had never been so strong and my heart felt light when I left the presidential residence. I was sure that nothing would eradicate faith in the republican régime from the Spanish people's hearts.

In Stockholm everybody had wanted to know how the Swedish-Norwegian medical unit was functioning. They had been granted a beautiful building inland, and I found them doing splendid work and delighted to be in Spain. One of their doctors said to me :

"I shall never forget these days in your country and with your people, Madame Palencia. They are wonderful." He had been amazed to see how the Spaniards appreciated Sweden and how grateful they were for its generous help. To be a Swede was the best introduction anyone could have those days. "I have not been able to pay for a single refreshment in a café," he went on to say, "the waiters always ask me my nationality, and when I tell them, they always say, *Ah, Suecia.* Then when I ask for my bill they invariably answer that it is already paid and I cannot get them to accept a cent."

At last I made up my mind I must leave. All my official work was done. I had received instructions and I had seen my boy, although for too short a time. Cefito was very loath to let me go but there were several reasons for my immediate return. I had promised to speak for the Help Committee in Oslo and besides Marissa was waiting for me to arrive for her wedding. Germán had made up his mind that he ought to be in Spain again by the end of April and when the time for the separation had grown near they had both seemed so upset that I myself suggested they be married and return to Spain together.

The decision had cost Marissa a struggle. She hated leaving me alone. On the other hand she could not bear the thought of letting Germán go, either. The balance turned in his favor.

They were to be married very quietly in the legation. None of us felt like making merry under the circumstances even to celebrate a wedding and a love match. Marissa had even refused to get a trousseau. She said she had quite enough clothes and would rather the money were spent on food for our people. Cefe was to come over from Latvia for the ceremony. At midday on a Friday I took the plane for Toulouse. Cefito took me down to the bus. I am afraid I gave him a very tearful good-bye. He put a large bunch of Valencian carnations into my two hands and smilingly cried out, *Salud*, as the bus drove off. I caught a last glimpse of his fair hair and two waving hands as we rushed along. Then a military convoy intercepted my view. War. . . The inevitability of destiny crushed me for a moment.

At four o'clock in the afternoon next day I was in Stockholm. Cefe was already there and came with Germán and Marissa to the airport to meet me. I spent the evening looking over Marissa's things and helping her to pack them.

"You haven't a single really appropriate frock to wear," I said. "You should have at least one simple tailormade."

"Don't bother, mother."

But I did bother. Germán had been appointed doctor of the air force and would have to be going from one town to another. If she went with him she would need a practical costume, not just the flimsy things she had. I wondered what I could do to get her a dress. The next morning was Sunday and the marriage was to take place at three o'clock Monday afternoon. I would try to find something Monday morning.

We had some trouble arranging the marriage so as to make it conform to Swedish laws. It was perfectly all right for Spain if it took place in the legation in accordance with our legal procedure and was duly registered afterward, but this did not make it legitimate in Sweden where the law required

all marriages to be registered in a church after the usual putting up of the banns. I was advised to consult the Legal Department of the Ministry of Foreign Affairs on the subject and,
after some discussion, it was decided that the marriage would
be valid in Sweden also if I requested the authorization of the
king. His majesty and the Swedish government granted my
petition in writing.

On Monday morning I drove with Marissa to the shopping
centre of the town and in spite of her protests indulged in the
purchase of a charming blue tailormade dress that we found
by chance in one of the shops. A few alterations were necessary but they promised we should have the frock in the legation
at two-thirty ; and so we did.

Very few people had been invited to the wedding, just our
most intimate friends besides the legation staff : the Brantings,
including Sonja's and Georg's eighty-year-old mother, the
widow of the great Hjalmar, still alert and bright in spite of
her years ; Doctor and Mrs. Perez Gil ; Madame Kollontay ;
Doctor Ruby Lind and some others. A pale April sun was
coming in through the windows of my study, trying to polish
the severe furniture with its rays and make the room look
cheerful, as we all stood round the table and the young couple
accepted each other as mates and good companions. Marissa
looked ridiculously young in her new blue dress, with a small
bouquet of rosebuds held between her two hands. Germán,
dark-skinned and dark-haired, looked very earnest over the
ceremony. This was not a scientific or research job like those
he loves. It was really much more formidable and he took it
very seriously. Cefe stood beside me. He turned and kissed
me as his daughter bent down to sign her name in the registry.
A spontaneous gesture like that of a child seeking comfort and
also meant to make up to me for the coming separation from
my little girl.

That night she and Germán left for Spain. They stopped at Copenhagen and Brussels and then went on to Paris where they had intended to stay for some days, but they were both so anxious to return to Spain, Germán, especially, that they cut short their honeymoon and flew to Valencia.

We kept all news of the wedding from the press but they found out about it somehow, and much to Marissa's indignation, for she hates publicity, some newspaper men turned up at the station and took snapshots. Those pictures were the first thing I saw next day. Nils, who was used to bringing my correspondence and the papers up to my room every morning, pointed them out to me. He smiled delightedly as he laid a huge finger on the column and chuckled to himself. Then he murmured, "Madame Somolinos."

Cefe stayed with me for two more days and then went back to Riga. I saw him off. The boat for Latvia lay in the docks waiting for the passengers who, with true northern slowness, passed over the gangplank and disappeared below.

There was still a good deal of snow on the ground but the trees were beginning to shake off their lethargy and waved their bare branches in the wind as though anxious to greet the coming spring. The ducks that had slept the winter through on the frozen water of the Mälar, not caring or needing to eat or move all those long months, had suddenly disappeared like the skaters and the skiers and the sleighs with their placid horses and soft tinkling of bells.

All Stockholm had changed.

In the street parterres some blossoms were forcing their way through the earth, hardened and dried up by the continued frost. Even the expression of the people's faces was different from what I had seen that day, four months ago, when I had come into the Swedish capital for the first time. Everybody seemed more gay, more awake. Like the trees and the flowers, they were preparing to welcome the spring, the season looked forward to by the people of the north as the herald of their beloved but all too short summer. A few days more and the snow would melt away entirely and Stockholm would wake up to find itself decked like a bride : masses of white lilac and cherry blossom resting against a background of tender green ; carpets of tulips and hyacinths spreading under her feet and high up in the clear blue sky whole processions of birds returning to their nests after a sojourn in warmer climates. The streets brightened up with colorful awnings made the whole town look different, more cordial, more receptive, more animated if not more beautiful.

Marissa's first letter from Valencia made me feel that we had done the best possible thing under the circumstances to let her marry and go. She was delighted to be in Spain again and was looking after Germán and Cefito like the true little mother she is.

"I should be quite happy if I knew you were not all alone in that huge house," she wrote. "I wish it had only two rooms instead of sixty." This allusion made me smile. The rooms of the legation had been counted by a lady who was so enthusiastic for republican Spain that she had felt quite annoyed when she heard the Italian minister's wife saying that Italy's legation was the finest foreign mission in Stockholm for it had forty rooms. This lady asked my leave to go through ours. She went from attic to cellar, through the hall and the salons, the kitchen and the scullery, and came back in triumph to announce that we had sixty rooms ! I suppose she lost no time in letting everybody know, but I should certainly not have gone to all that trouble myself.

In order to set Marissa's mind at rest, I asked one of her friends, Shanti Dussaq from Geneva, a niece of a very old friend of mine, to come and stay with me for a while. She and Anita, who turned up later and stayed all through the summer, kept the legation more lively than it would have been with just myself, poring over documents, signing papers, talking over commercial possibilities with Ugarte, looking over the press communiqués carefully prepared by Dethorey, paying and receiving indispensable calls, writing out reports, making extracts of the new and most interesting measures adopted by our government and having them passed to whoever might be interested, and listening in to the wireless when "news" came over the air. Such was my life day after day. A full life, yes, but one hampered by social requirements, by diplomatic limitations, by the necessity of being always careful of one's clothes, one's speech, and one's demeanor.

CHAPTER XXI

A few days after my return from Valencia I took the night train for Oslo. I had promised the Committee of Aid to Spain that I would give a lecture on Spanish culture. They were having a big drive for funds and thought my talk would help. I arrived early in the morning and came back the same night so I was not able to see much of Oslo. Enough, however, to wish I could have prolonged my stay among that fine sturdy people. The Norwegians are more passionate than the Swedes and because of it less reserved, more free spiritually. I thought that must be the reason why their art — their painting, writing and acting — is at present so much more progressive. I found everyone keenly interested in our problems and the generosity of the people on a par with the highest yet achieved.

When my all-too-short visit came to an end I promised myself to return, hoping that I would be able to tarry a little in order to appreciate more fully the many beauties of the rugged coast of Norway and the intellectual and social progress made throughout the country.

Stockholm was looking her prettiest when I returned and settled down to work with a will. As things were getting into shape at the chancellery, I thought it was time I studied Swedish methods and learned something about the country's past difficulties and its actual prosperity. The order and contentment that one saw all around could not be the result of spontaneous generation. Like most things, it must have come through strife and labor.

The Minister for Social Work who, in Sweden, is also the Home Secretary, Mr. Gustav Möller, and his wife, asked me to dine with them one night and I thought it would be a good chance to find out some of the inner workings of the system

337

by which Sweden had come to be what she is : the most highly civilized country of Europe, most civilized according to the modern social concept of the word, that is, where the greatest number of people, in proportion to the total population, are able to eat well, to dress well, to be decently housed and to receive the elements of culture, without — and this is the great test — being deprived, in exchange for those benefits, of the greatest of all human privileges : liberty ; without any of her citizens being forbidden to hear, to speak, to read and to think what they choose.   In one word, Sweden has reached her high level with as little sacrifice of individual liberties as possible. It is said that she has achieved this through compromise ; that, if not the individual liberties, she has immolated the other, perhaps, more essential things ; that the people have had to make concessions in order to preserve the benefits of peace.

There is a great deal to say on the subject.   It is true that Sweden, like other Scandinavian countries, has at times had to give in to the pressure of nations more powerful.   But which one is entirely free from blame in this sense ?   Brotherly love has not, unfortunately, become so universal and so deeply rooted that countries will sacrifice their own tranquility in order to help others in need, except when there has been something to gain by it or, perhaps, to save their own skin.   One of the cases where Sweden had to compromise was on the subject of Spain.   She, as every other country with the same concept of international law, should not have accepted the Non-Intervention Pact, but she ran, or believed she ran, great risks by refusing and so submitted.   Her judgment got the better of her feelings.   But, after all, the small countries were the ones that were least to blame.   In what refers to her own inner life Sweden may also have compromised.   The results have been excellent from a material point of view.   The system has perhaps failed in others.

That evening in the home of the social minister and his wife is among the pleasantest memories of my years in Sweden. Gustav Möller, tall, thin, with pleasant unaffected manners, is a socialist of the best type. Really progressive and sincerely on the side of the oppressed, his collaboration in the cabinet is a precious contribution to democracy. His wife, who writes under her own name of Else Kleen, is not only clever and original, she is also endowed with a sensitive understanding of human suffering that makes her rise above the common level. Her work for youthful delinquents has been the cause of controversy and opposition, but she is accustomed to carry things with a high hand and will not give in if she thinks she is right. She is a tall, distinguished, white-haired woman, with a whimsical smile and animated manner. She belongs to a conventional smart set but does not hesitate to defy it if, and when, she thinks it necessary.

Their tiny home is unpretentious to the highest degree, but charming. Minister Möller kindly explained many things to me about the social order in his country. He declared that great advances had been made in the standard of life of the people but that there was still much to be done, especially in the forest zones. His presence in the cabinet, I felt, was a guaranty that, no matter how difficult times might become, progress would continue or, at least, there would be no turning back.

I had already visited the headquarters of the Swedish co-operative societies, the K.F. (Kooperativa Förbundet) as they are known to every Swede. I had heard how they were started by a little band of determined men and women who had made up their minds that a way could be found to prevent the underdog and the middleman from being the victims of avarice or bad management.

Co-operative societies tending toward a total change in the buying and selling of home products had been functioning long before in England, but these were working toward a more ideal interchange between human beings. Their objective was utopian. The little group of Swedes was guided by reasons of a totally practical nature.

They first pooled their funds and proceeded to buy from wholesale merchants such commodities as their limited capital allowed. These commodities they would fetch and distribute themselves, by turns, after working hours. Soon others joined them and much to their surprise their adherents grew so many that new societies had to be set up in different parts of the country and later affiliated with the central group in Stockholm. The strong businesslike qualities of the Swedes were put at the service of the new movement. Small stores were opened and it was not long before their influence in the market began to make itself felt. Then began the struggle between the new organization and the retail merchants whose interests had been ignored to favor the buyer. The usual means employed in competitions of this kind, where the "sacred" rights of money-making concerns are endangered, were brought into play against the K.F. Boycott by wholesalers was leveled against the nascent social force that might have been strangled then and there had the K.F. not been led by men of indomitable will, and had the co-operators themselves not been ready to go to any lengths to save what they instinctively felt might be their salvation. They overcame the boycott by launching into wholesale buying, and they massed their strength in order to fight the "trusts" that were their chief enemies.

The first of these fights took place against the margarine cartel, a powerful Swedish organization that had all the business concerning this product in its hands. The K.F., after grave deliberation, made up its mind to take a definite step. It bought up a small margarine factory and began to sell at a lower price than the "trust." The people, observing the unequal struggle, looked with growing favor upon the "little man." The number of co-operators increased. The cartel was forced to bring down its rates, too, and victory in this field was assured.

The next battle was fought for a low price in bread. Here the opponent was even more powerful. The flour millers in the country had constituted a monopoly and managed things as they chose. The co-operators, after bringing into action their most able strategists, found it possible to buy a fine mill near Stockholm called *Tre Kronor* and under this emblem of their nation set out to destroy monopolist intentions.

It was achieved at the cost of great sacrifices. The K.F. had to maintain a low price against the even lower price suddenly adopted by their adversaries with the object of breaking up the new regulating factor. It was a bold game to play. People generally find it hard to resist the possibility of economizing a cent in their daily expenses even when they know that it will militate against them in the end. The society of flour millers continued to sell at reduced prices for a little while. The K.F. kept up its price to the level compatible with fair dealing and common sense. The Swedes again took sides with the brave co-operative society. A new mill was bought in Gothenburg. At last the K.F. won. The monopolists, unable to keep up their expensive game, were forced to put up their prices and the co-operators, by keeping theirs at the original level, found themselves selling at a cheaper rate.

The next step, by no means an easy one, was to interest the farmers. Here, too, success followed in unexpected proportions. After some hesitation a start was made. Membership in all the rural areas grew rapidly, each new group showing it was ready to lay aside its special interests in order to collaborate for the common good.

Another victory was obtained by the purchase of a factory for the manufacture of galoshes. The Swedish climate makes this item one of supreme importance so the public was amazed and gratified to find that, thanks to the co-operative organization, they could buy galoshes fully two crowns a pair cheaper than the powerful galosh trust sold them and they were quite as good if not of better quality. A shoe factory was soon added to the number of producing centres of the K.F.

Housing was another important question that the co-operative societies could not leave unsolved. New stores were built in order to carry on the business with as little cost as possible and then apartment houses were started so rapidly that between fifteen and sixteen per cent of Stockholm's nearly six hundred thousand inhabitants already live in dwellings of this sort. The K.F.'s factories lost no time in building houses for their workers and employees. Every device for simplifying labor is added to the houses built under the direction of the K.F. When possible small gardens are added, as well as playrooms for the children. This allows the mothers, most of whom are also workers, the necessary freedom.

And not the least important of the long list of achievements was the construction of the Luma Co-operative Electric-Lamp Factory by the co-operators of the four Scandinavian countries, forming a united front against the powerful Phoebus cartel and beating it by lowering the price of lamps from one crown-fifty to one crown and making a safe surplus margin in spite of it.

Needless to say, each and every success of the K.F. was the result of long and tedious struggling against manufacturers and business men. But the tenacity of the co-operators as well as their excellent management has so far won every time in the face of all opposition, and today the organization is respected by every sensible Swede, even those whose interests have been attacked.

One of the things I was most anxious to hear from Minister

Möller was whether any benefits had been obtained from the state control of some of the basic industries of the country. In many nations even the acquisition of such control is not achieved without a certain measure of violence. I was told that the Swedish government has for long been the owner of a great part of the forests of the nation and has been able to develop the industries derived from timber with important profits. In regard to the rich Swedish mines, the state has entered into partnership with other powerful firms for their exploitation and receives fifty per cent of the total net profits. The power system and most of the railways are also state controlled and their good management shows that the increase of bureaucracy is not always prejudicial to the country's interests. Gustav Möller smiled when I spoke of the high standard of living enjoyed by all the Swedes.

"Not by all yet," he said, shaking his head. "There is still much to do in that line also."

I could not, of course, contradict him, but my impressions so far had been that there were no underfed, ill-clothed, or uneducated people in the land. Stockholm is a capital not only with no slums but also without that disorder and ugliness that one so often sees when entering large or small cities, as though their inhabitants took pleasure in frightening away their visitors instead of attracting them. We spoke at length of the courage with which Sweden had taken the bull by the horns in applying her cure for the economic crisis by restoring (in 1924) the gold standard fully a whole year before Great Britain, as well as by attempting to stabilize her currency. Careful watching of her budget in the years that followed also helped her to overcome not only the effects of the general depression and the postwar difficulties, but also those of the Kreuger catastrophe which threw her into a situation any less-balanced nation would have taken years to overcome. Many a compromise had also to be made then but Sweden was saved for the Swedes, as she had been several times before, either from economic ruin or from destruction by war, or from both.

Remembering the tragedy that unemployment has brought to other countries and the enormous disadvantages of "relief" as a means of alleviating the ills derived therefrom, I asked Minister Möller what measures the Swedish government had taken so far in limiting the effects of this terrible modern scourge. He gave the following data showing how his cabinet had faced the issues and was solving the problem.

According to him, unemployment in Sweden had been highest in the years between 1931 and 1936 when it had begun to decrease, thanks to the more favorable business conditions. In 1933 the social-democratic government proposed a plan for the mitigation of unemployment by the creation, on a large scale, of labor facilities by the state and local authorities, at the usual market rates. The question of leveling wages to the current standard for unskilled labor gave rise to great discussion and to a strong opposition but, by means of compromise with both sides, the social-democratic government was able to overcome all difficulties.

Two hundred and eighty-four million crowns were appropriated for works at open market rates for the budget years 1933–1934 and 1936–1937. Part of these funds were used for financing such local and central enterprises as bridge building, electrification of railways, drainage and others. Private undertakings were kept going by means of subsidies and loans. Thousands of persons were employed by the national unemployment commission's "reserve work," chiefly in road making. The voluntary unemployment insurance was also helpful, for it covered a membership of over one hundred and fifty thousand. Benefit from this insurance is received without a need-of-means test for the members who have paid contributions for some time and who are ready to accept work and have applied to the labor exchange for it. Business recovery did not entirely obliterate the evils of unemployment ; for in 1937 there were still some depressed areas in the quarry and lumber districts, but well-distributed relief did wonders.

"Next time we shall not be caught napping," Minister Möller said. "The government will have a reserve fund large enough to absorb the workers without having to resort to extreme measures against the rest of the community."

He then proceeded to explain how everything was in readiness. The plans for public works were already drawn up. Evidently the arrangement was to take in the unemployed by degrees. The moment one industry closed up, its men would pass on to public works and would, in this way, not lose their purchasing powers. Thus the stoppage of many industries, not directly touched by world depression because depending on home consumption, would not be affected and their workers would not lose their employment.

The committee in charge of organizing these works had declared in its report that "caution should be observed in undertaking public works in times of prosperity but that they ought to be held on hand so that no time need be lost in putting them into practice."

At the end of 1937 Sweden was ready to begin utility projects to the extent of nearly three thousand million crowns were the necessity to arise. Great importance has been given in this plan to agricultural requirements such as ditching, drainage, clearage, improvement of livestock accommodation, wells and water supply.

Here the good common sense of the Swedes was useful. They know how important their agricultural development is and they mean to take advantage of the possibilities offered. Timber exploitation and forestry will, of course, also be well looked after. As much as one hundred and fifty million crowns were put aside for that. Other measures, studied with the object of counteracting unemployment and benefiting people at the same time, include "housing," that is, the construction and improvement of dwellings especially for those people who suffer from overcrowding and a low housing standard. In the budget years of 1933–1934 and 1936–1937 fifty million crowns were put by for this purpose. The local authorities have always seconded state efforts along these lines most effectively. One must bear in mind that Sweden is a country that is free from that other scourge called "graft" and that collaboration in this field always means disinterested planning for the good of the people.

According to the regulations, dwellings for families with many children can be built or administered by the local authorities, the statutes of which preclude private gains. The state lends the funds at cost rates of interest for mortgages lying between fifty and ninety-five per cent of the acquisitory value of the property. The commune provides the site free of charge so that it takes part of the cost on itself. It is responsible for losses from non-payment of rates as well as for the provision of that part of the building costs not covered by state loans. In this way the building has fewer expenses than it would have in the open market. Special laws regulating the size of the dwellings and made effective in January 1937, guaranteed more hygienic conditions in housing.

The social minister had also worked out a new law on pensions which improved the condition of aged people and invalids. All persons above sixty-seven years could draw a pension financed partly by compulsory insurance contributions, partly by the state and local authorities. These pensions sometimes amounted to four hundred crowns a year. The social-democratic government had succeeded in 1936 in grading pensions according to the cost of living. This measure had brought about the fall of the social-democrats a few months before that same year but their victory in the general elections of the following autumn insured its passing by parliament.

The pension reform expresses the general tendency to build up social welfare on the basis of insurance and bonus and to do away with the poor-law stigma. This tendency is also evidenced in the support of blind people, working mothers and small children.

Perhaps the most interesting of all the social measures adopted of late years are those relating to the population policy. During the last decades the Swedish birth rate has been rapidly declining. In 1935 a special committee of experts called the "Population Commission" was appointed to investigate the causes of this phenomenon. Toward the end of 1936 it published a memorandum in which it stated the need for adequate sexual enlightenment and for rational birth control, the eugenic, hygienic and ethical values of which were strongly emphasized. It alleged that :

"It [birth control] enables children to be born and grow up under the most favorable conditions, makes the adaptation of the number of children to the economic resources of the family possible and encourages early marriages."

The committee recommended the legalization of abortion on medical, humanitarian or eugenic grounds, but refused to accept abortion for purely social reasons because it believed that, in the near future, social measures and a changed attitude toward illegitimacy should considerably improve the moral and economic position of pregnant women of all classes.

During the 1937 session, parliament adopted a number of reforms based on the committee's recommendations, with the object of lightening the economic burdens of people with small incomes in connection with the maintenance of their children. It introduced different subsidies for mothers with a taxable income below three thousand crowns and other subsidies for prospective mothers. Other laws arranged for widows and unmarried or divorced women to be helped to support their children, and for the care of orphans.

The budget year for 1937 allocated two million crowns to a national fund out of which loans up to one thousand crowns could be made to young couples, anxious to get married, for their furniture and setting up of the home. It was expected that in the near future free meals would be given to all school children. Parliament also adopted the principle of "equal pay for equal work" in the new salary regulations for male and female teachers in public service.

My talk with Minister Möller lasted well through the dinner and the after-dinner coffee and we had barely finished our talk when Mrs. Möller gaily announced that Karl Gerhard was coming round to the house when his performance in the theatre was over. When he came in conversation turned into other channels. We spoke of the theatrical crisis in Sweden where the motion picture has almost killed dramatic art. And so we lingered on until long after we had partaken of the traditional cups of tea with more cakes and sandwiches, after which guests can say good-bye to their hostess without appearing to be discourteous. To go before tea is served is considered the height of impoliteness. That night we stayed on until the servant brought in the "hot dogs and beer" that are the last signal for one to take one's departure.

Minister and Mrs. Möller saw us off at the foot of their stairs. A very progressive couple yet observant of tradition. He had not failed to make the customary toast at the beginning of the meal to bid us welcome nor to rise at the end to kiss his wife and express his appreciation of the dinner. She, however, would not accept the usual *Tack för maten* (Thanks for a good dinner) guests in Sweden are supposed to tend to their hostess as they leave the table.

"Why should you thank me ?" she said brightly. "I think it is an absurd custom. I begged you to come, did I not ?"

The evening had been an interesting one and I felt as I drove home there were many things in Sweden that other countries might copy to their benefit. Evolution is no doubt a good thing. Best when, as in those northern countries, opposition is only a small brake that makes progress more solid and lasting, never a barrier that has to be broken down by force, by revolution.

CHAPTER XXII

"You must be in Geneva for the opening day of the labor conference," said a voice over the telephone one morning when I was getting ready to go to Spain where I, as all the other Spanish heads of mission in Europe, had been commanded to go by the Spanish government.

"But I can't go," I answered. "I am going to Spain."

"No, no, it is settled for you to come here. We need you."

I had been called up from Berne by our minister there, Señor Fabra Ribas, who had been acting as our permanent delegate to the League of Nations and the Labor Office.

"I count on your being here. You will receive the necessary orders from Valencia about it," he added, and with a few friendly words he rang off.

I confess I felt rather disappointed. I had been looking forward so much to going to Spain. A call from Valencia reassured me.

"Please go to Geneva first and then come on here for instructions," said my own chief, Señor José Girál, Minister of Foreign Affairs. "You are needed in Geneva."

I wondered what made it so urgent for me to go there. Well, I would find out when I arrived at the conference. The Spanish cabinet had just been reformed. Largo Caballero had been replaced by Doctor Juan Negrín as Prime Minister. Doctor Negrín had been doing very well as Minister of Finance, an able man, speaking five languages and well versed in international affairs. I felt he might perhaps command more attention from the hard-headed die-hard conservative British cabinet than a workers' representative like Largo Caballero. At least he would be able to handle matters in a more direct fashion. Señor Girál was still the Minister of Foreign Affairs, a quiet scholarly man and a great personal friend and loyal supporter of Azaña. The rest of the cabinet had been made up with three socialists, two republicans, two communists, one representative from the Catalonian party and one from the party of the Basques.

When I reached Geneva, Señor Fabra Ribas told me what the hurry was all about.

"The elections for the board of administration are to take place this year," he said, "and we must win them."

As everyone knows the Administration Board of the International Labor Office — the I.L.O. as it is familiarly called — has an executive board on which most industrial countries such as Great Britain, Germany, the United States, the Soviet Republic, Italy and Japan have permanent posts. The remaining seats were divided among the other nations by means of elections. The Scandinavian countries and the South American Republics usually secure one post for each group.

Spain has always been on the board as a semi-permanent member. Within the last few years, however, there had been a feeling that the latter arrangement was not fair. I had been sent once as delegate for the Spanish government to a meeting of the administration board and I knew pretty well what everybody thought about this, especially in the Scandinavian countries. They were opposed to the semi-permanent posts on principle and they were right, for such an arrangement was not authorized by the statutes of the office. They had been born from custom and they should disappear.

"But not now!" something in me cried out. "Not now! Not when Spain is engaged in a life or death struggle. Not when she has been despoiled of so many other rights. Next time it can be done but not this year!"

"I must go to Spain," Señor Fabra Ribas said to me the day of my arrival, "and I leave you with the rest of the delegation to work at this during my absence."

It was a grave responsibility.

"But the elections won't take place for about three weeks and I must go to Valencia," I said, with a cowardly desire to run away.

"You will go there later." He insisted that there were strict orders for me to help carry the thing through. I stayed, of course.

Next day I began to get my bearings and soon discovered what I would be obliged to do : lobby. Now, if there is any one thing I hate to a superlative degree it is lobbying. Besides, I am no earthly use at it. However, no less than Spain's prestige was in the balance so I had to do my best.

Some countries were unconditionally on our side or against us. Others were doubtful and therein lay the danger. The permanent members could not vote but they could influence the other nations although they were supposed not to do so.

There began a week of anxious sounding, trying to find out what everybody, particularly the South American Republics, intended doing. I knew I could count on Mexico but Chile had been against loyalist Spain all along. The Argentine, since Germany was no longer in the league, would probably do what England liked. Then there were the Scandinavian countries. They said they would all four meet later and decide. I began to feel that Sweden and Norway at least would stand firm for Spain.

I made lists. The other members of the delegation made lists. We counted the probable votes in our favor. Of China and Egypt we could now be sure.

Suddenly news reached Geneva that a Spanish airplane had hit a small German battleship lying in the rebel post of Ibiza in an attack against the foreign boats that were landing armaments and ammunition with which to kill our women and children. The battleship should not have been there. Probably it had come to protect the other boats. It was there at its own risk but to hit it was to hit German prestige. A prestige that, in fact, broken pledges and ruthless methods had done much more to hurt. Yes, German prestige must be saved. How? By shelling, without warning, an open and defenseless city where women and children and aged people had taken refuge and thought they were safe. That city was Almería, our much-loved Almería, with its Moorish flat-roofed houses and its gay and confiding people, the gracious town where Cefe had been civil governor for the republic. My heart bled for it.

The German attack caused a tremendous sensation in the conference. Perhaps it helped us among small and honest nations. We went on with our task. . . Two days before the elections Cefe rang me up from Valencia — he had gone there with all the rest of the diplomatic corps — he wanted to tell me that Marissa had come down with an acute attack of appendicitis and had had to be operated on at once. The way he told me was this :

"Nena, Nena, I have a very good bit of news for you." I naturally thought we must have had another Guadalajara.

"What is it ?"

"You are going to be so pleased."

"Well. . ."

"Marissa has just been operated on for appendicitis and is getting along beautifully."

I nearly fell off the little seat in the telephone booth. Then, in spite of my anxiety, I could not help smiling at Cefe's way of softening the news but I felt intensely worried. Marissa was not strong enough to stand a major operation. She was so weak and thin and to be in a hospital in a city that was under constant bombardment seemed terrible.

I felt inclined to take a plane and fly to her at once. Then I thought it over. It was impossible for me to leave Geneva just then when the elections were on the point of taking place. Some of the delegates, who had promised to give us their support, might be tempted to change their minds if I turned my back.

The situation had become much more delicate since Belgium had suddenly made up her mind to be a candidate for the vacant post, too. She was a dangerous rival, and had probably been advised to enter the lists by those who feared our victory. Fortunately we had a great friend in the Belgian delegation. The genial, kindly, loyal, socialist leader, Louis de Brouckére, had given us his word to vote for Spain and I knew he would not fail us.

I tried not to think about Marissa but it was difficult to put her out of my mind at night when I had to lie idle on my bed, trying to sleep.

On the day of the elections all our delegates were in their places in the assembly hall at an early hour. So was the Belgian delegation. Their seats were just behind ours. The Mexicans were several rows in front of us. One by one, all the delegates marched up to the stand to vote. The evening before, the four Scandinavian delegations had met at dinner. I was asked, too, and had been placed beside Minister Möller who was head of the Swedish group.

"How is everything getting on ?" he asked me kindly.

"Well, I hope."

"Are you sure you have votes enough to win ?"

"If everybody keeps his promise we shall win by seven votes."

He looked at me doubtfully. "And if they don't keep their promises ?"

I shrugged my shoulders.

"Would it not be better to retire ?"

"No," I said. "We shall not do that. If Spain is not elected, the shame will fall on the countries that did not vote for her at a time like this, not on us."

He smiled again. "You are right in principle."

And we were. Though there were moments in the long hour and a half before the results of the polling were announced when I wondered if we had been mistaken in staying on the field.

I observed that some people standing round the table where the counting was going on would turn and look encouragingly at the Belgians. My heart sank. Were they winning? But in a little while someone bent down and said something to Señor Fabela, the Mexican Minister, who at once looked round in our direction and smiled. He had been a staunch friend and had helped us with great tact and knowledge. The secretary went up to the stand and read out the names of the countries elected. Spain had won by three votes. Four delegations had played us false but what did that matter? We had won!

I rushed home, jumped into my traveling dress and caught the night train to Marseilles, where I boarded a plane for Barcelona at six o'clock in the morning. Cefe and Cefito were to meet me at the Catalonian capital and drive me down to Valencia.

The plane flew smoothly over the blue Mediterranean. Catalonia looked beautiful in the early morning sun. It was impossible to realize that the night before this coast had been the scene of bombardments by the Italian Savoia who did their deadly work easily enough, from the comfortable airport Franco had given them in Mallorca. I marveled once more at the blindness of France and Great Britain. How could they let the totalitarian countries take up those strategic positions? How could they let the passage through the vital route from

Africa to Europe and from the Atlantic to the Red Sea be dominated by their greatest enemies ? I could not then find an answer to my questions.

We found Marissa lying on her bed in the room she and Germán had taken in a little pension in Valencia. She was far from well. In fact two doctors were with her when we went in and they looked very grave. She should not have been moved so soon, they said, but the military hospital where she had been operated upon, there being no other, was so over-crowded with wounded men it was impossible for her to stay on there.

"The doctor says you should take her back with you to Stockholm until she is quite well again," said Germán to me in an aside. "I have to go back to my post in an airfield at the front the day after tomorrow," he added, "and she cannot stay on here alone."

I looked at Marissa. She seemed so thin and wan. "When can she be moved ?" I asked him.

"Not for a week or ten days."

That was just the time I needed to see the Minister of Foreign Affairs and get my instructions. Cefe left that evening for Riga via Paris and at midnight Valencia was bombed.

Like everybody else I had gone to bed, leaving my dressing gown and slippers on a chair beside me. I was wakened by the shrill whistle of the night watchman who went the round of our street, making as much noise as he could and knocking at the doors as he went along to arouse the people. Soon the sirens filled the air with their trailing lament and the wireless sets of the whole neighborhood screamed instruction after instruction, order after order.

"Women and children ! Women and children ! Go and

take refuge! Planes have been sighted from over the sea. Quick! Take refuge! Put out your lights!"

Over and over again the speaker repeated the same words. Lights that had gone up in different houses went out suddenly. Neighbors from the apartment above came down the stairs. They were all dressed in the most casual fashion. Some were wearing shawls, others dressing gowns, others had only a sheet round them. A few wore shoes, most only slippers. One man was barefoot. Almost everybody held a bag of some sort in his hands. They were all discussing whether they would go down to the refuge shelters or stay in our apartment which was on the ground floor. They all seemed calm. Some were even joking. One man insisted on going to see if the planes were coming. I rushed to Marissa's room and found Germán wrapping her up in a blanket.

"Do you think we should move her?" I asked in an agonized whisper. She looked so helpless.

"She seems safer against the wall," he answered.

I helped him lay her on the ground near the strong outer wall but as far as possible from the window for fear splinters might break through. We could hear people running down the street.

Suddenly there was a dull crash. It sounded rather far away.

"They are coming," said a woman's voice in a resigned tone. "It is too late to go down now."

Another crash! This time it sounded nearer. The door of our room opened and in came Cefito from his house, two blocks away. He was dressed in his dressing gown, a cigaret between his fingers.

"How are you feeling?" he asked Marissa, going over to where she lay.

"I am all right. Why did you come out?" she asked anxiously.

"I wanted to see how you and mother were."

Another crash! Another! They seemed to be coming closer.

Cefito put his arm round me. "Frightened?"

I shook my head. I do not know whether I was frightened or not. It all seemed unreal. One could hear the thunder of motors.

Crash! This time the noise took my breath away. Marissa did not move. I lay down beside her. Crash! A blinding light . . . a clatter and din as of things falling . . . a feeling that I was going under them . . . the shrill call of ambulances tearing down the street . . . the rattle of one solitary air-defense gun.

I sat up, stunned, and looked round. There was Cefito smiling. Crash! This time it sounded a little further off. Marissa lifted her head. Germán who had been lying on the bed got up.

Another crash in the distance. I listened. We all listened and one could guess that everybody was thinking the same thing. Will they come back? A moment's silence and then the voice of the speaker over the air:

"The planes have gone. You can retire to rest. Retire to rest. The attack is over." The voice ceased. There was a short silence. Then everybody began to move.

"Good night, good night!" Our neighbors began to leave the house. We put Marissa to bed and Cefito went away, too.

I lay down on my bed. This time I did not take off my dressing gown. There was a bitter taste in my mouth, the reaction of fear. I thought of Marissa. How light she was. Germán had carried her as though she were a baby. I must get her out of Valencia, away from the strain of the bombardments. She must be fed properly. But I knew by the way she had looked at Germán when the planes thundered over our heads that I would not be able to keep her long. She would come back to Spain as soon as she was well.

Before I fell asleep there was another alarm but this time the plane did not come to Valencia. It directed its bombs against the industrial town of Sagunto, a little farther along the coast.

Six nights out of the nine I spent in Valencia the same scene was enacted. Whistles. Sirens. A voice over the air. Crash! Crash! Crash! Houses falling, sometimes nearer us than others. Ambulances. Silence. The awful thing about bombardments is that you never know where the planes will go. You hear them drawing nearer and nearer and then, when you think they are going to strike, you find that you have been saved by a distance of metres. Shelling is not so nerve racking. My eyes burnt from lack of sleep but all those people who had stood this horror for months never complained.

Don José Girál, with whom I had a long talk before I left, informed me that the government had decided to extend my mandate to Finland. There was a rebel ex-minister barricaded in the legation there, too, and he must be got out as soon as possible.

We discussed the matter at length.

Besides food, butter and meat, cheese and milk must be brought from northern Europe to Spain and Spanish fruit sent up in exchange. But money on both sides was frozen. I was told I must try to get Sweden to come to some arrangement without loss of time. A commercial agreement might be drawn up that would allow interchange.

Two days later, Cefito and I went to lunch with Doctor Negrín and his eldest son, Juan. We drove out to a little res-

taurant beside the sea.   The prime minister spoke of the cruelty
of the Non-Intervention Pact and of the inhuman decision not
to allow air-defense guns to be bought at least to save the open
cities and the civilian population.

"The government would give every guaranty that they
would not be used anywhere else," he said, wondering if Sweden could not be persuaded to sell us some.   "They would
save so many lives."

But we both knew it would be useless to ask.   The great
European powers would never allow Sweden to sell guns to
us.   Their governments were anxious for Franco to win.   And
how was he going to do that if we were allowed arms ?   Why
we had nearly beaten him when we only had sticks and stones.

The insurgents and their allies considered it was very stupid
of us not to give in.   Evidently to them it seemed stupid of the
people to prefer war to living under a dictatorship as they had
done in Primo's time without having to think, or to speak out
their opinion, or to read.   Stupid of the women not to be content with what their mothers and grandmothers had been and
with having their modesty protected by rigid rules : no free
comfortable bathing dresses, no co-education that liberates spirit
and intellect in its daily competition against men's minds.   Stupid of the workers not to wish their wages to be brought down
and their working hours lengthened.   Stupid of the peasants
not to look forward to more days without land and with having to work, from sunrise to sunset, on another man's property,
for another man's gain.   Stupid of the children to prefer having schools and learning instead of having pigs and cows to look
after all their childhood.

Stupid !   Stupid !   Stupid !

Doctor Negrín went on talking and I dragged my thoughts
away from these things.

"Fortunately we now have an army," he said with pride.

It was true. I had seen troops marching through the town that morning. The men looked very fit, strong and alert and happy, as though they felt secure in their strength and their will to win. We rose to go. I looked round and sighed. It was such a lovely day — little waves swept playfully up to the beach and soaked it — a day to lie on the sand and rest and play, too. Instead of that we had sat and talked only of death and blood and of the horrors of totalitarian war.

Doctor Negrín who, even in the most difficult and anxious moments, is the perfection of courtesy — a warm-hearted courtesy, not just the conventional politeness — insisted on driving back with me and finding out how Marissa was.

Marissa and I left Valencia by car one morning. Germán had been given leave to stay with her until then. He and Cefito watched us drive away from them down the street. I dared not look back but I held my hand as high as I could for them to see, trying hard to swallow the lump in my throat. I did not succeed until we were well out on the high road, driving between cactus hedges and orange groves.

How I hated leaving it all : it was worse than the very worst thing that could happen to one in Spain, even to being hit by an Italian bomb. For the bomb brought death with it and that was the most it could do. Then, at least, one would be able to lie beside the others on Spanish soil. And if one were only wounded, one would be surrounded by Spaniards and would hear the language and the songs and the laughter, yes, and also the groans and the tears of one's own kin. It was worse to be alone away from Spain, having to face not only indifference but hatred, too, at times. Hatred for what one loves, which is the worst thing to bear. Then I thought of the people of Sweden and England and the United States who also loved Spain and I felt a little comforted but I wished that they, especially the women, would do a little more. They could protest against their governments, who they knew were wrong, and insist that Spain be given her rights.

I felt inclined to cry out to them sometimes, "If you let Spain go under you will be dragged under, too, some day. Don't do it! Don't do it! Ask only for what is legal but ask for *that*!" But I could not so speak to them. I was a "diplomat."

A fine thing, indeed. A diplomat! A figure of straw. Tied down to diplomatic etiquette. Unable to speak out what I thought. Unable to warn, not just unfeeling officials, but the people, the warm-hearted generous people of the world, who did not realize that they, too, were in danger of being sold, of losing their liberty.

The very thought of being tied down made me fling out my arms in a gesture of freedom. Marissa turned and looked at me in surprise. She lay against her cushions looking very weary. Well, I would have to look after her, to bolster up her courage, and she was not only a bit of myself, she was a tiny bit of Spain.

We stopped at Benicarló to have some luncheon. As we entered the terrace, where tables were laid out under the dazzling blue sky of Valencia and in hearing of the sea a few yards away, a group of men came forward to greet us. They were Spanish writers, waiting for colleagues from all parts of the world who were driving down to take part in the International Congress of Anti-Fascist Writers that was to be held in Valencia the next week.

"Could you not stay for it?" they asked me. I wished I could but I had been ordered away to try and get milk, butter and bacon for our people and the sooner I set about it the better. However, I looked at them all with something very much akin to envy. Writers who know how to keep themselves free are the freest people on earth.

We reached Barcelona in the afternoon. Our driver had

sung most of the way along the sunny roads while he looked out for enemy planes.

"If they come we shall have to throw ourselves down in the ditch," he said. I fervently hoped we would not have to do so for Marissa's sake.

"I would rather not move from the car," she said, but that would have been very dangerous.

Barcelona certainly did not look like a city in wartime. It was almost too gay, the people almost too happy. They seemed unconscious of the dangers, although they, too, were bombed sometimes but not as much as other towns, of course. The insurgents preferred to capture it in all its prosperous entirety. We had a cup of tea and went on again. The evening began to close in. Suddenly our car stopped. Down got the driver and examined the engine. He tried to make it go but did not succeed. He looked at me and looked at the motor and scratched his head. Then tried again. Off we went for a little and stopped once more. A car passed and hailed us.

"Anything wrong?" Two men got out and joined the driver beside the engine.

It grew later and later. We soon had three other cars round us and several men had inspected the motor.

One of them came up to me with his hat in his hand.

"Señora," he said, "the chauffeur tells me you wanted to get on to the French frontier tonight but I venture to advise you not to do that. The road after this is very winding and the motor is not safe. It would be better perhaps if you stopped for the night in a hotel in the town near by. The car can then be overhauled and you can continue your journey early to-morrow. If you will allow me I shall take you to the hotel in my car."

I accepted gratefully and as we drove along I could have

laughed outright. This peaceful courteous country was the Spain that Fascist propaganda was maligning, saying it was full of red assassins and that no woman could venture out of the house without danger to her life. Well, here were two women alone with a strange chauffeur on a road at night, being assisted by unknown men, none of whom seemed to have the slightest intention of assassinating them.

We spent the night at a funny little hotel in a village called Mataró, which a few days later was mercilessly bombed by Italian planes, and the next morning we went on, getting safely into France at midday. Anita and Shanti were waiting for us at the Stockholm airport and I went back to my work at once.

During my absence summer had chased dark night from Sweden. The days would wane toward nine o'clock into a soft twilight. I loved to walk in the garden at that time, the perfume of the roses was never so sweet. Then we would go upstairs and at eleven would look out of the window to see a narrow streak of light cross from west to east and slowly broaden as the night advanced until at around two o'clock in the morning the waters of the lake would light up, too, and the birds, cheated out of their sleep, would begin to sing lustily. I often thought they must feel puzzled at the short time they had to rest during those months.

Marissa recovered very rapidly. Everybody was delighted to see her again, especially Nils who racked his brains inventing excuses to get Madame Somolinos out into the open air. He finally hit on a grand way. He took her fishing.

They would go off early, armed with baskets and rods, and would come back several hours later looking brown and tired and generally with only a few tiny fish, but it did her a world of good.

Shanti had to leave us soon after our return but Anita stayed on and sometimes joined the fishing party.

During the weeks that followed we had no social life to speak of. My colleagues were either cruising round the islands or away on leave. Callers, however, were frequent, especially friends from the United States who were visiting Sweden. One day I had a call from Mr. and Mrs. Marquis Childs. He had already published his interesting book, *Sweden, the Middle Way*, and we found many subjects of mutual interest to talk about.

In August the days began to grow shorter. I was glad. The constant light was a little tiring and I found myself longing for the deep darkness of night when the ropes that tie down the spirit slide off, and thought and the heart are free.

The *kräftor* parties were almost over. Everybody had partaken of the tasty river crawfish that make their appearance on Swedish tables the first Sunday in August and can be eaten during one month only. Everybody makes quite a feast over their appearance. The houses are brightened up with red candles and red lampshades and red plates to be in harmony with the red boiled *kräftor*. But by the end of the month the Swedes had all drunk their summer schnapps and sung their songs and sailed and fished and bathed to their hearts' content, and were counting the sunny days they could still enjoy like misers counting their gold.

CHAPTER XXIII

Swedish politics are not difficult to understand. To begin with there are very few parties. First the right, conservative "die-hards." Then the people's party made up of liberals with different tendencies, none of which are radical. And the socialists, and the agrarians who for some time past have formed a coalition government with the socialists, helping them to constitute a parliamentary majority. The formation of such a cabinet was a master stroke of the social-democrats, for otherwise the agrarians would surely have been attracted by the right and even perhaps by Fascism as the peasants' and small farmers' groups have been in other countries.

In so doing the socialists had again to compromise, limiting their aspirations to a minimum program which was acceptable to both parties. Not being themselves a majority in the Riksdag they had to govern in a mild way while building up for the future with the help of the formidable Trade Unions Lands Organisationen, better known as the L.O. which, in a country of six million people, has a membership of seven hundred and fifty thousand and a capital of nearly eighty million crowns.

Two other small parties — the communists and the Nazis — are divided among themselves. The communists are divided into two dissenting factions, one with one seat in the senate and six in the lower house, the other, two seats in the lower and none in the senate. The Nazi party is not represented in parliament at all. Needless to say this simplicity of Swedish politics makes for order and for easy government as there are few internal conflicts.

I saw one strike in all the time I was there and in an industry which anywhere else would have created a serious problem, but not in Sweden. For several months during the winter the em-

366

ployees of hotels and restaurants throughout the country refused to work unless the employers accepted the rate of wages
they had proposed. Order was so well preserved that for days
I never even realized that the strike was on. Weeks and weeks
went by and there were no disturbances, no protests even on
the part of the press. Evidently everybody knew the hotel
owners would lose the strike. The L.O. had more than sufficient funds to help out the strikers for months, and when the
spring came along and the tourists began to come into the
country the hotels must necessarily be ready to receive them.
And so the strikers won.

That summer I was able to read a little and Stockholm is an
ideal place for reading. There are many bookshops, all well
stocked, and the National and the Nobel Libraries are a joy.

Marissa, too, was interested in seeing the Swedish schools.
The Spanish republic was doing marvels in this field in spite of
the war and Marissa, who is a graduate of the Teachers' School
in Madrid, wanted to contribute some ideas when she went
back. Sonja Branting, who was staying for the summer with
her mother and husband in a charming little house outside
Stockholm, coming in now and again to her lawyer's office in
the town, volunteered to show her around. Marissa found that
primary education in Sweden, based on methods similar to those
used in Germany and Switzerland, would be too uniform and
rigid in our country, but she was charmed with the bright
rooms and good equipment, and the fair-haired, blue-eyed,
earnest, little students. The measures taken to care for and
educate backward children she thought most interesting. No
child in Sweden can be said to be uncared for in an efficient
practical manner.

As to higher education I realized it was really of the very
best and highest type, entirely worthy of its world reputation

for thoroughness. I visited the University of Uppsala several times and in different seasons during my stay in Sweden, in the snow and ice of the winter and on the first of May when the students don their white caps and the legion of graduates from all the Swedish universities, however old they may be, also put on their white caps and walk about their towns, in memory of the happy days when they, too, were students and achieved the great distinction of becoming full-fledged members of the large brotherhood of graduates.

The whole town of Uppsala is interesting, from the castle of the Vasas down to the little village of old Uppsala, with its quaint church and its old inn, in which one is still offered honey water out of a silver-rimmed horn. The beautiful library, *Carolina Rediviva*, with its shelves of books and documents, the university and the cathedral and the palace of the Primate of Uppsala, who is head of the church in Sweden, are all redolent of the past and withal inspired with new democratic ideals. Religion and science walk hand in hand in Sweden toward different goals. Academic honors count for much in Sweden and those honors are not lightly granted.

Anybody and everybody can aspire to them. Every Swede has a right to try for honors but he must gain what he wants by perseverance and hard work. It takes as much as ten years to become a doctor of law or medicine, ten years of incessant study. The routine of the students follows simple but carefully considered lines. Clubs are favored and members of the faculty follow each individual case with keen interest, taking part in the life of the students and keeping in close touch with them and their problems.

The Swedish universities keep apart from all political strife. Perhaps the students are indifferent toward what is going on in the world outside, a world in which they soon will be called upon to take a place and direct their country along the paths that lead to welfare and prosperity, but, on the other hand, their attention is exclusively concentrated on the tasks they have in hand. Who can tell what is best ?

I was greatly interested in knowing something about Scandinavian folk arts. The costumes, pottery, songs and dances, that constitute the principal manifestations of a people's taste are, at least to me, the most fascinating landmarks one can find for the study of a country that is new to one. I had done much of this research work in our beloved Spain, a land so rich in these treasures that it would take years to exhaust its possibilities. I had also done a little in the study of the Czechoslovakian folk art and was busy looking up similarities of taste between the two peoples when the advent of the Spanish republic forced me into other paths.

Of course I could do very little in Sweden. My time was so taken up with other matters ; besides, my heart was absent and if there is one thing in which feeling must take part it is in the study of folk arts. How else is one going to discover the hidden meaning under all the coloring, the grace and beauty of these elementary forms of art that are not perfect if we measure them only by rigid formulas and conventional lines ?

When I had a spare moment, however, I found it pleasant to wander through the spacious rooms of the Nordiska Museum, quite close to our legation, and look at the fascinating collection of folk furniture, folk pottery and costumes. But that was almost the only thing I had a chance to do.

The Swedes love fine clothes, as they love fine housing and furniture and fine towns and parks. Their innate good taste needs to express itself in their surroundings but they do not follow just any passing whim of the mode. They like to keep in touch with tradition.   So you see them flock to any exhibition of folk music and dances.   Heirlooms are carefully placed in the most modern houses, and brides have not discarded the little gold crown that it has been customary for them to wear perched on the top of the head over the white veil.   Rarely is one of the innumerable novelties in the shape of diadems, nets of seed pearls or other ornaments that fashion has imposed elsewhere, substituted for it.

As in most places I came to know Swedish painting through Cefe, in the all too short holidays he took and during which we were together.   We had, of course, seen many pictures by Zorn, and the names of Arosenius, Bruno Liljefors and Milles were well-known to us.   But we still had much to learn and Cefe's visits to Stockholm were unfortunately far too rare and short to allow us to study these artists as closely as we should have liked and as their works deserved.   Mr. Gauffin, the Director of the National Picture Gallery, always made us welcome in his beautiful domain but I was too busy to take as much advantage as I should have liked of the opportunity.   My flying visits to Gothenburg did not allow for more than a passing glimpse of the treasures in the gallery there, and in Malmö it was the same.

However, I was able to become a little more familiar than I had been with the work of the painters we knew and with the pictures of Otto Hasselbom, Karl Nordström, Karl Larsson, Eugen Jansson and many others.   We found the new generation much influenced by the French schools.   This is not surprising, for all Sweden was dominated by France's philosophical, literary and artistic concepts until British methods and, more recently, North American influences made themselves felt.   German preponderance in educational methods had been very strong until the European war, after which it decreased considerably.   The study of the German language was subordinate to English and Spanish because trade with the South American Republics was more favored than it had ever been before.

The summer wore on and with a sinking heart I saw the day for Marissa's departure come closer. She was much better but I dreaded the lack of proper food she would experience again. Spain was already suffering terribly from want of essential nourishment. However, it was natural for Marissa to wish to be near her husband, so I did not complain and we arranged that Cefito's fiancée, Mary Morgan, should come and stay with me during part of my daughter's absence. Mary was at the time in London with her mother so it was an easy trip for her. Somehow I felt that her presence would bring my boy nearer to me, for we would be able to speak about him and that would ease my constant longing and anxiety. Spectres disappear when they can be discussed openly.

I have sometimes wondered why mothers should be jealous of their children-in-law. It is something to be grateful for to feel that one has escaped that disagreeable experience. I have always been glad that both Cefito and Marissa should think of building up their homes and I have not wanted to be first all the time. It is not good for the young generation to feel too dependent on the older and I was anxious to know it was not so with them, dear as I know I am to them both and much as they miss me when I am not with them.

Anita left us at the beginning of September. Our hearts were a little lighter. The Guadalajara victory had been followed up by military successes. A strong rebel offensive had been stopped in Pozoblanco and in Brunete and Belchite — both these last actions unfortunately at terrific cost.

The republican army was undoubtedly doing wonders. A little armament had been secured but, of course, could not make up for the overwhelming advantages of war material on the other side. The miracle as always was due to sheer courage, courage and a feeling that we had Right on our side, whatever official politicians the world over might care to say.

Just about that time a representative of the Swedish Committee to Aid Spain came to see me about an exhibition of drawings and paintings done by Spanish artists during the war, which was to be shown in Stockholm and other Swedish towns. I was consulted as to dates. After talking things over we came to the conclusion that instead of having an exhibition at one time, lectures on Spanish culture at another and so on, as they had been doing, it would be better to have one whole week dedicated to Spain. As the first anniversary of Madrid's resistance would be in November it was decided to choose the first week of that month for the different functions in honor of the Spanish capital.

The moment the plan was known offers of help came from people of all classes. Every paper in Stockholm that was not openly Fascist published head lines with the words *Spanska Veckan* (*The Spanish Week*) day after day, giving notice of the different activities.

The best-known writers of Sweden sent contributions that were collected in a pamphlet dedicated to Madrid. It was headed by a poem by Erik Blomberg, followed by articles, poems and drawings by men and women of the most varied political opinions but all moved to the heart by the heroism of the Spanish people. The novelist, Marika Stjernstedt, who afterward became a very good friend of mine, also contributed an article.

Karl Gerhard offered his theatre graciously for a daily performance in which he took part. Ernest Hemingway's magnificent film *Spanish Earth* was shown there, and one afternoon the well-known actresses, Naima Wifstrand, Anna Flygare,

Manda Björling and Sickan Karlsson, gave a performance of a little play of mine translated into Swedish.

The exhibition was a great success. It drew hundreds of persons who listened to the different lectures given in the salon, where the pictures were shown, with an increasing interest. I felt that the word Spain was indeed opening up the world to a realization of our tragedy and to the lurking danger for the future.

For some time past a group of industrialists, who were suffering from the effects of the war in Spain and the consequent freezing of credits and lack of business, began to speak of the convenience of having a commercial government agent in the Franco zone. The idea was not theirs. It had been suggested by a member of the staff of the ex-commercial attaché who was acting for Franco in Stockholm and was naturally in contact with the rebel representatives in other countries. His argument was that some nations had already sent an agent to Burgos. These agents promptly became official representatives near the insurgent authorities. But the Scandinavian governments had so far refused to take a step in that direction. Shortly after the activities of the Spanish Week, however, the Fascist press took up the matter again and insisted that there was no reason for refusing to send out to the Franco zone someone entitled to defend Swedish interests on that side of Spain.

I had more than sufficient reason to feel anxious. Compliance with the wishes of the industrialists and the Fascist press would extend a sort of indirect recognition to Franco himself. Would the Swedish government be able to withstand the pressure which would be exerted also from outside the country by international concerns almost as anxious for a Fascist victory as Franco himself?

I threshed the matter out with Minister Sandler. He assured

me that the Swedish government had not even considered such a possibility. But I knew that once the question had been brought up it would not be allowed to rest, that it would be pushed forward whenever an opportunity for it arose.

I had many arguments in favor of my point of view quite apart from all political considerations. By far the greater part of Sweden's commercial interests were on our side, not on Franco's. Apart from a few isolated towns in the insurgent zone, where special firms had been established, particularly for the importation of wood pulp, there was nothing much to defend there. On our side it was different. Spain had been carrying on a thriving trade with Sweden for many years, exporting oranges from Valencia, fresh peaches and plums and saffron from Catalonia, raisins and almonds from Alicante and mining products from other parts of loyal Spain. Both countries were anxious to keep on trading. Spain was in urgent need of the Swedish products and Sweden required fruit of all kinds, sun-ripe fruit with which to counteract the effects of continual cold weather and the lack of vitamines. The important thing was to intensify business. There was no better way to hush the vicious snarling opponents. The Swedish government would be careful not to offend the republicans if good commercial opportunities were developed.

Following orders from our government I began to open conversations for a new commercial agreement. This required meeting the minister of commerce and directing all my energies in that direction. Marissa had returned to Spain, so I was glad to have every minute of the day taken up and my thoughts absorbed by some useful task.

It was new ground I was treading on so I had to be careful, but the idea that real practical help could be extended to Spain by this means was stimulating. I found myself very soon really interested in what, some time ago, I would have deemed the dullest of matters. On the other hand it increased the feeling of unreality that so often invaded me since the war had broken out, a feeling that it was not myself who was acting this way. What has happened to me ? I would find myself asking at unexpected moments, when of a sudden I was again pulled back into the realms of my previous experiences. Am I the same person that I was ? Or by some strange transformation am I someone else ? Why should I be doing all these things ? And then the urge of business, the daily calls on my time brought with them the imperative necessity of doing, not dreaming, and of applying myself body and soul to the task before me. A task in which there could be no time for idle speculation, only for hard facts ; no time to be surprised about anything. We Spaniards should be cured of that. What bigger surprise could life ever offer us than what had happened and what was happening to our country ? We had believed and trusted and had wakened to find we were deceived and betrayed. Should we as human beings never be able to give credit to anyone again ?

A dismal outlook, indeed.

CHAPTER XXIV

Winter had come again. The north was being forced into the darkness of almost continuous night. The houses had taken on that hospitable air that only houses in cold countries ever manage to assume, when the courier brought me my credentials for Finland with orders to proceed to Helsinki as soon as I could manage it.

Fernando Careaga, a young diplomat of experience, who was to act as secretary to the legation during my stay in Helsinki and as chargé d'affaires in my absence, arrived in Stockholm in time for us to study the situation together before I went across to my new post.

We knew that Finland was not Sweden. In spite of the progress made by the left-wing parties over there during the past few years, in spite of the coalition government, similar, in a way, to Sweden's, that had been set up and in which the social-democratic party was strongly represented, in spite of the fact that the new President of the Finnish Republic, Kyösti Kallio, was not inclined to allow Nazism to try out in Finland its methods of devouring nations, there was undoubtedly still much to fear from the German influence that had dominated the country after the communist revolution and had "repressed" all subversive efforts for the future with a ferocity that has perhaps never been equaled in any country.

The Finnish government I knew approved of my appointment as chargé d'affaircs but, nevertheless, I had a feeling that it would not be as easy for me as it had been in the other Scandinavian countries.

Fernando Careaga went on ahead in order to get his bearings on several questions, especially the one regarding the Spanish ex-minister in Helsinki who, like Fiscowich, had decided to side with Franco and had, therefore, been dismissed from the service by the loyalist government. He was still occupying the apartment where the legation was installed and had all the files and documents in his possession.

On a cold wintry evening, the ninth of December, I took the boat for Finland. It would have been possible to fly but I was advised not to do so in such weather.

The trip was quite enjoyable — rough only for two hours between ten and twelve o'clock at night, and I was asleep at the time. At seven o'clock in the morning we found ourselves in the harbor of Åbo, where we took the train for Helsingfors or Helsinki and about three hours later drove slowly into the clean, well-built station of the capital of Suomi, the proper name for Finland.

About half way down to Helsinki several men and women reporters had jumped on the train in order to interview me on the Spanish situation. They were very anxious to have news and most of them revealed their sympathy for the loyalist cause. As in Stockholm they also wanted to know what I intended doing about the ex-minister's occupation of the legation. The question had also awakened curiosity in Helsinki itself and a good deal of expectation in the diplomatic corps, many of whose members were personal friends of my predecessor and had been giving him support.

At the Helsinki station I saw a large group waiting, from which Fernando Careaga promptly emerged to help me down from the car and introduce me to the other people who had come to meet me. He first presented the Foreign Affairs Chief of Protocol, a little man with a pleasant smiling face who told me that the Minister of Foreign Affairs would be pleased to see me at eleven o'clock the next morning.

Professor Lassila ; the Finnish deputy, Cay Sundström, whom I had seen in Stockholm before ; and other friends of Spain, among them a group of ladies, who bid me welcome and offered me a beautiful bouquet of carnations, accompanied us to the Torni Hotel where Careaga had reserved rooms for us both.

Most of that day was taken up making plans for the ejection of the rebel ex-minister and receiving callers anxious to express their sympathy and admiration for the Spanish people. Finland had certainly not been remiss in extending help. Besides the large sums collected from well-to-do persons the contributions of the workers had been most generous. I was touched to the depths of my heart to hear that a Finnish peasant had actually sold his little house and sent all the money he received for it to the "women and children of Spain."

We found that on the whole people were very indignant with the Non-Intervention Pact. But what could Finland do ? A little country with only three million inhabitants.

Punctually at eleven o'clock the next morning I drove up to the door of the Ministry of Foreign Affairs. The chief of protocol escorted me to the study of His Excellency, Minister Holsti, whom I had already had the pleasure of meeting in Geneva. A sincere democrat and very friendly to our Spain, I enjoyed my talk with him, little suspecting that, due it is said to German pressure, he would have to resign from his post a short time afterward. It seems he had made some disparaging remark about Hitler in an unguarded moment and it had been passed on.

We spoke at length about the Spanish situation and about the League of Nations. As to the legation in Helsinki, he advised me to appoint a legal adviser, first trying by friendly measures to persuade the ex-minister to go. Careaga had attempted this and failed, so we decided to put the whole matter in the hands of a lawyer and, meanwhile, take other rooms and furnish them so as not to keep the chancellery work paralyzed longer than necessary.

That afternoon we roamed about Helsinki. I found it to be a charming city, not so beautiful as Stockholm but gayer. The shops were all decked out for the Christmas sales and were filled with a bright well-dressed crowd. The streets were crowded to overflowing with people carrying parcels, evidently decorations for the traditional Christmas tree.

The next morning I called on the minister of finance in order to begin conversations for another commercial agreement on the lines of the one we were preparing with Sweden, by means of which we might get some benefit from our frozen credits.

I found Minister Tanner a most intelligent and well-informed man. He was then at the head of the Finnish co-operative societies which are quite as important as those of Sweden. A social-democrat and undoubtedly the strongest man in the cabinet.

He was quite ready to come to the desired agreement and told me he would speak to the minister of commerce himself. In the course of our conversation I was able to observe that Minister Tanner was not only a good friend of the British co-operators but in general a great admirer of Great Britain. He was intensely interested in Spain but pessimistic as to the final result of our struggle. British influence, I thought to myself, pondering over what he had said.

Two days later I was asked to have tea with the President of the Republic, His Excellency, Kyösti Kallio, and his wife. As I was not going to act as plenipotentiary minister in Finland but only as chargé d'affaires I did not have to present my credentials to the head of the state, only to the Minister of Foreign Affairs and I had already done that.

The palace of the Finnish president is a large rambling house situated in the centre of the town, an unpretentious but dignified building. I was not conscious of any guards as I went up the wide stairs escorted by one of the president's aides.

When I entered the large salon President Kallio, who was standing talking to his wife and two or three officers, came forward and shook my hand cordially. He then introduced me to Madame Kallio and to the rest of the group after which we went into another room where the table was laid for tea.

It was all charmingly simple and, as I was able to observe on the other occasions that I was invited to the palace, it was always so. A strong contrast to the etiquette and formality and magnificence of the Swedish court functions, but this seems natural when one remembers that Finland is a republic and a very small republic besides.

I found it very difficult to keep up a conversation with the president and his wife. Neither of them speaks any language but Finnish and I, of course, could not understand a single word of that most difficult-sounding language. They cannot or will not use even Swedish. As a matter of fact it was considered something to be proud of that the president should not speak the language of their past dominators or enemies. Of course, this often happens, especially in countries of newly acquired independence, but Sweden has done so much for Finnish culture that such an attitude strikes one as a little ungrateful. It may disappear in time, however. Meanwhile the Finns are giving a great impetus to their own culture and to works in their native tongue.

The president asked a great many questions about Spain and the person who was acting as interpreter must have given a very realistic translation of what I said about the horror of the bombardments of open cities, for Madame Kallio's eyes filled with tears and she pressed my hand sympathetically.

The Finns are as a rule a tall and strong-looking people. Perhaps not quite so big as the Swedes but big enough so that it was surprising to see how small the president and his wife were. Madame Kallio has a sweet round little face framed by

grey hair which is severely drawn back from her forehead.
The president has keen eyes, a beaked nose and a mobile mouth
shaded by a straight drooping mustache. They both look
what they are, a simple, kind-hearted, single-minded, democratic couple, and yet with a dignity all their own, the dignity
of race. I had observed it in other Finns I had met.

It would seem strange that people who have had to suffer
from constant domination should develop that great quality in
a more definite manner than others. But it is the same with
Spain.

It is one of the things every traveler that comes to our country remarks upon. "Spaniards are so dignified," you hear them
say. The reason for this, I feel sure, is that in spite of invasion,
in spite of forced temporary acceptance of foreign rule, some
peoples are never really dominated. Outwardly they may appear to be so. But what matters that? It is the light from
within that conquerors should beware of. The kernel of life
or of race can never be destroyed and on the day it bears fruit
domination is over.

History is full of examples of this. That is one of the reasons
why the men who try to subdue a people instinctively refuse
to give them anything more than a limited culture. They are
unconsciously afraid that in culture the vanquished will find
reason and that reason will make them rebel. Cultivated minds
cling to and defend freedom ; the ignorant are sure aspirants to
slavery. But there is something besides ; something, the source
of which is ignored, that keeps men alive and that no outsiders
have the power to kill ; something that recedes as domination
advances and suddenly springs up and rebounds with unexpected force.

The outward expression of that something is found in the
sayings and songs of the people. That is why at the moment
of a real liberation the first shouts of triumph are always ac-

companied not by the blast of trumpets or the roll of drums but by some simply worded songs, by poems that carry in them the essence of the hidden feeling that is like the grain of wheat to physical man, giving life to the race. The real nature of the Finns has been revealed to the world through their great poetic narrative, the *Kalevala*. It was first known only in fragments until about the middle of the last century when a village doctor, Elias Lönnrot, after careful research, assembled it and it was published. The argument of this poem is the struggle between two zones of Finland : the southern one, Kalevala, representing Suomi or Finland, and the northern one personifying Lapland. The whole struggle had only one object, that of obtaining man's happiness. This demanded that they strive against evil as represented by cold and ice and misery, and whatever is opposed to the full and free development of human life. The Finns of that time came up against all these ills in the North.

The publication of this great poem was the first demonstration of nationalist feeling in Finland and the point of departure for the new purely Finnish literary development. A humble peasant called Pietari Päivärinta later reaffirmed the national characteristics with his works on folk customs and Johan Ludvig Runeberg, the most national poet of Suomi, extended the knowledge of Finnish feeling with his creation, *Fänrik Ståls Sägner*, a collection of songs inspired by the heroic era of his country.

The Finns are fundamentally a musical people. Every facility is given the people to study this art and their great composer, Sibelius, by no means easily comprehended, is familiar to all.

They have as a rule beautiful voices. The Finnish choir is perhaps one of the finest in the world. I had a chance to listen to it at a reception given in 1939 by President Kallio on the occasion of the national holiday and was very much impressed with the power and harmony revealed.

Economically the Finns depend almost entirely on their forests and their land. Finland is the richest timber country in Europe after Russia. She has sixty million acres of forest, slightly more than Sweden and twice as much as Germany. Since the last European war she has developed all the industries related to wood to an almost unbelievable degree. A thriving trade in timber, tar and cellulose is carried on with other nations, the state itself being one of the biggest timber traders of the country. Wood is widely used for home industries such as the manufacture of furniture and building materials as well as for the match industry.

Timber exports and timber home industries absorb seventy-six thousand workers against ninety-three thousand six hundred that are employed in all other industrial occupations. A large number of small holders and landless laborers also manage to make a living by felling winter timber. As is the case in Sweden much wood is used for fuel in coalless Finland. Even the railway locomotives are in a large part fired by wood.

Another good source of income for the Finns is agriculture and its allied industries. They have made phenomenal progress in the last generation in regard to their home consumption, and forage cropping and dairy-farming have now become an all-important factor in Finnish economy.

The conditions of landownership have contributed largely to divert production in the direction of dairy-farming and its subsidiaries. Finland is a nation of small holders and this condition increases every day. The larger farms that were once useful in trying out new methods and machinery have almost entirely passed into the hands of the peasants. Or they have been divided up and distributed among the members of the different families to such a degree that one rarely meets anybody who hasn't a farm and who does not work or manage it personally.

Finland has very little capital to help her development. Her currency is extremely low : over ten marks to a Swedish crown when I was there, but the co-operative system has done wonders for the people from the point of view of home economy. This system has helped the small holders enormously and helps to maintain the high standard of living the Finns now enjoy at an extremely low cost.

The pioneers of co-operation in Finland were Dr. Hannes Gebhard, member of the Helsinki University staff, as Professor in Agriculture, and Mikael Soininen who became Chief of the State Education Department in 1899. They set up the Pellervo Society whose object, according to its constitution, is to "promote the economic improvement of the people by means of co-operation." The Pellervo, so named after the god of fertility and good harvest, spoken of in the *Kalevala*, has rendered a great service to the country under the direction of Dr. Gebhard who was the guiding spirit of the movement for many years.

Finland can thus show a really democratic economic life. All railways belong to the state, and gas, water and electrical supplies are publicly owned. Also much of the autobus traffic. Although there exists a difference of opinion within the country regarding the nature and extent of public enterprise that is most advantageous to the nation, there is general unanimity in favor of increasing the democratic control of trade and of separating it from all political strife. This opinion is naturally shared by the whole co-operative movement of Finland.

As in Sweden this movement has become national. It has contributed to the uplifting of the race in every field, material, spiritual and cultural, and has helped the whole country to develop in the surprising way one sees.

The morning after my tea with the Finnish president I began the usual round of calls on other members of the diplomatic corps in the order accepted by diplomatic protocol.

I wanted to pay as many as possible a day so as to get back to my post for, much as I was enjoying my visit to Helsinki, I could not afford to leave my work in Stockholm for long.

I was surprised to find that in spite of their friendship with our ex-minister my colleagues were in general less stiff and more friendly than in Stockholm. Was this due to the influence of Suomi and its *Kalevala*? Of course quite a number of the heads of foreign missions were, like me, also accredited in Sweden and lived there most of the time, only coming over to Helsinki on special business and on the sixth of December which is the anniversary of the proclamation of Finnish independence and a great national holiday.

I did not have to visit the German or Italian legations, of course, as their respective countries had already recognized Franco but I heard that Germany had an extremely active staff and that they were doing their best to preserve their influence over Finland, notwithstanding the change in Finnish politics and in public opinion.

Fear of Russia had begun to decrease it seemed, but the anti-communist feeling was strong, although small groups were sympathetic to the Soviet Union.

I met quite a number of interesting people those days. The writers, both men and women, struck me as much more alert and spiritually alive than the Swedes, certainly less reserved and shy. Finland is very progressive in regard to education. A most interesting modern school in Helsinki had as its head one of the finest men I ever met : Laurin Zilliacus who had done wonderful work and with unusual success. Illiteracy is practically non-existent and there is free access to the universities.

Women in Finland are very independent. They were emancipated long ago and have always taken an active part in public life. They are more frank and open in their manner than the women of other Scandinavian countries.

During the return trip to Stockholm I thought this over and wondered what it was that made people in Sweden so shy. It could not be an inferiority complex, for they are quite aware that they are superior to other people in many ways. Perhaps it is the result of overstrict education. This might apply to the men, for the women are brought up less rigidly. Whatever the cause, this strange reserve takes away from the joy of life in that it does not make them carefree even in youth.

"The Swedes are tied up in a knot just as I am now," I used to think to myself, "only for different reasons."

When my boat docked in Stockholm at seven o'clock in the morning I found the faithful Nils waiting with the car to take me to the legation. After coming from a country new to me Stockholm struck me as comfortingly familiar. And yet there were many things in Finland that I should not have found strange, for they were very like what I saw in Sweden : ice and snow, fir trees and islands, and fur-coated people with tall fur caps covering their fair hair and shading their blue eyes.

"I shall be with you on Christmas Eve," Cefe had said to me over the telephone the day I called him up, wild with joy, to know whether he, too, had heard the great news — the marvelous present Santa Claus had brought to Spain — the loyalist troops, the republican army had taken Teruel from the Fascists !

Cefe and I knew this town of Aragón perfectly for it had been his third post as civil governor. The last stand made by the rebels within the city was in a massive stone building where the civil governor had his residence and official headquarters.

Once more the world outside Spain listened with amazement to the news. Once more those who were always looking for our surrender, because they knew that we could not get the arms we needed and that the people on our side were suffering terrible privations, were disappointed.

Stockholm was ablaze with colored decorations and green wreaths and the *God Jul* wishes everywhere. Fir trees were piled up in most of the streets and sold for the home celebrations.

I thought we should keep up with tradition and so arranged to have a tree for the legation staff and the Spanish citizens with their children who lived in Stockholm.

Nils was as excited as a child. He brought the biggest tree he could find and set it up in the great hall, then spent hours hanging up the tinsel wreaths, the candles and toys and the presents that Mary and I had been getting ready all through the past weeks. He also insisted on hanging up bright red apples and painted fir cones and on placing the customary stag made of straw at the foot of the tree.

We had a large party between three and seven in the afternoon with a general distribution of presents. We drank to Spain's victory and then just a small group of us sat around the fire before partaking of the usual Christmas dinner.

I wanted the servants to observe Christmas the way they were accustomed to, and they had ordered the traditional soup and fish and cakes, and I sent in mountains of Spanish oranges and grapes and nuts of all kinds.

After our dinner we again sat round the fire listening to the radio, on the watch for news. The rebels, we heard, were still holding out in the civil governor's residence of Teruel.

Soon after eleven our guests left us. Mary, Cefe and I stayed on beside the fire, talking of other Christmases in Spain, with the children singing the *villancicos* (Spanish Christmas carols) to the accompaniment of guitars and castanets. We talked of the house, redolent with the perfume of fir trees brought down from the Guadarrama Mountains and with the lavender, incense and storax burnt on the ashes of the braziers to make the rooms warm and fragrant. We spoke of the Christmas trees we had decorated and the *nacimiento* we had set up with the naive clay figures, of Christ in the manger between the mule and the ox, of shepherds and peasants dancing before the cave, of little washerwomen wringing out their linen beside a stream made of silver paper and of the hill built up with cork and brown paper down which the Wise Men of the East and their suite of slaves and camels wended their way along a narrow path, guided by a glittering tinsel star. Herod's palace was always placed on the top of the hill so as to dominate the landscape.

In Cefe's house and in mine, as in all Spanish homes, the *nacimiento* is the great feature of the season. The figures are kept from one year to another and sometimes handed down through several generations. I remember Aunt Maria used to put up the one that had belonged to her grandmother and with which her own mother had played as a child.

We thought of Cefito and Marissa and Germán and wondered whether they would manage to spend that evening together. The fir trees of the Guadarrama would not perfume the houses of Madrid. They were doing better. Laid across the road, they were acting as barricades against the people's foes.

"Will they have put up the *nacimientos* in Spain this year?" I asked Cefe. He shook his head. We both knew that Franco was sure to choose that night, as he chose all great religious feasts, to bombard the open cities more implacably than at other times.

Did he do it as a punishment from God, with the same spirit that had inspired the insurgent authorities to have the new tanks, made in Germany to kill Spaniards, blessed by the bishops and priests and named after different advocations of the Blessed Virgin, *Our Lady of Sorrows, Our Lady of the Pilar* and *Our Lady of the Immaculate Conception*, who was the patroness of the Spanish army in olden times ?

I wondered how such things could be made to harmonize with the idea of the angels' message to men and with that of the little Child in the manger who was to preach brotherly love among all men. Surely He would never have wished people to use bombs to destroy little children ; and on that night of all nights !

We waited impatiently for the clock to strike twelve and wish each other a happy Christmas as we had always done at home. I waited also to read a letter from Marissa which I had received that morning and had saved to enjoy with Cefe when we were alone.

Midnight. I broke open the envelope and with Cefe's arms around me, I read out all the news.

Germán had been sent to Barcelona. He might be staying there for some time. They thought Cefito would be with them for Christmas. Cefe and I decided we would try and get a long distance call through to them the very next day.

Then Marissa went on to give us a description of the visit she and Germán had made to Madrid at the beginning of the month. She spoke in thrilling terms of the wonderful defense of the capital, of the work of destruction that the bombardments and continued shelling had done, of the marvelous way in which the people were standing up in spite of the cold and the hunger that everybody had to suffer.

"People have to cook with paper fires or on the ashes of burnt rubbish," she said. "There is no wood and, of course, no coal, and the cold is appalling."

What touched Cefe and me most of all, however, was what she said of the dear old servants, Maria and Asunción, who had refused to come to Stockholm with me or even to follow the children to Valencia and Barcelona because they were afraid something might happen to our house.

"Father and mother built it," they said, with the stubborn love for family property that peasants from their region of Galicia, the northwest coast of Spain, so often have. "And if we leave it something might happen to it." Orders and prayers had been equally unavailing.

"No, we shall look after the house. Mother does not need us just now. There is no war where she is," they had told Marissa when she begged them to go back with her.

But that was not all. She had arrived in the house late at night and they had asked her what she would like to have to eat.

"Anything," Marissa answered, thinking she would be thankful to get a plate of lentils cooked in water. It was the only thing most people had to eat. Her surprise was enormous when she saw Maria and Asunción march into the dining room with their arms full of parcels of chocolate, butter, cheese, coffee, preserves of all sorts, and sugar.

"What is this?" she asked.

"This is all that mother has been sending us," they answered proudly.

"But why have you not eaten it? That's what mother sent it for."

"Oh, we manage all right. We would not eat these things for anything. A pretty pass it would be if mother or any of you had to come to Madrid and we had nothing for you to eat!"

I could not keep back my tears to think of those frail little women lacking everything and yet so strong in their affection for us all that they preferred to keep what they must have hungered for rather than that we should not be fed some day.

Marissa told them she was very angry with them and that I would be terribly disappointed to know that they had not eaten the food I had taken the trouble to send. She made them promise they would never do such a thing again, but I am sure they did not keep their word.

CHAPTER XXV

In spite of the capture of Teruel, the year 1938 had not come in under the best auspices. Teruel had been taken, certainly, and the action had been a marvel of strategy. But tactics are not everything in war, the invading armies had accumulated vast quantities of armaments to force an entrance into the city and the republicans were holding it from them at the cost of terrible sacrifices.

Day after day I waited for news in an agony of suspense. Marissa's letters showed signs of the awful strain the people in Spain were going through, not that the possession of Teruel was of basic importance but that the weakening of the resistance there showed we were again suffering from a heart-rending shortage of means to defend our positions. Every morning when I read the press I felt my heart literally go down into my heels, into the depths from which it had to be hauled out afterward for the brave front I needed to face either pity or indifference or unholy joy with calm equanimity. I did not want Teruel to be recaptured by the insurgents and yet I could not bear to think of the thousands of men who were being torn into pieces by bullets and bombs or at best having their nervous system wrecked by the constant tension.

At last a day came when we heard that the enemy had opened a great gap in our forces and that we had had to retreat from a position that so many lives had been sacrificed to gain. It was about this time that I gave a dinner party for the Swedish government. His excellency, the prime minister, was not fond of going out to dine among the diplomatic circle but he had graciously accepted my invitation.

After dinner we lingered over the coffee, talking about Spain. Per Albin Hansson had a realistic vision of politics and though he was deeply moved that night, by our descriptions of the destruction caused by modern warfare, it seemed to me that this knowledge, far from weakening his decision to keep Sweden out of every possible conflict, made it firmer than ever.

Nowadays it is relatively easy to frighten people, even the finest, into the most abject positions, for fear has been one of the curses of our time. Some people say that the real trouble has been selfishness, but I do not agree. Selfishness on the part of those high up, perhaps, but in the masses, who have nothing to gain by keeping quiet, it is fear that has moved them, or rather, prevented them from moving onward of late. The great psychological superiority that Hitler has shown over his contemporaries, in other lands, is that he has known how to wield the instruments for engendering fear with a really masterly mind.

Fear of suffering, fear of dying, fear of losing, fear of having to endure, fear of fear itself, has led the world into chaos. The recommendation that we should "cast fear out of our hearts" shows that this is one of men's greatest weaknesses and, when it is allowed to take root not in one heart alone but in millions, the result is catastrophic.

From the very first day of our war I felt that absence of fear was what carried the Spaniards along ; what allowed us to keep our senses, what prevented us from becoming insane, insane like the rest of the world. What else but insanity can have prompted the greatest nations of the world to behave like overgrown children subdued by a madman's whip ? What else but insanity, born from fear, could have led upright men to betray their principles and allow moral values on which civilized peoples had laid the highest price to be trampled under the clay feet of presumptuous "gods" ? Fear, fear, fear. There were moments when one felt it was in the very air one breathed.

In February Marissa wrote that she was coming back to Stockholm. She tried to tell me the great news in a round-about way but Germán spoke out : "Marissa is going to have a baby and she cannot remain here." He said no more, but it was enough to awaken a whole legion of thoughts and of both hopes and fears.

"Marissa is going to have a baby."

My little girl. I trembled to think of her under bombard-ments and without food. I knew that shortly after she re-turned to Spain after the summer, she had had nothing to eat for twenty-three days but mushrooms boiled in water. She had not complained. In fact, she insisted that those days, following Germán from one airport to another, were among the happiest experiences of her life.

I wrote the news to Cefe, wondering what he would say to this change of category within the family circle ; whether he would think he was being relegated to the background, marked with the sign of old age. But he was delighted and gave me no peace until I assured him Marissa was on her way to Stockholm.

I could not help thinking of so many other expectant mothers going through all the privations of war at such a time. The government did its best for women in that condition and for young children, too. Whatever milk and good food could be had was given to them. But it was so little.

Donations from peoples of the whole world kept pouring in but they were not enough. And my heart nearly burst with thankfulness when I had my little girl safely with me once again.

I had been working very hard over the two commercial agreements and hoped that during the coming season we would be able to derive some benefits from them. But my attention was often absorbed by international events. German pressure on Czechoslovakia, over the Sudeten question, was becoming unbearable. England and France, instead of picking up courage, were letting themselves go slowly down that hill of complacency one might call by the name of *laissez faire, laissez passer,* hitherto applied to commercial policy, but which is admirably adapted to the political methods that have been followed by the great powers during the last twelve years.

"What is going to happen in your country?" I said one day to a Czechoslovakian friend, a great sympathizer with Spain, who had just come from his country.

"God alone knows," he answered. "The situation is growing more difficult every day."

"Well, if you have to go to war, and I still hope you may not need to, for we know what modern war is, remember one thing that may bring some comfort to you. The resistance of Czechoslovakia will ease the pressure that is being brought to bear upon Spain."

"Madame Palencia," he answered, shaking his head dolefully, "I wish I could be comforted that way. But I am sure of one thing, there will be no war in my country."

"Then do you believe that Germany will respect your independence?"

"Certainly not. What I believe is that there will be no war because my country will be betrayed."

"Ah! You do not think that France . . ."

"Oh, it is not only that. Czechoslovakia will be betrayed from within."

His words puzzled me at the time but later events proved that he was right.

The Committee of Experts on Slavery was to meet in the second half of March and I had been told by our government to be sure and be present at its conference. I had also been given leave to go to Spain when it was over and spend a few days with Cefito whom I had not seen for nearly a year.

Marissa at once jumped at the chance of seeing her husband, too, and decided she would go with me. I demurred at first but as Mary was planning to go to Barcelona also, having returned to London first to see her mother, I gave in. After all, it was only natural that Marissa should want to see Germán, especially as he would probably not be able to be with her when the baby came.

When we left Stockholm the news from Spain was not encouraging. Our troops were retreating before the iron pressure of the invaders who were now centring their efforts on one objective, that of cutting off Catalonia from the rest of Spain. The four provinces which form what is called the Catalonian regions constitute the richest industrial zone of Spain. The land is carefully cultivated, divided into small properties, and is rich in fruits and cereals, so that to deprive the rest of Spain and the army of the Catalonian products and her industry was little short of condemning them to death.

Marissa and I stopped at Brussels for a couple of days on our way in order to see my sisters Maria and Inez once more. I found Maria much less intolerant toward the republic than she had been the year before. Evidently she was discovering that we were not so wicked after all and certainly not so wicked as Hitler who, she confided to me, must be the Antichrist. "He is a very bad man, in any case," she told me gravely.

By the time we reached Paris, the situation in Spain had grown much worse. In order to smash the Catalonian people into submission, the Fascists had begun a totalitarian air attack on Barcelona.

For three consecutive days and nights this beautiful capital was bombed every two hours. We heard that the whole city rocked under the explosions. There was not a single corner that could be considered safe. People were killed by thousands, killed and maimed, and the latter was worse than dying.

Someone I knew told me some time later he had found a woman kneeling on the pavement of a Barcelona street a little while after a school for very young children had been hit. She was leaning back against the broken-down wall of a house and crying out in a dull despairing way. My friend stopped to ask her whether she had been hurt. The woman shook her head and moaned. Then she held up something that she was holding between her two hands. The man bent down to see what she was showing him and raised his head again in horror. What she held was a little hand, a child's tiny hand that an explosion had cut off from the arm near the wrist.

The woman told the story. Her little boy was in the school that had been bombed and when she heard the explosion she had run out to look for him. That hand had almost fallen into her lap. The fingers were closed over a small school book. On the flyleaf was the name of her boy.

When my friend finished his story I felt quite sick and then I thought sadly of the longing for culture that my people had shown, of the efforts that had been made by the republic to satisfy their hunger, of the ruthless destruction of that culture the Fascists were carrying on. But I knew now that they would not succeed. The people, like that little child, would hold on to their treasure in spite of fire, in spite of bombs, in spite of death. The tiny hand was the emblem of the new Spain that might be temporarily beaten but would not let go what she had prized above all things.

Señor Ossorio Gallardo, the Spanish Ambassador in Paris, looked very grave when we called upon him the moment we arrived in Paris. Catalonia was being mercilessly destroyed because we had no means of defense, almost no cannons and no planes.

"Why doesn't France send us some?" I exclaimed desperately.

"Dear Isabel," said the ambassador, who was an old friend, one of Spain's greatest lawyers and a fervent and faithful Roman Catholic, "you are speaking like a heretic. What of that *safeguard of civilization* called the Non-Intervention Pact?"

The embassy teletype worked incessantly. And always it was the bearer of bad news. The enemy was very close to Lérida. They were advancing in the south, trying to cut their way through to the Mediterranean. The loss of life in Barcelona was appalling but the people kept very calm. That is what we heard. The people, always the people, giving gallant proofs of their courage.

That night I dined at the embassy. Mr. Paul Boncour, who had just been appointed Minister of Foreign Affairs, was the guest of honor. There were a great many people there; among them, Mr. François de Tessan whom I had known for several years and who was undersecretary in the same department.

We sat down to our meal in the luxurious dining room. Liveried servants attended our slightest wants and every now and again conversation was interrupted by the arrival of the latest bulletin. They all said the same, "Another raid." The twentieth or twenty-fifth since the morning. "Many persons killed." We went on eating, rather, I should say, making believe to eat.

Paul Boncour, who was sitting beside me, bent his head and murmured, "*C'est affreux. C'est affreux.*"

At last I could bear it no longer. I felt I was going to

scream at him, that I was going to tear the diplomatic bonds that forced me to be prudent and silent and courteous, and shout :

"*Oui, c'est affreux*, but not only the bombs. What is more *affreux* is the apathy, the cruelty, the blindness of the democratic countries and of France in the first place. No, not of France, but of the French government which would not let the arms we needed so sorely cross the frontier in a rush as they should have done. She only allowed them through sometimes when she thought fit, one by one, drop by drop. France might have lent us a few planes those days just to ward off the attacks that were blasting the Spanish people into empty space."

"The truth is that France cannot do it because she has no planes," someone murmured to me that night. Subsequent events proved this was true. True, she could not have lent us whole fleets of bombers and pursuit planes, but she might have spared fifty decent machines and they could still have saved Spain for democracy.

Marissa and I left for Geneva the next day. The news from Spain followed us all the way into Switzerland. There was not a paper that did not remind us of the danger our troops were in.

"The Spanish government army in danger of being cut in twain," said one. "Catalonia in imminent danger of being separated from the rest of Spain," said another. "Barcelona in the dark," said a third. This last news was quite true. The Fascists had managed to take Tremp and its great electric power station and had condemned Barcelona not only to darkness but to industrial inactivity at a moment when we needed the factories kept going even more than we needed food.

Fortunately the government showed it was capable of managing the situation and was generating power by means of coal. The cost was enormous but it saved the people from total darkness at least during some hours of the night and allowed the factories to go on producing a little.

I do not know how I ever lived through the two weeks that followed. The news grew worse and worse. Our army in Aragón was simply routed. What could it do with no arms? The enemy kept on advancing at lightning speed. It was difficult to concentrate on the question of slavery. However, I did my best.

The day after our arrival in Switzerland our consul general in Geneva telephoned me to say there had been a reshuffling of the Spanish cabinet. The socialist leader, Indalecio Prieto, who had been acting as Minister of the Defense, had not been included in it. Many people had for some time past shown their disapproval of his methods. Naturally very pessimistic, and physically sick at the time, he had lost hope in the possibility of resisting and he would speak discouragingly even to the officers coming in from the front. No army could keep up its morale indefinitely under such an influence.

Doctor Negrín undertook the gigantic task of keeping loyal Spain together in the face of disaster. He would be Prime Minister and Minister of War with the words, "To resist is to win," as his motto.

Señor Alvarez del Vayo was again given charge of the portfolio of Foreign Affairs in place of Señor Girál, one of the representatives of the republican party, who was made minister without portfolio.

That night I spoke to Alvarez del Vayo over the telephone.

"We have lost a good deal of ground," he said to me, "but we are beginning to stop the advance."

"May I go to Spain for a few days?" I asked.

For a time there was no answer then a voice said hesitatingly :

"If you want to."

"Of course I do. Besides, I must talk some things over with you."

"Very well then, come when you have finished your work at Geneva. I shall send a car to the frontier to meet you."

When the permanent Mexican delegate to the league, Señorita Palma Guillén, whom I had known several years before in Madrid and who had been minister for her country in Denmark, heard that I was going to Barcelona, she proposed that she and Marissa and I should drive down together in her car. She was going to fetch the children of some friends of hers and take them back with her to Geneva where they would be safe from bombs.

My great anxiety was Marissa. She would not hear of being left behind and I was terrified of the risk she might be running if she went in her condition. However, she grew so nervous and upset fearing I might not let her go that at last, against my better judgment, I gave in. Mary, who was still with her mother in London, I thought had better wait until another time. I felt that, not being my daughter, I should not take the responsibility and her mother shared my point of view.

The Committee of Experts on Slavery was dismayed when I told them I was going to Spain the moment our work was done.

"Madame Palencia, we beg of you to think it over," they said. "You know one can be too courageous."

As a matter of fact, I did not need to be courageous for I really was not a bit afraid, or was it that I did not realize the danger? Perhaps that was it.

At last we finished our task in the committee. The morning we finished discussing the report Gouverneur Marchand, who always made some courteous allusion to my presence, expressed the thanks of the whole committee for the interest I had shown and the co-operation I had given them in days of such distress as those had been for me. They all said good-bye as though I were going to the scaffold and hoped I would come out of Spain safe and sound, but they looked rather dubious. Sir George Maxwell begged me once more not to go to Barcelona and waved a sad farewell from the door of the hotel, where we were both staying, as the car with Palma Guillén, Marissa and I started off. His last kind words, however, were cheering, "Good luck to you!"

The news that morning was a little better. The republican army was being brought into shape again. Negrín's firmness looked as though it might save the day.

Marissa sang Spanish folk songs for the benefit of Señorita Guillén on the way to Spain, and I found myself repeating Negrín's motto over and over to myself : "To resist is to win. To resist is to win."

CHAPTER XXVI

I found the car the minister had sent, waiting for me in the French frontier town of Perpignan. The driver turned out to be a man who had been Cefe's chauffeur when he was Civil Governor of Teruel. We filled the empty seats with parcels of food and tobacco and sewing materials to give away and, followed by Señorita Guillén and Marissa in the other car, we drove down the highroad to Barcelona, looking out for threatening planes the whole way.

The road was almost blocked at times with lorries carrying men and armament to the front which was now, of course, much nearer Barcelona than it had been. Lérida had fallen and down south of Tarragona, between the regions of Valencia and Catalonia, the enemy was smashing through our line, and just a thin wedge of land still separated them from the Mediterranean.

In spite of the imminence of danger everyone we talked to seemed calm and confident. Down we drove through the lovely well-kept villages and past the rich fields decked out in all their fresh spring garb.

"I should like to get into Barcelona before it is dark," the driver said.

I echoed his wish, for we had telegraphed to the boys that we were coming and I feared Cefito might only have a few hours' leave. Germán's headquarters were in Barcelona so we were sure to see him.

Night, however, soon began to fall, and we did not seem to be anywhere near the city. However, it was impossible to see anything in the dark.

"Barcelona," said the driver suddenly, with an accent of pride in his voice, as though he were showing off some priceless treasure.

Marissa's voice floated up behind us. She was still singing, and evidently she was very happy. There were no lights anywhere and the car lamps were so shrouded with dark cloths I have not yet understood how it could be safe to drive. After a while we felt we were off the road and driving over paved streets. The chauffeur managed to advance slowly.

After what seemed to me a very long time, the car stopped before a house. A man seemed literally to jump out of a doorway and I found myself being helped up from my seat by Cefito. Still holding me by the arm, he went to get his sister out of the other car. We both said good-bye to Señorita Guillén and, half laughing, half crying with excitement, we reached the apartment where Cefito and Germán were staying and where we were to stop for the night. Both of them had made up their minds that we were not to go up to General Hidalgo Cisneros' house, as we had arranged when he and Connie had come through Stockholm about a month or so before on their way to Spain after their visit to Moscow where Ignacio had gone to recover his health, sadly impaired by overwork and tension. For that night at least, the boys wanted us all to themselves.

"I want to see you and speak to you alone for a little while," Cefito said pleadingly, before he rushed out to get Germán who was waiting for us at the Foreign Press Bureau with Connie, thinking we would stop there first.

Connie understood the situation quite well. She came round to see me for a few minutes and we arranged that I would go to them the next day. I was in such a state of nerves I could hardly speak or think. We had been so anxious about the boys and it was such a relief to see them safe, it almost took my breath away.

The moment we were able, we unpacked our parcels, laying by what was to be given to other people and sent up to Madrid.

What jokes the boys made while they fell like young wolves on the dainties and tobacco !

After a curious, impromptu supper, with the strangest assortment of food, we went to our rooms to try and get some sleep, but it was not long before Cefito came and sat on my bed. We talked until daylight and then, utterly worn out, he lay at my feet and fell into a heavy slumber.

My fatigue had disappeared. Visions of the past seemed to rise up before me. I saw Cefito as a baby, holding on to my hand as he toddled along, as a schoolboy showing me off proudly to his friends, and as a man, taking his part in the life of Spain. Now, asleep, he seemed a child again. I dared not move lest he wake up. And in my heart I breathed a passionate prayer that the precious burden lying at my feet would come to no harm.

Early the next morning I hurried down to the Ministry of Foreign Affairs to see Alvarez del Vayo. There was room for thought in all I saw as I went down. Barcelona seemed completely changed from the years before. Now it was indeed a city at war, streets and avenues full of horrible blackened streaks like huge scars, masses of stone and mortar and empty spaces. I know of nothing more terrible than the sight of a city that has been bombed. Of course, Barcelona, being a great city — at that time it held almost two million people — was not completely destroyed. Many of its fine thoroughfares were still intact but even they showed signs that the awful "black birds," as the people called the bombers, had flown over them. I looked up at the blue sky over us. How could war dare to defile its purity ?

The people, too, I found very much changed, gaunt, emaciated men and women who, one could see, had not had a decent meal for months. The greatest shock I got in this sense was coming across the painter, Roberto Fernández Balbuéna, President of the Commission to save the Spanish Artistic Treasures, and Vice-Director of the Prado Museum. He was almost like a brother to us and it made me anxious to see how terribly ill he looked. No wonder the food at the legation had seemed to choke us as we thought of the hunger at home.

In spite of this, I found all the persons I spoke to as determined to go on with the war and win as ever. The past bombardments had told on their nerves but had not demoralized a single one of them. On the contrary, there was a smoldering rage beneath the calm exterior that revealed a decision not to give in, whatever happened.

"You will have to go to London on your way back to Stockholm," said Alvarez del Vayo, as he shook my hand and made me sit down near his desk.

"To London?"

"Yes. I have been asked whether you would go and speak to the members of the House of Commons. And I said I was sure you would be pleased to go." The minister looked at me rather quizzically.

I kept silent.

"Well, what do you think about it?"

"I must go if you say I should, although I do not believe it will be of the slightest use."

Del Vayo laughed bitterly. He looked rather tired after the past strenuous days. His desk was covered with papers and he tried to look them over as we talked. Some men were setting up a microphone in the room for a speech he was to deliver that afternoon.

"Thanks," he said curtly, and then, "yes, it *will* do good. I am sure people who would not otherwise hear the truth will go and listen to what you have to say. How long do you intend to stay here?"

"As long as I am allowed."

"Well, you may stay over the fourteenth."

The fourteenth of April was the anniversary of the Proclamation of the Republic, our national holiday. This year I was again going to spend it in Spain.

The minister then proceeded to give me an outline of all the political and military events that had taken place since the beginning of the retreat in Aragón.

"I should like to see you every day during your stay in Barcelona," he said, "so that you are able to inform people in London, as well as in Sweden, of what has happened and of what they may still expect." He spoke firmly and with hope.

"Doctor Negrín will get things going very soon," he added. "Why, you would never have thought so much could have been done in such a short time. Last week everything was in disorder. The army on this front was completely disorganized. Today we have everything under control again."

By something that was little short of a miracle, Catalonia had got hold of herself. The disbanded troops were coming back of their own accord. Everybody knew the troops were not to blame. The enormous superiority of the enemy in arms and ammunition had broken down the lines. The men had lost contact with their officers and they had been pushed back day after day before they were able to regain their foothold.

The people understood it all perfectly and were ready to make allowances and to do their part of the job by keeping firm. Perhaps they did not know the full extent of the danger they ran, nor that for some days there was nothing between them and the enemy, no men, no guns, nothing. Perhaps the enemy itself did not know it. In any case, now it was too late for Franco to take advantage of it. The republican army was falling into line and was ready to carry on the fight, still with insufficient arms. Down south the insurgents still kept on

advancing toward the sea, but the ground had to be fought for
step by step.

That evening we moved up to General Hidalgo de Cisneros'
house, Germán, too.   Cefito went just for one night, for early
the next morning he got the order to go to the Segre sector on
the Aragón front.   I felt very anxious.   Fierce fighting was
going on there at the time.   Besides, I had hardly seen him and
would probably be going before he got another leave.

We went down to his rooms, together, to get his kit.

"Don't worry, mother," he said suddenly, while he was lac-
ing his boots.

"I am not worrying," I answered.

"Oh, yes, you are."   And he looked up at me in the funny
little way he had when he wanted to tease.

He and several other doctors were supposed to start at midday.   I went down to his barracks with him and was introduced to his colleagues.   Then I said good-bye.

Next morning I received a note from him.   After all, they
had not started until four o'clock in the morning.   I could have
wept to think we had missed being together all those hours.

My time was filled to the last minute during the next few
days.   In the mornings I went down to the Ministry of Foreign
Affairs and heard the latest news, and the afternoons I spent
going the round of the other departments for matters connected
with Sweden : to the Ministry of Education for books and
information on the latest schools opened ; to the Labor Department for copies of the new regulations for women's and
children's work ; to the Department of Commerce to discuss
the commercial agreements with Sweden and Finland.   I also
tried to get in touch with my nephew Juan, but he was away
with his ship, carrying on the strenuous task our navy had been
charged with and which, being a silent one, was generally ig-

nored. Our naval men certainly did not get so much credit for their work as they deserved.

I dined with Doctor Negrín up in the War Ministry one day. He seemed very calm and one could see he had the situation well in hand. His exceptionally strong physique certainly helped him to get through those awful days. He was anxious to get my impressions of the reaction in the northern countries and insisted on the necessity of getting food sent to Spain as soon as possible.

After a few days in Barcelona it was plain to me that the food problem was very serious ; if Valencia was cut off the situation would become much worse. And boats with victuals were being sunk in sight of land every day. It was criminal.

The fourteenth of April was a lovely day, as lovely as that other one seven years before when we had hailed the advent of the republic in the midst of general rejoicing and without bloodshed. The public buildings of Barcelona were all decorated with flags and, although no one dreamt of stopping work, there was quite a holiday feeling throughout the town.

I had had a private interview with the President, Señor Azaña, the day before and had given him an account of how things were going in the Scandinavian countries. I thought he looked ill and very depressed.

I have known Don Manuel Azaña for many years, long before we ever suspected that the monarchy would be overthrown in our time and that he would be the President of the Spanish Republic. He is an extraordinarily intelligent man and generally misunderstood, believed to be strong, but really a weak character, supposed to be cruel and hard but really softhearted. He is the finest orator, bar none, that I have ever heard, but not a speaker for the masses ; a fine statesman, but not in troubled times. He has a mind in which logic becomes destructive through sheer clarity. It is wasted at moments like those Spain was then going through in which everything illogical, everything arbitrary, unexpected, incomprehensible, was happening.

Ignacio Hidalgo de Cisneros, who would give us the latest news of the front when he came in to dinner, looked grave that night. The retreat of the republican army, south of Tortosa and toward the Mediterranean, was going on. The tiny strip of land that still kept Catalonia bound to Valencia was getting narrower and narrower.

"I am going to fly over tonight," he said.

Connie looked up anxiously.

"I must see that they have everything they need on the other side before we are cut off."

We all felt worried. He would have to fly over enemy ground part of the way and it was extremely dangerous at such a time. I felt very sorry for Connie.

"Do you think the road will be cut soon?" I asked.

"Any moment now."

But it took them two more days. Our men held their ground although the lovely little villages on the coast, with their white-washed houses and their exquisite gardens, were just a mass of blackened ruins.

I wanted to stay on and see for myself the effect that the cutting of the road would have on the people's morale. Many people in Barcelona had their families in Valencia and Madrid or in places farther south. What would they say of the severing of communications with those towns?

When the news came, when it was known that the loyalist territory had been cut in half, the people looked grave. They knew that it was a serious development in the war but they kept that unbreakable spirit which had carried them along for two years.

Marissa and I had to move on at last. Looking back on the days we spent in Spain at that time, I can still sympathize with Cefito when I asked him what he was anticipating most in the way of comfort when the war was over. He did not mention food or tobacco or even warmth in winter. He said :

"I long to see the shop windows lit up at night."

I understood it so well ! The darkness in the streets those nights we were in Barcelona had made me more nervous than anything else. I could not get accustomed to the stumbling and the groping, the feeling of helplessness.

When Marissa and I started on our way again the enemy had, for the time being, stopped bombing the town. The Fascists had been concentrating their efforts on other places so as to help the invaders in their task of breaking through to the sea. We had, therefore, slept pretty well most nights. Besides, Connie's house was out of the usual range. The enemy pilots liked to do their work and use their bombs where they were most sure of causing damage : the centre of the town that was thickly populated and the port where they tried to sink ships, especially if they carried food.

We left by car. I felt that the elation and faith in human solidarity that had characterized the first months of our struggle were over. We were now up against the stark, grim truth that we were outnumbered in everything, that our resources were dwindling, that our people were worn out, and worse still, that we were misunderstood, that we were alone.

The spirit of resistance invoked by Negrín was there. It was the only bulwark of democracy now. We could count only on our own efforts. If help came it would indeed lead to rapid victory. But where was that help ?

As we drove along, always looking out for enemy planes, I turned my thoughts away from the future and tried to make the most of every minute that I still had in Spain.   I tried to look down on the rich red earth of Catalonia, to feel the perfume of the thyme on the rugged hillside of the "Costa Brava," the most beautiful coast in Europe — to look upon the faces of the people and to answer their wan smiles and the long-drawn-out republican password *Salud*.   It is such a Spanish word ; such an old-fashioned way of wishing you the best in the world, "Good health."

Paris, where we had to stop on our way up, irritated me beyond measure.   The indifference, real or feigned of those in power, for our struggle, their wilful ignorance of the gravity of the situation for all Europe, made me wonder why I was going to London.   The men in office there were working hand in hand with France.   Rather, they were the leaders down the road of destruction over which they were pushing democracy.

Turning to personal considerations I found comfort in the thought that Marissa had borne the trip wonderfully well considering her condition and that this new parting from Germán had been a great trial.   He was now doing work which carried him constantly from one town to another so every bombardment was a terror to her.

"How can I tell he was not there just then ?" she would say when we looked over the papers and read the names of the places that had suffered from the bombings by Italian planes.

Savoia bombers were most generally employed for attacking open cities in Catalonia.   It was so easy for them, they had only to hop over from the Balearic Islands and they could be sure they would not meet any opponents on the way.   The few planes we had were at the front.

We flew to London from Paris in fifty minutes.   The car from the embassy and two members of the staff had been sent to meet us. I was struck, as always, with the smallness of everything : houses, fields, fences. England certainly does not care to make a show of her strength. She does not glory in parades. She keeps her colossal dreadnoughts and her boundless wealth discreetly in the background. Her officers do not care to swagger about in uniform until the moment comes when those things are needed. But one feels the great underlying force all the time that one is in the British Isles.

We had been asked to stay at the embassy. Pablo de Azcárate, who had given up his comfortable post in the League of Nations the moment the war broke out and had offered his services to Spain, is a charming host. So is his tiny, intelligent wife, Amelia, whose careful eye was always on the watch to prevent her husband from getting overtired, for he had not been strong for some time and tension now was growing.

Azcárate gave me an outline of the situation in England that evening. Everything was ready for me to speak in one of the committee rooms of the House of Commons next day. He was as skeptical as all of us about the results we might obtain, but we should at least let them hear the truth as often as possible. The British parliament, like most things the English possess, is unique. The buildings are beautiful and the old traditional customs soften the unavoidable feeling of routine that other institutions show.

I was met at the entrance of the House of Commons by the Duchess of Atholl, Miss Ellen Wilkinson, and a group of sympathizers with the Spanish cause. Mrs. Corbett Ashby, President of the International Alliance of Women for Suffrage and Equal Citizenship, was there also ; rather a delicate-looking woman, she had been actively present in every movement for justice and democracy in the world. I have known her for many years and appreciated the fine stand she was always ready to maintain even during the most difficult moments.

The Duchess of Atholl introduced me to the group of parliamentary members who had assembled to hear about Spain. Such a variety of types : red-headed stocky men sprung from the people ; thin-lipped, thin-limbed representatives of the "upper class," well-set-up men from the banking and business world, scholarly-looking men from the intellectual circles.

I gave an outline of the situation in loyal Spain, of the real reasons for the war, of the difficulties we had come up against and of the possibilities for the future. I did not mince my words, told the truth straight out without adding or subtracting anything, and then waited for some questions.

I had instinctively felt which of the men among the audience were with us and which were not, and I was ready to hold my own against whatever argument was brought up. But what I certainly did not expect to meet at that late hour was the ignorance of the matter on hand revealed in the questions posed by one or two of the conservative members. - They were so lacking in understanding, so empty of logic, that for a moment I believed that they were intending to disconcert me. But no indeed. . . It really was ignorance : the ignorance of men who can never for the life of them look at a thing from two different angles.

"Do you think," one man asked, "that when Franco wins the Germans and Italians will retain their influence over Spain ?"

I looked at him in amazement. Was it possible that a man in his position could be so badly informed on world affairs ? Was he not aware yet of the threat that was hanging over Europe, Great Britain included ? That the "man in the street" should not know these things, was natural. But it was inconceivable that a member of parliament, a man whose people had made him responsible for their welfare and for that of the future and safety of the empire, should be so ignorant. I could understand the Chamberlains and the Halifaxes and others "making believe" that they were ignorant of these facts. Such an attitude was part of their tactics to avoid war at that moment, but they *knew*.

This man did not. He was undoubtedly a well-meaning soul, scrupulously anxious to do his duty by his country but misled by propaganda and by that now almost used-up scarecrow of "communism." He held on to the belief that Germany and Italy were really carrying out a beneficent task in Spain, beneficent for the whole world. He had evidently never realized that the wings of the altogether too "protective angels" Mussolini and Hitler were already casting their shadows over his own country.

"I suppose you mean *if* Franco wins," I answered.

He looked at me in astonishment. Any other possibility than a Franco victory had never, of course, come into his head.

"*If* Franco wins," I repeated, "Germany and Italy will certainly keep the influence they are now fighting so hard to obtain. They will stay in the Balearic Islands so as to cut off, or at least hamper, France's communications with her North African possessions. They will control Ceuta and Algeciras in order to make the Strait of Gibraltar a dangerous spot for Great Britain. They will install cannon along the Pyrenees to threaten the allied armies and close in on France from the south. They will stay on in Coruña and Vigo so as to have good observation posts over the Atlantic. They will settle in Bilbao and Huelva and Almadén so as to be sure of the iron ore and the copper and the quicksilver of the mines in those places, and they will keep a hold on Barcelona and Valencia so as to have access to the fruits and fields of those regions."

I saw him take down notes and shake his head in a puzzled manner. He had never heard of such a thing! I remembered my talk with Sir Stafford Cripps the evening before. The labor leader had come round to the embassy to see me and had been referring to the lack of political conscience and the ignorance of world affairs many Britishers had. Well, here was good proof.

The Duchess of Atholl, who that very day had announced her intention of abandoning her party because she could no longer back its leaders, looked up at me with an apologetic smile for her countryman.

"Would you advise Great Britain to give up such advantages *if*," I asked my puzzled interlocutor, laying special stress on the last word, "she had obtained them ?"

He said nothing. New questions were brought up. I answered one after another with arguments that no one could contradict or lay aside. They were irrefutable. But I left the House of Commons feeling sure that nothing would be gained by my talk except, perhaps, the enlightenment of some sincere persons. Perhaps I had sown doubts in their minds and had put those who were behind the scenes in a still more uncomfortable position by that enlightenment, but nothing else.

When I got back to the embassy I found Marissa lying on her bed. She was not feeling well. Mary Morgan and Trudy Araquistain's lovely little daughter, Sonia, were keeping her company.

"We are going on to Sweden tomorrow," I said to her. She looked relieved. The long trip and the excitement and worry were telling on her. But she had seen Germán and Cefito. So had I. We both felt it was a great deal to look back on, a memory to cherish and cling to in those days, with another long separation before us and always : doubt.

So many questions were continually being asked about the fate of our works of art, especially the pictures from the Prado Museum, that immediately after my return I set about arranging some lectures to be delivered throughout the Scandinavian countries by Roberto Fernández Balbuéna whom our government had decided to send for some time out of Spain, hoping that in this way he would rest and be properly nourished and thus his life be saved.

The responsibility of looking after those priceless treasures that the commission, under Roberto's chairmanship, had taken upon itself, had exacted an effort he was physically not in condition to stand. It was thought that a complete change, at a time when the pictures were for the moment out of danger, would allow him to continue his work later on.

The Director of the Stockholm Picture Gallery and those of Copenhagen and Oslo, as well as the Universities of Uppsala and Lund, answered that they would be only too glad to avail themselves of the chance of profiting by Roberto's experience. It is probable that many of the measures taken lately in various European capitals to safeguard their artistic treasures are the result of his observations. For Roberto was interviewed on the subject not only in the Scandinavian countries but also by persons who were responsible for the safety of the museums in London and Paris, as well as in other towns of Europe.

The moment we reached Stockholm Marissa had to be put to bed. She was suffering from severe kidney trouble. Our dear doctor, Ruby Lind, who took her at once under her care, did not disguise the fact that she was worried about the case. Marissa's slight strength had been sapped by her condition and the tension of the war. And any ailment at the time was fraught with danger, a new cause for anxiety.

One would think that when the mind is taken up with a great many problems and the heart is full because of many sorrows, the intensity of apprehension and feeling for each individual motive or subject would diminish. I found it was not the case. On the contrary, they increased as though they were nourished one by the other.

CHAPTER XXVII

Any observer, even the most indifferent, could have sensed at the beginning of June 1938, that very serious trouble was looming ahead, trouble for every country. Already thunderous black clouds were gathering over the Baltic. The first visible sign of the storm was to be found in the question of the Åland Islands. In the same way that a tiny spot on human flesh is the herald of a deadly disease, so these small, inoffensive-looking little islands, surrounded by the grey-blue northern waters of the Baltic Sea, which had been feeling secure in the autonomy that other nations had granted them, believing that the battles waged for them in the past between Russia and Germany and Sweden and Denmark were over for good, found themselves again converted into a strategic position coveted by two great powers. They found themselves an important factor in the ominous silent struggle already going on behind the scenes of the European stage.

Many, many years have passed since a Swedish monarch built the powerful fortress of Kastelholm and fortified the islands to protect his kingdom from his enemies in the east. A long time, too, since that castle and other fortifications, erected by Russia when the islands formed part of her empire, were demolished. Twenty odd years since Åland was put under the care of Finland, in spite of Sweden's natural desire to control the islands herself.

In order to keep them safe from all complications in the future, a pact was this time set up between the European countries providing that the Åland Islands could not be fortified without the consent of all the signatory nations.

Suddenly, however, the Swedes and the Finns observed that Germany was excessively fond of visiting the Åland Islands.

418

Nazi engineers and naval experts would spend days measuring the depth of the sea around them. Russia began to grow nervous. The isles were the approach to Leningrad. In possession of a powerful foe, the Soviet territory would be easily accessible. Germany was at that time the Soviet's most feared opponent, for they both wanted to obtain supremacy in the Baltic. On the other hand, Sweden and Finland began to feel that the islands, not being fortified, might any day fall into the hands of one of the two rivals. Their occupation would be the easiest thing in the world and a terrible threat to the independence of their nearest neighbors. After prolonged discussion and weighing of pros and cons, for neither country is apt to make a decision lightly, Sweden and Finland came to the conclusion that the only way to protect Åland, and themselves, by the way, was to fortify the isles between them.

The moment this plan became known the peoples of the two countries began to grow restless.

They feared that Germany and Russia would come to blows near their shores, that Åland, having become once more a bone of contention, might be the spark destined to set the world on fire.

As to the inhabitants of the islands, they did not take long to voice strong protests. They did not in the least want to be fortified and submitted to conscription. It meant losing their much-cherished autonomy and being exposed to invasion. Commissions from Åland visited the Swedish and Finnish governments which did their best to appease the frightened Ålanders.

Meanwhile the knowledge that, although the Finnish law prevents land from being sold to foreigners, Finns who sympathized with the Reich were buying properties in the Åland Islands and passing them on to the Germans, increased everybody's nervousness. It was feared that the acquired land might be used in the case of war to establish bases for the Reich's pocket submarines.

After great discussions, all the other countries except Germany and the Soviet Republic agreed that the islands could and should be fortified. Germany seemed at that time ready to agree also, but on condition that the fortifications should be exclusively under Finnish control, that Sweden, of whose friendship the Reich was not too sure, should be eliminated from the field.

Sweden for years has kept apart from all international conflicts, bent only on the maintenance of the Baltic *status quo*. She now began to be afraid that she might be caught in the meshes of this vital problem, a wrong solution of which would be sure to endanger the neutrality that has been the only foreign policy she has followed for years. Consultation followed consultation. Interview followed interview, but Russia would not give in. One could understand her opposition, in a way. The situation dragged on and on and has never reached a satisfactory settlement. In any case, the fortifications that were being built have lately been demolished.

On the sixteenth of June 1938, King Gustav celebrated his eightieth birthday. Preparations had been going on for months in anticipation of an event that to most Swedes was a matter for calm congratulations. Every shop window in Stockholm and, I dare say in every other Swedish town, exhibited a picture of the king. The blue and gold Swedish colors flew over every house, street and garden, and from the topmast of every boat, large and small, sailing on Swedish waters.

The time of the year was perfect for outdoor celebrations and the presence of the King and the Crown Prince and Princess of Norway and the Crown Prince and Princess of Denmark was the excuse for a number of social affairs.

The Swedes are not fond of making a display of their feelings. And in regard to the royal family they are content to show their affection in a very tranquil way. The king and the crown prince know that they are both loved and trusted but there is never any wild cheering or demonstration as it is the fashion to offer the head of the state in some countries nowadays. It appears that if there is no wild enthusiasm for royalty neither are there any republican outbursts. At least I have never heard of any.

The royal family can walk or drive about without any escort. Evidently they have nothing to fear from their subjects. On the occasion of the king's birthday the people were as undemonstrative as usual. I am sure they felt sincerely glad to see their sovereign reach this ripe old age but thought there was no need to make any more fuss about it than at other times. And they heartily appreciated his majesty's gift of the money collected as a national present to him to the fund for the fight against cancer.

The celebrations within the Royal Palace comprised a supper and concert to which all of the diplomatic corps were invited. I had been more than usually busy those days, sending parcels of food to Spain where the need for victuals was more pressing every minute. The committee was doing its best to help me but, in spite of the good spirit of collaboration I was meeting, I found it very hard to reconcile myself to the brilliant scene in the large Hall of State that night.

The ladies in waiting and the wives of the cabinet ministers had discarded their black court dresses for white lace or gauze gowns. All the other guests were naturally in full evening garb. Jewels and decorations of all sorts glittered on uniforms and dresses. King Gustav of Sweden and King Haakon of Norway towered above the heads of their retinues. The two sovereigns and other members of the royal family took their places.   The guests occupied the two sides of the hall in rows. I found myself sitting exactly opposite Prime Minister and Mrs. Hansson.

While the music played my thoughts wandered to Spain and I suddenly realized that I was unconsciously staring at Per Albin Hansson and mentally addressing him.

What are we doing here, you and I ?   What have you, with your honest eyes and your kindly face — a man of the people — to do here while your comrades in Spain are dying for want of help ?   Why am I here and not with them ?   What have I to do with all this luxury and brightness and elegance, lights and jewels, when the women of my country are hungry and homeless, widowed and childless ?   I could find no satisfactory answer either for him or for me.

In the interval between the two parts of the concert the royal family mingled with their guests.   When Princess Ingeborg came up to our side of the hall she smiled at me and said :

"Well, Madame Palencia, are you feeling more at home now in Sweden ?"

"I should be ungrateful if I did not, your highness," I answered, "for Sweden has been very kind to me."

"And do you like the house ?" she asked.

"Very much, your highness.   I like it because it is not just an official residence.   There is something homely about it, too."

"Ah, yes," she said with a rather sad smile.   "That is what it was intended to be."   Then, coming closer, "Did you read what was written on the window ?"

I nodded.   "I read it the very first day and it touched me deeply.   Finding myself as I did in a strange land and with the tragedy of my country on my heart, it seemed almost like a welcome."

On her way to present her credentials to the King of Sweden

"That is exactly what it was meant for, Madame Palencia, and I hope that you will be very happy there."

Again I marveled at her generosity of soul.

Alvarez del Vayo had given me leave to go and spend a few days with Cefe in Latvia so, taking advantage of a lull in my work, I boarded the ship for Finland where I found Careaga well settled and looking after the affairs of the legation with success.

From Finland I went on by air to Tallin and stayed there for a little while, not only to see the town, perhaps the most typical and interesting city on the Baltic, but also to find out what possibilities there were for a more active interchange of products between Estonia and Spain.

It did not take me long to discover that the Germans were taking complete hold of the country. Although, as in Finland, it was not easy to buy property, the Nazis were, through sympathizers and friends, getting possession of a very large part of the land. They controlled business and politics and were fast becoming masters of the whole country, in fact, if not in name.

My train left Tallin at midnight and was due in Riga at six o'clock the next morning. I had told Cefe not to trouble to come down to meet me so early but, of course, he was waiting at the station. We drove to the legation which was installed in a large ground-floor apartment with fine reception rooms, well heated with the tiled stoves that are so typical of the northern countries. But in Sweden one finds them only in the older buildings and houses, not in modern apartments where central heating is quite common.

Cefe had been lucky enough to find an excellent housekeeper, Erna, who saw that everything in the legation was in good order. She could speak French perfectly and often acted as interpreter with salesmen and in answering the telephone out of office hours. It was she who opened the door for us and took our wraps.

The first thing Cefe did was to blindfold me and lead me into the big salon where he stopped, uncovered my eyes and bade me look. I gave a gasp. Facing me was a lovely oil painting of a nude figure. It had been painted for me by Cefe as a surprise. I knew he had been working a little with his brushes during his spare moments. He had told me that drawing and reading were the only things that could keep his mind away from the anxiety and tension of the war but I had not suspected that he was doing anything so lovely.

After I had been shown round the apartment and introduced to the maids and the legation staff, Cefe gave me a list of the engagements he had made for us both during the time of my stay. There were so many invitations to lunch and dine at the houses of Cefe's colleagues that I began to fear we should not have a minute to ourselves. I told him so.

"I tried to keep some days free," he said, "but it was impossible." Then, with ill-concealed pride, "They are all so anxious to know you."

I wasn't surprised. Cefe had evidently talked so much and so constantly about me that, either to please him or out of curiosity, they had sent all these pressing invitations.

"Never mind, we shall manage to find time for ourselves, too," I said.

The first evening we had a big dinner party in the legation. Erna had arranged the table beautifully and Cefe had ordered a bouquet of flowers with the colors of her country for each one of the ladies who were our guests. My bouquet was made up of red carnations, yellow pansies and dark purple violets. The idea was so charming that I copied it for the dinner party

I gave a few weeks later in the Stockholm legation to the members of the diplomatic corps and in honor of Minister and Madame Sandler.

I have often thought that, had it not been for the war, those days in Latvia would have been among the happiest in my life. Cefe made a perfect host and to be in a new country with him, looking at things together, then discussing them in our long talks at night, after we came in from our daily parties, and seeing him painting and making plans, would have been bliss had the spectre of our struggle not cast a shadow over everything.

Cefe tried to make up for it in every possible way. We would have our breakfast in a little room leading into the dining room and every single morning of my stay I found a present from him lying on my plate : either perfume, or gloves, or books, or dainty underwear. The wives of some of his colleagues had helped him to choose the presents and were always greatly interested to hear how I had liked them.

At last I felt I could not possibly stay any longer. There was a great deal to do in Stockholm and, besides, I felt Marissa needed me. There were still many things to prepare for the new little Spaniard we expected, and although one of her friends, Marie Luisa Vilches, who was staying with her for a while, would be good company for her, I knew she would be missing me very much.

I left Riga by plane. Cefe stood staring at my airship with such a disconsolate air that I was glad the minister of Rumania and his wife, who were among his best friends, were with him. They would be sure to take him along to lunch at their house after I left and would look after him as they had been doing all along. My visit had certainly been a charming experience and an unforgettable one. When I reached Stockholm I found to my relief that Marissa was able to be up and about.

One morning, a few weeks after I got back to Sweden, Dethorey walked into my study in the chancellery almost without asking permission to enter.

"Señora! Señora!" he exclaimed. "I have just heard a wonderful bit of news!" Then very haltingly — he always stuttered when he was excited — he told me that, according to a press agency which had just rung up the legation, our army, the Spanish republican army that had been driven back a few weeks ago from Aragón and had only just been reorganized and put into shape, had accomplished one of the most daring and well-thought-out feats that have ever been registered. With the aid of little boats belonging to the fishermen from all down the Catalonian coast, our men had crossed the river Ebro in the night, had captured several villages from the Italians, before they had even had time to look round, and were advancing into the invaded territory.

The object of this extraordinary action was to stop the enemy's pressure on Valencia where a strong offensive was expected and feared. During four long months the Spaniards kept their positions in an unceasing battle, being blasted by the Italian planes day and night and attacked by an army that was overwhelmingly superior both in numbers and equipment.

The bridges that kept the communications open with the rear-guard were bombed every day and built up again every night, protected by our one plane to their every nine or ten, by our one cannon to their fifteen or twenty, by our one tank against their twelve or fifteen.

Man after man fell, the best and bravest of our troops. It was due to them that the offensive against Valencia did not take place, but the price paid was terrific. Our forces were almost as large in numbers as theirs and very much better in quality, for ours were all men picked for their courage and their devotion to the cause and for their fighting qualities.

They were not just poor ignorant peasants brought over by force from the Italian fields and valleys, whose lives were of course as precious as Spanish lives but whose death did not constitute such a loss from a military point of view.

Europe was again amazed. When would Spain stop being a surprise ? I could read this amazement in the faces of my colleagues and in their questions. I could also see that many of them were annoyed that the situation created by our war should be prolonged so long. It kept the atmosphere too tense and the possibilities of a general conflict increasing through it. But Spain could not stop and give up just to please them. . .

One morning, on August the eighteenth, Doctor Ruby Lind and I took Marissa to the maternity hospital. She had been suffering for some hours so I hoped with all my heart that her deliverance would not be long delayed. I sat near her bed all through the afternoon and the early part of the evening, trying not to remember when Cefito was born, not to think of the awful crushing pain that I had endured then. I did my best to fix my mind on other things but it was difficult with Marissa's pale face there before me.

Then I began to count up the days Marissa would be in the clinic. How nice it would be when she came back to the legation. The baby's room was all ready, waiting, and the little wardrobe and chest were full of the daintiest, cunningest little things. There were fifty-four pairs of little shoes. I had counted them that very morning. They and some other articles had been sent by friends from different countries : from France, from England and from the United States, from Russia, from Latvia, and Finland and Norway and Czecho-slovakia, from Barcelona and Valencia and war-torn Madrid and from China. Yes, there were two little pairs of shoes from China, one in red and the other in yellow, all embroidered with flowers. I tried to make Marissa talk about these things and she did occasionally. Then she would turn her head away and moan until I felt I could bear it no longer.

At nine o'clock she was taken down to the operating room. Doctor Lind went with her. Before they lifted her out of the bed she kissed me and murmured :

"Oh, mother, I hope it is not going to be a boy. I don't wish him to go to war."

How many young mothers have thought and said this same thing and yet children go on coming into the world to be used as cannon fodder in war. I sat up in the room for a little while and then thought I would go out for a walk. Doctor Lind had said it would take a little time yet and in any case they would keep her downstairs for two hours after it was all over.

I put on my hat and walked out of the clinic. Nils had gone back to the legation with the car and would not return, by my orders, until I rang him up. Besides, I wanted to walk, not drive.

Down the garden and out into the street I went. It was a lovely night. I strolled about for what seemed a very long time, then feeling tired, I went into a small coffee shop and had a glass of milk. The woman in charge began to put up her shutters. That meant it was eleven o'clock, time to close in Stockholm. I walked out again. What would Marissa be doing ? Would she be in pain ? The doctor at the clinic had promised he would give her something to ease her suffering and Doctor Lind would see that he did. But could that pain really be eased ? I remembered how I had hoped my first baby would not be a little girl so that she should not have to go through such awful agony.

I went on walking under the stars, looking at my watch every now and again. A quarter past eleven . . . half past. . .

How slowly the hands went round ! My thoughts, which had been riveted to the hospital operating room, turned to Spain. I wondered what my boy was doing. And Germán. He always thought of Marissa as though she were still a baby herself. He little knew . . . Neither did Cefe, why make him anxious ? I would telephone in the morning if all went well. A sudden terror overwhelmed me. Go well ? Why should it not go well ? It had never struck me that Marissa . . . I held my breath for a minute and then ran, yes, ran back to the clinic, my heart beating violently at the idea that something terrible might have happened to her.

There was no one at the door. I took the elevator. No one there either. At last I met a nurse near Marissa's room. I asked her if she knew how Marissa was. She did not know. She said she was not in charge of that room. I felt impatient. How could anyone in the whole clinic not know about Marissa ? I had just entered the room when Doctor Lind, breathless from having run up the stairs instead of waiting for the elevator, took me by the arms and exclaimed :

"A boy ! A beautiful boy !"

A boy ? And Marissa had wanted a girl. Then suddenly I began to cry. I don't know quite why I cried but Doctor Lind seemed to think it was natural. She was crying herself. She patted my hand for a little and then she began to tell me that everything had gone beautifully and that Marissa would be brought up after a while.

So I sat and waited until we heard the elevator coming up, and then we went to meet the stretcher. Marissa looked like a little Madonna with her hair in two long plaits on either side of her face and her baby in her arms. Such a tiny little baby ! Doctor Lind had assured me that he had the making of an athlete : a broad back and chest and narrow hips, but he seemed very small to me.

After Marissa had been comfortably settled in her bed by the nurse, she begged me to go and have some sleep. Doctor Lind volunteered to take me home in her car. She called up Nils and told him he need not come to fetch me, and also, I gathered, told him it was a boy, for when he opened the door of the legation for me he was grinning from ear to ear and saying :

"*En poike, Madame Minister, en poike.*" ("A boy, Madame Minister, a boy !")

Before going to bed I went into the baby's room and looked around. I felt very queer being a grandmother. Of course, most things seem strange when we go through them for the first time. Being a mother should be queer, also, and yet it isn't so strange as being a grandmother. I came to the conclusion that this is because you become a mother yourself and you are made a grandmother by someone else.

I went over the baby's name, over and over again. It had been decided that if it were a girl she would be called Ana for my mother, and if it were a boy he would be named Juan Enrique after his two grandfathers. Juan Enrique was a lovely name but, as a matter of fact, since he had been born in Sweden, we got into the way of calling him Jan, and Jan he probably will always be.

As I passed the room next to mine I saw the evening papers that Nils had left on my table and there on the front page were the dreaded headlines *Spanska Kriget*. The Spanish war. And Marissa had borne a boy !

Then I was struck with a sudden desire to telephone to Cefe. I was longing to give him the news and, selfishly, I did not resist the temptation, but I had not realized what an impression it would make on him.

"How is Marissa ?" he kept on asking. "Has she suffered very much ?" His voice sounded worried, anxious. I wished he were near me. He said he would call me in the course of the next few hours to hear how she was getting on.

I was thoroughly awake by that time so I sat down to write out telegrams to Germán, to his father and mother, to Cefito, to Inez, to Anita. Afterward I went through Marissa's room and automatically straightened out her bric-a-brac. At last I thought I really must get to my bed.

CHAPTER XXVIII

I had not recovered from my surprise after Cefe rang me up to say that the government was going to suppress the Latvia legation and that he was packing up in order to leave for Barcelona as soon as possible, when I heard that I would have to leave in order to look after business in Norway and Denmark until the re-organization that was taking place in the Ministry of Foreign Affairs should be finished. It was not an easy task.

Norway had been giving in to outside pressure very much of late and the Norwegian government was on the point of sending a commercial agent to the Franco zone. This meant that the same influences would be brought into play in Sweden, too. In Denmark there were questions of a different order to be discussed, the proprietorship of boats that were docked, and complicated legal matters that I could only watch from afar.

Cefe had been telling the Minister of Foreign Affairs for some time that the legation in Riga could be suppressed, or at least closed for a while, with no great loss. The régime in Latvia, a dictatorship of an extremely reactionary character, did not allow much, if any, useful work to be done. He had come up against the authorities constantly, denying false news and trying to publish the truth about our situation, but the censorship of the press was so strict it was next to impossible to succeed to any useful extent. Besides, sympathizers with our cause were closely watched and often arrested when leaving the legation, for no other crime than having gone to offer a little help for the women and children of Spain. Cefe naturally felt in a way responsible for the peace and welfare of those people, for landing in a Latvia prison, at that time, was like falling into a well.

He had not yet seen his grandchild for all the legation furniture and archives, by order of the minister, were to be deposited in Stockholm and it was a job that could not be carried out in just a few days.

"I am desperate," he would say over the telephone. The despair being due to the fact that either the carpenter had not finished taking down the pictures, or the cases had not been brought in, or Erna was sick and could not help pack the linen.

When at last he reached Stockholm, he stayed with us only four days. Nothing would induce him to wait although he had been given leave to be gone some time. I have never seen him in such a hurry to go anywhere.

"I wish to be in Spain," he would say, over and over again. "Now that I have no job to do or duty to perform outside, I want to be with our people."

Germán, who had come over on leave to see his baby, was also impatient to get away. He and Cefe decided they would go to Barcelona together.

I kept trying not to think about their departure. In addition to the hardships I knew Cefe would have to suffer and which others were already suffering, it was my own loneliness I dreaded and my anxiety that would naturally be increased a hundredfold.

Marissa felt the same way about Germán so we never spoke about our concern. The only thing was to hold on and to be doing something all the time.

At last the day for our farewells arrived. "If the government would only let me go to Spain, too," I said to Cefe as we went down the stairs together to the car.

"It is not for us to decide," he murmured, unconsciously repeating the very words Alvarez del Vayo had used when he sent me to Stockholm. "You have your work to do for Spain and you have to look after Marissa."

Yes, all that might be true, but I wanted to be with Cefe and

Cefito, to share their lives and their dangers. It was much worse to be up in Sweden all alone, hungering for news and knowing that they were going to be bombed continually, that they might be killed while we were safe in Stockholm.

One day they left us and Marissa and I turned to each other more than ever. The news from Spain was not good. Our men were still holding on in the Ebro sector but every day they slipped back a little, leaving the ground covered with their dead.

I used to feel furious when I thought that while Germany was trying out all her new models of bombers on our people, Goering was offering Sweden an ambulance plane in the place of one that Sweden had just lost through an accident. His offer gave rise to a great many comments.

It appears that the "second in command" in the Reich had offered the Swedish people this gift in memory of his first wife who was a Swede, but it struck many people as insufferable that he should try to impress the world with this apparently humanitarian gesture while planes under his orders were smashing into atoms a people who had done him no harm.

Sweden had the good taste not to accept the gift. It was refused first by the government, and parliament later ratified this decision.

Sweden like every other country in Europe was almost in hysterics during the fateful Munich days. Men and women quaked in their shoes as political prophets announced the imminence of war. The press, although in general sympathetic to Czechoslovakia, was not too critical of the Reich, nor of England and France, though they were really the responsible factors.

Chamberlain's wild flights over the British Channel, which were to culminate in the biggest defeat yet suffered by democracy, were made the object of a few sarcastic comments. But, as a rule, everyone just waited. As a matter of fact, that is what the people of the whole world, except the Germans, were doing : waiting. In spite of the presage of my Czechoslovakian friend, I was still naive enough to believe that he had exaggerated. Not that I had any doubt as to what France and England were going to do, but I had faith in Czechoslovakia, in her spirit of independence, in her love of liberty, in the principles that Masaryk had inculcated in the people.

"They will not give in," I said to myself and to everybody I spoke to at that time. "If France does not help them, or Russia, they will fight alone."

At times, way down in my subconscious, something went on repeating, "She will be betrayed, she will be betrayed from within." But I refused to listen. Instead, I said to myself that the Czechs had a wonderful army of nearly two million men and splendid armament and a strong line of defense. Two days before Czechoslovakia signed her death sentence I rang up the minister, Doctor Kučera.

"I do wish to express my sympathy and feeling for you at this difficult moment," I said, "and also to tell you what faith I have in your people." I was dismayed when I heard his voice in answer to my words — faint, dispirited, like a man who has given up hope.

"I thank you, Madame Palencia," he said, "but it is not easy to have hope these days."

"But surely you, knowing your countrymen, are as confident as I am that they will win."

"Madame Palencia, there is no good fighting under these conditions."

"They are no worse than ours and look how we have kept on."

"Yes, but we are completely surrounded. Spain at least has the sea behind her."

I could not see that this helped us and felt inclined to say that the Mediterranean in possession of the Italians was not of much use except for us to drown in.

I felt sorry for him and his wife, a very interesting woman and an architect by profession. Wishing to cheer them up, I asked them to come for luncheon the next day and invited other good friends of their country. Through the next twenty-four hours everything seemed a little brighter. Some people really appeared to believe that Czechoslovakia would defend herself. We sat by the wireless set day and night. It was most important for us that the attention of the Reich should be diverted from Spain. The pressure of the totalitarian countries against us would have to slow up, which would give us time to get our breath.

It seemed terrible to wish another country to go through the agony that Spain was suffering, but, on the other hand, it was time someone helped us.

Then, crash, came the blow. Czechoslovakia, with her fine army and her splendid armament and her fine defense line, had given in. Why? Because France broke her word? Because Russia did not help? No, those are reasons that cannot justify the mental and physical paralysis of the country itself at such a time. Undoubtedly it had been betrayed from within. I felt very downhearted and could not keep myself from thinking that had the people defended themselves and had the worst happened, that worst would have been defeat. But there was, putting everything at the very lowest, one chance in a hundred that they might have won in the long run. Won, after, thanks to their resistance, the conflict had spread to other countries. Well, the dismemberment of the Czechoslovakian republic, the slavery to which the whole nation would surely be reduced, was surely as bad or worse than that possible defeat with its one in a hundred chance of winning. In any case, the spirit of the people would not have been crushed, for there is nothing so uplifting as to feel that one has known how to preserve one's self-respect.

Who betrayed Czechoslovakia? Who refused to give the orders for the defense? Who misled public opinion? Time alone will give an answer to these and many more questions. To me at that moment it was disappointment enough to realize that my Czechoslovakian friend had known what he was talking about. I wished that he had not.

"Oh, Madame Palencia, could you call on His Excellency, Minister Sandler, this morning? He would like to have the pleasure of seeing you."

"Yes. Will twelve o'clock do?"

"Perfectly. Twelve o'clock then."

I let the receiver of my private telephone drop with a bang. It was Minister Sandler's secretary who had just called. I was wanted at the Ministry of Foreign Affairs that morning. Well, I had been expecting this for some weeks now. Sandler was evidently going to tell me what I had been expecting daily, that the Swedish government, unable to resist the pressure of the big industrial firms, together with other influences from outside, had decided to send a commercial agent to the Franco zone. I had been fighting against this for exactly one year. Several countries, powerful ones, too, had already thus recognized Franco. Could I be surprised that Sweden should follow suit?

Everybody knew about the pressure inside Sweden. Many articles, evidently inspired by the industrialist group, had been published within the last fortnight in favor of the measure. They had been answered by others against it. No one could be so sure of the outside pressure. It may have taken the shape of a mere suggestion, but this means of persuasion can be very powerful at times. In any case, it was obvious that Minister

Sandler's anxiety to see me that very morning must be prompted by some very weighty reason.

The military situation in Spain favored the plans of those who had demanded the appointment of the agent. Had we advanced instead of retreated on the Ebro front, or had we obtained another smashing victory, as at Guadalajara, the government would have been willing or able to stand firm. But the news from Spain had been far from good lately and our opponents were taking advantage of it.

I finished my most pressing business and drove down to see the Minister of Foreign Affairs. There was nobody else waiting in the large ante-chamber hung with portraits of all the Ministers of Foreign Affairs that have ever taken charge of Sweden's international policy.

Rickard Sandler received me almost at once. He smiled nervously, asked me to be seated and cleared his throat.

I waited. There was some satisfaction in not helping him out in what was undoubtedly a disagreeable task. After all, he was a social democrat. I wondered whether all the members of the cabinet had approved of the official decision. I afterward heard that one had refused to sanction it. Why was I so sure that what Minister Sandler had to tell me was that Sweden, democratic Sweden, was going to send a commercial agent to the enemies of democracy in Spain? His manner revealed it. He smiled uncertainly and asked after my health, then after Marissa's and the baby's health. He asked if I had good news of Cefe. I kept on waiting in silence. Well, at least his conduct showed he did feel some remorse.

"Madame Palencia, the government deeply regrets . . ."

At last! I sat in my chair with my hands tightly crossed. I thought of Spain and a wave of bitter disillusionment swept over me. So this was the reward offered my people for their brave struggle, for their generous sacrifice? The remembrance of all the suffering endured by our men, our women and our children was too much. My eyes smarted. Was I going to cry ? No, never that ! Not before him ! Besides, the pain was too deep to come to the surface.

When somebody asked me some days later what I had felt about this decision of the Swedish government, I answered at once :

"I felt as if I had had a sick child in my arms and someone had given it a blow."

Minister Sandler went on speaking. The agent would enjoy no diplomatic privileges. He would merely be in charge of the interests of the Swedish industrialists and business men.

I did not answer. To what use ? I had exhausted all my arguments in previous discussions. Besides, the decision was a compromise, a concession that Sweden had to make. At least the government thought so. Words in these cases are superfluous.

I waited until Minister Sandler had finished speaking. Then I rose.

"*Eh bien, au revoir,*" I said, not a syllable more. Then I walked out of the room. What else could I do ?

When Marissa saw me come in she guessed what had happened. "Never mind, mother. You did your best."

Yes, I had done my best to prevent this. So were our people doing their best to save the world from future catastrophe. I fervently hoped they would succeed better than I had done. The feeling of bitterness lasted a long long time.

Marissa and Matica Goulard, the Spanish lecturer in the Stockholm University, who had arrived from Spain a few days before to take up her post and meanwhile was staying with us in the legation, were very anxious to be present at the ceremony which every year, on December tenth, assembles all the cultural, social and financial personalities of Sweden in the Concert Hall of Stockholm to see the Nobel Prizes awarded. I had hurried back from another visit to Helsinki for the occasion. One of Marissa's and Matica's friends had given them two tickets. I was supposed to sit with the diplomatic corps. Sharply at four o'clock in the afternoon of the important day, the three of us entered the vast room already filled with women and men in evening dress.

The prize winners that year were an Italian whose name escapes my memory and who had been granted the prize for physics, and the well-known American writer, Pearl Buck, who was to receive the much-coveted literature prize for her famous books, including *The Good Earth.*

We had hardly had time to sit down when the king and all the other members of the royal family took their places in the front row of the seats on the ground floor of the hall. I was sitting just behind his majesty. Madame Kollontay and the Italian minister were a little further up. The members of the cabinet were also near by. On the stage, decorated with plants and flags, was the bust of Alfred Nobel, the generous donor of the funds that allow two hundred thousand crowns to be awarded to each of the five winners of a prize every year. Round the bust were seated the members of the Swedish Academy of Letters, of the Academy of Sciences, and of the Caroline Medical Institute.

When Pearl Buck and the Italian scientist appeared on the stage everybody, from the king downward, rose to greet them in the midst of a great ovation. It was the most touching moment of the afternoon.

Pearl Buck, looking very dignified in her gold lamé dress, with her hair simply drawn back from her forehead, stood beside the little Italian with whom she was sharing these honors. But she received the most attention. The audience seemed to me to take delight in showing that people of totalitarian countries were less welcome. As a matter of fact, I was told that the scientist, who had come to Sweden with his whole family, apparently in order to allow them to participate in the festivities held in his honor, left Sweden for the United States the moment he had pocketed the two hundred thousand crowns, with the intention of remaining in America. I did not hear the report confirmed but were it to be true one cannot help sympathizing and rejoicing with him. In any case, I was told that though small physically, he was great in his special science.

Perhaps Pearl Buck's popularity was due to the fact that everybody had read her books. Whatever the reason, I was glad to see her as she stood, tall and stately, hailed by the Swedes with what was, for them, an uproarious enthusiasm.

It is not easy for a woman to stand or sit calmly on a stage, the focus of the gaze of hundreds of persons, most of them belonging to a distinguished class, many of them her own colleagues, without becoming nervous. But her demeanor was perfect throughout ; even when she came down the narrow little staircase to receive the prize from the royal hand ; when King Gustav rose to give it to her, she seemed absolutely self-possessed !

I had the pleasure of meeting her and her husband a few days later at a reception given in her honor by Minister and Madame Sandler at their residence. Pearl Buck came forward when she heard Madame Sandler greet me and took my hand in her warm, sympathetic clasp. She was full of sympathy for my Spain.

Cefe's letters from Barcelona were very comforting. I had been worried lest he find conditions there difficult, too difficult to become accustomed to suddenly. The other people, who had been there all the time, had been adapting themselves to the privations gradually. But Cefe had fallen from a land of plenty into the desert of hunger. However, he did not seem to mind it. His letters were cheery, much more optimistic than they had been from Riga.

Yet the news that came to us from Spain showed that the situation was growing more and more difficult. I kept working furiously in order not to think about it, and Marissa had her hands full learning how to look after the baby properly from Sister Julia, a charming Swedish nurse who was to stay on with us until Jan was six months old. It was difficult for us to become accustomed to the strict nursery ways of Sweden : not to take the precious morsel out of his cradle and hug him and dandle him was a great trial. But Sister Julia looked so severe when we dared suggest fondling him that we had to submit to her orders.

One night, on the twelfth of December, I wondered what was going on in the legation. The servants, who were used to retiring very early, kept moving about the house, running up and down the back stairs, and talking in subdued whispers. I sat up until quite late writing and in the silence of the night these unusual sounds were quite audible.

At last I went to bed and at four o'clock Matica burst into my room.

"Doña Isabel ! Doña Isabel ! Do you hear ?"

I sat up in bed. She and Marissa were talking in low tones. "What is it ?" I said to them.

Then through the doors of my room that Matica had opened wide came the sound of sweet singing. Nearer and nearer it came. A few minutes later I saw the twinkle of lights and the strangest of processions met my astonished gaze.

Sister Julia, dressed in a long white robe, her fair hair hanging over her shoulders, and carrying Jan in her arms, appeared at the door, followed by all the other servants, even the gardener and his wife and their two daughters, all clad in white and carrying lighted candles in their hands. She seemed crowned by a circle of light.

Jan had on a little white robe and a high peaked cap, and from his neck hung a flat brown biscuit in the shape of a huge heart. Two tears rolled down his tiny face. Evidently he had been frightened at first.

The white-robed group stood at the foot of my bed, singing all the time in Swedish to the tune of the Neapolitan song, *Santa Lucia*.

My heart was strangely moved by this quaint old custom which I had read about. On the thirteenth of December the young daughter of the house, dressed in white and wearing a crown of candles, wakens her parents at dawn, singing words of hope that the dark night of winter will be followed by light and warmth.

Tears that had been suppressed for very long suddenly welled up and bathed my face. I stretched out my arms for our baby and Sister Julia gave him to me. Then she went back and they all continued to sing in a low sweet caressing way that moved me to the very depths. It seemed to me that they were telling me that Spain, too, would emerge from the darkness of night and soon see the dawn of peace.

After a little the singing ceased and we were served coffee and biscuits like the one Jan had on his little breast. When we had finished, the group retired, singing again.

I was told by friends that it was a great compliment to have been made the object of this touching attention on the part of the staff. It showed I was looked upon as a sort of mother of the household.

Christmas drew near. I made up my mind that we would celebrate it the same way as we had the year before. A Christmas tree for the staff and the children and a quiet supper for ourselves.

It was difficult to feel interested in even these very limited celebrations when the news from Spain was so disquieting. Our troops had been forced to retreat entirely from the Ebro and the hunger in all Spain was worse than the year before. However, there was nothing for us to do but go ahead.

After all, it was Jan's first Christmas and we had him to be thankful for. He acted as host for the children, having been dressed by Sister Julia for the occasion as a little goblin in a grey suit and red cap.

The children had gone away and we were sitting round the hall fire when Marissa was handed a letter from Germán.

"Mother," she cried out in anguish, coming over to my side, "Germán is in Madrid. He has flown there."

Germán had flown over enemy territory to see his widowed mother, his father having died suddenly from angina pectoris. The letter was heart-breaking. The lack of wood in Madrid had increased the tragedy of the situation. Germán's family had not been able to buy a coffin in which to bury the father. Some friends hunted the town over until they found a few empty fruit crates and with them they built a rough box for him to lie in.

Marissa was very upset. The knowledge that Germán would have to fly back to Barcelona in some old machine — the better ones could not be spared for such cases — haunted her and the idea that she should not be with her husband at such a time made the blow seem doubly hard. I could not get out of my mind the memory of the dead man lying on those pieces of wood hastily put together. How many, how very many,

of our people were going through such suffering, through the
same gruesome privations and worse ? Germán's father was
dead. Suffering was over for him. The others had to go
on living.

CHAPTER XXIX

At the king's dinner that year Doctor Kučera seemed very downcast. The situation in Czechoslovakia was tragic. A total occupation by Germany was expected any day. I marveled at the Czechoslovakian minister's calm when he went up to greet the German representative. Those bonds of diplomacy! They had never seemed so heavy. I felt positively bowed down under mine and yet our situation was very different. I did not need to feign satisfaction over a meeting with the men whose countries had invaded mine. It was bad enough to have to bow to some others who had only "looked on."

The remembrance of those January days is very vague. I have a memory of feeling my throat go dry every time the news from Spain came over the wireless or the newspaper was brought in. Telephone calls would startle one, too.

The only thing that kept one from having a nervous breakdown was to bend over one's desk and work. A steamer, laden with ripe Valencia oranges, had reached Sweden safely. I had held armfuls of the lovely fruit and hugged them. They came from Spain! At other times I would wander round the house wishing, as on one other occasion of my life, that I could open a hole in the earth and bury myself in it, just to get away from the voices and the sounds round me, just to forget. And then my heart would rebound from the thought. Forget? How could I wish to forget? Could I possibly drive out of my mind my people, who were as dear as my own children?

Toward the end of January we knew that the enemy had advanced so near to Barcelona that the Catalonian capital would have to be abandoned if we did not wish the people to be caught as rats in a trap. I tried not to think of Cefe and Cefito and Germán. I knew Cefito had been sent to Vich as head of the hospital there. The others were in Barcelona.

446

Then, suddenly, one day we heard that Barcelona had fallen, that the invaders were entering the Catalonian capital. I was not surprised. We had been expecting it but the blow was very hard, as when death comes to someone dear to us who has long been sick.

The press began to speak of the exodus of our people. It was said that the army had retreated to a new line and that it would make a new stand, but I had a map of Spain on my table and every day the line, according to the news, changed. It did not stand. We were retreating all the time.

Details and pictures of the forced march of the people up toward the French frontier began to come in. Marissa was wild with anxiety. So was Matica whose mother was in Barcelona when she had last heard from her. Back went the line. Down went the towns, all along the coast and the northern provinces of Catalonia.

"The Spanish cortes is meeting in Figueras on February first," the papers said one day. The Spanish cortes was meeting in the midst of that awful retreat? Evidently even at such a moment Doctor Negrín would take no decision against the will or without the knowledge of the Spanish people. He was ready to offer peace terms but they must have the support of the members of parliament. Those peace terms were : "first, that the independence and sovereignty of Spain be guaranteed ; second, that all the foreign pressure cease and a plebiscite be allowed for the people to choose their own government ; third, that no reprisals be taken on the population."

The offer was such as any honorable man could have accepted. If it were refused then the Spanish people would go on fighting. They had lost Bilbao and fought on. They had lost Gijón and had gone on fighting. The loyal territory had been cut in two and neither of the two pieces of loyalist land had surrendered. Now Barcelona and probably the very last little bit of Catalonia were lost, too. Well, they would go on fighting in Madrid, Guadalajara, Valencia, Murcia, Cuenca, Ciudad Real, Jaén, Albacete, Alicante, Almería.

Yes, they would go on struggling for every inch of ground, blasted and shelled and withered by fire though it might be, for it was consecrated by the blood of the men who had died rather than let Spain lose her freedom.

The hours of each day dragged on. I had no official news, no instructions, of course. I realized that each and every member of the government had only one duty to perform those days and nothing could be allowed to interfere with it. That duty was to see that the people got out, that they were not trapped, to cover the retreat of the army so that as many lives as possible should be saved. And this had to be done under incessant bombing, as plane after plane pelted the ambulances carrying the wounded and the cars and the trucks and the lorries loaded with ammunition, and the people ! The helpless famished people as they scurried up the roads or lay dying in the ditches, compact masses of men, women and children, fleeing for safety and pursued by those merciless instruments of war right up to the very limits of republican Spain ! We heard that a few trains with civil employees had left Barcelona — we wondered whether Cefe was on one — that the air force had moved up to Figueras — Germán might be there — that Vich had fallen. But we had no news of where Cefito might be.

Marissa sat all day hunched up in an armchair. Her eyes with their piteous expression haunted me. Matica roamed nervously from room to room. The rest of the staff had no near relatives to worry about. They did their best to comfort us.

At last, on February fifth, we had a telegram from Germán. He, with all the Spaniards who had defended democracy, had been thrown into a concentration camp the moment he had entered France. His younger brother, who had fought in Guadalajara and Madrid and through all the Ebro campaign, was with him. "He is wounded," Germán said in his telegram. I called up some friends near Perpignan and asked how Germán and his brother could be got out of the camp. Everybody there was frantic, looking out for their own men. It would be necessary to see the *préfect,* they said ; but he was refusing all petitions.

The next day a telegram came from Cefe. He was safely over the frontier, too, but was asking me if I had news of Cefito. He promised to look after the other two boys.

Two more days wore on and brought no news. At last we had another telegram. Germán and his brother Alejandro were out of the French camp. Information poured in through the press. President Azaña was in Paris, so was part of the loyalist government, but not Premier Negrín nor Alvarez del Vayo. They were still hanging on to a tiny strip of Spanish soil. The prime minister had refused to leave Spain until every loyalist Spaniard from the Catalonian zone was safely over the border. The last appeal made by the Minister of Foreign Affairs to the League of Nations had failed, too. The press headlines suddenly took on another tone. "The fight will go on in the other sectors of Spain. The men of the Catalonian army are getting ready to go to the remaining loyalist territory. The government of Negrín intends flying to Madrid," they said.

No news from Mrs. Goulard. No news from Cefito. At last Matica had a telegram from Perpignan, her mother was safe. There was only Cefito left behind. I could not sleep or rest. I knew there would be thousands of women going through the same strain, thousands of them asking the same question, "Where is my boy ?" But there are moments in life when the sheer animal instinct in us makes us selfish to the verge of cruelty. There were moments when I could not think of any-body's children but my own. My boy !

Could he have been caught ? The thought was maddening. I kept on thinking that if he had not managed to escape he would be shot, tortured like all those that fell into the in-surgents' hands. I felt sometimes that I could not stay on in the legation. I was sure that if I looked for Cefito myself I should find him. But it was impossible to leave at such a mo-ment. The secretary — one that just recently had come — had already said he was giving up his post. Rats leaving the sink-ing ship ; I would not be one of them.

One evening Cefe rang me up. "I have spoken to someone who saw Cefito the other day in Figueras. He was all right and said he would leave Spain only after he had finished bring-ing out the wounded men under his care." I breathed for a little.

That night the press agency that gave us the last news of the day said there was nothing special to communicate. "Except," they said at the last moment, "except that the worst bombard-ment since the war began was carried out today in Figueras."

This misery lasted for eleven days. At last I had a wire to say that Cefito had just crossed the border and that, with all the others, he had been taken to a concentration camp in the south of France. I knew Cefe would rescue him sooner or later if he died in the effort.

The next few days were very full, seeing people and answer-ing questions. Our friends in Sweden were terribly depressed and wanted to know exactly what had happened. From that moment until the end of the war I had to let myself be guided exclusively by intuition. . . The confusion in Perpignan where the Spanish government was staying before flying to Madrid must have been enormous. It was impossible to get instruc-tions or information on any subject whatsoever.

I would receive an occasional ciphered cable but not one of the really important questions was covered. Del Vayo had other far more essential matters on hand to attend to. I thought the best thing I could do, under the circumstances, was to try and raise more help for the Spanish refugees. The want, from all accounts, was appalling. Georg Branting telephoned to me one morning. He was just back from the south of France and wanted to see me.

I shall never forget the things he told me about the exodus of our people.

"I do not believe Dante's *Inferno* would be an adequate description," he said. "It was so terrible, so inconceivably terrible, that at times I thought I must be looking at a film, that nothing so frightful could be really happening."

He gave me news of some of our friends and told me what was being done in other countries to help the Spaniards. Needless to say, Sweden was ready, as always, to do her part. I knew that under his chairmanship they would not fail. We waited to hear more news from the boys, expecting at any moment to be told that they had left for Madrid, but their letters were vague. They did not know what was going to be done, when they would be called. Before leaving for Madrid, Negrín and del Vayo had been having heart-breaking talks with Azaña in Paris.

The president, who was staying in the Spanish embassy, wanted to resign. I had always felt he would never come well out of a crisis of this sort. Fundamentally timid, he might have been a great statesman in times of peace, but not now when rapid, courageous and decisive action was necessary. He insisted that the only thing to do was to surrender. Negrín tried in vain to make him see that to surrender at once was to hand over thousands of loyal Spaniards into Franco's hands, that it was his duty to go with the government to Madrid and make a stand until an honorable peace could be arranged. He was sure they could resist long enough for that. But Azaña refused to listen. He insisted that his duty as President of the Republic was to make peace, that it was mad to resist. He could not be made to see that his resignation would provoke the immediate recognition of Franco by Great Britain and France and that such a measure would strengthen Franco's hand and weaken our position even more.

I could only imagine what was going on from the press news, but I knew all the actors in this awful tragedy well enough to guess what was happening. It was very difficult to know what to say to people in Sweden. I was seeing Minister Sandler quite often those days and I always had to give the same answer to his questions.

"I have no official news yet. Besides, the communications are very sparse, but I am sure that tomorrow or the day after tomorrow I shall receive detailed information."

Some days passed and, at last, we heard that the government had flown to Madrid. Hope surged again in our hearts. I refused to discuss possibilities. The only thing that mattered was that the fall of Catalonia had not destroyed the last chance. The word "Madrid" rose again before the astonished gaze of the world. Perhaps the great epic of November 1936, was going to be repeated. At all events, the government would see that all the people who were most in danger in that zone would get out. Negrín had the confidence of the army. His presence over there could do wonders.

I devoured the papers but only the vaguest news was published. Then, on the evening of March fifth, when we were sitting listening to the Paris station over the air, we heard that the republican navy had had to leave the port of Cartagena. The artillery officers in the town had rebelled and threatened to fire on the ships. Soon after a communiqué of the Spanish government was read. It said that, reinforcements having been sent to Cartagena, the rebellion had been suppressed and that everything there was calm again.

I went to bed not knowing what to think, with dark foreboding in my heart. Why had those officers risen ? Could it be that a plot was prepared in all the loyal zone ? Could it be the workings of the fifth column, of traitors within our ranks ?

The very next day I got my answer. A rumor that General Casádo had risen in Madrid and that the movement was directed against Negrín spread like fire. The legation telephone did not cease ringing all day. News reporters, friends, at times mere acquaintances and even people we did not know, wanted to hear what I had to say. It was difficult to hold out hope. I did not know myself what it was all about. I had never heard of General Casádo, evidently some obscure officer whose ambition had gotten the better of him.

A little later we heard that he had constituted a junta in Madrid with Julián Besteiro, the reformist socialist leader. Besteiro is a distinguished scholar but he had not been playing a clean game during the war. He had refused to accept any post and insisted on remaining in Madrid, working on the committee for the reconstruction of the capital. But this. . . What he was doing now was treason !

The next thing we heard was that the government had had to fly back into France and that Casádo was beating down the slightest intent to oppose the junta with terrible harshness. In one word, loyalists were being treated by Casádo as though they were enemies.

A few days later I had to see Minister Sandler again in order to obtain permission for some Spaniards to come into Sweden and for my own family as well. In view of the fact that the return to Spain was impossible, we had decided that they should all come to Stockholm until we had determined what they ought to do in the future.

"Madame Palencia," Sandler said to me with real feeling in his voice, "you do not require any permission for your family to come here."

"They are not all relatives," I answered.

"It makes no difference."

He then asked about Casádo. I spoke quite plainly.

"I have no direct news yet," I said, "but I can say one thing. I am the representative of the legal constitutional government of Spain, not of any rebel general or officer, be he named as he may."

There could be no doubt now in his mind that I did not recognize the Madrid junta.

In the following week I was supposed to go to a dinner at the Royal Palace. Every winter the crown prince was in the custom of giving several dinner parties and inviting to each one five or six members of the diplomatic corps and a number of outstanding Swedes from the different ways of life : aristocrats, business men, high-grade officers, artists and professional men of all kinds.

My invitation for 1939 was for the twenty-first of March. I had decided that I would stick to my guns until the very last minute, but — in view of the turn of events and that practically every country in Europe except the Soviet Republic, and in America with the exception of Mexico, had recognized Franco — I felt sure that Sweden would have to do the same. In that case, I would, of course, give up my post and leave the legation at once. Two weeks before this the Czechoslovakian minister had had to excuse himself from attending the dinner because the very day he was invited, Germany had taken possession of his entire country and he — rather precipitately, I thought — had resigned. Something like this might happen to me.

It did not, however. Perhaps the government waited to recognize Franco until after the dinner party was over so as not to have a recurrence of Doctor Kučera's case. At all events, no step had been taken by the twenty-first of March. Few things in my life have cost me more than to dress and attend that dinner party. I was feeling far from well and the knowledge of what the refugees were experiencing was heartbreaking. How could I go and smile and talk about indifferent things?

However, it would not have done for me to keep away at such a moment, even with the excuse of ill health. And certainly that evening the crown prince and princess went out of their way, more than usual, to be courteous and kind to me. When I returned home I felt sure that the dinner that was just over would be my last official function.

One day a friend came to see me.

"Madame Palencia," she said, "I have been with Minister Sandler this morning, shortly after you yourself had been to see him, and I want to tell you that he spoke about you with the greatest respect and with the greatest admiration for your courage. He told me he would like you to know that if Sweden had to change her policy in regard to Spain, you and yours are to feel that you will always be welcome in this country." My friend told me that she had taken advantage of the occasion to ask the minister whether he thought Sweden would be changing her policy soon.

"We shall hold out as long as we are able," he had answered.

I fully appreciated Minister Sandler's kindness. Besides, I felt that what he said was quite true. The Swedish people would always make me welcome.

It was not until a good many days later that I was officially informed that Sweden was going to recognize Franco. I had already prepared for my departure and had decided to tell

Minister Sandler that I would give over the legation to a representative of the Foreign Affairs Department and for them to pass it on to my successor later.

With the inventory made out by the notary public, I personally went through each room and saw that every single thing was in its place. My heart was much lighter regarding my own personal worries. Cefe, Cefito, Germán and Alejandro were with me. The first impression I got when I saw them arrive was terrible. They were just skin and bones, and oh, so tired! As for clothes, they had nothing but the most indispensable things. Cefe was the only one of the lot who had been able to save a suitcase and he had had to provide the others with part of his own wearing apparel. The three younger ones had lost absolutely everything — clothes, medical kit — everything.

"Don't worry, mother. All the Spaniards are in the same plight," said Cefito.

Marissa had quite a time supplying what they needed. It was pathetic to see them eat. They had gone without proper food for months and found everything delicious.

I thought with remorse of the times I had turned away from food which in Spain would have been considered the height of luxury.

Cefe was a greater cause of worry than any of the others. They were young and would recover, but he had received a terrible shock.

"You do not know," he said to me, "what the last hours before getting into France were. You cannot conceive what it is to see bodies of women and children strewn all over a road and having sometimes to walk over them." It took a long time for him to get over this vision — this nightmare.

ONCE more Minister Sandler's secretary telephoned me to

say that his excellency wanted to see me. I felt quite differently from the way I had when he told me that Sweden was going to send a commercial agent to the Franco zone. Then we were still fighting and the blow to us was a vantage point to Franco. Now we had, for the time being, given up the struggle. The insurgents were in possession of the whole country and the other nations were free to do as they pleased. They could, of course, withhold recognition. Some countries had not yet recognized the Soviet Union and twenty years had elapsed since their revolution. Why all this hurry to recognize the totalitarian revolutions? Whatever may have been the reasons that were pushing Sweden, as they had done other nations, into an official acceptance of the destruction of Spanish democracy, there was nothing more that I could do.

I spent the last days in the legation alone. All the others had gone down to the lovely summer resort of Saltsjöbaden, where kind friends had taken rooms for us in the hotel and begged us to stay there as their guests until we decided what we were going to do. Except for Cefito, who spent the last night with me in the legation, only the servants and I remained in the house. During those days I received the most touching proofs of Swedish friendship. Letters of sympathy with the kindest offers of help poured in all the time and my rooms were a mass of flowers.

Willingly would I give the names of all the men and women who, in writing those feeling notes, rendered homage to the heroism of my people, but the times are not propitious for making such things public. A *beau geste* can be turned against its author nowadays. However, I should like those staunch friends of Spain to know that I have not forgotten that they, at least, had the courage to be sincere.

The morning of April first, Dethorey accompanied the representative from the Foreign Affairs Department about the house, checking everything on the inventory ; a copy of which was afterward signed for me as a proof that all had been found to be in order.

Several reporters had tried to interview me during the previous day and renewed their petition that morning, but I refused. I was not the representative of the Spain that Sweden was going to recognize and had, therefore, no official position and, above all, no official duties ; although the Swedish government did me the courtesy of recognizing my diplomatic status during the whole of my stay in the country.

I left the legation with my arms full of flowers and my head held very high. There was nothing I need be ashamed of. On the contrary, like my Spain, I had tried to do my best. Strange to say, the dominant note within me, as I crossed the threshold of the legation that had been my home for nearly three years, was the sensation that once more I was free.

Cefito was in London. He and Cefe and I had many talks as to what should be done about his engagement to Mary. The boy thought they should be married before leaving Europe.

"I have waited so long, mother," he said. "And Mary's presence will mean a great deal to me in the new life we are going to begin."

I tried to make him see he should first make sure that he would be able to make a home for her. He answered with the usual confidence of youth that he was sure that everything would come out all right.

"I can work and will work," he said.

However, I thought that Mary should not be exposed to all the discomforts of the first uncertain months. The others had to come along because there was no place they could stay, but she was in London with her mother and could wait until we saw where we were going to settle and how things were turning out. I myself wrote to her about this and she agreed that I was right. So it was decided that she and Cefito would be married and enjoy a short honeymoon, after which she would stay with her mother until it was time to come to Mexico. Being married to a Spaniard, there would be no difficulty about her quota in Mexico.

Cefito and I went together to get all the things he required and I saw him off at the Central Station one afternoon with the feeling that we had done what was best for them. Certainly in the wildest flights of optimistic fancy I never dreamt that two months after our arrival we would be able to tell Mary that she could come to Mexico and share her husband's modest home and, with her moral support, help him to build up their future.

During the weeks that followed we were all able to recover, partly, at least, from the strain of the past months. We had callers constantly, and pressing invitations to spend some of our time with other friends. One of the suggestions, perhaps the most warm-hearted of all, came from Fröken Elisabeth Tamm who wanted us — the whole family — to spend as long as we liked on her beautiful property in Fågel Stad — the city of the birds. I hesitated for some time. There were really too many of us, but she was so graciously insistent that at last Marissa, the baby, Germán, Alejandro and I went to her for some days before leaving Sweden. I was glad to have the chance of knowing this interesting type of Swedish woman at home.

Fröken Tamm, who has been an invalid for some years, is nevertheless able to manage her estate herself. She now goes into Stockholm rarely, and only when there is something useful to do, either helping some private person or a cause she may be interested in. These visits are always of a humanitarian character.

I used to marvel at the spiritual force that was required for this delicate, almost bedridden, woman to get up and drive three or four hours just to be present at some meeting or to act as chairman of some charitable organization. Her home, a beautiful old-fashioned rambling house, was a pleasant place to visit. The quaint old bedsteads and comfortable furniture, the pictures and miniatures and the wonderful library gave one a happy picture of country life in Sweden.

Fröken Elisabeth Tamm is an ardent feminist as well as a fervent upholder of peace. In those all too short days we stayed with her we would sit and talk in her beautiful library about the ways and means that could and must be found to end war.

Sometimes her friend and physician, Doctor Ada Nilsson, who was staying with Fröken Honorine Hermelin, would drop in, and then the conversation would turn to other subjects, first and foremost the summer course on social subjects held every year at Fågel Stad under the direction and rectorship of Fröken Hermelin.

The conditions in Europe were not encouraging to our hopes yet there was the underlying conviction that something new must and will come to the world. A new cycle is to begin, perhaps : something future generations may benefit from. And so the days passed by and the end of our stay in Sweden drew ever nearer.

We had had many discussions as to what we should do about our future. Cefe hated the idea of leaving Europe and hesitated between staying in Paris or in Stockholm — a very favorite city of his — but the great problem was what to do with the boys. They had to work, to begin life anew, and in Europe we knew that it would not be easy.

In addition we had to think of the difficulties derived from most countries' immigration laws, particularly in the case of Spanish refugees, the "reds" as we were called. Mexico was the only country that had thrown open its doors to our people.

The three boys and Marissa agreed that the most sensible thing they could do was to take advantage of Mexico's generosity and see if they could open up a way for themselves there in their professions.

I made up my mind that I would go with them. It seemed absurd to separate again after having had the luck of gathering them all together. Besides, I was sure that war would soon break out in Europe and that would make our reunion in the future still more difficult if we were apart. After a little, Cefe made up his mind to come with us.

Before leaving, however, I had to arrange affairs for my nephew Juan. I had received a letter from him after his ship, with the rest of our navy, left Cartagena. He was now in Tunis and expected to be interned with the rest of the officers and crews in a camp six hundred kilometres inland, on the edge of the desert.

He had written me a courageous letter, saying he was ready to work at anything, but as "a free man." It took two months to get him out of the concentration camp, although we, of course, had said we would pay all his expenses. Had it not been for Fröken Tamm, Minister Sandler, the French Minister in Stockholm, and the Committee of Aid to Spain, I am sure we would never have succeeded. Everything was arranged for him to come to Stockholm and follow us on a Swedish ship. The committee and the section of the Lands Organizations that looked after refugees had also helped me with the other boys.

When the moment of our departure arrived we found it difficult to say good-bye to friends like Fröken Tamm, Doctor Ruby Lind, Kerstin Hesselgren, Naima Wifstrand, Sonja Branting, Madame Kollontay, Barbro Alving, and other loyal kind-hearted women, the remembrance of whom stands out now among my other memories with a distinctness that hurts.

June first we left by the *Drottningholm* of the Swedish-American Line for New York. Word had gone round that I was leaving and when Cefe and I reached the station — the others, who were still at Fröken Tamm's, were to join us half way — we found the platform full of people. Bouquet after bouquet was laid in my arms as I shook hands all round, then, just as I was about to board the train, Georg Branting stepped forward and made a short speech in French, wishing me Godspeed.

I looked at Cefe and saw that he was thinking, as I was, that I must speak a few words, too, that I could not go away without once more thanking them all in my own name and in the name of Spain. I felt it was going to be hard to speak just at that moment. However, I did manage to say a few words. Then I jumped up on the train steps, and as we moved out I stood at the window waving my hands, with tears — the first I had shed in public since my arrival in Stockholm — streaming down my face. There is nothing so upsetting as kindness in such times.

In Gothenburg we were met at the station by other groups of friends and members of the local Committee to Aid Spain who drove us to the boat and stayed with us until the bells rang for visitors to leave. The *Drottningholm* began to move from the dock. We all stood near the side of the ship, with our eyes fixed on the friends we were leaving. The band played a gay tune. The deck steward came along with trays of serpentines in the Swedish colors. Soon streamers of these frail gay-colored papers had reached land and the ends were being held by the people on the pier. The boat moved very quickly. The bunch of streamers I held — which were the last visible

As Minister to Sweden she accepts the banner given by
Stockholm to Madrid

Isabel de Palencia, in 1936
receiving American reporters in her hotel in New York City

ties that bound us to Europe, to Sweden and to Spain — broke one after another in my hands. When the last of the blue and yellow paper ribbons fell into the sea I covered my face with my hands and sobbed. I felt the weight of a hand on my shoulder. It was Cefe. I had not noticed he was so near me.

The days went by and every hour brought us nearer to the new world. As at the time of my first visit to America, I was going toward an unknown country, toward a new life, a life still wrapped in mystery. It might be a happy and prosperous one, it might hold nothing but sorrow. Impossible to know. Only one thing was sure, that although we were all together, the ship was taking us farther from Spain, from the Spain we had loved, from our people who were now prisoners in Franco's hands or in French concentration camps.

We, ourselves, might come up against all kinds of unexpected difficulties, but at least we were free. I felt that whatever destiny might bring my way I could never be happy until every single Spaniard was free, too.

We reached New York on a broiling July day. It was the first time that Cefe and the boys were to set their feet in the United States. The sight of New York harbor with its magnificent background of skyscrapers brought cries of admiration from them all.

Anita, with some other friends, was on the pier, waiting impatiently until we were through the passport formalities, trembling lest at the last minute, like so many other refugees, we would not be allowed to land in the city, even on a transit visa.

We stayed in New York only twelve days but in that short time I saw Alvarez del Vayo and Luisi, who were leaving for Europe after a short stay in the United States, and all the old friends : Berta and Elmer Hader, Bertha Gunterman, Jean May, Bessie Beatty, Bill Sauter, and many others who still wanted to help Spain, who were helping our people. Among them were Jay Allen and Ruth, friends from the good old times in Madrid when Jay and I were both foreign correspondents there. He had done splendid work for democratic Spain all through the war and was now devoting his time to getting refugee Spaniards started in the new life.

Before we left New York, it was arranged that I should go back to the United States in the fall to give some lectures and to speak for Spain. The possibility of my writing a book, perhaps two, was also discussed. My life, to my great relief, seemed to be shaping itself again along the old familiar lines.

We left for Mexico by boat. Once more we went down the New York harbor, waving a good-bye to crowds of friends on the pier. Once more we passed close to the Statue of Liberty.

CHAPTER XXX

Before making up our minds to leave Sweden I had often asked myself what would be the better way : to live in a country where nothing would be like our native land or in one where everything — the language to begin with — would remind us of Spain.

The moment I reached Mexico I realized that we had been right in coming. The first moments were of course very difficult. No one who has not been an exile or, worse still, a refugee, can have an adequate idea of what it means. The first strange impression is to find oneself adrift in the world, with only one's clothes packed in a box or in a couple of suitcases, that is, if one has been lucky enough to have even them. Under very fortunate circumstances a few books may have been added to these limited possessions. But such is the contrariness of human nature that such reduced belongings constitute a problem when, as in our case, a whole crowd of people travel together. Cefito and Juan, who arrived in New York after us, did not join the party until Mexico. However, Cefe and Marissa and Germán and baby Jan and Alejandro and I were a large enough party to be difficult to manage.

We landed at Vera Cruz on a sweltering hot day and I was staggered when I saw our luggage. Two suitcases apiece, twelve in all, and Jan's pram and his food basket and toys that had been presented to him on the way. However, everything was fitted into place on the train and we reached Mexico City without having lost a single parcel.

We went straight to a hotel and the first thing in the morning we set out to try and find an apartment. There would be time enough later to look around and see the city. To rent a dwelling place in our circumstances is not always easy. House owners are as a rule suspicious of refugees. They are afraid that, in the most favorable of cases, they may not be able to pay their rent but there are political reasons, too. Refugees nowadays, due to the destruction of all moral values, are not looked upon with the sympathetic respect they used to enjoy in olden times. Now they are considered outlaws of a sort when, as in the case of the Spanish refugees, they have had to go into exile because they observed and defended the law of their land. This is all very confusing but attention ought to be called to it if we do not want future generations to think that we have been quite mad. They will probably think so in any case, even if we do point out the anomalies.

After several days spent in finding an apartment that was big enough, and cheap enough, and pretty enough, and healthy enough, to satisfy the needs of an artist, a housekeeper, two doctors and a baby, we found a really charming place with sufficient space and a beautiful terrace in a good location in the residential part of Mexico City.

No sooner had we found this prize and rented it, paying several months in advance, so as to convince the owner — who, by the way, turned out to be a Frenchman — that although called "reds" we were not given to the practice of larceny, than we hurried to a store, ordered cots and mattresses and bed linen for us all, and that very night Marissa and Germán and Jan moved in. We followed them the next day with Anita who had come over from the United States to help us settle. Cefito and Juan had also arrived and everybody was eager not only to find a home of some sort but to get something to do.

The first morning I opened my eyes in our new home I did not see the bare floors and walls nor the empty rooms. I saw only the Mexican sky lit up by the rising sun and being turned into a gem of many colors — colors of rubies and emeralds and opals and topaz. I have had this same sensation every day since. It has never failed me nor have I grown weary of it. I expect I never shall.

When we began to make lists of the things we needed, Cefe and I were simply overwhelmed. It is extraordinary what is required in a house. I don't count the partially superfluous things but the indispensable items like chairs to sit on, and plates, tumblers, knives and forks to eat and drink with, and tables to write and lay your things on. Besides everything had to cost so very little we felt pessimistic at times of ever getting them. We came to the conclusion that the best we could do to get on quickly was to assign a task to each one. In a cheap market in Mexico City called "la Lagunilla" — where one can find everything that is needed for everyday life if one is not too particular — we bought a large assortment of plain kitchen tables and chairs at one, three, and four pesos each. In order to have a variety we cut them down to different heights and distributed them in the different rooms. The dining-room table, big enough for ten persons, with twelve chairs and two little china closets, cost thirty pesos the lot. Other kitchen chairs for the other rooms were only one peso a piece, and a small bench with two little armchairs for the hall cost six pesos.

We began to feel optimistic. By buying just kitchen furniture we would be able to have all we needed and the folk art in Mexico, as in Spain, offered vast possibilities for brightening up things afterward at a ridiculously low price. The dining-room furniture we left unstained, all the other pieces were taken to the terrace and every member of the family took up a brush and began to paint the wood a warm brown tone. This kept us busy several days.

The house had a large number of windows and the strong light was trying to the eyes. Besides it prevented one from sleeping after five o'clock in the morning, so we looked around, trying to find a solution for this problem. Everything in the stores, however, was quite out of our reach so we went back to the market and there we found a thick cloth of a creamy white tone, striped in gay colors, that is used in Mexican houses for scrubbing floors.   We were sure it would do beautifully so we bought it and brought home at least eighty yards, ready to begin to sew them up at once.   This had to be done by hand, for we had no sewing machine.   As luck would have it just at that moment I came down with a severe attack of kidney trouble that kept me in bed for nearly two months during which I sewed most of the curtains while the others went on with the outside buying.

Soon our floors were strewn with the lovely straw *petates* — mats — that the Indians use to sleep on.   A few pieces of folk pottery brightened up the rooms with their brilliant tones, and charming tin and glass lanterns hid the ugly electric bulbs.   We were settled !

As I lay in my bed and heard the street vendors call out their wares under my window I could sometimes almost delude myself into thinking that I was back in Spain.   Not the Spain of the years after my marriage and, of course, not the Spain we had now left behind.   But the Spain I had known as a little girl in Malaga, with its flat-roofed houses and its beautiful gardens, its parks full of palms and pomegranate and pepper trees and huge hibiscus bushes, and roses and carnations and sweet-smelling lilies and the tuberoses.   Even the way the Mexicans talked reminded me of home for they do not use the pure but harsher Castilian pronunciation.   They lisp their words softly like Andalusians.

To make things even more homelike we found we could not walk along the principal streets of Mexico without coming up against Spaniards from Madrid, from Barcelona and Valencia : our close friends, and many of our dearest.

After a time, however, the young people began to grow restless. They wanted to do something. Cefito was naturally anxious to begin to earn a living and to bring his bride to Mexico. So was Juan, whose young wife is still in Spain. It was not easy to get a job, however. We looked over the advertisements in the papers and answered many of them, but the days went by and no progress had been made. This was the most difficult time to get over. Cefe, who of all the family has turned out to be the least adaptable to life in the new world, hungered for his books and his brushes and for his home in Spain. The boys fretted all the time. War is destructive in many ways : disillusion is one of them and our young people had every reason to have lost their faith in the virtue of civilization and progress — they had served but to destroy our Spain. Besides their attitude after the war was over was another disappointment. With the exception of Mexico no country in the world had respected international law in the Spanish question.

"One begins to think that it is better policy to be a gangster than an honest man," Cefito said one day. The other boys agreed, but not Marissa, who generally feels very responsible.

"Perhaps it is unfortunate you did not bring us up that way," Cefito added, half laughing but with a certain bitterness.

At last Alejandro came in one day to tell us triumphantly that he had been given work. Alejandro is the youngest of the group and had begun to study agricultural engineering when the war broke out. His job in a baker's shop consisted of moving heavy bags of flour from one place to another and helping in the shop itself. He had some funny experiences the first few days, for there were such a number of different kinds of loaves he kept mixing them up. After some time he was able to give up that uncongenial work and find employment in a factory as a draughtsman. He seems to have a future before him now. Germán and Cefito also got started. They had to do it on their own, however, and we found it very difficult. We took a small apartment under ours and Germán, having been assistant to the head of the laboratory in the Faculty of Medicine of Madrid, set up a little laboratory in one room while Cefito arranged a small consulting room in another. Marissa helped her husband.

The first big difficulty they came up against was the lack of instruments and of course Germán could do nothing without a microscope. This they thought they would never find, at least not one which we could afford to buy but, after looking everywhere, they discovered what they wanted in an old curiosity shop. They were asked a very reasonable price for it so they paid for it and fled, lest the man in the shop change his mind. Though a little old-fashioned it has a good lens and was all Germán required at first. When they had all that was absolutely necessary they sat down and waited for patients who now are slowly coming in.

Juan, finding nothing else to do, sat down to write the history of the Spanish navy and got an offer from a publishing house before he had finished it. He did some translations, too, even of English hymns into Spanish.

Mexico is not a rich country. Salaries are very low and everything takes time but, at least, the young people have found a road leading to the activities they themselves had chosen before the war.

Had it not been for the news from Spain and from the French concentration camps, for the torturing knowledge of the suffering of thousands of our fellow Spaniards, we could have found a little rest. But each step forward, each small achievement, is a stab in one's heart. Every family we know has suffered some heavy loss, not only of a material kind but of precious human life or freedom.

Every refugee looks toward the land of his birth with anguish, but not with despair. As the Arab who sits before his tent, waiting for the corpse of his enemy to go by, the refugee, too, is waiting to see the corpse of tyranny and oppression pass by and to see Spain and the world live again. When that happens, he shall be content and at peace.

I often weep. Tears ease the heart when they are not the fruit of bitterness. I can also laugh at times and play with Jan and tend the flowers on the terrace and write and dream, more of the past, perhaps, than of the future.

But I am bewildered at times because of the conflicting emotions within myself that have not been the least of my trials during the Spanish war. The emotions of wishing for peace and yet for my country's sake anxious that others should come to our defense, of condemning armaments yet begging for arms, of feeling reverence for human life yet almost longing for its destruction at times : these contradictory sentiments have affirmed others. Among them the conviction that democracy is the only political system under which people can be happy. That hatred is the most destructive force that nations can suffer from and that liberty is the most priceless of gifts. I do refer not only to political freedom which is, of course, essential. I also mean economic freedom and that other freedom which allows man to grow and develop according to the desires of his heart. There are many ways of being enslaved and not the least degrading is the one that prevents us from using our creative possibilities.

No democracy is worthy of its name if it does not provide human beings with the chance to create . . . great works of art or simple manifestations of beauty, but man's own. I firmly believe a day will come when this will be possible, and because I believe it I am convinced that life is worth while. In spite of all the struggling and the suffering and the unsatisfied hopes with which my past years, like those of most other people, have been burdened, I am thankful to have been and *to be*.

Thinking and wondering about these things and more, I look around at those who make up my little household, still gratefully amazed that they are safe. Three Mexican women, Antonia, Lupita and Alberta, look after us, the consulting room and the laboratory. They have not taken the place of Maria and Asunción ; that would be impossible. But they are affectionate and trustworthy, too, and help to make life easier with their care and happier with their childlike gaiety and their sweet songs. Maria and Asunción will be with us some day again when Spain revives as she is sure to do.

If the young people are still impatient at times, and Cefe also, I say to myself that these are just the last sighs of the wind after a storm.

Another great gift has been given to me of late, rather has it been returned. When I look out of my window and see the great mountains rising all round the city and the snow-capped volcanoes, Ixtaccihuatl and Popocatepetl, I feel my heart melting under the influence of nature again. The feeling of indifference for everything beautiful that the earth has to offer us, that numbness I had experienced throughout the war, is disappearing. I am no longer tied up in a knot. It is not that I am resigned. Resignation is the fruit of hopelessness and I do have hope and also faith. Therefore, I can accept what came before and what has come now : the good and the bad, the light and the shadow. I can look out of myself and, hand in hand with Cefe, begin life over again : thinking of Spain, sure of Spain, and with my heart full of gratitude for Mexico.

INDEX